Archaeology
An Introduction to the World's Greatest Sites

Eric H. Cline, Ph.D.

PUBLISHED BY:

THE GREAT COURSES
Corporate Headquarters
4840 Westfields Boulevard, Suite 500
Chantilly, Virginia 20151-2299
Phone: 1-800-832-2412
Fax: 703-378-3819
www.thegreatcourses.com

Copyright © The Teaching Company, 2016

Printed in the United States of America

This book is in copyright. All rights reserved.

Without limiting the rights under copyright reserved above,
no part of this publication may be reproduced, stored in
or introduced into a retrieval system, or transmitted,
in any form, or by any means
(electronic, mechanical, photocopying, recording, or otherwise),
without the prior written permission of
The Teaching Company.

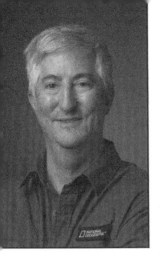

Eric H. Cline, Ph.D.

Professor of Classics and Anthropology
Director of The George Washington
University Capitol Archaeological Institute
The George Washington University

Dr. Eric H. Cline is a Professor of Classics and Anthropology, the former Chair of the Department of Classical and Near Eastern Languages and Civilizations, and the current Director of The George Washington University (GWU) Capitol Archaeological Institute. He is also a National Geographic Explorer, a Fulbright Scholar, a National Endowment for the Humanities (NEH) Public Scholar, and an award-winning teacher and author. He holds a Ph.D. in Ancient History from the University of Pennsylvania, an M.A. in Near Eastern Languages and Literatures from Yale University, and a B.A. in Classical Archaeology modified by Anthropology from Dartmouth College. In 2015, he was awarded an honorary doctoral degree (*honoris causa*) from Muhlenberg College.

An archaeologist and ancient historian by training, Dr. Cline's primary fields of study are biblical archaeology, the military history of the Mediterranean world from antiquity to the present, and the international connections among Greece, Egypt, and the Near East during the Late Bronze Age (1700–1100 B.C.E.). He is an experienced and active field archaeologist, with more than 30 seasons of excavation and survey to his credit in Israel, Egypt, Jordan, Cyprus, Greece, Crete, and the United States. Dr. Cline is currently codirector of the renewed series of archaeological excavations at the site of Tel Kabri in Israel, which began in 2005. The project is run by the University of Haifa (with Assaf Yasur-Landau) and GWU. Dr. Cline was also a member of the Megiddo Expedition in Israel, excavating at biblical Armageddon for 10 seasons over a 20-year period, from 1994 to 2014. In 2015, Dr. Cline was named a member of the inaugural class of NEH Public Scholars, receiving the award for his next book project.

At GWU, Dr. Cline has won the Oscar and Shoshana Trachtenberg Prize for Teaching Excellence and the Oscar and Shoshana Trachtenberg Prize for Faculty Scholarship; he is the first faculty member at GWU to have won both awards. He also won the national Excellence in Undergraduate Teaching Award from the Archaeological Institute of America. Dr. Cline teaches a wide variety of courses at GWU, including Introduction to Archaeology, History of Ancient Greece, History of Egypt and the Ancient Near East, and History of Ancient Israel, as well as various smaller honors and freshmen seminars. He has also served as the advisor to undergraduate archaeology majors at GWU since 2001.

Dr. Cline's most recent book, *1177 B.C.: The Year Civilization Collapsed*, received the 2014 Award for the Best Popular Book from the American Schools of Oriental Research and was considered for the 2014 Pulitzer Prize. Three of his previous books have won the Biblical Archaeology Society's award for Best Popular Book on Archaeology. His books have also been featured as a main selection of the Natural Science Book Club, a main selection of the Discovery Channel Book Club, a *USA TODAY* "Books for Your Brain" selection, and a selection of the Association of American University Presses for Public and Secondary School Libraries.

A prolific researcher and author with 16 books and more than 100 articles and book reviews to his credit, Dr. Cline is perhaps best known for such books as *The Battles of Armageddon: Megiddo and the Jezreel Valley from the Bronze Age to the Nuclear Age*; *Jerusalem Besieged: From Ancient Canaan to Modern Israel*; *From Eden to Exile: Unraveling Mysteries of the Bible*; *Biblical Archaeology: A Very Short Introduction*; and *The Trojan War: A Very Short Introduction*. His books have been translated or are being translated into 14 languages. His research has been featured in *The Washington Post*, *The New York Times*, *U.S. News & World Report*, *USA TODAY*, *National Geographic News*, CNN, the London *Telegraph*, the London *Mirror*, the Associated Press, and elsewhere, His books have been reviewed in *The Times Literary Supplement*, *Times Higher Education*, *The Jerusalem Post*, the *Cincinnati Enquirer*, the *History News Network*, *Jewish Book World*, and many professional journals.

Dr. Cline has also appeared in more than 20 television programs and documentaries, including those on ABC, the BBC, the National Geographic Channel, HISTORY, and the Discovery Channel. Dr. Cline has been interviewed by syndicated national and international television and radio hosts on such shows as ABC's *Good Morning America*, Fox News Channel's *America's Newsroom*, the BBC World Service's *The World Today*, NPR's *Public Interest*, and *The Michael Dresser Show*. In addition, he has presented more than 300 scholarly and public lectures on his work to a wide variety of audiences both nationally and internationally, including at the Smithsonian Institution in Washington DC, The Metropolitan Museum of Art in New York, and the Skirball Cultural Center in Los Angeles. ∎

Table of Contents

INTRODUCTION
Professor Biography i
Course Scope 1

LECTURE GUIDES

LECTURE 1
The Origins of Modern Archaeology 3

LECTURE 2
Excavating Pompeii and Herculaneum 21

LECTURE 3
Schliemann and His Successors at Troy 40

LECTURE 4
Early Archaeology in Mesopotamia 58

LECTURE 5
How Do Archaeologists Know Where to Dig? 78

LECTURE 6
Prehistoric Archaeology 96

LECTURE 7
Göbekli Tepe, Çatalhöyük, and Jericho 115

LECTURE 8
Pyramids, Mummies, and Hieroglyphics 133

LECTURE 9
King Tut's Tomb 151

LECTURE 10
How Do You Excavate at a Site? 169

LECTURE 11
Discovering Mycenae and Knossos 187

LECTURE 12
Santorini, Akrotiri, and the Atlantis Myth 207

LECTURE 13
The Uluburun Shipwreck 226

LECTURE 14
The Dead Sea Scrolls 245

LECTURE 15
The Myth of Masada? 264

LECTURE 16
Megiddo: Excavating Armageddon 282

LECTURE 17
The Canaanite Palace at Tel Kabri 300

LECTURE 18
Petra, Palmyra, and Ebla 317

LECTURE 19
How Are Artifacts Dated and Preserved? 335

LECTURE 20
The Terracotta Army, Sutton Hoo, and Ötzi 353

LECTURE 21
Discovering the Maya 373

LECTURE 22
The Nazca Lines, Sipán, and Machu Picchu 392

LECTURE 23
Archaeology in North America 411

LECTURE 24
From the Aztecs to Future Archaeology 430

SUPPLEMENTAL MATERIAL

Bibliography 449
Image Credits 463

Archaeology: An Introduction to the World's Greatest Sites

Scope:

What, exactly, is it that archaeologists do? Although tremendous numbers of people are fascinated by the idea of archaeology, many have little idea what is involved. Indeed, many people picture an archaeological excavation as an Indiana Jones movie.

This course is meant to set the record straight. It is an introduction to archaeology for the general public that provides answers to the questions archaeologists are asked most frequently: How do archaeologists find ancient sites? What happens during an actual excavation? How do we know how old something is?

In answering these questions, this course provides the inside story of what it is that archaeologists actually do and how they do it. We will learn how what began as a haphazard search for famous sites of ancient history evolved into a highly organized, professional, and systematic study of the peoples and cultures of the past—progressing from the first crude excavations at Herculaneum to the high-tech methods being used at Teotihuacan today. We'll also get firsthand insight into how cutting-edge technology has forever changed the field.

In addition, we will discuss some of the most famous archaeological discoveries of all time, including the tomb of King Tut, the Uluburun shipwreck, the Nazca Lines, and the amazing terracotta warriors. These discoveries are arranged thematically, both chronologically and geographically. We'll travel the world—from Ur in Mesopotamia to China's Shanxi Province, from Masada in Israel to the ancient town of Akrotiri in Greece, from Sutton Hoo in England, to Machu Picchu in Peru. We'll also include forays into Spain and France, Italy and North America, Africa, Mexico, and Turkey.

Whether you're new to the subject or you're an archaeology enthusiast, this course will provide an unparalleled glimpse into a critical source of historical knowledge. ■

Lecture 1

The Origins of Modern Archaeology

The field of archaeology began as a haphazard search for ancient statues and famous sites of history but has evolved into a highly organized, professional, and systematic study of the peoples and cultures of the past. In this course, we'll explore some of the most famous archaeological discoveries of all time, and we'll look at how cutting-edge technology has changed the field. By the end of the course, you'll be an expert in excavation, and you'll possess a deeper appreciation for why saving the past matters. Archaeology not only teaches us about the past, but it also connects us to a broader range of human experience and enriches our understanding of our present and our future.

Ancient Archaeologists

- The first archaeologist we know of lived more than 2,500 years ago. He was the Neo-Babylonian king Nabonidus, who ruled in ancient Iraq and Syria during the middle of the 6th century B.C. Nabonidus is known to have excavated ancient buildings and even set up a museum so that he could display the objects he found.

- Nabonidus wasn't the only person in antiquity who was interested in what had come before him. The Greek writer Hesiod, who wrote a poem called *Works and Days* in about 700 B.C., before the time of Nabonidus, referred to the earlier periods in Greece as the Age of Gold, the Age of Silver, and so on. Hesiod lived during a period of regeneration after centuries of the world's first Dark Age, and he called his own time the Age of Iron. Archaeologists still call that period the Iron Age, thanks in part to Hesiod.

Early Modern Archaeologists

- In terms of the modern world, one of the first people to try to look back at the stretch of human history was Archbishop James Ussher. In the 1600s, he went through the Bible and added up the various dates for people mentioned there, such as Noah, Joshua, Abraham, and so on, and came up with the idea that the world had been created about 6,000 years ago—specifically, on October 23, 4004 B.C.

- The origins of modern archaeology probably go back to the early 1700s, when people first started exploring the ancient Italian ruins that had been buried by an explosion of Vesuvius in 79 A.D.
  - Credit here usually goes to a man named Emmanuel Maurice de Lorraine, who was the prince (and, later, duke) of Elbeuf, in Austria. He was living in Italy near Naples at the time and underwrote the first efforts to tunnel into the ground at Herculaneum, a town near Pompeii.

  - His men happened to dig right into the ancient Roman theater at Herculaneum and were able to extract a number of marble statues. Most of these were used to decorate Emmanuel Maurice's estate; others were distributed elsewhere in Europe, including to some museums. Proper excavations at Herculaneum and Pompeii began a few decades later.

- Interestingly, Thomas Jefferson also did a bit of archaeology in the late 1700s. In fact, some think that what he did should count as the first real archaeological excavations conducted in the New World.
  - In about 1784, he excavated a Native American burial mound on his property in Virginia. He was able to tell that there were different layers in the mound and that the bodies in it had been buried at different times.

  - In this, Jefferson was far ahead of his time. Today, the idea of separate layers is known as *stratigraphy*, but it wouldn't become an established part of archaeology until the time of Sir William Matthew Flinders Petrie, who excavated in Egypt and Palestine a century later.

Archaeology in the 19th Century
- By the mid-1800s, serious excavations were underway at a number of ancient sites in the Near East, underwritten by such institutions as the British Museum and the Louvre and conducted by Sir Austen Henry Layard, Paul Émile Botta, and others. They excavated in what is now Iraq at such places as Nineveh and Nimrud and shipped magnificent pieces back to the museums for display. These

pieces include the colossal winged bull and lion statues from the palaces of Sargon II and Ashurnasirpal II that are currently on display at the British Museum.

- Other 19th-century archaeologists, such as John Lloyd Stephens, went exploring in the New World. Stephens, along with a British artist named Frederick Catherwood, traveled in the Yucatan, in modern-day Mexico. They published beautiful books about their travels in the 1840s, in which they reported the discovery of previously unknown Maya sites.

- The fledgling field of archaeology, as it began to grow and solidify, borrowed heavily from other disciplines, especially geology. James Hutton and Charles Lyell, considered to be among the fathers of geology, had suggested theories concerning the stratification of rocks.
  - They believed that the lower down in the earth one went, the earlier the rocks would date; that is, the earlier rocks had been laid down in the strata first, with later levels coming in on top of them.

  - This is similar to what Thomas Jefferson had concluded; it's also a premise that would form the basis of Petrie's excavations.

- Another advance came from a Danish museum curator named C. J. Thomsen, who began cataloguing the objects in the National Museum of Denmark in the 1830s. His results were published in an English edition just before 1850. Thomsen split the museum's collections of antiquities into three periods: the Stone Age, the Bronze Age, and the Iron Age.
  - This system—known as the *three-age system*—was soon adopted throughout Europe and remains in use to this day, though it now has a number of subdivisions. For instance, the Stone Age is divided into the Paleolithic, that is, the Old Stone Age; the Mesolithic, which is the Middle Stone Age; and the Neolithic, the New Stone Age.

- The Bronze Age is frequently subdivided even further, according to location. The timing of the Bronze Age varies depending on where you are in the world; for example, the Bronze Age in China took place at a different time than either the Bronze Age in Europe or the Bronze Age in the ancient Near East.

- By the 1860s and 1870s, Heinrich Schliemann was searching for the legendary city of Troy. Going against the scholars of the day, most of whom didn't think the Trojan War had taken place, Schliemann began excavating at the site of Hisarlik in northwest Turkey and soon announced to the world that he had found Troy. Later, he also announced that he had uncovered the ruins of Mycenae, home to Agamemnon, who led the Greek army in its assault on Troy.

- At around the same time, various people were working to decipher ancient languages. Probably the most famous person in this field is Jean-François Champollion, the brilliant French scholar who is credited with deciphering Egyptian hieroglyphics in 1823.
  - Another language scholar was Sir Henry Rawlinson, who helped to translate the cuneiform script in Mesopotamia in the 1850s. Cuneiform is a wedge-shaped writing system that was used to write Akkadian, Babylonian, Hittite, Old Persian, and other languages in the ancient Near East.

  - Rawlinson cracked the cuneiform system by translating a trilingual inscription written in Old Persian, Elamite, and Babylonian. Darius the Great of Persia, in about 519 B.C., had carved the inscription into a cliff face at the site of Behistun in what is now Iran.

Sir William Matthew Flinders Petrie

- By the end of the 19th century and into the 20th, some of the great early archaeologists began to appear on the scene. One of the most important of these was Sir William Matthew Flinders Petrie.

- Petrie first dug in Egypt, where he trained a group of workmen from a village near modern-day Luxor. To this day, the descendants of those men, known as *guftis*, still provide much of the skilled labor for archaeological excavations in Egypt. Each *gufti* does the same task that his family has always done; some are pickmen, some are trowelmen, and so on.

- Petrie also dug in what is now modern Israel but was Palestine in his day. Here, he was responsible for the introduction or popularization of a number of concepts that are taken for granted in archaeology today. For example, he applied the concept of stratigraphy, adopted from geology, and argued that earlier things are usually found lower down than more recent things, especially in the man-made mounds known as *tells* that can be seen throughout the Middle East.
  - Of course, Petrie was right; tells are actually made up of one ancient city on top of another, built up over centuries or millennia, and the earliest city is always at the bottom.

The tell (ancient mound) at Megiddo, which is the site of biblical Armageddon, is made up of 20 different cities in layers.

- For example, at Megiddo, the 70-foot-tall mound has no fewer than 20 different cities hidden within it, with the first one, at the bottom, dating back to at least 3000 B.C. and the most recent one, at the top, dating to about 300 B.C.

- Petrie is also one of the people responsible for realizing that broken pieces of pottery removed while digging can be used to help date different levels of a mound. Because styles of pottery go in and out of fashion, certain types can be correlated, especially in conjunction with radiocarbon dating, with fairly specific dates and periods. Petrie also realized that if the same type of pottery is found at two different sites, the levels in which they are found at each site are probably equivalent in time. This has proven to be an extremely useful point.

The idea of separate layers representing successively earlier periods on an archaeological site is known as stratigraphy.

Sir Mortimer Wheeler and Dame Kathleen Kenyon

- Sir Mortimer Wheeler excavated at Maiden Castle in England and Harappa in India. At both sites, he excavated in 5-meter squares, with a 1-meter-wide balk in between the squares, on which excavators could walk, push wheelbarrows, and so on. Wheeler's student Kathleen Kenyon, who is probably best known for digging at Jericho and Jerusalem, brought this method with her when she began excavating in what was then Palestine in the 1930s. It is now known as the Wheeler-Kenyon or Kenyon-Wheeler method.

- This method allows the archaeologist to keep control of the stratigraphy, by looking at the interior sides of each square to see what has already been dug through and to get a visual idea of the history of the area.

- At the end of each season, most archaeological teams in the Near East draw and photograph each of these sections so that they can publish a record of it for others to see and discuss. The reason for this step is that archaeologists destroy the very things they are studying as they dig; thus, it's important to record every detail of the process.

Suggested Reading

Bahn, *100 Great Archaeological Discoveries*.

Fagan, ed., *The Great Archaeologists*.

Fagan and Durrani, *In the Beginning*.

Questions to Consider

1. Might there be a better way to divide and subdivide the periods of antiquity rather than the three-age system that Thomsen created?

2. What do you think of the excavation techniques introduced by Petrie, Wheeler, and Kenyon? Can they be improved upon?

Lecture 1 Transcript

The Origins of Modern Archaeology

When you hear the word archaeology, what comes to mind? Do you think of searching for lost treasures and traveling to exotic locales? Do you think it's like in the movies—like what Indiana Jones does? Well, if that's the case, then I'm going to have to break it to you gently. Indiana Jones isn't really an archaeologist, and most of what he does isn't even close to archaeology.

I'm sorry, but it's true. Most of us wear baseball caps rather than fedoras, and archaeologists don't carry whips. We wouldn't even know how to use one, even if somebody gave it to us. In fact, you can usually tell the over-eager volunteers who are on their first dig because they've all got fedoras rather than baseball caps. So let's take off the hat. We'll take off the man-purse and because it gets very hot by 6:00 or 7:00 AM, we'll take off the jacket as well.

Hello and welcome. My name is Eric Cline. I'm both axn ancient historian and an active field archaeologist. I'm also a National Geographic Explorer. Even if my job isn't like the movies, being an archaeologist is still one of the most interesting jobs that you can have. In fact, in my office, I've got two bumper stickers that are pasted to the wall. The first one says simply, "Archaeology, I'd rather be digging." The second one says, "Archaeologist, the coolest job on earth. I save the past. What do you do?"

Now to me, the bumper stickers do a couple of things. First, just as bumper stickers should, they encapsulate my feelings about archaeology in a nutshell. I really would rather be digging. But they also issue a challenge to the rest of the world. Archaeology is not only about finding the remains that have been left from past civilizations; it's about preserving and curating those remains for future generations.

As I mentioned, I'm a National Geographic Explorer because they were gracious enough to fund our excavations at Tel Kabri in Israel. I've also had the good fortune to be featured on a number of National Geographic television shows, and I've published a book with National Geographic, and I've served as a consultant on several others.

I've been digging almost every summer since I was a sophomore in college, which was longer ago than I care to imagine. I'll just say that I've participated in 30 different dig seasons, and I'll let you figure out the math. I've dug in Israel, Egypt, Jordan, Cyprus, Greece, and Crete, so most people consider me to be an Old World archaeologist. But I've also excavated in California and Vermont in the United States, which is considered the New World in archaeological terms.

Most recently, I have been co-directing two digs, both of them located in Israel. One is at Megiddo, which is biblical Armageddon, and yes, it's a real place; it's not just a place mentioned in the Bible as the final battle between good and evil. I've retired from that excavation just now, though, after spending 10 seasons there. The other dig where I am still co-director is at a site called Tel Kabri, which is up in the north of Israel and has a Canaanite palace that dates back almost 4,000 years. That's the dig that's received funding from the National Geographic Society, which is why I'm proud to call myself a National Geographic Explorer in addition to everything else.

So what is it exactly that archaeologists do? Well, that's what we'll answer in this course. A lot of people are fascinated by the idea of archaeology but they've got no idea what's actually involved, so together we'll explore how what began as a haphazard search for ancient statues and famous sites has evolved into a systematic study of the peoples and cultures of the past. We'll also take a look at how cutting-edge technology has changed the field, and we'll explore some of the most famous archaeological discoveries of all time, including the tomb of King Tut, the Uluburun shipwreck, the Nazca Lines, and the amazing Terracotta Warriors.

By the time we're done, not only will you be an expert on how to excavate and know a little bit more about some of the famous sites, but you'll also possess a deeper appreciation for why saving the past matters. Archaeology not only teaches us about the past, but it also connects us to a broader sample of human experience and enriches our understanding of both our present and our future.

Before we go any further, though, allow me to tell you a little bit more about myself. I decided that I wanted to be an archaeologist when I was seven years old. My mother had given me a copy of a biography about Heinrich Schliemann, which was written just for kids. It's called *The Walls of Windy Troy*. After reading it, I announced that I was going to be an archaeologist. I actually still have that book. Later, when I was in junior high school, I read John Lloyd Stephens' book *Incidents of Travel in Yucatán,* and then I read C. W. Ceram's book *Gods, Graves & Scholars*, and that cemented my desire. Looking back, I have to say it's been a lot of fun so far with hopefully more years and many more adventures still to come.

What's amazing to me is that my trowel is now older than most of the students who come to dig with me these days. It's a Marshalltown trowel, which many archaeologists favor. My mother gave me the trowel back in 1981. I hate to say it, but if I dropped it by accident at a site now and somebody dug it up, it probably would be considered an artifact at this point. Now, in all those years of digging, I've unearthed some pretty remarkable things. And, believe me, the thrill of discovery never gets old. For example, at our excavations at the Canaanite palace at Kabri, my team and I discovered a roomful of jars in 2013.

I remember it well. When the first jar began to emerge out of the dirt towards the end of the first week of our dig, we nicknamed her Bessie. I took a lot of pictures of her during those first few days since I'm the excavation photographer as well as the co-director, but I had no idea at the time that she was just the tip of the iceberg. Bessie was lying on her side, and we didn't think very much about that until, as we dug a little bit deeper and more of her began to appear, some of her friends also began to appear, one by one by one by one.

By the time we had most of Bessie uncovered, we also had 39 other jars in the same room, all lying on the floor of what turned out to be a store room in the palace. And when we did some organic residue analysis of the interior of those jars, it turned out that they all contained wine. Of course, the wine was almost 4,000 years old, so it had a bit of an earthy taste to it.

I'm kidding; that's an archaeological joke. The wine that had actually spilled out and then evaporated long ago, but enough residue was left so that we could tell by analyzing the insides of the sherds that there had also been things like mint, juniper berries, and honey that had been added to the wine. We're hoping that someday we might even be able to re-create the wine and find out what it really tasted like in ancient Canaan during the Middle Bronze Age—that would be about 1700 B.C., just after the time of biblical Abraham. However, my co-director, Assaf Yasur-Landau, thinks it'll taste a little bit like Greek retsina flavored with cough syrup, so it might not be something to actually look forward to.

So while I may not be Indiana Jones, my team has found the oldest and largest wine cellar yet discovered in the ancient Near East. That's pretty cool, especially since we made all the papers, including the *New York Times*, the *Wall Street Journal*, and the *Washington Post*, plus *Time* and *Smithsonian* magazines. Of course, archaeological discoveries have been grabbing headlines for quite a while now. And even before there were newspapers, people were experiencing the same thrill of discovery that I've experienced across my career. So let's spend the rest of this lecture meeting a few of these people—some of the notable archaeologists who helped lay the foundation for the discipline that I call the coolest job on earth.

And by the way, for those of you interested in reading more about what I'm going to discuss in this course, I can tell you that there are dozens, if not hundreds, of books available out there for you. I'm especially partial to two of them. One is Brian Fagan's textbook called *In the Beginning,* and the other is Paul Bahn's book called *100 Great Archaeological Discoveries*. Fagan and Bahn are both scholars whom I greatly admire for their ability to make archaeology understandable and accessible to the general public. And that's why I've organized many of the topics in this course around their two books.

OK, let's turn our attention to those notable individuals I mentioned a moment ago. The first archaeologist that we know of lived more than 2,500 years ago. That would be the Neo-Babylonian king, Nabonidus. He ruled in ancient Iraq and Syria during the middle of the 6th century B.C., just before the time of Cyrus the Great of Persia.

Nabonidus is known to have excavated ancient buildings, and he even set up a museum so that he could display the objects that he had found. Now, it took a while for modern archaeologists to understand what they were finding when they excavated his museum. "Wait a minute," they said, "we're digging in a 6th-century Neo-Babylonian level, so what's this object from the Sumerian period 2,000 years earlier doing in this room? And what's it doing next to this other object, which is from a completely different time period?" It was only later that they realized that they were excavating an ancient museum. Now, I have to sympathize with them, because imagine what it's going to be like to excavate the Metropolitan Museum in New York or the British Museum in London or the Louvre in Paris in another couple thousand years if our civilization has collapsed in the meantime.

At any rate, Nabonidus wasn't the only one in antiquity who was interested in what had come before him. The Greek writer, Hesiod, who wrote a poem called *Works and Days* back in about 700 B.C.—even before the time of Nabonidus—referred to the earlier periods in Greece as the Age of Gold, the Age of Silver, and so on. Even today, of course, we'll sometimes still refer to an earlier decade as a golden age. Hesiod lived during a period of regeneration after centuries of the world's first Dark Age, and he called his own time the Age of Iron. Archaeologists still call that period the Iron Age, thanks in part to Hesiod and in part to a Danish museum curator whom we'll meet in just a moment.

Now, in terms of our modern world, one of the first people to try and look back at the whole stretch of human history was a man named Ussher—Archbishop James Ussher. He lived from 1581–1656. He went through the Bible, and he added up the various years for the people mentioned there, like Noah, and Joshua, Abraham, and he came up with the idea that the world had been created about 6,000 years ago—quite specifically on October 23rd in the year 4004 B.C. Some people still cite this number and the date today, especially those who don't agree that evolution and geology indicate that the world is an awful lot older than that.

But if we're looking for the origins of modern archaeology itself, we probably should go back to the early 1700s. That's when people first started poking around in some ancient Italian ruins that had been buried by the eruption of Mt. Vesuvius back in 79 A.D. Credit usually goes to a man named Emmanuel Maurice de Lorraine, who was the Prince, and later the Duke, of Elbeuf, which is in Austria. He was living in Italy near Naples at the time, and he underwrote the first efforts to tunnel into the ground at Herculaneum, which is a town near Pompeii. His men happened to dig right into the ancient Roman theater at Herculaneum, and they were able to extract a number of ancient marble statues. Most of these were used to decorate the Count's estate, but others were distributed elsewhere in Europe, including some to museums.

Interestingly, Thomas Jefferson, the third President of the United States, also did a bit of archaeology in the late 1700s. In fact, some think that what he did should count as the first real archaeological excavations conducted in the New World. Around 1784, he excavated a Native American burial mound that was on his property in Virginia. He was able to tell that there were different layers in the mound and that the bodies in it had been buried at different times. He was very far ahead of his time, though, for we now call this idea of separate layers stratigraphy, and it wouldn't really become an established part of archaeology until the time of Sir William Matthew Flinders Petrie, who excavated in Egypt and Palestine a century later.

By the mid-1800s, serious excavations were underway at a number of ancient sites in the Near East underwritten by institutions like the British Museum and the Louvre, and they were conducted by people like Sir Austen Henry Layard and Paul Émile Botta. They excavated in what is now Iraq at such places like Nineveh and Nimrud, and they shipped magnificent pieces back to the museums for display like the colossal winged bull and lion statues that are from the palaces of Sargon II and Ashurnasirpal II. These pieces are now on display at the British Museum.

Other 19th-century archaeologists, like John Lloyd Stephens, went exploring in the New World. Stephens, along with a British artist named Frederick Catherwood, went traveling in the Yucatan, in modern day Mexico, in that region. They published beautiful books about their travels in the 1840s in which they reported on their discovery of various Maya sites that were previously unknown. It was one of those books that first got me interested in archaeology, as I mentioned. When I saw, for example, Catherwood's depictions of the stone idols at Copán, I was mesmerized by the thought of a long-lost civilization just waiting to be discovered in the jungle. It was like something out of an adventure novel, but it was real life.

The fledgling field of archaeology, as it began to mature, borrowed heavily from other disciplines, especially geology. Men like James Hutton and Charles Lyell—they are considered to be among the fathers of geology—they had suggested theories concerning things like the stratification of rocks. They believed that the lower down in the earth the one went, the earlier the rocks would be; that is, the earlier rocks had been laid down in the strata first, with later levels then coming in on top of them. This is similar to what Thomas Jefferson had concluded, and it's also a premise that would form the basis of Petrie's excavations later, as we'll see in a minute. Their geology books also influenced Charles Darwin, who reportedly read the first volume of Lyell's *Principles of Geology* during the famous voyage of the *Beagle*.

Another advance came from the museum side of things. In the 1830s, a Danish museum curator named C. J. Thomsen began cataloguing the objects in the National Museum of Denmark in Copenhagen. His results were published in an English edition just before 1850. What he did was actually very simple. He split the museum's collections of antiquities into three periods: the Stone Age, the Bronze Age, and the Iron Age.

This system which is known as the Three Age System was soon adopted throughout Europe and it remains in use to this day, although by now we've made a number of sub-divisions. For instance, the Stone Age is now divided into the Paleolithic—that is, the Old Stone Age—and the Mesolithic, which is the Middle Stone Age, and the Neolithic, which is the New Stone Age. The Bronze Age is frequently subdivided even further, but here it really depends upon where you're working in the world because the timing of the Bronze Age depends upon where you are. For example, the Bronze Age in China took place at a different time than either the Bronze Age in Europe or the Bronze Age in the ancient Near East.

Where I work now, in Israel, the Bronze Age goes from 3000 B.C. to about 1200 B.C., and it's split into the Early, Middle, and Late Bronze Ages. It's also been further refined and subdivided even more from there. So my particular time period of specialization is the Late Bronze Age, which is the period from about 1700–1200 B.C., but within that I am mostly focused on the first half of the 14th century B.C. In Greece, this is called the Late Helladic IIIA1 period, while in Israel it's called the Late Bronze IIA period. If your head is starting to spin, believe me, I sympathize. I've got a friend whose specialty is the LH IIIC1b period, which I kid you not, is basically the first decade or so of the 12th century B.C.

Anyway, by the time we get to the 1860s and 1870s, we find Heinrich Schliemann searching for the legendary city of Troy. Going against the scholars of the day, most of whom didn't think the Trojan War had taken place, Schliemann began excavating at the site of Hisarlik in northwest Turkey, and he soon announced to the world that he had found Troy. Later, he also announced that he had uncovered the ruins of Mycenae, home to Agamemnon, who led the Greek army in its assault on Troy.

In the meantime, we've also got various people working to decipher the ancient languages that were being found. Probably the most famous person is Jean-François Champollion, the brilliant French scholar who gets credit for deciphering Egyptian hieroglyphics in 1823.

But there's also the British scholar, Sir Henry Rawlinson, who helped to translate the cuneiform script in Mesopotamia in the 1850s. Cuneiform is a wedge-shaped writing system. In fact, the very word cuneiform comes from the Latin, and it means wedge-shaped. It was used to write Akkadian, Babylonian, Hittite, Old Persian, and other languages in the ancient Near East, much as we now use the Latin alphabet to write English, French, German, Italian, Spanish, and so on.

Rawlinson cracked the cuneiform system by translating a tri-lingual inscription. It was written in Old Persian, Elamite, and Babylonian. Darius the Great of Persia, in about 519 B.C., carved the inscription into a cliff face at the site of Behistun, in what is now Iran. Even after the inscription was copied down, it still took Rawlinson 20 years to decipher the cuneiform and to successfully read the whole inscription.

By the time we get to the end of the 19th century and into the 20th, some of the great early archaeologists appear on the scene. One of the most important is also a man who has one of the best names in all of archaeology: Sir William Matthew Flinders Petrie. I wanted to name one of my kids after him, but my wife wouldn't allow it. Even so, my daughter will still sometimes claim to gullible friends that her full name is Hannah Sir William Matthew Flinders Petrie Cline. It's amazing how many people believe her, at least at first.

In any event, Petrie first dug in Egypt, where he trained a whole group of workmen from the village of Quft, which is near modern-day Luxor. To this day, the descendants of those men, known as guftis, still provide much of the skilled labor for archaeological excavations in Egypt. Each gufti does the same task that their family has always done. Some are the pickmen; some are the trowelmen; some are the overseers. Guftis are a very talented group of workmen, and I had the pleasure of working with some of them when I was on a dig in the Nile Delta region back in the mid-1980s.

Petrie also dug in what is now modern Israel but which was Palestine in his day. Here, he was responsible for the introduction, or in some cases the popularization, of a number of things that we basically take for granted in archaeology today. For example, he applied the concept of stratigraphy, adopted from geology, and he argued that earlier things were usually found lower down than more recent things, especially in the man-made mounds that we call tells, which can be seen throughout the Middle East today.

Of course, he was right, because these tells are actually comprised of one ancient city on top of another, built up over centuries or millennia, and the earliest city is always at the very bottom. For example, at Megiddo, where I used to excavate, the 70-foot-tall mound has no fewer than 20 different cities hidden within it, with the first one at the bottom dating back to at least 3000 B.C., and the most recent one, at the top, dating to about 300 B.C. When you're looking at a side profile that's been cut into one of these mounds, you can easily see the different layers because they're full of dirt, and stones, and other materials, with all sorts of different colors, textures, and consistencies.

Petrie is also one of the people responsible for realizing that all of the broken pieces of pottery that we find with almost every bucketful of soil that we remove can be used to help date the different levels of the mound. It turns out that certain types of pottery go in and out of fashion, just like clothing and shoes today. And so pottery can be correlated, especially in conjunction with radiocarbon dating, with specific periods. In fact, it's frequently pottery styles that give their names to our archaeological periods, so that we have, for example, Late Helladic IIIA1 pottery, which dates to the first half of the 14th century. Petrie also realized that if you find the same type of pottery at two different sites, the levels in which they are found at each, probably are equivalent in time. This has proven to be an extremely important, and useful point.

Perhaps the most interesting about Petrie, though, is that when he died in 1942, he willed his head and his brain to science. He had died in Jerusalem, and the rest of him is still buried there, but his head was shipped back to London. At some point, when it had been stored in a basement for quite a while, the label on the jar fell off so that nobody actually knew whose head it was, but it was eventually re-identified and is now reportedly somewhere in a storage room at the Royal College of Surgeons in London, though I haven't actually gone to look for it personally.

There are many other famous archaeologists from this early period in the development of the field, but let me just mention two more: Sir Mortimer Wheeler and his best-known student, Dame Kathleen Kenyon. Wheeler excavated at Maiden Castle in England and at Harappa in India, and he invented a new excavation method which he employed during his excavations in both countries. He decided to excavate in five-meter by five-meter squares, with a meter-wide balk in between the squares. On this, the excavators could walk and push wheelbarrows, and so on. Kathleen Kenyon, who's probably best known for digging at Jericho and at Jerusalem, brought this method with her when she began excavating in what was then Palestine in the 1930s, so it's now known as the Wheeler-Kenyon or the Kenyon-Wheeler method.

Very simply, this method allows archaeologists to keep control of the stratigraphy by looking at the interior sides of each square to see what they've already dug through and to get a visual idea of the history of the area. Trust me, it can be quite easy to dig right through a patchy plaster floor, but afterwards you can see it very plainly as a white line stretching straight across the side of your square of the balk, or the section, as we call it. At the end of each season, most archaeological teams in the Near East will draw and photograph each of these sections so that they can publish a record of it for others to see and discuss. After all, archaeology is destruction. We destroy the very things that we're studying, even as we're digging through them. So we need to record every little thing in the process.

Well, today, we've looked at the origins of modern archaeology, and we've met several prominent individuals who contributed to the development of the discipline. Some of their methods and techniques are still used, especially those introduced by Petrie, Wheeler, and Kenyon. Every time we go out excavating in the field, we are not only digging up our past, but we're doing so using tried and true procedures that have been honed by the successors of the people we've met today.

But even beyond their methods and techniques, I'm impressed by the spirit of curiosity that drove these early archaeologists. They wanted, quite literally, to get beneath the surface of things—to uncover and retrieve the hidden records of the past. And it's that spirit that has inspired archaeologists ever since—generations of men and women who would join with me in saying, "I'd rather be digging."

Lecture 2

Excavating Pompeii and Herculaneum

Mount Vesuvius is located near the modern city of Naples, Italy. It is the only active volcano on the mainland of Europe today; as we know, it erupted on August 24, 79 A.D., killing at least 2,000 people in Pompeii, plus others in nearby towns, such as Herculaneum. At the time, Pompeii was a wealthy Roman town; in fact, it may have been something of a resort city—used as a getaway for wealthy members of society wishing to escape from Rome. Herculaneum, too, was a wealthy city, perhaps even more so than Pompeii. In this lecture, we'll look at the destruction and later excavation of these sites.

The Eruption

- We actually have an eyewitness description of the eruption of Mount Vesuvius, contained in two letters written by Pliny the Younger and sent to the Roman historian Tacitus. Pliny was 17 years old at the time and had been staying with his uncle, Pliny the Elder.

- The elder Pliny was in charge of the Roman fleet, which was stationed across the Bay of Naples from Vesuvius, at Misenum. During the eruption, the older Pliny attempted to sail to the rescue and save some of the fleeing survivors, but he died while doing so. The younger Pliny remained at Misenum, watching the eruption. His letters are full of details, based both on what he observed and what was later told to him by the men who had been with his uncle on the ships.

- Pliny's second letter, in particular, brings the story of the eruption to life:

    Behind us were frightening dark clouds, rent by lightning twisted and hurled, opening to reveal huge figures of flame. ... I look back: a dense cloud looms behind us, following us like a flood poured across the land. ... [Then] a darkness came that was not like a moonless or cloudy night, but more like the black of closed and unlighted rooms. You could hear women lamenting, children crying, men shouting. ... Many raised their hands to the gods, and even more believed that there were no gods any longer and that this was one last unending night for the world.

- As we know, for centuries afterward, Pompeii, Herculaneum, and other towns lay buried beneath several meters of ash and rock. Pompeii was the first of these towns to be discovered (in 1594), but Herculaneum was the first to be excavated. In the early 1700s, the duke of Elbeuf ordered his men to tunnel into the ground at Herculaneum after he bought the site specifically because ancient pieces of marble had been recovered from the area. The workmen happened to dig into the Roman theater and extracted a number of ancient marble statues.

- The earliest excavations at Pompeii were unprofessional, to say the least, frequently involving simply digging tunnels until something ancient was unearthed. Rather than archaeology, it was more like looting, but it was the first known excavation done in the modern era. However, proper excavations at Herculaneum and Pompeii began a few decades later and have essentially been ongoing ever since.

Herculaneum
- In addition to being hit with ash and pumice, Herculaneum seems to have been the victim of a 30-foot mudflow, known as a *lahar* in geological terms. This filled up the buildings and completely buried the city. Being buried in such a manner essentially preserved Herculaneum, freezing it just as it had been on that August morning in 79 A.D.

- Archaeologists working in 1981 discovered that Herculaneum had suffered yet another horror during the eruption of Vesuvius.
  - Until that point, relatively few human remains had been found, and it had long been assumed that most people had successfully fled or been evacuated. However, in excavations that year and again in the 1990s, archaeologists found the bodies of at least 300 people who had taken refuge in what seem to be boat houses on the shore.

- The people were probably waiting to be picked up by ships from the Roman fleet; however, a blast of heat, estimated at 1000° F, swept through the area. According to forensic anthropologists, the people were probably killed instantaneously. Only their skeletons remained; their skin and internal organs were destroyed by the heat and the hot ash that covered the bodies almost immediately.

- The same intense heat and ash also destroyed other organic material in the town, including private libraries and documents written on scrolls. These were turned into what are described as "cylinders of carbonized plant material." Up to 300 of these scrolls were found intact during the earliest excavations at Herculaneum (in 1752) in a villa that probably belonged to the family of the father-in-law of Julius Caesar.
  - In looking at photographs of these scrolls, it's difficult to see how they could possibly be unrolled or read in any way. But recent investigators have discovered a technique for making out letters written on the scrolls without unrolling them.
  - The technique involves using X-rays in a "laserlike beam," which allows researchers to detect "the ... contrast between the carbonized papyrus ... and the ... ink." It is not yet known whether the technique will work well enough to allow the carbonized scrolls to be read in their entirety, but it is an exciting development in archaeology.

Pompeii

- Excavations at Pompeii first began around 1750. Here, the ash and pumice that covered the town mixed with rain and eventually hardened into the consistency of cement, encasing hundreds of bodies. Over time, the flesh and inner organs of each body decayed slowly, forming hollow cavities in the ash in the shape of the body that had once been buried there.

- In 1863, Giuseppe Fiorelli, the Italian archaeologist in charge of excavating Pompeii, directed his team to pour plaster into these

Early excavators in Pompeii found a town frozen in time from 79 A.D.; bread was still on the tables, a dog remained chained up outside, and bodies were in the streets, some still clutching jewelry and other objects.

cavities, yielding an exact cast of what had originally formed the cavity. In this way, Fiorelli's team recovered the remains of hundreds of bodies, as well other organic materials, such as wooden furniture and loaves of bread. They also recovered nonorganic objects, ranging from jewelry to silverware to jugs made of precious metals.

- The houses in Pompeii were quite elegant, and just as in Herculaneum, they are extremely well preserved. One called the House of the Faun features a bronze statue of a faun, the satyr-like creature that is usually depicted playing the double-pipe. This same house also has the famous Alexander Mosaic, which uses hundreds of thousands of small stone tesserae to depict Alexander the Great fighting the Persian king Darius III.

- The eruption of Vesuvius also buried the gardens that belonged to some of the houses in Pompeii. In 1961, the archaeologist Wilhelmina Jashemski excavated an open area in Pompeii and found the remains of root cavities from the plants that had once been there. In fact, she was able to figure out the planting pattern in what was once a vineyard.

- Elsewhere in Pompeii, archaeologists have uncovered the remains of bath houses, tanneries, shops, and other dwellings that one would expect to find in a city from the period. Some of the most recent findings come from the excavations of Steven Ellis, a professor at the University of Cincinnati. In 2014, after digging in an area by the Porta Stabia, one of the main gates into the city, Ellis announced that he had found 10 separate building plots with 20 shopfronts from which food and drink were sold or served. Such an arrangement seems typical in Pompeii, where even the private houses frequently had shops installed on the street.

- Even more interesting, perhaps, were the drains, latrines, and cesspits that Ellis and his team excavated. In these, they found the remains of "grains, fruits, nuts, olives, lentils, local fish, and chicken eggs, as well as minimal cuts of more expensive meat and salted fish from Spain." In another drain, they found the remains of "shellfish, sea urchin, and even delicacies, including the butchered leg joint of a giraffe."

Paintings, Advertisements, and Graffiti at Pompeii

- The sudden burial of Pompeii preserved the paintings on the walls of the houses and buildings, including scenes that now give their names to the structures. For instance, the Villa of the Mysteries—referring to the mystery cult of Dionysus—gets its name from a scene of bacchanalian revelry on the walls of a small room.

- Outside some of the shops in Pompeii, we can also see written advertisements. One promises a gladiator combat on April 8 through 12, featuring 20 pairs of gladiators and "a full card of wild beast combats." Another specifies the market days for Pompeii, Nuceria,

Atella, and other towns. Outside a pub, yet another advertises the types of drinks and ales served 2,000 years ago.

- Hundreds of campaign notices from a recent or upcoming election have also been found. These notices concern people who were running for vacant offices, such as the office of aedile, which was a relatively lowly job in charge of public buildings, baths, water, sewers, and public festivals. Another was the office of duovir, which was a higher judicial office. Some of these endorsements include: "The goldsmiths unanimously urge the election of Gaius Cuspius Pansa as aedile," and "I ask you to elect Marcus Cerrinius Vatia to the aedileship. All the late-night drinkers support him. Florus and Fructus wrote this."

- Perhaps most interesting are the graffiti that we would usually think of as scrawled on bathroom walls today.
   - For example, one reads: "Take your lewd looks and flirting eyes off another man's wife, and show some decency on your face!" Another was obviously written by someone whose heart had just been broken: "Anybody in love, come here. I want to break Venus' ribs with a club and cripple the goddess' loins. If she can pierce my tender breast, why can't I break her head with a club?"

   - Finally, signaling that some things never seem to change, we find what is apparently a prostitute's sign: "I am yours for 2 asses cash."

- Indeed, looking into the past at such sites as Pompeii and Herculaneum—sites that have been frozen at a precise moment in time—we note a great number of similarities between the past and the present. Of course, we now have iPads and cell phones, but our houses today are not all that different from theirs back then; our food is similar; and we have the same dependence on roads, elected officials, and stores that stock items we need. On the whole, the excavations at these two sites teach us that the ancient inhabitants of the Mediterranean were not that different from people in the same area today.

Suggested Reading

Beard, *The Fires of Vesuvius*.

Berry, *The Complete Pompeii*.

Ellis, *The Making of Pompeii*.

Questions to Consider

1. If we did not have the words of Pliny the Younger, would archaeology alone be enough to reconstruct what happened in Pompeii when Mount Vesuvius erupted in 79 A.D.?

2. What are some of the similarities between life in Pompeii during the 1st century A.D. and life today in terms of diet, housing, elections, and other aspects of city life?

Lecture 2 Transcript: Excavating Pompeii and Herculaneum

When I was a kid growing up in San Francisco, there was a family who lived down the street; they had been to Pompeii. I was fascinated by this fact as I was with Pompeii itself, and so when I was in sixth grade, I interviewed them about what it had been like to visit Pompeii. I also wrote a fictional story about what it must have been like to be in the city when Mt. Vesuvius exploded in the year 79 A.D. So you can see, I've had a long-time relationship with this famous buried city, including visiting it myself, and it's rather near and dear to my heart.

So let's go to Italy now, near the modern city of Naples, where Mt. Vesuvius is located. Mt. Vesuvius is the only active volcano on the mainland of Europe today. It's erupted several times since 1900. The most recent one was in 1944 during World War II, but that was a pretty small one. In 1906, though, there was an eruption that lasted for days and killed several thousand people. That one was probably similar to what happened on August 24th back in 79 A.D. when about 2,000 people were killed in the city of Pompeii. Others died in nearby towns like Herculaneum.

At the time, Pompeii was a wealthy Roman town, well known for its fish sauce called *garum*, and for its opulent villas and houses. In fact, it may have served as something like a resort city, kind of like a getaway for wealthy members of society who wanted to escape from Rome. Some Romans may actually have had a second home in Pompeii that they used on weekends or during the summer.

In contrast, I've always thought of Herculaneum as being Pompeii's poorer cousin, almost as if the people who actually worked in Pompeii couldn't afford to live there, so they lived in Herculaneum instead and commuted. But as it turns out, Herculaneum may actually have been an even wealthier town than Pompeii, at least if the density of nice houses and the amount of marble that was used is any indication.

In any event, in late August of 79 A.D., Mt. Vesuvius blew its top, and a fierce volcanic eruption began. This resulted in the destruction of Pompeii, Herculaneum, and other towns in the vicinity, including one called Stabiae. We actually have an eyewitness description of the eruption which is contained in two letters written by Pliny the Younger. He sent them to Tacitus, the Roman historian, who had asked him for details. Pliny the Younger was 17 years old at the time, and he'd been staying with his uncle, whom we now call Pliny the Elder.

This older Pliny was in charge of the Roman fleet which was stationed across the Bay of Naples from Vesuvius at a place called Misenum. During the eruption, the older Pliny attempted to sail to the rescue and save some of the fleeing survivors, but he died while doing so. The younger Pliny, fortunately for him, didn't go with his uncle on that rescue mission. He stayed back at Misenum watching the eruption. His letters are full of details, based both on what he observed and what was later told to him by the men who had been with his uncle on the ships.

In his first letter, Pliny vividly describes the events surrounding his uncle's death. But let me read to you a few paragraphs from his second letter, which is a first-hand account that really brings the story of the eruption to life. Pliny writes:

> Behind us were frightening dark clouds, rent by lightning, twisted and hurled, opening to reveal huge figures of flame. Now came the dust, though still thinly. I look back. A dense cloud looms behind us, following us like a flood poured across the land. Then a darkness came that was not like the moonless or cloudy night, but more like the black of a closed and unlit room. You could hear women lamenting, children crying, men shouting. Some were calling for parents; others for children or spouses. It grew lighter though that seemed not a return of day, but a sign that the fire was approaching. The fire itself actually stopped some distance away, but darkness and ashes came again, a great weight of them. We shook off the ash, again and again. Otherwise, we would have been covered with it and crushed by the weight.

Bear in mind, young Pliny was describing these horrifying scenes at Misenum, which was spared the brunt of the eruption. Other towns weren't so lucky. For centuries, they lay buried beneath several meters of ash and rock.

Even though Pompeii was discovered first when an irrigation trench accidentally exposed some of the ancient ruins in 1594, it was Herculaneum that was the first of these buried cities to be excavated, if we can call it that. It was the duke of Elbeuf in the early 1700s who ordered his men to tunnel into the ground at Herculaneum. He had bought the site specifically because ancient pieces of marble had been recovered from the area. His men happened to dig right into the ancient Roman theater there, and they were able to extract a number of the ancient marble statues. Some of these were used to decorate the Count's estate; others were distributed elsewhere in Europe, including to some museums.

The earliest excavations at Pompeii were unprofessional, to say the least. They frequently involved simply digging more and more tunnels until something ancient was unearthed. It wasn't exactly what we would call archaeology; it was more like looting, but it was the first known excavations done in the modern era. However, proper excavations at Herculaneum, and then at Pompeii, began a few decades later and have essentially been ongoing ever since.

In addition to being hit with ash and pumice, Herculaneum seems to have been the victim of a thirty-foot-high mudflow, known as a *lahar* in geological terms. This smashed into the city, filling up the buildings, and completely burying it. We hear of similar things happening when volcanoes erupt today, like Mount Pinatubo in the Philippines back in 1991, or Nevado del Ruiz in Colombia where a mudflow killed more than 23,000 people out of the almost 29,000 that were living in the village of Armero back in 1985. The U.S. Geological Service reports that such mudflows can move as fast as about 40 miles an hour, and they can reach as far as about 60 miles away from the actual volcano.

Being buried in such a manner essentially preserved Herculaneum, freezing it just as it had been on that August morning back in 79 A.FD. Andrew

Wallace-Hadrill, the former Director of the British School at Rome, has pointed out that we've been able to recover upper floors, even to two levels; wooden structures including beams, doors and flimsy partitions; wooden objects, cupboards, shrines, screens, beds, even a cradle; and fabrics, also papyrus scrolls and wooden tablets.

From a distance, it can actually be rather difficult to distinguish where the ancient buildings end and the modern town begins because the bricks and other materials from which the structures are made look very similar. The walls still stand to the second story in many of the ancient houses, and the decoration on the walls, including in the bathhouses, is still extremely vivid.

But archaeologists working in the town in 1981 discovered that Herculaneum had suffered yet another horror during the eruption of Vesuvius. Until that point, relatively few human remains had been found. It had long been assumed that most people had successfully fled or been evacuated. However, in excavations that year and then again in the late 1990s, archaeologists found the bodies of at least 300 people who had taken refuge in what seem to be boat houses on the shore.

The people were probably waiting to be picked up by ships from the Roman fleet like those that were commanded by Pliny the Elder, but a blast of heat swept through the area. Its temperature is estimated to have been nearly 1,000 degrees Fahrenheit. The people were killed pretty much instantly—in less than a fraction of a second—according to the forensic anthropologists who studied them. Only their skeletons still remain; the skin and their internal organs were destroyed by the heat and then by the hot ash that covered the bodies almost immediately.

The same intense heat and ash also destroyed other organic material in the town, including private libraries with books and documents written on scrolls. These were turned into what are described as cylinders of carbonized plant material by the hot gases that swept through the town. About 300 of these scrolls were found intact during the earliest excavations at Herculaneum, way back in 1752. They were discovered in a villa that probably belonged to the family of the father-in-law of Julius Caesar. In looking at these, it's actually quite hard to tell what they are. In photographs, at least, they look more like lumps of wood than papyrus scrolls, and it's very hard to see how they could possibly be unrolled or read in any way, shape, or form.

It's not surprising that it was thought that nothing could be done with them for the longest time—despite occasional attempts—since they were so carbonized, but all of that may now be changing. There's still no telling what the scrolls contain, but since they're considered to be part of a library, they may well include things like the lost books of Livy's history of Rome, at least according to a *New York Times* article that was published in January 2015.

The article describes the work of investigators. They've been able to make out letters written on the scrolls without actually unrolling them. The technique involves using X-rays in a laser-like beam, which allows them to detect the contrast between the carbonized papyrus and the ink even though the ink is also made out of carbon. We don't know yet whether the technique is going to work well enough for us to read the carbonized scrolls in their entirety. But if we can, it's going to be fantastic, so stay tuned.

Over at Pompeii where excavations first began about 1750, time also froze during that late August morning in 79 A.D. Bread is still on the tables, a dog remains chained, graffiti is still on the town walls, and bodies are in the streets, some of them clutching jewelry and other objects. In fact, these bodies are one of the most interesting things about excavating at Pompeii. But how have they endured?

Well, as the ash and pumice rained down upon Pompeii, the ash mixed with rain and eventually hardened into the consistency of cement. So essentially, you've got hundreds of dead bodies encased in this hardened ash. Now over time, the flesh and the inner organs of each body decayed slowly, as opposed to being scorched away in an instant like happened in Herculaneum. As a result of this slow decay, hollow cavities formed in the ash, each cavity bearing the shape of the body that had once been buried there.

OK, fast forward to 1863. This is when Giuseppe Fiorelli, the Italian archaeologist in charge of excavating Pompeii, had an idea. Whenever his team came across a cavity while digging, Fiorelli had them stop what they were doing so he could pour plaster into the cavity. The plaster filled up the cavity, and when the ash was excavated away, they had an exact cast of whatever had been in there originally. In this way, they recovered the remains of hundreds of bodies, including entire families, huddled together, as well anything else organic like wooden tables and other furniture, as well as buns and even loaves of bread. They also recovered other non-organic objects, of course, ranging from jewelry to silverware to jugs and juglets that are made out of precious materials.

The problem with using plaster of Paris is that you can't see the bones from the skeleton, or if any artifacts might have been left in the cavity even after the body disintegrated. Let's say, for instance, that somebody had run back to their house to grab a small leather bag of jewelry and had then been overcome by the superheated poison gas that came through the town or by the ash and pumice that was raining down. The skin and the organs of the body, and the leather bag will have disintegrated long ago, but the bones and the jewelry should still be intact. So some have suggested using resin, like for skateboards or surfboards, instead of plaster of Paris because it's transparent, but that's very expensive. In fact, it's been used in 1984 for only one victim of Vesuvius, a woman who is now forever known as the Resin Lady. She was found in the basement of a villa in a suburb of Pompeii still wearing her gold jewelry and with her hairpin in her hair.

Most recently, in late September of 2015, it was announced that a team had started to restudy the plaster casts that had been made of the victims. This team included not only archaeologists and anthropologists but also other specialists like radiologists. They're doing laser imaging and DNA sampling of the bones, but it's the CAT scans that have already made the news. They revealed amazing details, including a young boy about four years old who was found with his parents and a younger sibling. In the scans, you can see just how scared and in shock he must have been just before he died. The scans also show that many of the people had suffered head injuries, perhaps from collapsing buildings or perhaps even from rocks falling from the sky. And they indicate that the victims included people of all ages, not just the young, or the old, or the sick city dwellers.

I tell my students that I feel very sorry for the people who died, of course, but I feel even worse about the dog that was found still chained up where his owner had left him. The poor dog climbed up the ash as it fell until he reached the extent of his chain and then he strangled to death. His body was found upside down in a contorted position with the collar still plainly visible in the plaster cast that's now all that remains of the dog.

Elsewhere in the city, there's a happier portrait of a different dog, which is one of my favorite parts of ancient Pompeii. This is a floor mosaic of a really cute black and white dog, with a nice red collar. The mosaic is in the entryway to the House of the Tragic Poet, as it's called. Since it's in the entryway, it's probably not surprising, and perhaps it's even fitting that beneath the dog's paws at the very edge of the mosaic, it says C-A-V-E C-A-N-E-M—pronounced Cah-way-Cah-num, which is Latin for—you guessed it—Beware of the Dog.

The houses in Pompeii were quite elegant. Just as in Herculaneum, they're extremely well preserved since they were covered over and entombed underneath meters of hardened ash and pumice for almost 2,000 years before the archaeologists arrived and began revealing them once again. We see men's quarters, women's quarters, inner atriums, and backyard gardens in these dwellings. I'm especially partial to the one that's called The House of the Faun. This features a bronze statue of a faun, a satyr-like creature with horns on his head and a tail, who's usually depicted playing the double-pipe. This particular faun is located within a large basin that served to catch rainwater in an open area of the house.

The house also has the famous Alexander Mosaic. This depicts Alexander the Great fighting the Persian king Darius III. It used to be thought that this depicted the battle fought at Issus in 333 B.C., but now some scholars have suggested it could be a depiction of their second meeting, at the Battle of Gaugamela two years later in 331. Either way, the mosaic is a masterpiece, with hundreds of thousands of small stone tesserae—little cubes—used to depict the action. Somebody in Pompeii knew their Greek history and could afford to hire a master craftsman to depict it. And the House of the Faun also has a marvelous backyard. Today it's filled with trees and plants of all kinds and it actually reminds me of southern California where I grew up, which has a very similar climate.

In fact, the eruption also buried the actual gardens that belonged to some of those houses in Pompeii. One archaeologist, Wilhelmina Jashemski, who taught at the University of Maryland, specialized in these gardens. Back in 1961, she was allowed to excavate an open area in Pompeii and quickly found the remains of root cavities from the plants that had once been there. In fact, she was able to figure out the planting pattern, as it's called, in what was once a vineyard. Subsequently, she published several volumes on the gardens of Pompeii and Herculaneum, and in the process, she basically started a whole new subfield of archaeology.

Elsewhere in Pompeii, archaeologists have uncovered the remains of bath houses, both for men and for women. They've also found tanneries, shops, and other dwellings that one would expect to find in a city from that period. Some of the most recent findings have come from the excavations of Steven Ellis, a professor at the University of Cincinnati. In 2014, after digging for several years in an area by the Porta Stabia, one of the main gates into the city, Ellis announced that he had found 10 separate building plots with 20 shop fronts. From these, food and drink would have been sold or served. Such an arrangement seems typical in Pompeii where even the private houses frequently had shops installed on the street side.

Even more useful, perhaps, were the drains, and latrines, and cesspits that Ellis and his team excavated. In these, they found the remains of grains, fruits, nuts, olives, lentils, local fish, and chicken eggs, as well as smaller cuts of more expensive meat and even salted fish from Spain. In another drain from a more centrally located property, probably belonging to a member of the upper society, they found the remains of shellfish, sea urchin, and delicacies like the butchered leg joint of a giraffe. All of this, of course, gives us an idea of what people were eating in Pompeii at the time of the eruption, including the fact that the different classes ate different types of food which, of course, is not at all surprising.

By the way, just in terms of new technology being used on excavations, Steve Ellis's University of Cincinnati team was one of the first in the world to use iPads on-site. They directly recorded the excavation information using apps instead of pen and paper, and then later they uploaded the data to servers back in Cincinnati, even while they were still at Pompeii.

The sudden burial of Pompeii also preserved the paintings on the walls of the houses and buildings, including scenes that now give their names to the structures. So one scene of a bacchanalian revelry featuring Dionysus and lots and lots of wine is in a house called the Villa of the Mysteries, because if you weren't a member of the cult of Dionysus, it was a mystery to you as to what they did. In this case, we're shown a scene that goes around all four walls of a small room, maybe a dining room. And it depicts what appears to be the initiation of a young woman into the mysteries of Dionysus. Other scenes found on walls in other houses are much tamer, including what look like ballet dancers and less exotic, or even erotic images.

One of the most interesting things to me is the amount of graffiti that can still be seen painted on the walls of Pompeii's buildings on either side of some of the main streets. Don't get me wrong, these are not graffiti in terms of kids tagging buildings or railroad cars like they do today, but instead, it's graffiti that served a purpose. Some of these have been collected together in a sourcebook by Naphtali Lewis and Meyer Reinhold.

For instance, outside some of the shops, we can see advertisements written. One says that a gladiator combat is upcoming, or rather was. The dates that are given are April 8–12, but it's not clear if that was in the past or still in the future for Pompeii in 79 A.D. It reads:

> Twenty pairs of gladiators of Decimus Lucretius Satrius Valens, lifetime flamen of Nero son of Caesar Augustus, and ten pairs of gladiators of Decimus Lucretius Valens, his son. They will fight at Pompeii on April 8, 9, 10, 11, and 12. There will be a full card of wild beast combats, and awnings [for the spectators]. Aemilius Celer [painted this sign], all alone in the moonlight.

I like the fact that the guy who painted this sign is quite literally moonlighting. I wonder if he had a day job as well?

Another bit of graffiti tells us about the market days: Saturday in Pompeii, Sunday in Nuceria, Monday in Atella, Tuesday in Nola, Wednesday in Cumae, Thursday in Puteoli, and Friday in Rome. So if you wanted to go get fresh vegetables, you knew where to go depending upon what day it was.

One of my favorites is written outside of what must once have been a bar or a pub. It reads: "Pleasure says: 'You can get a drink here for an as—that's a few cents—a better drink for two, and Falernian for four.'" So we know what types of drinks and ales they were serving 2,000 years ago and how much they cost. And outside a shop that apparently had just suffered a theft is written: "A copper pot is missing from this shop. 65 sesterces reward if anybody brings it back, 20 sesterces if he reveals the thief so we can get our property back."

There were also hundreds of campaign notices from a recent or an upcoming election. The most interesting to me are the notices concerning people who were running for a few of the vacant offices. One of these is the office of aedile, which was a fairly lowly job in charge of things like public buildings, baths, water, sewers, and regulation of public festivals. Two people were elected to this each year. Another was the office of duovir. This was a higher judicial office to which two people were also elected each year. Some of the endorsements that we find written on the walls of the building include things like: "I ask you to elect Gaius Julius Polybius aedile. He gets good bread." And another one: "The worshippers of Isis unanimously urge the election of Gnaeus Helvius Sabinus as aedile."

My two favorites, though, are the following: "I ask you to elect Marcus Cerrinius Vatia to the aedileship. All the late-night drinkers support him." And the other one: "The petty thieves support Vatia for the aedileship." For the life of me, I can't decide which of those two I like the best. Tell me, if you were running for office, would you rather be endorsed by the late-night drinkers or by the petty thieves? I'd say that it's kind of a toss-up, at least for me, but, at least, this guy Vatia is supported by both groups, so that's good.

But then, we still have the people running for the office of duovir. Here's one: "His neighbors urge you to elect Lucius Statius Receptus duovir with judicial power; he is worthy. Aemilius Celer, a neighbor, wrote this. May you take sick if you maliciously erase this." Note that this is the same guy who also wrote the advertisement about the gladiator fight all alone in the moonlight, so maybe he does have a day job.

But perhaps of the most interest are the graffiti that we would usually think of as scrawled on bathroom walls today. One is in three parts. The first part reads: "The weaver Successus, he loves the innkeeper's slave girl, Iris. She doesn't care for him, but he begs her to take pity on him. Written by his rival. So long." And then underneath it is a response, an answer from the rival: "Just because you're bursting with envy, don't pick on a handsomer man, a lady-killer, and a gallant." Then we've got the first guy replying again: "There's nothing more to say or write. You love Iris. She doesn't care for you."

Another piece of graffiti simply says: "Take your lewd looks and your flirting eyes off another man's wife, and show some decency on your face." I'd love to know the backside of that story and exactly where it was written—is it outside a house, outside a store? Is it somewhere else?

One piece of graffiti was obviously written by someone whose heart had just been broken: "Anybody in love, come here. I want to break Venus's ribs with a club. If she can pierce my tender breast, why can't I break her head with a club?"

Our final two examples include one that reads simply: "I write at Love's dictation and Cupid's instruction. But damn it. I don't want to be a god without you." And the last one is apparently a prostitute's sign: "I am yours for 2 asses cash." Based on that last bit of graffiti, I think it's safe to say that some things never change. In fact, what we've learned from more than 250 years of on-again, off-again excavations at Pompeii and Herculaneum is that archaeology is a useful tool to find out more about ourselves as human beings.

Looking into the past at sites like these where they have been frozen at essentially a precise moment in time, indicates to me that we really haven't changed all that much during the past 2,000 years. Sure, we have iPads and cell phones now, but our houses today are not all that different from theirs back then. Our food is basically similar. We've got the same dependence upon roads and elected officials, and stores that stock items that we need. We keep the same pets. We wear similar jewelry. We eat from similar dishes and use similar utensils.

Now, we may not eat peacock's tongues as a delicacy anymore, and we might not clean our clothes using urine, but on the whole, the excavations at these two sites teach us that the ancient inhabitants of the Mediterranean were not that different from people in the same area today. And it's thanks to archaeology that we can confidently say such things.

Lecture 3: Schliemann and His Successors at Troy

Our information about the Trojan War comes to us mainly from the Greek poet Homer. According to Homer, during the Late Bronze Age, the Greeks believed that Helen, the wife of a king named Menelaus, had been kidnapped by Paris, a prince of Troy. For their part, the Trojans claimed that Helen went with Paris willingly because she was in love with him. Led by Menelaus and his brother Agamemnon, the Greeks sent a fleet to besiege Troy and get Helen back. After 10 years, the Greeks destroyed Troy and returned with Helen. The question Heinrich Schliemann and others sought to answer was: Was there a historical Trojan War that served as a basis for Homer's epic?

Heinrich Schliemann's Quest and "Discovery"

- The classical scholars of the 19th century in Europe were pretty firmly convinced that the Trojan War had not taken place and was completely invented by Homer. Thus, when Heinrich Schliemann, an amateur in the field of archaeology, decided that he was going to go look for the site of Troy, he was going against the thinking of most scholars of his day.

- By all accounts, Schliemann was not a man whose word could be entirely trusted. But by the time he was in his 40s, he had earned enough of a fortune so that he could retire and devote himself to finding evidence for Troy and the Trojan War.

- In 1868, Schliemann traveled to Greece and Turkey, searching for a site that would match the description of Troy given by Homer. In his travels, he met the American vice consul to Turkey, Frank Calvert, who had also been looking for Troy and believed that he had found it. In fact, he had already bought the ancient mound, which now had the modern Turkish name Hisarlik, meaning "Place of Fortresses."

- Calvert had already begun excavations at the site but didn't have enough money to continue the work. Schliemann had plenty of

Heinrich Schliemann was intent on finding Troy and proving that the Trojan War had taken place, claiming that the quest had been a childhood dream.

money and was happy to join forces with Calvert. However, once they began excavating and Schliemann decided that the mound was indeed the site of ancient Troy, he deliberately left Calvert's name out of all subsequent official announcements, lectures, and publications, thereby claiming the fame and glory for himself.

Schliemann's Early Excavations

- In 1872, Schliemann began his greatest assault on Hisarlik. Using a large team of local workmen, he dug a huge trench across most of the mound and down to a depth of about 45 feet. Although archaeology was a relatively new field at the time, there were still people who were knowledgeable enough, including Calvert, to warn Schliemann that such reckless digging might result in catastrophe—and they were right.

- Schliemann and his men dug deeper into the trench, through buildings and stratigraphic levels. It turned out that there were nine cities buried on top of one another in the mound, although Schliemann thought at first that there were only six.
    - He stopped at what turned out to be the second city from the bottom, which he called the Burnt City. He was convinced that this was the city ruled by the Trojan king Priam, and his discoveries the next year confirmed to him that he was correct.

    - We now know, on the basis of pottery and carbon-14 dating, that Schliemann's Burnt City dates to 2400 B.C., during the Early Bronze Age, which is more than 1,000 years before the Trojan War would have been fought.

    - If you stand at the bottom of Schliemann's Great Trench today, at the level where he and his men stopped digging, and look straight up, you can see a level that contains a building made out of huge blocks of stone. This building dates to the period of city VI and was reused in city VII. It is all that's left of a palace that dates to the Late Bronze Age, that is, the time period for which Schliemann was looking.

Priam's Treasure

- What convinced Schliemann that city II was Priam's Troy? For one thing, he found a huge city gate, which he identified as Homer's Scaean Gate. He also reported that he had found Priam's Treasure.

- According to Schliemann, he and his wife, Sophia, dug out the treasure themselves. The objects they discovered included gold jewelry, bronze tools, gold and silver cups and bowls, a golden vessel in the shape of a pomegranate, and stone hilts that probably belonged to bronze swords. The Schliemanns brought the objects home from the site and catalogued them.

- They subsequently smuggled the treasure back to their residence in Athens. But soon thereafter, Schliemann donated it to the Berlin Museum. The treasure disappeared in the aftermath of World War II and was presumed lost for nearly 50 years. In the early 1990s, the Russians admitted that they had taken it as part of the spoils of war.

- Today, Priam's Treasure is in the Pushkin Museum in Moscow. It remains there despite the fact that four countries now lay claim to it: Turkey, Greece, Germany, and Russia. Interestingly, the question of who owns the treasure is irrelevant because it's neither Priam's nor a treasure.

- Given that the objects were found in city II, which dates back to about 2400 B.C., they are 1,000 years too early to have belonged to Priam. In addition, some scholars have suggested that Schliemann didn't even find the treasure in one place. Instead, they think he gathered the best of his finds from the season and announced that he had found them all together. In fact, we may never know what actually transpired.

- The objects bear a great deal of resemblance to objects found elsewhere, from the islands of the northeast Aegean to the so-called Death Pits of Ur. The gold earrings, pins, and necklaces that Schliemann found may not have belonged to Priam, but they did belong to a class of jewelry that was in fashion across much of the Aegean and the ancient Near East at the end of the 3rd millennium B.C.

The Excavations of Dörpfeld and Blegen

- Schliemann continued to dig at Troy throughout the 1870s and 1880s with the assistance of Wilhelm Dörpfeld, an architect with some previous archaeological experience. Dörpfeld eventually persuaded Schliemann that they should investigate city VI or city VII. Schliemann made plans for an additional attack on the mound, focused on these later levels, but he died in 1890.

- Dörpfeld concentrated on excavating the remains at Hisarlik that Schliemann had left untouched, mostly around the edges of the mound. He unearthed tall stone walls, each several meters thick, and large gateways allowing entrance to the interior.

- These were the remains of city VI, which seems to have lasted from about 1700 B.C. to 1250 B.C. Dörpfeld found numerous phases to the city, which he categorized A through H. The last phase, Troy VIH, showed signs of almost complete destruction. For Dörpfeld, this was definitive evidence for the Trojan War. He ended his excavations and published his results.

- However, Carl Blegen, an archaeologist at the University of Cincinnati, examined Dörpfeld's results and correctly concluded that an earthquake, not warfare, had caused the destruction of Troy VIH. Blegen believed that city VII had been besieged and destroyed by an army; thus, he reopened the excavations at Hisarlik in the 1930s.

- Blegen found enough evidence, including arrowheads, bodies, and other indications of battle, to convince himself that city VII had been destroyed by humans in a protracted siege.
    o He also found that the large buildings and palaces of the previous city had been subdivided to allow several families to live where only one had been previously. Further, he noted that the storage capacity of the city had been increased tremendously, with large jars buried up to their necks in the ground.

- To Blegen, all this indicated a city that was under siege, just as Homer had said. The fact that the city had been destroyed about 1180 B.C. also put it in the timeframe suggested by the ancient Greeks.

- Moreover, the material culture of the city showed continuity between Troy VI and VII. In other words, there was no evidence of a new group of people in city VII; rather, it appeared that the people in city VI had rebuilt their city. For these reasons, Blegen was convinced that an earthquake had destroyed city VI, while the Mycenaean Greeks had destroyed city VII during the Trojan War.

Recent Excavations

- Beginning in 1988, an international team of archaeologists decided to investigate the mound of Hisarlik again. This team was led by two men: Manfred Korfmann from the University of Tübingen, investigating the Bronze Age remains, and Brian Rose from the University of Cincinnati, investigating the post–Bronze Age remains.

- Korfmann's team surveyed the agricultural fields around Hisarlik using a magnetometer, which enabled them to detect walls, ditches, and buildings lying below the surface of the earth. Thanks to this device, the researchers realized that they had found an entire lower city of Troy beneath the agricultural fields. All the earlier archaeologists had simply been excavating the citadel—or upper part—of the city. The remains found by Korfmann's team increased the size of the city at least tenfold and established it as a site that would indeed have been worthy of a 10-year-long siege.

- Although Korfmann's team misinterpreted some of their initial results—mistaking a large ditch for the great wall of the city—some of their findings seemed to confirm Blegen's work. For example, in both the citadel and the lower city, they also found evidence for earthquake destruction in city VI and human destruction—warfare—in city VII.

- In addition, Korfmann's work confirmed Blegen's findings that after the city was destroyed in about 1180 B.C., the next city was occupied by what seem to be new people. In this phase, called Troy VIIb, we see new types of pottery, new architecture, and other material culture—all indications that the inhabitants of the previous city had been replaced by a new group.

- As the Hisarlik digs continued, the post–Bronze Age team, led by Brian Rose, found a great deal of material, too, including a statue of the Roman emperor Hadrian and a marble head of Augustus. The Hellenistic Greeks and then the Romans had built on the citadel and established a nicely gridded city below. These later inhabitants were also convinced that this was the site of ancient Troy; in fact, they gave it the name New Troy in both Greek and Latin.

- Korfmann died suddenly in 2005, but the international excavations continued. Interest both in digging and remote sensing in and around the site continues even now, which means that Hisarlik may reveal even more secrets about the ancient town that inspired one of the greatest epics ever written.

Suggested Reading

Cline, *The Trojan War: A Very Short Introduction*.

Strauss, *The Trojan War: A New History*.

Wood, *In Search of the Trojan War*.

Questions to Consider

1. Do you believe that Schliemann actually found Priam's Treasure?

2. Do you think that Troy VIh or Troy VIIA is more likely to be Priam's city?

Lecture 3 Transcript
Schliemann and His Successors at Troy

Let's talk about excavations, specifically at the site of Troy, starting with Heinrich Schliemann and then bringing them up to the present. This is actually a topic that got me started in archaeology in the first place. When I was seven years old, my mother gave me a book by Marjorie Braymer. It was called *The Walls of Windy Troy*. It was a biography of Heinrich Schliemann, written for children. And I announced to my parents there and then that I was going to be an archaeologist. And when I graduated from college with a degree in archaeology, my mother gave me the exact same book all over again, and I still have it.

Things have now come full circle. Not only have I published a very short introduction to the topic of Troy and the Trojan War, but I also wrote, in collaboration with the wonderful Jill Rubalcaba, a book specifically for young adults, called *Digging for Troy*. And I hope that at some point, some young person, whether they're 7 years old or 17 years old, will read that book and decide that they too want to become an archaeologist.

So, let's begin at the beginning. I don't know that we really need to go through the entire story of the Trojan War, so let me just give you the CliffsNotes version, down and dirty, which we get from the Greek poet Homer and a few other epic poets. We do need to keep in mind, though, that the story probably wasn't written down until about 500 years after the actual events.

Now, it seems that back in the Late Bronze Age, probably in the 13th or the 12th century B.C., the Greeks and the Trojans went to war for 10 years over a woman named Helen. At that time, Helen was the wife of a man named Menelaus, who was a king in an area in the southern part of the Greek mainland. His brother is Agamemnon, king of kings, who ruled from the city of Mycenae. And it's from this city, Mycenae, that we derive the name Mycenaeans, by which we mean the Greeks of that time.

Now, a delegation from Troy came to visit Menelaus. Among its members was a man named Paris, who's also sometimes referred to as Alexander. He was a prince of Troy, the son of King Priam. When the delegation returned home to Troy, which is located on the western coast of Anatolia—that is, modern Turkey—Helen was among them. The Trojans claimed she had come with them willingly because she was in love with Paris. The Greeks claimed that she had been kidnapped.

Led by Agamemnon and Menelaus, along with other Mycenaean heroes like Odysseus and Achilles, the Greeks sent a large fleet of ships and men to besiege Troy and get Helen back. It took 10 long years before they were able to do so, and even then it was only by using the trick of the Trojan Horse that they were able to succeed. In the end, the Greeks destroyed Troy; they burnt it to the ground, and they returned home with Helen. Now, it took some of them longer to get home than others, including Odysseus—and for him, it took an additional 10 years.

So that's the story in a nutshell. But now we come to an important question: Was there an actual, historical Trojan War that served as a basis for Homer's epic? Well, even the ancient Greeks were divided on whether the Trojan War had actually taken place, and even if it had, what was the actual date? In the end, the most generally accepted date for them was 1184 B.C., which as it turns out is actually just about the time when the entire Late Bronze Age came crashing down, and it may be that the Trojan War was part of a much larger catastrophe. However, the classical scholars of the 19th century in Europe were pretty firmly convinced that the Trojan War hadn't actually taken place and that it was completely made up by Homer.

So when Heinrich Schliemann, who was basically a complete amateur in the field of archaeology, decided that he was going to go look for the site of Troy, he was going against the thinking of most of the scholars of his day. But Schliemann was intent on finding Troy and proving that the Trojan War had taken place. In a book written much later, Schliemann claims that he had first decided to do this at about the age of eight or nine. His father had given him a history book for Christmas and in the book was an artist's rendition of Aeneas fleeing from the burning city of Troy. Aeneas is headed for Italy, where his later descendants Romulus and Remus founded the city of Rome—at least according to tradition. Schliemann says he decided there and then that he was going to find Troy.

Now, I'm sympathetic to Schliemann's story—because it's actually similar to my own—but other scholars have called it into question. That's because Schliemann never mentions this earlier in his life, despite leaving quite literally volumes of diaries, and notebooks, and letters, and even other books. In any event, it took Schliemann until he was in his 40s to earn enough of a fortune so that he could retire and then devote the rest of his life to finding evidence for Troy and the Trojan War. Now, we don't have time to go into all of the shenanigans that Schliemann did while accumulating this fortune, but let's just say for now that it seemed he was not a man whose word could be entirely trusted, either in his personal life or his professional life.

Let me give you just one example. It's relevant because it pertains directly to Schliemann's discovery of Troy—and I would definitely put discovery in quotes. In 1868, Schliemann took a trip to Greece and then he proceeded on to Turkey. He says that he traveled around northwestern Turkey, with Homer in one hand, looking for a site that was small enough so that Achilles could've chased Hector around it several times and that also had both hot and cold springs, again to match the description given by Homer. Now, Schliemann looked at a number of sites that had been suggested previously, but none of them seemed to him to quite fit the bill.

However, he then met the American vice consul to Turkey, a man named Frank Calvert. Calvert had also been looking for Troy, and he thought that he had found it. In fact, he had already bought the ancient mound, which now had the modern Turkish name Hisarlik, meaning Place of Fortresses. Calvert had already begun some initial excavations at the site, but he didn't have enough money to continue working properly. Schliemann, on the other hand, had plenty of money and was happy to join forces with Calvert. But once they began excavating and Schliemann thought the he had found enough to decide that the mound really was the site of ancient Troy, he deliberately left Calvert's name out of his subsequent official announcements, and lectures, and publications, and he thereby claimed the fame and glory for himself. It was only in 1999, with a book published by Susan Allen, that Calvert was restored to his rightful place in history.

At any rate, the first excavation season by Schliemann at Hisarlik began in April 1870. He didn't yet have an official excavation permit from the Turkish authorities, but that didn't stop him. He didn't find much that season, or the next. And so in 1872, with the help of a large team of local workmen, he launched his greatest assault on the ancient site. Now, this took the form of a huge trench that his men dug right across most of the mound and down to a depth of about 45 feet. Today it's known as Schliemann's Great Trench, and it's still visible as a huge gash right in the middle of the site.

Now, do bear in mind, archaeology was still relatively in its infancy in that time. Even though excavations had been ongoing at Pompeii for over a century by that point, there wasn't that much digging going on elsewhere in the 1870s. But, there were people who were knowledgeable enough, including Calvert, that they warned Schliemann that such reckless digging might result in catastrophe. And sure enough, they were right.

In the Great Trench, Schliemann and his men went down, down, down; right through all sorts of buildings and stratigraphic levels. It turns out there were nine cities buried one on top of another in the mound, although Schliemann thought, at first, there were only six. He stopped at what turned out to be the second city from the bottom, which he called the Burnt City. He was convinced that this was the city that Priam had ruled, and his discoveries the next year confirmed to him that he was correct. But, he wasn't correct. We now know, on the basis of pottery and carbon-14 dating, that city number two dates to 2400 B.C., during the Early Bronze Age. That's more than 1,000 years before the Trojan War would have been fought.

Now, if you stand at the bottom of the Great Trench today, at the level where Schliemann and his men stopped digging, and you look straight up, you can see—way high above—a level that contains a building made out of huge blocks of stone. This is a building that dates to city number six and was reused in city number seven. It's all that's left of a palace that dates to the Late Bronze Age; that is the time for which Schliemann was looking. Most of that palace, though, is now missing, and it's missing because of Heinrich Schliemann. In his haste, Schliemann and his men dug right through it and they threw most of it out on their back dirt pile. So if we were to go dig in that spoil heap of dirt, I can almost guarantee that we would find all sorts of things, including perhaps clay tablets used by the ancient scribes.

So, what was it that convinced Schliemann that city number two was Priam's Troy? Well, for one thing, he found a huge city gate that he identified as Homer's Scaean Gate. And then came his report that he had found a great treasure, which he identified immediately as Priam's Treasure. And he told a great story about finding it, too; one that has long been repeated in introductory archaeology textbooks, though now it's been called into question. I've written about this at length elsewhere, especially in my introduction to the Trojan War, so here I'll just give you the most relevant and salient details.

It seems that Schliemann was wandering around the mound one morning in May 1873, observing his workmen digging, and he says that he noticed one of them unearthing a copper pot, behind it, he could see the glint of gold. Now, he doesn't say exactly where it was, and indeed, the location seems to move around in his later publications, but the impression is given that it was found somewhere near that Scaean Gate. He then says that he dismissed all the workman, and he and his wife Sophia dug out the treasure all by themselves, even though a large section of earth that was above them looked like it was about to fall down on them at any moment.

According to the most popular account, Sophia then gathered the objects together in her shawl and carried them into the house. At that point the two of them catalogued the objects and realized just what they had found: a King's treasure of gold necklaces, rings, earrings; bronze tools; gold and silver cups, bowls, other vessels, and included within these are a solid gold sauceboat, which is one of only two that's ever been found. There's also a golden vessel in the shape of a pomegranate, stone hilts that probably belonged to bronze swords, and a multitude of other objects the like of which has rarely been found together anywhere else in the world.

Now, Schliemann and his wife subsequently smuggled the treasure onto a boat and sent it back to their house in Athens. There, Sophia put on most of the jewelry that they had found, and they took a picture of her, which remains one of the most iconic images in archaeology to this day. Interestingly, soon thereafter, Schliemann donated Priam's Treasure to the Berlin Museum, perhaps in exchange for being granted his doctorate in archaeology at a German university. But the treasure disappeared in the aftermath of World

War II, and it was presumed lost for nearly 50 years. It was only in the early 1990s that the Russians admitted that they had it. They had taken it back to Russia as part of the spoils of war and claimed it as recompense for the losses that they had suffered during the war.

So today, if you want to go see Priam's Treasure, you have to go to the Pushkin Museum in Moscow. And it remains there despite the fact that four different countries now lay claim to it. Those four are Turkey because that's where Troy is; Greece because that's where Schliemann first stored the treasure; Germany because Schliemann gave the treasure to Berlin Museum, and Russia because they claim it as reparation for Nazi aggression.

So, who really owns it? That hasn't been resolved, and Russia shows no signs of handing it over to anybody else. But you know what? In some ways, it doesn't matter because it's not Priam's Treasure anyway. In fact, as I tell my students, "Priam's Treasure is neither Priam's nor a Treasure; discuss."

The treasure was found in city number two. That dates back to the Early Bronze Age, about 2400 B.C., so it's 1,000 years too early to have even belonged to Priam. And some scholars have even suggested that Schliemann didn't even find the treasure all in one place. They think he actually gathered the best of his finds from the entire season and then announced to a gullible public that he had found them all together as one single treasure.

The debate is ongoing, and we may never know what actually transpired though Schliemann later admitted that he had lied about Sophia's role in his story. She wasn't even at the dig on the day that he claims to have found the treasure; his own diaries and journals show that she was in Athens at the time. Schliemann explained that his intention was to involve her more in his career, in the hopes that she would become more interested in what he did. So he wrote her into the story so that she could share in his triumph. Now, it's very unlikely that an archaeologist today would dare to do what Schliemann did, or that he or she would be able to even get away with it.

For me, though, what's most interesting about these objects is that they bear a great deal of resemblance to objects found elsewhere, from the islands of the northeast Aegean, for example, and all the way over to the so-called

Death Pits of Ur that Sir Leonard Woolley excavated in what is now Iraq. The gold earrings, pins, and necklaces that Schliemann found may not have belonged to Priam, or to his wife or daughter, but they did belong to a class of jewelry that was in fashion across most of the Aegean and the ancient near East toward the end of the 3rd millennium B.C. This, in turn, may give us hints about ancient trade and the interconnections at that time—and that, to my mind, makes them even more interesting.

At any rate, Schliemann continued to dig at Troy throughout the 1870s and 1880s, though he was also digging at Mycenae by that time, where he was looking for Agamemnon. To help him at Troy, he hired Wilhelm Dörpfeld, an architect with some previous archaeological experience, and he eventually persuaded Schliemann that Schliemann had been wrong, and it was city number six or city number seven at Troy that he should've been investigating all along. So Schliemann began to make plans for an additional attack on the mound, focused on these later levels. But on Christmas Day in 1890, Schliemann collapsed in a street in Naples, Italy, and he died the next day.

It was left to Dörpfeld to carry on. And so he did, with the financial assistance of Sophia Schliemann, who wished him to continue her husband's work at the site. He concentrated on excavating the remains at Hisarlik that Schliemann had left untouched, mostly around the edges of the mound. And as it turned out, those remains were extremely impressive. Dörpfeld unearthed tall stone walls, each several meters thick, which would've stymied any attacker, and large gateways allowing entrance to the interior, but only once you got past the guards.

These were the remains of city number six, which seems to have lasted for nearly 500 years, from about 1700 B.C.–1250 B.C. Dörpfeld found numerous phases to the city, so he numbered these A–H. The last phase, Troy VIH; it shows signs of an almost complete destruction of the city. For Dörpfeld, this was the evidence for the Trojan War that they had been seeking; he ended his excavations and published his results. His methods of excavation had been far better than those of Schliemann, plus he had a good eye for both architecture and stratigraphy.

However, not everyone was convinced that city number six was Homer's Troy. Carl Blegen, an archaeologist at the University of Cincinnati, examined Dörpfeld's results and concluded that an earthquake had caused the destruction of Troy VI, not warfare. He decided this because of a number of walls that were found off-kilter; and large stones that had been thrown about and so on, which he thought could only have been caused by Mother Nature. And, as it turns out, he was right. On the other hand, it looked to Blegen like city number seven was a city that had been besieged and then destroyed by an army. So, Blegen reopened the excavations at Hisarlik in the 1930s in an effort to see if he was right.

Now, there was even less left for him to dig since Dörpfeld had excavated much of what Schliemann had left behind. But, Blegen found enough to convince himself that city number seven had been destroyed by humans, and in a protracted siege. His evidence is fairly convincing, including arrowheads buried in walls, bodies left lying in the streets, and other indications that a major battle—or several battles—had taken place.

Blegen also found that the large buildings and the palaces of the previous city had been subdivided so that several families could now live where only one had been previously. And he also found that the storage capacity of the city had been increased tremendously, by burying very large jars up to their necks in the ground. To Blegen, all of this indicated a city that was under siege, just as Homer had said. And the timing was still OK; this city had been destroyed about 1180 B.C. or thereabouts, and that was still within the timeframe suggested by the ancient Greeks.

Moreover, the material culture of the city—that is, the pottery and other artifacts—indicated to Blegen that there was continuity between Troy VI and VII. That is, there's no evidence in city number seven that a new group of people were living there; rather, it appeared that the people in six had renovated and rebuilt their city as seven. In fact, it's so similar that both Blegen and Dörpfeld, who was still alive, thought that what the archaeologists were calling the first phase of the seventh city was actually more likely to be the last phase of the sixth city—so Troy VIi, rather than Troy VII—but by that time it was too late to change the terminology.

And so, Blegen was convinced that an earthquake destroyed city number six; while the Mycenaean Greeks had destroyed city number seven while trying to get Helen back. Now, Blegen may well have been correct. But, 50 years went by, a new generation of archaeologists emerged, and a new team decided to investigate the mound of Hisarlik all over again, starting in 1988. This time, it was an international team of archaeologists, led by two men: Manfred Korfmann from the University of Tübingen investigated the Bronze Age remains, and Brian Rose from the University of Cincinnati investigated the Post-Bronze Age remains.

Apart from cleaning up Schliemann's Great Trench and reexamining the stratigraphy of the mound, probably the most important thing that Korfmann's team did was to survey the agricultural fields around Hisarlik. They employed a magnetometer, which enabled them to detect walls, and ditches, and even buildings lying below the surface of the earth. Now, thanks to this device, Korfmann and his team soon realized they had found an entire lower city for Troy, which lay beneath those agricultural fields and which nobody had previously suspected was there.

It turns out that all of the previous archaeologists, from Schliemann through Dörpfeld to Blegen, had simply been excavating the citadel—or the upper part—of the city, where the king and his direct family and retinue would have lived. The remains that Korfmann's team found increased the size of the city, at least, 10-fold and established it as a city that would indeed have been worthy of a 10-year-long siege.

However, there are other lessons to be learned here as well. The use of magnetometers was still not widespread in the 1990s, and so Korfmann's team misinterpreted some of their initial results. For example, in 1993, they announced, with great fanfare, that they had discovered a huge wall that ran around the ancient site at a distance of about 1,300 feet from the citadel. They said this was the great wall of the city that had kept Agamemnon and Achilles, and the other Mycenaean Greeks, out for 10 years.

However, when they went to actually excavate the wall, it wasn't there. In its place was a ditch, measuring up to six feet deep in places. Over the centuries, the ditch had filled up with all sorts of junk, from broken pottery to stones to random bits of garbage, and all of this combined to show up as a solid mass running around the city on their magnetic images. The moral of the story: beware of holding press conferences to announce your remote sensing findings until after you've also done some excavating to confirm those presumed discoveries.

In the aftermath, the team argued that a ditch is as good as a wall in protecting the city, but I for one, I'm not so certain about that. Still, I'll admit that a ditch, perhaps in combination with a wooden wall or palisade that has long since disappeared, might be reasonably effective. I'd rather have a wall, though, or at least, some additional spears with their bottom ends stuck into the ground and pointing outward so that horses and chariots would run straight into them.

Now, other findings by Korfmann's team seem to confirm Blegen's earlier work. For example, in both the citadel and the lower city, they also found evidence for earthquake destruction in city number six and human destruction—that is, warfare—in city number seven. And in one case, they found a house from city number six that had been destroyed by an earthquake and then a house from city seven that had been built right on top of it, only to be destroyed in warfare. How's that for destruction stratigraphy?

Now, among the evidence for warfare, Korfmann found more unburied bodies, including one body of a young girl about age 17 who was partially burned, and also arrowheads of an Aegean or Greek type. There's also a quantity of what appear to be sling stones, which were gathered in at least one pile, perhaps to be thrown at the attackers by somebody inside the walls of the city.

Korfmann's work also confirmed Blegen's earlier findings that, after the city was destroyed in about 1180 B.C., the next city was occupied by what seem to be a completely new people. In this phase, which archaeologists call Troy VIIb, we see completely new types of pottery, new architecture, and new material culture, including an inscribed seal that has the first writing ever found at Troy. Now, these are all indications that the inhabitants of the previous city had been completely replaced by a new group. And therefore, for me, I see the human destruction of the seventh city as being part and parcel of what Homer would call the Trojan War. But I also believe that he added in elements from the sixth city, and he thereby compressed the two cities into one, telescoping things, but that was his prerogative as an epic poet.

It may even be that the Trojan Horse is a poetic metaphor for the earthquake that leveled the sixth city, for the Greek god of earthquakes was Poseidon. And, just as the goddess Athena was represented by an owl, so a horse represented Poseidon for the Greeks. It's conceivable, at least in the poetic imagination, that earthquake equals Poseidon equals the Trojan Horse. At least, that's what one German scholar has suggested, and so I leave it out there for all of you to think about.

As the Hisarlik digs continued, the post-Bronze Age team, led by Brian Rose, found a lot of material too, including a larger-than-life statue of the Roman emperor Hadrian. They found that in 1993, and then in 1997 they found a large marble head of Augustus. The later Hellenistic Greeks and then the Romans had built upon the citadel, as well as establishing a nicely gridded city down below. These later inhabitants were also convinced that this was the site of ancient Troy and, in fact, they gave it the name New Troy in both Greek and Latin. Alexander the Great came here to visit and pay his respects, as did Julius Caesar and others over the centuries.

Now, Temples to Athena and Jupiter were also built on top of the mound itself, and that explains why Schliemann had trouble understanding the stratigraphy and why Priam's Troy was far closer to the top of the surface than he expected it to be. Because it turns out that builders in both the Hellenistic and the Roman periods had shaved off the top of the mound as it stood in their time. This gave them level ground on which they could build their temples, and theaters, and other structures that went with their cities number eight and nine, which were the last to be built at the site.

Now, Manfred Korfmann died suddenly in 2005, but the international excavations continued under new directors. Interest in digging and doing remote sensing in and around the site continues even as we speak, so perhaps Hisarlik has even more secrets to reveal about this ancient town that inspired one of the greatest epics ever written.

Lecture 4

Early Archaeology in Mesopotamia

The site of ancient Ur is situated on the Euphrates River in modern Iraq, north of where the river empties into the Persian Gulf. This is the region known as ancient Mesopotamia, a name that means "between the rivers"—that is, the Tigris and Euphrates. Ur was a site famous in antiquity, with all the typical features of a Bronze Age Mesopotamian city, including religious structures known as ziggurats. Beginning in 1922, the site was excavated by Sir Leonard Woolley and his right-hand man, Max Mallowan. But it wasn't until the fifth field season, in 1926–1927, that they began digging the cemetery at the site—the famous Death Pits of Ur that had captured the attention of Europe.

Royal Burials at Ur
- Between 1927 and 1929, Sir Leonard Woolley and Max Mallowan uncovered 16 royal burials at Ur. The royal burials date to about 2500 B.C. and were quite impressive compared to the many other burials found in the cemetery at Ur. Each tomb usually had a stone chamber, either vaulted or domed, into which the royal body was placed. The chamber was at the bottom of a deep pit, with access possible only via a steep ramp from the surface. Precious grave goods were mostly found in the burial chamber with the body, while wheeled vehicles, oxen, and attendants were found in both the chamber and in the pit outside.

- Numerous attendants were found in the Death Pits: One tomb had more than 70 bodies that went with their master or mistress into the afterlife. Most of these were women, but men were present, as well. Woolley assumed that they had drunk poison after climbing down the ramp into the pit, but CT scans of some of the skulls done in 2009 indicate that at least some of these people had been killed by having a sharp instrument driven into their heads just below and behind the ear while they were still alive. Death would have been instantaneous.

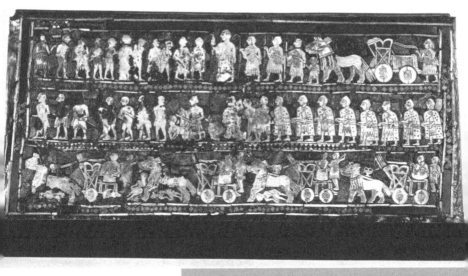

Scenes on the Standard of Ur found in the Death Pits seem to depict a battle, followed by presentation of loot to the king and a victory banquet.

- The grave goods that Woolley and Mallowan found with the royal bodies were amazing, despite the fact that many of the graves had been looted in antiquity. Among the finds were gold tiaras, gold and lapis jewelry, gold and electrum daggers, and a gold helmet. There were also delicate sculptures, the remains of a wooden harp with ivory and lapis inlays, and a wooden box with inlays that Woolley dubbed the Standard of Ur.

Henry Rawlinson and Paul-Émile Botta
- Among the first modern scholars and archaeologists who worked in Mesopotamia was Sir Henry Rawlinson, who helped to decipher and translate cuneiform script in the 1830s. Cuneiform is a wedge-shaped writing system that was used to write Akkadian, Babylonian, Hittite, Old Persian, and other languages in the ancient Near East.
  - Rawlinson, who was a British army officer posted to what is now Iran, cracked the secret of cuneiform by translating a

trilingual inscription that was written in Old Persian, Elamite, and Babylonian. Darius the Great of Persia had carved the inscription 400 feet above the desert floor into a cliff face at the site of Behistun in about 519 B.C.

- By 1837, about 10 years before the copying of the entire inscription was completed, Rawlinson had figured out how to read the first two paragraphs of the part that was written in Old Persian. It reportedly took him another 20 years to decipher the Babylonian and Elamite parts of the inscription and successfully read the whole thing.

- Along the way, however, Rawlinson was able to use his knowledge of cuneiform to begin translating some of the inscriptions that British archaeologist Sir Austen Henry Layard was finding at his excavations in what is now Iraq. In fact, Rawlinson was able to confirm that Layard had found two ancient sites that, up until that point, had been known only from the Bible.

- Paul-Émile Botta was an Italian-born archaeologist who worked for the French. In December 1842, he began the first archaeological excavations ever conducted in what is now Iraq. Botta's first efforts were concentrated on the mounds known as Kuyunjik, which are across the river from the city of Mosul. However, he didn't find much there and quickly abandoned his efforts.
  - From one of his workmen, Botta learned that some sculptures had been found at a site called Khorsabad, which was located about 14 miles to the north. In March 1843, he began excavating there and, within a week, began to unearth a great Assyrian palace.

  - At first, Botta thought that he had found the remains of ancient Nineveh, but now we know that Khorsabad is the ancient site of Dur Sharrukin, the capital city of the Neo-Assyrian king Sargon II (r. 721–705 B.C.).

Austen Henry Layard

- Beginning in 1845, Sir Austen Henry Layard undertook his initial archaeological efforts at Nimrud, which he first thought was ancient Nineveh. Amazingly, on the first day of digging, his team of six local men found not one but two Assyrian palaces! Today, they are usually called the Northwest and Southwest Palaces.

  o From the inscriptions Layard found, it eventually became clear that the Northwest Palace was built by Assurnasirpal II (r. 884–859 B.C.), and the Southwest Palace was built by Esarhaddon (r. 680–669 B.C.). Later, a Central Palace was discovered at the site, built by Tiglath-Pileser III (r. 745–727 B.C.). Shalmaneser III (r. 858–824 B.C.) also had buildings and monuments constructed at the site.

  o Layard published a book about his amazing discoveries at Nimrud. The book was called *Nineveh and Its Remains*, but when the inscriptions from the site were finally deciphered, they confirmed that it was actually ancient Kalhu (biblical Calah), rather than Nineveh.

  o As it turns out, Kalhu was the second capital city established by the Assyrians, the first being Assur itself. It served as their capital for almost 175 years, from 879 to 706 B.C. After that, Sargon II moved the capital to Dur Sharrukin for a brief period, and then Sennacherib moved it to Nineveh.

- In 1849, Layard returned to Mosul for another round of excavations, but this time, his primary focus was Kuyunjik, the mound that Botta had abandoned seven years earlier. Layard's men immediately began unearthing walls with reliefs and images, and translation of the tablets found there confirmed that this was the actual site of ancient Nineveh. By the time Layard and several other excavators were done, a palace of Sennacherib (r. 704–681 B.C.) had been uncovered, as well as a palace of Assurbanipal, Sennacherib's grandson (r. 668–627 B.C.).

  o Sennacherib, who had moved the Assyrian capital from Dur Sharrukin after he came to the throne, built what he called the

Wall reliefs and tablets found by Austen Henry Layard helped confirm the identity of Kuyunjik as the ancient site of Nineveh.

Palace without Rival at Nineveh. Today, the palace is probably most famous for the Lachish Room. Here, Layard found wall reliefs showing Sennacherib's capture of the city of Lachish in 701 B.C. At that time, Lachish was the second most powerful city in Judah; Sennacherib attacked it before proceeding on to besiege Jerusalem.

- The capture of Lachish is described in the Hebrew Bible, as is the siege of Jerusalem. Layard's discovery was one of the first times that an event from the Bible could be confirmed by extrabiblical sources.

- Twentieth-century excavations at the site of Lachish, in what is now Israel, not only confirmed the destruction of the city in about 701 B.C. but also revealed an Assyrian siege ramp, built of tons of earth and rocks and looking similar to ramps depicted in Sennacherib's reliefs.

- o The Nineveh reliefs are full of gruesome scenes, including captives having their tongues pulled out and being flayed alive, along with decapitated heads displayed on a pole. It is universally accepted that the Assyrians actually committed such atrocities, but the depiction of them in Sennacherib's palace is most likely meant as propaganda—a means to deter other kingdoms from rebellion.

- It's important to note that Layard was not a trained archaeologist. He frequently left the middle of rooms unexcavated and wasn't particularly interested in any of the pottery his men uncovered. He was, however, interested in the inscribed slabs that made up the walls of rooms, as well as the colossal statues. Many of these were shipped back to the British Museum, where they can be seen today.

Continuing Excavations
- In 1853, Hormuzd Rassam, Layard's protégé and successor at Nineveh, discovered Assurbanipal's palace, literally under the nose of Botta's successor, Victor Place, who was digging in the same spot.
  - o Rassam and his men dug secretly for three straight nights in disputed territory on the mound; when their trenches first revealed the walls and sculptures of the palace, Place could do nothing but congratulate them on their finds.

  - o Within the palace, Rassam found a tremendous library of cuneiform texts, just as Layard had done previously in Sennacherib's palace. In fact, it is generally considered that the state archives were split between the two palaces, even though they were two generations apart. Apart from state documents, Rassam found religious, scientific, and literary texts, including copies of the Epic of Gilgamesh and the Babylonian flood story.

- In 1872, nearly 20 years after Rassam first found the tablets, a man named George Smith was employed at the British Museum, sorting out the tablets that Rassam had sent back from Nineveh.
  - At one point, Smith discovered a large fragment that gave an account of a great flood, similar to the deluge account found in the Hebrew Bible. When Smith announced his discovery at a meeting of the Society of Biblical Archaeology in December 1872, all of London was abuzz with excitement.
  - The problem, though, was that a large piece was missing from the middle of the tablet. A reward was promised to anyone who would go look for the missing fragment, and Smith himself decided to take on the challenge, even though he had never been to Mesopotamia and had no training as an archaeologist.
  - Amazingly, just five days after he arrived at Nineveh, Smith found the missing piece by searching through the back-dirt pile of previous excavators. He also found about 300 other pieces from clay tablets that the workers had discarded.

- The 19th-century excavations at Nimrud, Nineveh, Khorsabad, Ur, Babylon, and other sites began an era of excavation in the region that continues to this day. As recently as 1988, spectacular discoveries were made at Nimrud by local Iraqi archaeologists. They uncovered the graves of several Assyrian princesses from the time of Assurnasirpal II in the 9th century B.C. Foreign excavations were suspended in Iraq around 1990 but are now being resumed and may lead to yet more exciting discoveries.

Suggested Reading

Fagan, *Return to Babylon.*

Lloyd, *Foundations in the Dust.*

Roux, *Ancient Iraq.*

Questions to Consider

1. Was it proper for the British Museum and the Louvre to sponsor expeditions to acquire material for their collections?

2. How can we protect antiquities in lands that are ravaged by civil wars and/or invaders bent on destruction?

Lecture 4 Transcript

Early Archaeology in Mesopotamia

At my wedding, back in 1990, my late mother toasted us by quoting Agatha Christie's immortal words: "An archaeologist is the best husband any woman can have. The older she gets, the more interested he is in her." Agatha knew well of what she spoke. I presume that many of you are familiar with her and that some of you may even have read one or more of her many mystery books, but I bet that most of you don't know that she was married to the archaeologist Max Mallowan. She met him in 1930 when she came to visit the site of Ur in Mesopotamia where he was excavating. They got married six months later. From then on, she came with him on most of his digs and wrote many of her books while there, when she wasn't helping him process the material that they were finding.

Mallowan was Sir Leonard Woolley's right-hand man at the site of Ur in what is now modern Iraq. Agatha Christie, along with most of the rest of England at that time, was entranced by the announcements of their finds from the famous Death Pits of Ur. She had come to see them for herself. She found herself even more entranced by Mallowan than she was by the Death Pits. However, it seems that after she married him, Agatha was no longer welcome at the site. And as a result, he left Ur soon thereafter to start his own excavations.

The scuttlebutt is that Woolley's wife, Lady Katharine Woolley, didn't want to share the attention of the men on the dig with anyone else. And that's why Lovely Louise, the first person killed off in Agatha Christie's book *Murder in Mesopotamia*, is believed by many to be based on Lady Woolley, especially since she's described as a "beautiful but difficult archaeologist's wife." Reportedly, those who were in the know instantly recognized Louise as Lady Katharine, and Louise apparently, or rather Lady Katherine didn't apparently mind at all.

The site of ancient Ur is situated on the Euphrates River, north of where the river emerges into the Persian Gulf. This is the region known as ancient Mesopotamia, a name that comes from the Greek words "meso" and "potamia," and it means literally the area between the rivers—and that would be the Tigris and the Euphrates rivers. Ur was a site famous in antiquity, with all of the typical features of a Bronze Age Mesopotamian city, including religious structures known as ziggurats that reached up to the sky. Woolley identified the site with Ur of the Chaldees, which the Book of Genesis mentions in association with the patriarch Abraham. But it's still anyone's guess whether Woolley was actually right about that.

Woolley and Mallowan began excavating at Ur in 1922, but it wasn't until the middle of their fifth field season, 1926–1927, that they began digging the cemetery at the site. And thereafter, between 1927 and 1929, the two archaeologists uncovered the 16 royal burials that would make them famous. All told, including the later excavations that Woolley conducted without Mallowan after 1931, there were about 1,850 intact burials that were found in the cemetery. The royal burials thus make up only a small percentage of the total graves that they excavated.

These royal burials at Ur date to about 2500 B.C., give or take. And although many of the other burials in the cemetery were very simple, the royal tombs were quite impressive. They usually had a stone chamber that was either vaulted or domed into which the royal body was placed. The chamber was at the bottom of a deep pit, with access only possible via a steep ramp from the surface. The precious grave goods were mostly found in the burial chamber with the body. Wheeled vehicles, and oxen, and attendants were found in both the chamber and in the pit outside.

There were numerous attendants that were found in these Death Pits. One had more than 70 bodies who went with their master or mistress into the afterlife; another held more than 60 bodies, and still another had 40 bodies. Most of these were women, but there were men as well. Woolley assumed that they had drunk poison after climbing down the ramp into the pit, but CAT scans of some of the skulls that were done in 2009 at the University of Pennsylvania indicates that at least those people had been killed by having a sharp instrument driven into their head just below and behind the ear while they were still alive. Death would have been instantaneous.

The grave goods that Woolley and Mallowan found with the royal bodies were amazing, despite the fact that many of the graves had been looted long ago, in antiquity. They found gold tiaras, gold and lapis jewelry, gold and electrum daggers, even a gold helmet—though that was probably ceremonial because gold helmets aren't very good at stopping a sword or an axe in battle. But there were also delicate sculptures, such as the pair of figures that depict a ram in a thicket. One of these lovely sculptures is now in the British Museum; the other one is housed at the Penn Museum in Philadelphia.

The excavators at Ur also unearthed the remains of a wooden harp with ivory and lapis inlays, which Woolley had reconstructed. One of the royal tombs contained a wooden box with inlays on front and back, which Woolley dubbed the Standard of Ur—thinking that maybe it had been carried on top of a pole into battle in front of the troops, much like the Romans had their banners centuries later. He suggested this because of the scenes that are depicted; which include a possible battle, followed by loot being presented to the king, and then a victory banquet. Among the figures in the banquet is a musician holding a harp, and it's partially that which was the basis for Woolley's reconstruction. Of course, these scenes could also be a depiction of something else entirely, and this might just be a simple wooden box rather than a standard. The discussions and debates about this and some of the other objects still continue today, even though it's almost a century after Woolley and Mallowan found the royal graves.

Now, Woolley and Mallowan were not the first archaeologists to find amazing things in the ancient sites of Mesopotamia. So let's go back in time to the 19th century, and let's talk about the first modern scholars and archaeologists who worked in the region. The first individual that we should mention is the British scholar Sir Henry Rawlinson. He helped to crack and then translate cuneiform script in the 1830s. Cuneiform is a wedge-shaped writing system that was used to write Akkadian and Babylonian, Hittite, Old Persian, and other languages in the ancient Near East. Rawlinson, who was a British army officer posted to what is now Iran, cracked the secret of cuneiform by translating a tri-lingual inscription; it was written in Old Persian, Elamite, and Babylonian. Darius the Great of Persia, in about 519 B.C., carved the inscription 400 feet above the desert floor, into a cliff face at a site called Behistun.

The story that's often repeated is one that was originally told by Rawlinson himself. It seems that after spending as many as 12 years, from about 1835–1847, in copying the inscription by climbing up and down rickety ladders and scaffolding, he eventually hired what he called a wild Kurdish boy to shimmy down a rope from the top of the cliff in order to copy down the final lines of the long inscription. The boy actually had to swing from side to side and run along the cliff face in order to copy down the last couple of bits.

In any event, already by 1837—a good 10 years before the copying of the entire inscription was completed—Rawlinson figured out how to read the first two paragraphs of the part that was written in Old Persian. He presented his findings in official papers that were published in 1837 and 1839, just ahead of other scholars who had also been working on deciphering the inscription. Even then, it reportedly took him another 20 years to decipher the Babylonian and Elamite parts of the inscription and to successfully read the whole thing.

Along the way, though, Rawlinson was able to take his knowledge of cuneiform and begin translating some of the inscriptions that British archaeologist Sir Austen Henry Layard was finding at his excavations in what is now Iraq. In fact, Rawlinson was able to confirm that Layard had found two ancient sites that, up until that point, had been known only from the Bible. And that brings us to the first archaeologists who were working in Mesopotamia. We'll get back to Layard in a moment, but let's first turn to Paul Émile Botta—an Italian-born archaeologist who was working for the French.

In December 1842, Botta began the first archaeological excavations ever conducted in what is now Iraq. In his day job, he was the French Consul at Mosul. But that was a position that essentially left him free to conduct archaeological fieldwork on behalf of the Louvre in Paris. That's what he spent most of his time doing, with the active endorsement of his higher-ups back in France.

Botta's first efforts were concentrated on the mounds known as Kuyunjik, which are right across the river from the city of Mosul. However, he didn't find much there and quickly abandoned his efforts rather prematurely as it turned out. From one of his workmen, he learned that some sculptures had been found at a site called Khorsabad, which was located about 14 miles to the north. So in March 1843, he began excavating there instead—with immediate success. Within a week, he had begun to unearth a great Assyrian palace there. At first, he had thought he had found the remains of ancient Nineveh, but now we know that Khorsabad is the ancient site of Dur Sharrukin, which was the capital city of Sargon II—the Neo-Assyrian king who ruled from 721–705 B.C.

As for Austen Henry Layard, he didn't mean to undertake excavations in Mesopotamia, at least not at first. In 1839, at the age of 22, he had been traveling with a friend to Ceylon, which is now Sri Lanka, overland from England. They had gone through Turkey and had visited Jerusalem, Petra, Aleppo, and other ancient cities when they reached Mosul in May of 1840. There, the archaeology bug bit him, but it was a few years before he was able to return and actually begin to excavate.

Layard's initial archaeological efforts began in 1845. They were at the site of Nimrud, which he first thought was ancient Nineveh. It was located a few miles downstream from Mosul. In order to fool the local ruler—who was a one-eyed, one-eared despot named Mohammed Pasha—Layard pretended to be going on a hunting expedition, but he secretly included some excavating equipment among his supplies.

When he got to the site, he spent the first night in the hut of a local sheikh, dreaming of what he might find. He described it later as "visions of palaces underground, of gigantic monsters, sculptured figures, and endless inscriptions." As it turned out, that was more of a premonition than a dream because he found all that and more in the coming years.

The next morning he began to dig. His team consisted of six local men, whom he split into two teams. They began digging in two different areas, far apart on the mound. Before the very first day had even ended, both groups uncovered rooms with walls covered in carved inscriptions. As it turned out, the rooms belonged to two different palaces. In a single day, Layard had found not one, but two Assyrian palaces! Today, they're usually called the Northwest and the Southwest Palaces. As a result, Layard doubled the size of his team to 11 men. And later he expanded again, to a total of about 30 workmen.

From the inscriptions that Layard found, it eventually became clear that the Northwest Palace was built by Assurnasirpal II, who reigned from 884–859 B.C. Esarhaddon, who reigned 200 years later, from about 680–669 B.C., he built the Southwest Palace. There's also a Central Palace at the site, which was only discovered later. That one was built by Tiglath-Pileser III, who was in power from 745–727. Shalmaneser III, who ruled from 858–824, and was the son of Assurnasirpal II, also had buildings and monuments constructed at the site.

Layard published a book about his amazing discoveries at Nimrud, including the Black Obelisk of Shalmaneser III that mentions Jehu, the king of Israel. The book appeared in 1849, and it instantly cemented his reputation as an archaeologist, as well as an intrepid adventurer and an engaging writer. He called the book *Nineveh and Its Remains* since that's what he thought he was excavating. However, this turned out to be an unfortunate choice for the title when the inscriptions from the site were finally deciphered. They confirmed that the site was actually ancient Kalhu, biblical Calah, rather than Nineveh.

As it turns out, Kalhu was the second capital city established by the Assyrians; the first one being Assur itself. It served as their capital for almost 175 years, from 879 until 706 B.C. After that, Sargon II moved the capital to Dur Sharrukin for a brief period, and then Sennacherib moved it to Nineveh.

Other archaeologists have excavated at Nimrud since Layard, almost up until the present day. In fact, it was in the news as recently as March 2015, when videos were released by ISIS militants, showing them taking a bulldozer and a sledgehammer to the ancient remains at the site and also destroying artifacts from Nimrud that were in the Mosul Museum. Heartbreaking images indeed.

In 1849, Layard returned to Mosul for another round of excavations, but this time, his primary focus was Kuyunjik, the mound that Botta had abandoned seven years earlier. And he didn't come back with empty pockets either. In fact, Layard now had enough money to hire up to 300 workmen at a time—ten times more than he had ever had at Nimrud.

Layard had better luck than Botta did. His men immediately began unearthing walls with reliefs and images. This time, translation of the tablets found there confirmed that this was the actual site of ancient Nineveh, finally. By the time he and several other excavators who followed him were done, a palace of Sennacherib—who was in power from 704–681 B.C.—had been uncovered; as well as a palace of Assurbanipal, Sennacherib's grandson—who was in power from 668–627.

Sennacherib, who had moved the Assyrian capital from Dur Sharrukin after he came to the throne, built what he called a Palace Without Rival at Nineveh. At first, Layard knew it only as the Southwestern Palace. However, within it, he found what is referred to now as the King's Library. These were two large rooms in which he found clay tablets piled a foot deep on the floor. When the translation of these began, the real name of the palace became clear.

Today, Sennacherib's palace is probably most famous for what is called the Lachish Room. In here, Layard found wall reliefs with both pictures and inscriptions carved into the stone slabs, showing Sennacherib's capture of the city of Lachish in 701 B.C. At that time, Lachish was the second most powerful city in Judah; Sennacherib attacked it before proceeding on to besiege Jerusalem. The capture of Lachish is described in the Hebrew Bible, as is the siege of Jerusalem. Layard's discovery was one of the first times that an event from the Bible could be confirmed by what we call extra-biblical—that is, outside the Bible—sources.

Almost 30 years before Layard found Sennacherib's palace, Lord Byron had immortalized the biblical account in his poem, which is called "The Destruction of Sennacherib." And that was published in 1815. It reads:

> The Assyrian came down like the wolf on the fold,
> And his cohorts were gleaming in purple and gold;
> And the sheen of their spears was like stars on the sea,
> When the blue wave rolls nightly on deep Galilee.

Twentieth-century excavations at the actual site of Lachish, in what is now Israel, not only confirmed the destruction of the city in about 701 B.C., but it also revealed an Assyrian siege ramp, built out of tons of earth and rocks, and looking very similar to the ramps that are depicted in Sennacherib's reliefs. The Nineveh reliefs are also full of gruesome scenes, including captives having their tongues pulled out and being flayed alive, along with decapitated heads shown on a pole. It's universally accepted that the Assyrians practiced what they preached, and they actually committed such atrocities. But the depiction of them in Sennacherib's palace is most likely meant as propaganda—a means to deter other kingdoms from rebelling against the Assyrians. Foreign ambassadors were probably shown the room in the heart of the palace and then allowed to take the message back home that they probably shouldn't try to rebel or cross the Assyrians in any way, shape, or form.

At this point, though, I need to note that Layard was not a trained archaeologist by any stretch of the imagination; nor was Botta, for that matter. Brian Fagan has said bluntly, "Botta and Layard were appalling excavators by today's standards." In particular, Layard excavated by chasing walls, which we don't do in archaeology today. This means that his men dug a trench straight down into the mound until they hit a stone wall, and then they followed the wall by digging a tunnel. When that wall met another one, they turned the corner, and they tunneled along that wall, and so on until they had burrowed along all four edges of the room. And Botta and his men did essentially the same thing.

Concerning the excavation of Sennacherib's palace at Nineveh, Layard noted, "In the magnificent edifice I had opened no less than 71 halls, chambers, and passages, whose walls had almost without exception been paneled with sculptured slabs of alabaster." He estimated that his men had dug enough tunnels to expose almost 10,000 feet—or about two miles—worth of such walls, along with 27 doorways which were formed by colossal winged bulls and lion-sphinxes.

However, this also means that Layard frequently left the middle of the rooms unexcavated. And he also wasn't particularly interested in any of the pottery that his men uncovered during the course of their excavations. What he was interested in were the inscribed slabs that made up these walls, as well as the colossal statues. Many of these were shipped back to the British Museum, where they can be seen on display today. Others that were found both here and at Nimrud and Khorsabad wound up in museum collections around the world, including some at Dartmouth and Amherst Colleges in the United States.

It took a tremendous amount of effort to get the pieces back to the British Museum, or the Louvre in the case of Botta and his successor Victor Place. Botta's finds went on display in the Louvre starting in May 1847. He beat Layard and the British Museum by a matter of months because their pieces didn't go on display until September of that year. In order to get his finds back to France, at one point, Botta had a wagon built with wheels that were three feet wide; only to find out that it was too heavy to be moved, even by more than 200 men. Layard had similar problems in transporting his finds back to England.

However, it was Victor Place, who replaced Botta at Khorsabad, and had the worst misfortune of all. It was on his watch, in 1853 and 1855, that two separate shipments of antiquities were lost in the Tigris while being sent back to France. In 1853, bandits intercepted the shipment. When they realized that the cargo wasn't gold, they spitefully capsized and sank the boat and four rafts, complete with their cargo of precious and irreplaceable ancient finds.

In 1855, the shipment of antiquities was too heavy and sank because of the weight of the artifacts. Of the more than 200 crates that were lost, nearly 120 contained artifacts from Khorsabad; and another 68 had sculptures from Sennacherib's palace at Nineveh, which Place had been allowed to take for the Louvre, even though the British team had excavated them. There was also material from elsewhere in Mesopotamia, which had been retrieved by a French expedition to Babylonia.

Seton Lloyd, one of the greatest British archaeologists of recent times, called this one of the most appalling disasters in the history of archaeology. Only a few of the pieces were recovered right away, so I'm pretty sure that dredging the river in this location might still be very worthwhile. However, the finds kept coming. Two years before the disaster on the Tigris, Hormuzd Rassam—Layard's protégé and successor at Nineveh—had discovered Assurbanipal's palace at the site literally under the nose of Victor Place, who was also digging there. Rassam and his men dug secretly for three straight nights in disputed territory on the mound, and when their trenches first revealed the walls and the sculptures of the palace, Place could do nothing but congratulate them on their finds.

Within the palace, it was Rassam's turn to find a tremendous library of cuneiform texts, just like Layard had done previously in Sennacherib's palace. In fact, it's generally considered that the State Archives were split between the two palaces, even though they were two generations apart. The two sets of tablets, together, number about 25,000 in all; they're now at the British Museum.

The texts that were found by Rassam in Assurbanipal's palace came from what is often called the Royal Library. Apart from the State documents, they include religious, scientific, and literary texts, which Assurbanipal had instructed his scribes to collect or to copy from all over the empire. They form one of the great libraries of the ancient world, perhaps to be mentioned in the same breath with the much later libraries at Pergamon and Alexandria. Included among the tablets were copies of the *Epic of Gilgamesh* and the Babylonian Flood story. In fact, speaking of these, I should mention here the story of George Smith, which is one of my favorite examples of the excellence of accidental archaeology.

It was in 1872, nearly 20 years after Rassam first found the tablets, that a man named George Smith was employed as a banknote engraver in London. He also moonlighted at the British Museum, sorting out the numerous tablets that Rassam had sent back from Nineveh. As I tell my students, by day, Smith was a banknote engraver; by night, he was an Assyriologist. He wasn't quite Batman or Superman, and he wasn't just an Assyriologist at night, but the students get the picture.

At one point, Smith began reading a large fragmentary tablet as he was piecing it together. He was rather astonished to realize that he was reading an account of a great flood, very similar to the Deluge account found in the Hebrew Bible—you know, the one that Noah had survived. Only in the account that Smith was reading, which turned out to be the 11th tablet from the *Epic of Gilgamesh*, the survivor was not Noah, but a man named

Utnapishtim. When he announced his discovery at a meeting of the Society of Biblical Archaeology in December of 1872, all of London was abuzz with excitement.

The problem, though, was that a big piece was missing from the middle of the tablet, right at the part where everything gets interesting. So, the *Daily Telegraph*, one of the newspapers of the day, promised a thousand British pounds to anyone who would go and look for the missing fragment. Smith decided to go himself and take them up on their offer, even though he had never been to Mesopotamia and he had no training as an archaeologist. Nevertheless, within a week after he arrived at Nineveh, he found the missing piece.

How on Earth could he have done that? It turns out that it was very simple, actually. He reasoned that perhaps the workmen who had found the other fragments had missed this big one. So, rather than digging into the mound again, he searched through the back dirt pile, as it is called by archaeologists—that is, the huge artificial mound that had been created by the archaeologists and their workmen when they dumped out the earth that they had excavated at the site.

The dirt in these piles should be empty of ancient objects, but the pile at Nineveh was full of them because the workmen dug so fast and were frequently careless in picking out the pieces that they came across—whether they were pottery or clay tablets. So, not only did Smith find the missing piece that he had come for, but he found something like 300 other pieces from clay tablets that the workers had also missed and thrown out. And, when he got back to London, the missing piece fit perfectly into his Flood tablet.

Interestingly, something rather similar just happened again in 2014, when another Assyriologist at the British Museum, Irving Finkel, announced that he had found a copy of the Akkadian version of the Flood story. In this version, the survivor is a man named Atrahasis. What's interesting about Finkel's tablet is that it appears to describe the ark as being round in shape, as opposed to the way that we usually think of it. The tablet is in a private collection. The owner first brought it to Finkel in 1985, but he wouldn't leave it with him long enough for him to translate it. It was only in 2009 that Finkel was able to gain access to it again and actually translate it.

The 19th-century excavations at Nimrud, Nineveh, Khorsabad, and then at Ur, Babylon, and other sites, began an era of excavation in the region that continues to this day. Max Mallowan and Agatha Christie reopened the excavations at Nineveh starting in 1931 after they parted ways with Woolley. In addition to other sites, they also dug at Nimrud beginning in 1949.

As recently as 1988, spectacular discoveries were also made at Nimrud by local Iraqi archaeologists. They uncovered the graves of several Assyrian princesses from the time of Assurnasirpal II in the 9th century B.C. These included incredible gold necklaces, and earrings, and other treasures. They nearly disappeared during the Second Gulf War, but turned out to be safely hidden in a bank vault. With the assistance of National Geographic, they have since been recovered.

And I'm happy to say that foreign excavations are now being resumed in Iraq, after having been suspended since about 1990 because of the ongoing wars and chaos in the region. So we have a lot to look forward to. It'll be interesting to see what the next century of expeditions will uncover in the region.

Lecture 5

How Do Archaeologists Know Where to Dig?

In their textbook *In the Beginning: An Introduction to Archaeology*, Brian Fagan and Nadia Durrani define a *site* simply as a place "where traces of past human activity are to be found." Some sites are fairly obvious. For example, when you look at the Athenian acropolis or the mound of Megiddo in Israel, you know that you're looking at an ancient site. But other sites can be almost indiscernible—as small as a scatter of flakes where someone once made a stone tool. In this lecture, we'll explore the concept of archaeological surveying, that is, the process of looking for sites. We'll also learn about the various types of remote sensing now being used by archaeologists.

Ground Reconnaissance

- There are two basic ways to find sites: doing reconnaissance on the ground and doing it from the air or from space. Ground surveys first began to be popular in the 1960s and 1970s and gained speed in the 1980s, in part because they are usually a much cheaper alternative to digging and can cover a great deal more ground. They also allow archaeologists to ask and answer different types of questions than they can when digging a single site.

- For instance, we might want to investigate how intensively a specific area in Greece was occupied during the Bronze Age. Did that settlement pattern change during the following Dark Ages? What happened when things began to return to normal and we get into the eras of Archaic and Classical Greece? What happened in the region when the Romans arrived? What was it like in the Byzantine period, the Ottoman period, or the modern period?

- Ground surveys can help answer these kinds of questions. By doing surveys and identifying various sites from different periods in the area, we can construct a history of the region without ever digging at a single site. Of course, many surveys lead to an excavation afterwards.

Aerial Surveys

- These days, instead of leading with a ground survey, it generally makes more sense to start with aerial surveys. This type of survey can be as simple as buying aerial photographs or satellite images or as complicated and expensive as arranging for overhead flights using light detection and ranging (LiDAR. a remote-sensing technology) to survey an area. Among the images that can be purchased are declassified military satellite images, high-resolution images sold by private companies, and images taken from the space shuttle.
    - Interestingly, buried walls, earthworks, and other large constructions associated with settlements can often be seen more easily from the air than they can be seen on the ground, even if you are walking right over them. Often, aerial images reveal *crop marks*, which mark the precise locations of buried items, such as ditches, walls, and other structures.

    - Such buried structures affect the soil and, thus, the vegetation that grows directly above them. Very simply, if there is a buried ditch below the modern surface, the vegetation growing directly above it will be higher and more lush than the surrounding vegetation because there are more nutrients in the soil in that spot. If there is a buried wall below the modern surface, the vegetation growing directly above it will be less dense and lush than the surrounding vegetation because there are fewer nutrients in the soil.

    - Although these differences in height and density might be almost imperceptible at ground level, from the air, they are immediately obvious, especially in the spring.

- Recently, archaeologists who have enough funding have been using LiDAR, a remote-sensing technology that works like radar but uses light from a laser to produce highly accurate measurements. LiDAR is especially useful in such places as Central America, because it can quite literally see through the trees in a jungle or rain forest and can provide images of lost temples, buildings, and even cities that are completely overgrown and almost inaccessible.

- Some archaeologists are now also using small drones to fly above areas of interest. These allow investigators to take either low-level or high-level photos of a region and have the results sent directly to a computer.

Other Remote-Sensing Techniques
- Ground-penetrating radar works exactly as you might imagine, by having radar signals bounce back from buried objects, such as walls. The newest versions of this technique are extremely powerful and able to "see" down nearly 4 meters (about 12 feet). This has resulted in some incredible discoveries being reported from the area of Stonehenge in England in 2014 and 2015, including the fact that Stonehenge was apparently once a complete circle.
    - Using ground-penetrating radar, as well as magnetometers and other remote-sensing techniques, archaeologists have been involved in the Stonehenge Hidden Landscapes Project. In just a few years, they have detected Bronze Age burial mounds, Iron Age shrines, and enclosures for cows and other livestock that are either Bronze Age or Iron Age, none of which had ever been noticed before. Most exciting is that they have also found another megalithic monument that is less than 2 miles from Stonehenge and probably dates to about the same time, that is, 4,500 years ago.

    - Some are now calling this site Superhenge. It consists of more than 50 giant stones that formed a large C-shaped enclosure. The stones are each about 10 to 15 feet long and about 5 feet wide. All of them are buried horizontally, rather than standing upright, and are about 3 feet below the surface, which is why they hadn't been spotted before. It is only through remote-sensing techniques that they have now been discovered and recorded.

- In addition to ground-penetrating radar, another technique involves electronic resistivity or conductivity, which basically works by running an electric current through the ground between two poles. If a buried wall or similar structure is in the way, it will interrupt the current; if there is nothing buried in the location, the current won't be interrupted. The result is a rather fuzzy picture of what is belowground with little information about its exact location under the surface.

- Magnetometers measure the magnetic field in areas that are of interest to archaeologists. Buildings, ditches, or other archaeological features that are buried underground may show up on magnetometer readings because such things affect the magnetic field in the area. In some cases, however, these structures may not appear; the success rate depends on characteristics of the soil and the type of magnetometer in use.
  - At David Schloen's excavations at Zincirli in Turkey, for example, using a magnetometer worked so well that the results look like a photograph of excavated ruins—except that the ruins are still buried!

  - In contrast, attempts to use a magnetometer at Tel Kabri in Israel have failed rather miserably so far, probably because of the nature of the soil at the site. Sometimes, archaeologists just have to dig to find out what is beneath the surface.

Ground Surveys
- In cases where satellite imagery and other high-tech solutions don't work, archaeologists must resort to the tried-and-true methods of finding sites by conducting ground surveys, usually on foot.

- There are two types of ground surveys. One is the large-scale *reconnaissance survey* that is intended to cover a large area quickly. The other is the *intensive survey*, which usually involves returning to a single site or a small area that was identified during the reconnaissance survey as being particularly promising.

- In areas where the number of sites or the time period is unknown, archaeologists usually start with a general reconnaissance survey. Typically, this involves team members painstakingly walking over every square meter of an area.

- The team may divide into groups of about six people each. After identifying the site, the group members spread out, about 30 feet apart, and start walking forward. Usually, they cover about 100 yards at a time in this fashion. This technique is known as *walking a transect*.

- As they walk, the group members look at the ground for pottery sherds, stone tools and flakes, ancient walls, or anything else that might mark the remains of an ancient settlement. They keep track of the number of artifacts they find using "clickers," and by the time they reach the end point of the transect, they have a record of the number of the artifacts seen during each stage of the 100-yard walk.

- Pottery is not biodegradable, and broken pieces always work their way to the surface of the ground. Thus, if you're walking across a site that was inhabited in the Bronze Age, the Iron Age, Roman times, and Byzantine times, you will see sherds from all those periods on the ground. And as you record the sherds on your clicker, the numbers will increase as you enter the boundaries of the site on one side, then walk through the middle of what had been the inhabited area. Then, after you exit the boundary of the site on the other side, the numbers on the clicker will drop.

- The team members give their numbers to the team leader, who records them in a notebook and marks the probable site on the map for later examination by the follow-up team.

- This process is repeated in 100-yard increments until the team reaches the end of the designated area for the day. Once the team members have reached that end point, they turn around and repeat the process, going back toward where they started. In this way, a team can traverse and record all the sites in a chosen area.

- Back at camp, the results of each day's survey are recorded, and from these results, a running list is developed. The list indicates how many sites have been found, the periods they represent, and where they are located. The most promising of these possible sites then receive a visit from a team of experienced surveyors.

- There are many variations of this kind of surveying, including those that cover specific portions or randomly chosen portions of an area that is simply too large to survey in its entirety. In such cases, statistics are used to decide the areas to be sampled.

- Finally, targeted surveys involve revisiting sites that have been previously discovered; essentially, a targeted survey is similar to the second half of the ground survey just described, except that the sites may have been found by more than one project and over a number

Surveyors collect diagnostic pottery sherds, including rims, handles, bases, and anything decorated, to allow pottery experts to identify the periods represented at a site.

of years. The goal of such a survey may be to confirm or refine the dating previously assigned to a site or answer similar questions.

Suggested Reading

Howard, *Archaeological Surveying and Mapping*.

Leach, *The Surveying of Archaeological Sites*.

White and King, *The Archaeological Survey Manual*.

Questions to Consider

1. What do you think of the increasing use of satellite photographs, LiDAR, and other high-tech imaging to find ancient sites? Is it a good use of resources?

2. Is it enough to simply find and locate ancient sites, then end the project? Should excavating always follow surveying?

Lecture 5 Transcript

How Do Archaeologists Know Where to Dig?

I'm frequently asked, "How on earth do you know where to dig?" Well, that is a great question. And it actually bears on some of the tools and the methods that archaeologists employ. So, I'm going to talk about the concept of archaeological surveying—that is, the process of looking for sites. I'm also going to introduce you to the various types of remote sensing that are now used by archaeologists.

First of all, let's define what we mean by a site because these come in all shapes and sizes. Within their textbook, *In the Beginning*, Brian Fagan and Nadia Durrani define a site simply as a place where traces of past human activity can be found. And these are normally identified by the presence of artifacts. Some of them are pretty obvious. For example, when you look at the Athenian acropolis or a huge mound like Megiddo in Israel, you know that you're looking at an ancient site. But others can be very tiny and almost indiscernible. A site can be as small as a scatter of flakes where somebody once made a stone tool, or as large as Machu Picchu in Peru. The trick is to find the ones that aren't so easy to detect.

There are two basic ways to find sites: doing reconnaissance on the ground, and doing it from the air or even from space these days. Ground surveys first began to be popular in the 1960s and 1970s, and then they gained speed in the 1980s, in part that's because they're usually a much cheaper alternative to digging, and they can cover a lot more ground. They also allow you to ask and to answer different types of questions than you can when you're digging a single site. So for instance, you might want to investigate how intensively a specific area in Greece was occupied during the Bronze Age. Did that settlement pattern change during the following Dark Ages? Now, what happened when things began to return to normal, and we get into the eras of Archaic and then Classical Greece? What happened in the region when the Romans arrived? What was it like in the Byzantine period? And how about the Ottoman period or the modern period?

Ground surveys can help you answer these kinds of questions. By doing surveys and identifying the various sites from different periods in the area, you can actually construct a history of the region without ever digging at a single site. Many surveys, though, do lead into an excavation afterward, as the archaeologists zoom in on one or more of the most promising new sites that they've just found and get a permit to dig there. These days, though, instead of leading with a ground survey, it actually makes more sense to start with aerial surveys, if you can afford them. This can be as simple as buying aerial photographs or satellite images from specific companies or as complicated and expensive as arranging for overhead flights using LiDAR to survey your area.

We will return to LiDAR in a moment, but if you want to buy imagery, which is by far the easiest way to go, you do have some options. One option is to purchase declassified military satellite images like the ones taken by the Corona program. Corona was a surveillance operation that was conducted by U.S. intelligence agencies from 1960 to about 1972. Images from the program were declassified by an executive order in 1995, and they're now used for all sorts of things, including finding archaeological sites. If you don't want to work with old black-and-white photos, you now also have the option of getting up-to-the-minute, high-resolution, color satellite images from companies like DigitalGlobe. There are also images that have been taken from the space shuttle. For example, there's a fairly well-known picture of the city of Angkor, in Cambodia, that was taken from the shuttle, in which you can see all of the buildings very clearly.

My friend Sarah Parcak, a National Geographic explorer who calls herself the Space Archaeologist, is a great example of someone who does surveys using satellite images. The newer images allow her and other archaeologists to use all kinds of fancy techniques, like infra-red imaging, to illuminate some features and take away others. And that's how Sarah found several hundred new sites in Egypt a few years ago. New techniques with satellite imagery have also enhanced our ability to see ancient paths still marked in the desert. That's how the lost city of Ubar, in Oman, was found back in 1992. The space shuttle Endeavour had taken a picture of the area and archaeologists noticed where the ancient paths converged. They subsequently excavated there and found the ancient site.

Interestingly, buried walls, earthworks, and other large constructions associated with settlements can often be seen more easily from the air than they can be seen on the ground, even if you're walking right over them. Especially in a raking light, or if an aerial photograph is taken at a slight angle, you can sometimes see shadows that are cast by buried walls. More usually, though, what you can see are what we call crop marks. These mark the location of the buried items precisely, whether they're features like ditches or structures like buildings and walls.

The simple reason is that those buried items affect the soil, and thus the vegetation that's growing directly above them. Of course, this won't work if there's something built on top of them, like a modern parking lot, but it will work if you're looking at a field in which grass, or wheat, barley, or even just thick weeds are growing. Very simply, if there's a buried ditch below the modern surface, the vegetation growing directly above it will be higher and more lush than the surrounding vegetation because there are more nutrients in the soil right there. If, though, there's a buried wall beneath the modern surface, the vegetation growing directly above it will be lower, less dense, and less lush than the surrounding vegetation because there are fewer nutrients in the soil right there.

While these differences in height and density might be almost imperceptible at ground level, from the air, they're immediately obvious if the season is right. No, you're not going to see anything in the dead of winter, and you're unlikely to see anything in the middle of summer either. But in the spring, when things are growing, you should be able to see much more easily. Therefore, you could possibly see the outline of a building sometimes, as well as ditches that were once there. If you're in England, or somewhere in Europe—especially, say, in Italy—and you see a crop mark that's about three feet wide and running straight as an arrow across the fields, you can pretty much bet that you're looking at a buried Roman road.

In fact, I often amuse myself when I'm on a flight that's landing somewhere in Europe by looking out the window of the airplane as we're descending, and trying to see if I can discern any crop marks in the fields surrounding the airport. You'd be amazed how many times I've seen something that I'd love to go back and excavate, in order to figure out what it was.

At one point, Sarah Parcak and I bought some satellite imagery of the area right around Megiddo in Israel, just as an experiment to see what we might be able to locate. Almost immediately we saw the outlines of what looked like a large building in a field right next to the actual mound. When we compared the outlines to other known sites and buildings, we found an almost perfect match with the Roman camps that were built around the site of Masada, when the Romans besieged it back in 73 or 74 A.D. It was clear to us that we were looking at the site of Legio, where the sixth Roman legion had their headquarters right by Megiddo from the 2nd century A.D. on.

And indeed, when Yotam Tepper and Matt Adams began excavating in that field in 2013, they immediately came down upon the remains of ditches and walls, along with coins, and bits of scale armor, and most importantly—fragments of roof tiles. The tiles were actually stamped with the legion's insignia, thereby confirming that this was indeed their camp. Most recently, archaeologists who have enough funding have been playing around with LiDAR, which stands for Light Detection and Ranging. It's a remote sensing technology that works like radar, but it uses light from a laser to produce highly accurate measurements. We've actually used it at Tel Kabri in Israel to quickly and accurately record the wine cellar that we found in 2013, but it's more usually used from an airplane.

LiDAR turns out to be especially useful in places like Central America because it can quite literally see right through the trees in a jungle or rain forest, and it can provide images of lost temples, buildings, and even cities that are completely overgrown and almost inaccessible now. Probably the best-known example is a team that used LiDAR to map the Maya city of Caracol in Belize, back in 2010. But other teams have found additional Maya cities hidden in the Yucatan as recently as 2014.

One other thing that some archaeologists are now doing is using a little drone, flying it like hobbyists fly model airplanes. If you can get one of these drones successfully through customs in whatever country you're working, you can then fly it above the area that you're interested in. And then you can take either low-level or high-level photos of the region, sometimes even sending the results directly to your computer. Of course, you do always run the risk of having your drone suddenly fall 300 feet straight down to the ground, as happened to a friend of mine recently. I don't think that the drone survived the crash.

But that brings us to other remote sensing techniques that are, in fact, more ground based. These include ground-penetrating radar, which works exactly as it sounds like, by having radar signals bounce back up from buried objects like walls. The newest versions of this technique are extremely powerful and are able to see down nearly 4 meters—about 12 feet. This has resulted in some incredible discoveries being reported from the area of Stonehenge in England, for example, in 2014 and 2015—including the fact that Stonehenge was apparently once a complete circle.

Here, using ground-penetrating radar, as well as magnetometers and other remote sensing techniques that we'll talk about in a minute, archaeologists have been involved in something called the "Stonehenge Hidden Landscapes Project." In just a few years of work, they have detected Bronze Age burial mounds, Iron Age shrines, and enclosures for cows and other livestock that are either Bronze Age or Iron Age; none of these had ever been noticed before. Most exciting is that they've also found another huge megalithic monument that is less than two miles from Stonehenge, and which probably dates to about the same time—that is, about 4,500 years ago.

Some are now calling this Superhenge. It consists of more than 50 giant stones that form a C-shaped enclosure. They are each about 10–15 feet long and about 5 feet wide. All of these stones are buried horizontally rather than standing upright, and they're about three feet below the surface, which is why they haven't been spotted before. It's only through these remote sensing techniques they have now been discovered and recorded.

In addition to ground-penetrating radar, there's also electronic resistivity or conductivity, which basically works by running an electric current through the ground between two poles. If there's something like a buried wall in the way, it will interrupt the current; if there isn't, it won't be interrupted. You end up with a rather fuzzy picture of what's below ground; but frequently, you've got no idea just how far below ground it is.

The same thing can happen with magnetometers. These measure the magnetic field in areas that are of interest to archaeologists. If there are buildings, or ditches, or other archaeological features that are buried underground, these can show up on a magnetometer reading because such things affect the magnetic field in the area. Then again, they might not show up. It all depends on what the soil is like and what type of magnetometer you're using.

At David Schloen's excavations at Zincirli in Turkey, for example, using a magnetometer worked so well that the results looked like a photograph of excavated ruins, except that you're looking at ruins that are still buried and haven't yet been excavated. At the famous site of Troy in Turkey, though, excavators had tried several different types of magnetometers before they finally found one kind—a cesium magnetometer—that yielded the same great results. They suddenly realized that there was an entire huge lower town at Troy, buried under the agricultural fields around the mound. Teams had been excavating the mound since the days of Schliemann in the late 1800s, but nobody had thought to excavate in the fields next to it because it looked like nothing was there.

On the other hand, our attempts to use a magnetometer at Tel Kabri in Israel have failed rather miserably so far, probably because of the nature of the soil that we have at the site. Rather than getting beautiful pictures of what lies below, we get things that look like amoebas. So, magnetometers don't always work well, and sometimes you just have to dig in order to find out what lies below.

In fact, while there have been big advances made in remote sensing in the past couple of decades, sometimes even satellite imagery and other high-tech solutions won't help you at all. In those cases, archaeologists must resort to the tried and true methods of finding archaeological sites by conducting a ground survey, usually on foot. These take us back to the original days of surveying, back in the 1960s and 1970s. In fact, the methods used for ground surveys today are pretty much the same ones that I employed when I was surveying in Greece, back in 1981 and in 1992. So I can tell you just exactly what's involved in slogging over the ground by foot—or in a car if you're lucky—when you're doing a site survey in an area.

First of all, I should tell you that there are two types of ground surveys. One type is the large-scale reconnaissance surveys that are intended to cover large areas quickly. The other type is the intensive surveys that usually involve coming back to a single site or a small area that was identified during the reconnaissance survey as being particularly promising. If that's the case, then you'll probably do a very detailed investigation of the area that may or may not involve picking up and bringing back to the camp every single artifact that you find there.

If you're dealing with an area where you don't have any idea how many sites might be there, or from what time period they might be, then you'll want to start with a general reconnaissance survey. Typically, this involves your team members painstakingly walking over every single square meter of the area, or at least over every square meter of selected portions of it. This is what we did in the region of Boeotia, near the city of Thebes in Greece, back in the early '80s, when I was in college. And again, it's what we did near the Mycenaean palace of Pylos in the early '90s, just after I had finished my Ph.D. In both cases, we had no real idea what sites were in the area that we were surveying, but I'll focus on the survey that we did by Pylos. There, I was actually a team leader rather than simply a field walker—as I had been before—so I was more privy to some of the decisions that were being made by the directors and why.

First off, we were split into three teams of about six people each. I was in charge of Team A, which, of course, we promptly renamed The A-Team. At first, we were assigned to survey the mountain heights on one side of the valley, despite my protestations that I'm afraid of heights—which I am. Sure enough, on the very first day, as we began our survey, I froze in place at one sheer drop and had to be manhandled back into the car—hardly an auspicious start for the team and the team leader. Later, we were able to move lower down, and I had no problems from then on; but I learned a valuable lesson which I use to this day—listen to your team members, especially if they tell you about a phobia that might impact their duties.

In any event, once we started to get into the swing of things, we got our routine down. As I said, we had about six people on our team. First, we would find our location on the map using a readily discernable feature like a road. Of course, this is much easier today with GPS systems; but remember, this was back in the early '90s when such devices were very expensive and quite rudimentary. We would then spread out, about 30 feet apart. When I shouted or blew a whistle, each person would start walking forward in the designated direction and walk in a straight line until they reached a specific pre-determined point. Usually, it was another road or a boundary wall that was also marked on the map. This usually meant walking about the length of an American football field at a time—that is, about 100 yards—because more than that became too complicated.

This is what is known in archaeological surveying terms as walking a transect. And when I say walking in a straight line, I mean quite literally walking in a straight line, regardless of whether that means fording a stream, rappelling down a small cliff, or facing down a bull, or a local farmer with a shotgun who didn't want us on the land. All of those things actually happened, either to me or other people on our team at one point in time. But what was much more frequent was ripping your legs to shreds, even through your pants, because you had to walk through the underbrush. In Greece, this is called the macchi, and that stuff can be nasty

But the point was not just to walk, but to walk while looking at the ground for pottery sherds, or stone tools and flakes, or ancient walls, or anything else that might have marked the remains of an ancient settlement. By the way, you can always tell someone who has just spent several weeks on an archaeological survey because they're always the one who spot the pennies and other loose change on the ground when they get back to civilization.

So, the secret to all of this is that you also have a clicker in your hand, like those clickers set into the turnstiles that count people going into a stadium. Every time you see a pottery sherd or a worked piece of stone, you click it once. At the end of about every 10 steps, you write down the number that's on your clicker, and you start counting again from 0. By the time you've reached the end point of the transect, you have a record of the number of the artifacts that you saw during each stage of your hundred-yard walk.

So, why is that important? Well, pottery is not bio-degradable, and broken pieces will always work their way up to the top. So if you're walking across

Lecture 5 Transcript—How Do Archaeologists Know Where to Dig?

a site that was inhabited in the Bronze Age, the Iron Age, Roman, and Byzantine times, you'll see sherds from all of those periods on the ground. And as you record the sherds on your clicker, the numbers will increase astronomically as you enter the boundaries of the site on one side, then walk through the middle of what had been the inhabited area. And then after you exit the boundary of the site on the other side, the numbers on your clicker will drop. Your clicker counts—again, recording the number of pieces of pottery and worked stone that you saw every 10 paces or so—will look something like this: 1, 5, 25, 107, 510, 423, 298, 152, 87, 0. The numbers for the people on either side of you will probably be similar because they're likely to have walked across that same site. Those further out from you, however, if their transects did not cross the site, then they'll just have normal background scatter counts like 1, 6, 4, 12, 0, 5, 3, 8, 5, 0.

The team members give their numbers to the team leader, who records them in a notebook and marks the probable site on the map so that the follow-up team can find it again and examine it more thoroughly a day or so later. And then, the team members spread out again, so that they're in the same approximate positions in a line as before; and again, they march a predetermined distance, clicking as they go, repeating the process again and again until they reach the end of the designated area for that day. Once they've reached the end part, they swing around, though, and they repeat the process going in the other direction; returning the entire length to where they started out, only now they're a good way farther down the road. So, you do one transect here, then you swing around, and you come back again; at the end of that, you swing around again and go through again. That way you can traverse and record all of the sites in a square mile, or kilometer, or whatever you've chosen for that day until the entire region has been covered after six weeks or so of surveying.

Now, back at camp, the results of each day's survey are recorded; and from these results, a running list is developed. The list indicates how many sites have been found, the periods they represent, and where they're located. The most promising of these new possible sites then receive a visit from a team of experienced surveyors who are tasked with doing an intensive survey of the newly-discovered area. These surveyors record the surface finds more carefully and bring back the most diagnostic of the pottery sherds—rims, handles, bases, anything decorated—so that the pottery experts on the team can tell them what periods the pottery comes from.

So, those are the survey methods that we used near Pylos in the '90s, and they're the same methods that are often employed elsewhere today. Besides the excitement of locating possible sites, I think it's also worth mentioning the camaraderie and the bonding that come with being in the field with the same people for a period of several weeks. In fact, I'm still in touch with many of the people that I surveyed with in the '80s and '90s, including several who now hold senior positions in academia.

Now, there are many variations of the kind of surveying that I've described, including those that cover only specific portions, or even randomly chosen portions of an area that's simply too large to survey in its entirety. Here, statistics frequently enters into the situation because it's an art form in and of itself to decide whether you're going to sample entirely random areas, or stratified unaligned areas, or stratified random areas, and so on. As I've said, these types of surveys were especially popular from the 1960s onward, in part because of the arrival of processual or "new" archaeologists. These archaeologists wanted archaeology to be more scientific than it had been. It was also the case that surveying an entire area for six weeks was frequently much, much cheaper than the cost of excavating a single site for six weeks.

There's one other type of survey that I'd like to mention before we end. This is a targeted type of survey, which only involves revisiting sites that have been previously discovered. Essentially, it's like the second half of the survey that I just described, except that the sites might have been found by more than one project and over a number of years. This is the type of survey that we did in the area around Tel Kabri in Israel, in 2006 and 2007. We had already been digging at the site in 2005, and we had determined that we wanted to do a long-term excavation of the site. But first, we wanted to understand its context—what did the area around Tel Kabri look like before, during, and after its heyday in the Middle Bronze Age?

Fortunately, it was easy for us to do such a targeted survey of known sites because the western Galilee of Israel, where Kabri is located, has been surveyed intensively by several teams of archaeologists in almost every season and under almost every condition imaginable over the past 30 years or more. So, we already had maps of the area, with all of the known Middle Bronze Age sites marked on them. We also had access to the pottery and other artifacts that had been collected and stored by previous teams of archaeologists. We could have gone out and resurveyed the entire area again, but that probably would have been a waste of time for the most part. So instead, we elected to drive to the sites that were already known and simply to do an intensive survey of each of these.

Our goal? Our goal was to confirm and refine the dating previously assigned to each of these sites, so that we would know, for example, if they had been inhabited in the Middle Bronze IIA or the Middle Bronze IIB period, but not in the Middle Bronze I period. We also wanted to recheck how large, or how small, each of the sites were. In some cases, we were able to ascertain that a site was much bigger than previously thought; other times, it turned out to be much smaller than expected. And, in the end, we were able to produce a map showing the sites that were inhabited in the area just before, during, and after the time that Tel Kabri had flourished as a major center, from about 1800–1500 B.C.

So, that's the long answer to the very brief question that I posed at the beginning of this lecture, namely, "How on earth do you know where to dig?" What it all boils down to is surveying. Because, as we've seen today, once you have surveyed an area, it's really pretty easy to know exactly where you want to dig. Now, as for how you actually dig; well, that's a whole different story, which we'll tackle a little later in the course.

Lecture 6

Prehistoric Archaeology

In this lecture, we'll explore prehistoric archaeology, otherwise known as paleontology or palaeoanthropology. This field allows us a unique glimpse into the earliest times of hominid and human history. In particular, we'll look at several discoveries of hominid remains and footprints, and we'll explore paintings on the walls of caves in France and Spain dating to at least 30,000 years ago. As we'll see, palaeoanthropology is a fast-moving field of research, with more discoveries made every year.

Hominid Finds
- The most famous family in prehistoric archaeology is the Leakey family, with Louis and Mary in the first generation; their son Richard and his wife, Meave, in the second generation; and their daughter Louise in the third generation.
  - Louis was the founder of the dynasty, along with Mary. He was one of the first people to argue that human origins should be sought in Africa rather than in Asia, which had been the generally accepted theory. He turned out to be correct, though it took a while for others to adopt his point of view. His case was helped by the finds that he and Mary made beginning in 1948 and, later, in 1959. At that time, they were working in a canyon or ravine known as Olduvai Gorge in Tanzania.

  - Here, Louis and Mary found skeletal fragments that they identified as coming from a new species of hominid, which they ultimately named *Australopithecus boisei*. The Leakeys originally thought that it dated to about 600,000 years ago, but another dating technique showed that it was closer to 1.75 million years old. The Leakeys promptly followed this discovery by another one the next year of another new hominid species, *Homo habilis* ("handy man").

  - After Louis died in 1972, Mary made what is considered to be her most significant discovery: the hominid footprints at

Laetoli, found in 1978 and 1979. The site is located about 45 kilometers southeast of Olduvai Gorge. The famous footprints were made by several individuals who were walking across freshly fallen ash from a nearby volcano about 3.5 million years ago. In all, Mary Leakey and her team found about 70 human footprints that go on for almost 90 feet. It is usually suggested that the footprints were made by hominids called *Australopithecus afarensis*.

- These are not the only footprints that we have now, however. A team led by Dave Braun and Brian Richmond found another series of footprints in 2007 and 2008 at Koobi Fora. These are about 1.5 million years old and were probably made by *Homo erectus*, a direct ancestor of modern humans.

- In 1974, Donald Johanson found Lucy at the site of Hadar in Ethiopia. Lucy died about 3 million years ago at about the age of 20. She has been identified as an *Australopithecus afarensis*, similar to the individuals who left their footprints at Laetoli 500,000 years earlier. It is believed that she would have stood about 3 feet, 6 inches to 4 feet tall and weighed about 65 pounds.

- Today, the discoveries keep coming. The October 2015 issue of *National Geographic* magazine featured a story about a find made by Lee Berger and his team in a South African cave called Rising Star. They discovered more than 1,500 bones from at least 15 individuals, which Berger thinks belong to previously unknown hominin species, now named *Homo naledi*. These bones may be up to 2.8 million years old.

- Just a few years earlier, Berger had announced another discovery of early hominin fossils from a cave near Johannesburg in South Africa. These were excavated in August 2008 and were officially named *Australopithecus sediba* in 2010. Berger dates them to about 1.78 to 1.95 million years ago.

Cave Discoveries

- Dorothy Garrod is widely recognized as one of the most important early female archaeologists; she specialized in the Paleolithic period, or Old Stone Age (from about 2.6 million years ago to 12,000 B.C.). In the 1920s and 1930s, she investigated a cluster of caves located on the slopes of Mount Carmel, south of the modern city of Haifa.
    - From 1929 to 1934, Garrod excavated the Tabun Cave and another cave, known as el-Wad. She showed that the two caves were occupied almost continuously for about 500,000 years. Tabun Cave was occupied first, from about 500,000 years ago to 40,000 years ago; the occupation of el-Wad began just before Tabun was abandoned, about 45,000 years ago.

    - In Tabun Cave, there is a burial of a Neanderthal woman, dating to about 120,000 years ago. Although the skull indicates that her brain was about the same size as ours today, she had no real chin and a very low forehead, which means she probably looked similar to Hollywood's depictions of Neanderthals.

- There are also burials from nearby Skhul Cave. However, these burials, about 14 in all, are what are called *anatomically modern people*, that is, *Homo sapiens sapiens*. These have generated much discussion among scholars, who include this evidence in the debate about whether Neanderthals and modern humans lived side by side for a time.

- From 1982 to 1989, Harvard archaeologist Ofer Bar-Yosef excavated in Kebara Cave. There, he and his team found a Neanderthal burial: an adult male who lived about 60,000 years ago. Nicknamed Moshe, he may be the most complete Neanderthal skeleton found to date. The bones in his throat indicate that he was probably capable of speech.

Cave Paintings

- Even closer to us in time are other caves with evidence for Neanderthals and other hominid inhabitants. In particular, three are rightfully famous for their cave paintings: Chauvet Cave in France,

Lecture 6—Prehistoric Archaeology

The exquisite paintings in Chauvet, Lascaux, and Altamira caves depict a wide variety of animals, including horses, lions, woolly rhinos, owls, mammoths, bears, and many others.

dating to at least 30,000 B.C., if not 6,000 or 7,000 years earlier; Lascaux Cave, also in France, dating to approximately 15,000 B.C.; and Altamira, in Spain, dating to about 12,000 B.C.

- Lascaux Cave is located near Bordeaux in southern France. It is about 650 feet long, with at least 600 paintings and another 1,500 engravings on the walls. When Willard Libby was first experimenting with the technique of radiocarbon dating in 1949, one of the first trials of the new method was done on a piece of charcoal found at Lascaux. In part as a result of the new technique, the cave is now generally dated to about 17,000 years ago, or 15,000 B.C.

- The current entrance—possibly the original entrance—leads into the huge Hall of the Bulls, which has four bulls more than 5 meters long painted on the cave wall. Straight ahead is the Axial Gallery, which has paintings of cattle, deer, and horses. A passageway to the right of the Hall of Bulls has almost 400 more engravings, mostly of horses. Lascaux also features the Chamber of the Felines, which has six large felines among dozens of other engravings.

- The cave was never really excavated but was simply prepared for tourism and opened to the public in 1948. However, having more than 100,000 annual visitors quickly began to take its toll on the paintings. Today, a replica of the cave has been built nearby that the public can visit instead.

* The paintings in the cave at Altamira, in northern Spain, are usually dated to about 12,000 B.C., the end of the last Ice Age, though some have argued that they could be a good deal older.
  - The cave at Altamira is about 300 meters long, with a number of passages and chambers. Of the animals that are painted or engraved on the walls, the most famous are those on the Polychrome Ceiling, which include a herd of bison, horses, a deer, and possibly other animals.

  - Like those at Lascaux, the paintings in the cave at Altamira have suffered damage as a result of too many tourists. A nearby replica of the cave attracts up to 250,000 people per year, while a very limited number of visitors are allowed to tour the actual cave for brief periods.

* Chauvet, located in the Ardèche region of southern France, is the oldest of these three caves, but it is also the most recently discovered. The cave may be as much as 400 meters long and cover more than 8,000 square meters.

Lecture 6—Prehistoric Archaeology 101

- Nearly 4,000 artifacts and animal bones have been found in the cave so far, as well as 1,000 images on the walls. The drawings and paintings here include some of the earliest and best-preserved cave art in the world, depicting at least 13 different species, ranging from lions, horses, and woolly rhinos to owls, mammoths, bears, and other animals.

- The generally accepted dates for the paintings from radiocarbon analysis put most of them in the Aurignacian period, between 30,000 and 32,000 years before the present. The cave was then abandoned for several thousand years before being reoccupied during the Gravettian period, between 25,000 and 27,000 years ago, at which time dozens more paintings were added. However, even these dates have been pushed further back as a result of DNA and radiocarbon tests on the skeletons of cave bears found inside; these confirm that they date between 37,000 and 29,000 years old, after which a rockslide closed off the cave entrance so that nothing could enter.

- The cave has a number of different parts. The original entrance chamber leads into a huge area, named the Brunel Chamber for Éliette Brunel, the first person to enter the cave in 25,000 years. Next is the Chamber of the Bear Hollows, which has evidence of occupation by cave bears.

- Two galleries can be reached from the bears' chamber: the Cactus Gallery and the Red Panels Gallery, so-called because most of the paintings here are in red. Turning left from the Red Panels Gallery leads to the Candle Gallery, which is the beginning of the second part of the cave system.

- The system also includes the Hillaire Chamber; the Skull Chamber, where a bear skull was carefully placed on a stone fallen from the ceiling; the Gallery of the Crosshatching; the Megaloceros Gallery, with depictions of an extinct type of giant deer; the End Chamber, featuring a painting of 16 lions hunting a herd of bison; and the Sacristy, which has drawings of a horse, a bison, a large cat, and a rhinoceros. This chamber is the end of the cave system, at least as it is currently known.

- In late April 2015, a replica of Chauvet Cave was opened to the public. Each of the images is an exact replica of the original, created by using three-dimensional models, digital images, and other techniques, ranging from scientific to artistic. The original limestone walls are now reproduced in concrete, and the stalagmites and stalactites have been re-created in resin. Reportedly, the results are stunning.

Suggested Reading

Curtis, *The Cave Painters*.

Johanson and Edey, *Lucy*.

Leakey and Lewin, *Origins*.

Questions to Consider

1. Do you think it was a good idea to build replicas of all three caves so that tourists can see what was in the original ones without unintentionally destroying them?

2. Can you come up with a list of equipment and personnel that you would want if you were to excavate at a place such as Koobi Fora?

Lecture 6 Transcript **Prehistoric Archaeology**

Let's talk about prehistoric archaeology, otherwise known as paleontology or paleoanthropology. Archaeologists in this field study a period that covers millions of years—from our hominid ancestors, right up until the beginnings of recorded history.

The most famous family in prehistoric archaeology are the Leakeys, with Louis and Mary Leakey in the first generation; their son Richard and his wife Meave in the second generation; and their daughter Louise in the third generation. All of them have received grants from the National Geographic Society, and Meave and Louise have been National Geographic Explorers-in-Residence as a mother-daughter team.

Louise reportedly holds the record of being the youngest person ever to find a hominid fossil. She was 6 years, in 1977, when she found a tooth that was 17 million years old. Fast-forward 22 years to 1999, when she and her mother found a 3.5 million-year-old skull belonging to an early human. Louise has also been involved since 1993 in the Koobi Fora project in northern Kenya, where her father Richard first began digging in 1968. Dave Braun, one of my colleagues at GW, currently runs the Koobi Fora project; it's a small world.

Louise's mother, Meave, started her career by working for Louis Leakey—who was first her dissertation advisor and then her father-in-law after she married Richard in 1970. Richard became well known in his own right, with a long and distinguished career. I still remember reading his book *Origins* when I was in college. Among the more notable discoveries made by his teams were the nearly complete 1.6-million-year-old skeleton that was found in 1984. Turkana Boy, as he was initially known to the general public, was probably between 7 and 15 years old when he died.

Louis was the founder of the dynasty, along with Mary. He had grown up in Kenya and was one of the first people to argue that human origins should be sought in Africa rather than in Asia, which had been the generally accepted theory until then. He turned out to be correct, although it took a while for others to come around to his point of view. His case was helped by the finds that he and Mary made beginning in 1948, but then especially beginning in 1959. At that time, they were working in a canyon, or a ravine, that was 30 miles long and 300 feet deep known as Olduvai Gorge in Tanzania. Here, Louis and Mary found skeletal fragments that they identified as coming from a new species of hominid. Actually, it was Mary that found the first fragment, because Louis was back at the camp with a fever. She went out with their two Dalmatians to check on a site that they hadn't been to since 1931 and promptly found a fragment of skull and two teeth in a hominid jaw. She jumped in the Land Rover and drove back to get Louis. The two of them then found even more bone fragments and were able to reconstruct much of the skull.

They initially named it *Zinjanthropus boisei*, after their primary sponsor at the time, Charles Boise. Subsequently, however, the official name was changed to *Australopithecus boisei*. They originally thought it dated to about 600,000 years ago, but a dating technique that was new at the time showed that it was more like 1.75 million years old. At the time, the discovery caused a sensation. They promptly followed it up the next year by another discovery of another new hominid species, *Homo habilis*. This time, they didn't name it after a sponsor; *homo habilis* translate roughly as handyman. It would be hard for us to imagine what it was like for the Leakeys in those early days, except that we have photographs of them working from that period. We see them picking carefully at the dirt, in extremely hot conditions, with a huge umbrella planted for shade and several Dalmatian dogs keeping them company.

It was after Louis died in 1972 that Mary made what is considered to be her most significant discovery—the hominid footprints at Laetoli, which were found in 1978 and 1979. The site is located about 45 kilometers southeast of Olduvai Gorge. The first footprints were actually found at the site a few years earlier, in 1976, by team members who were throwing elephant dung at each other for fun, but those footprints were all made by animals. The famous footprints were made by several individuals who were walking across freshly fallen ash from a nearby volcano about 3.6 million years ago. In all, Mary Leakey and her team found about 70 human footprints that go on for almost 90 feet.

It's usually suggested that the footprints were made by hominids that we call *Australopithecus afarensis*. However, it's not clear whether they were made by all three individuals walking together, or if they came through at separate times, or if two were together plus a third unrelated one. In any event, judging from the footprints, two of them were about four foot eight tall and the third one was just about four foot tall.

These are not the only footprints that we have now. A team led by Dave Braun and Brian Richmond found another series of footprints in 2007 and 2008 at Koobi Fora. These are only about 1.5 million years old, so they're more recent by 2 million years than the ones that Mary Leakey found. However, they were probably made by *Homo erectus*—that is, a direct ancestor of modern humans. They're also about a size 9 in terms of today's men's shoes.

It was also soon after Louis Leakey died that Donald Johanson, an American colleague and a rival of Richard's, made a discovery in 1974 that ensured his membership in the Archaeology Hall of Fame. This was Lucy, who was found at the site of Hadar, in Ethiopia. As frequently happens in such circumstances, it was a chance discovery. Johanson and a colleague had been surveying in another area, and they began walking back to where they had parked their Land Rover. Rather than go back the way that they had come, he suggested going a different route, through a gully that they hadn't gone through before.

As Johanson tells the story, first he spotted a bone from a hominid forearm; and then, in rapid succession, a skull fragment, a leg bone, ribs, a pelvis, and a lower jaw. Within two weeks, they found several hundred pieces of bone, all belonging to Lucy.

Lucy died when she was about twenty years old, which was about 3 million years ago. She has been identified as an *Australopithecus afarensis*, similar to the individuals who left their footprints at Laetoli 500,000 years earlier. It's believed that she would have stood about three foot six to four foot tall and weighed about 65 pounds at most. That's just an estimate, though, since we only have about 40 percent of her skeleton. The origin of her name is now a trivia question among archaeologists and paleontologists. The simple answer is that the Beatles' song "Lucy in the Sky with Diamonds" was playing over and over again at the party that night back at the camp when they first returned with the skeletal remains. Sometime that evening, they began referring to her as Lucy. At least, that's the story that's always been told, and so I guess that we'll stick with it.

And, the discoveries keep coming. The October 2015 issue of *National Geographic* magazine featured a story about an exciting discovery made by Lee Berger and his team in a South African cave called Rising Star. They found more than 1,500 bones from at least 15 individuals, which Berger thinks belong to a previously unknown hominin species. They've been named *Homo naledi*, after the cave in which they were found. "Naledi" means "star" in the Sesotho language.

Now, it's not yet known how old the bones are, but they may be up to 2.8 million years old. They were all found in an almost inaccessible chamber in the cave in 2013 and 2014 after two spelunkers told Berger what they had seen through a crack in the cave wall. The six scientists who actually retrieved the bones were all women who were slim enough to fit through the cave passage—which, at one point, narrows to only seven and a half inches.

Just a few years earlier, Berger had announced another discovery of early hominid fossils from a cave near Johannesburg in South Africa. These were excavated in August 2008, after Berger's nine-year-old son had found the first two by accident. They were officially named *Australopithecus sediba* in 2010. Berger dates them to about 1.78–1.95 million years ago.

So caves are extremely important sites for prehistoric archaeology. They play a crucial role in helping us understand our connections to the deep past. In fact, Berger's discoveries are part of a long line of discoveries centered around caves. So for the rest of our lecture, let's do a bit of spelunking.

And let's start with an archaeologist named Dorothy Garrod, who in the 1920s and 1930s was investigating a cluster of caves located on the slopes of Mount Carmel, south of the modern city of Haifa. Garrod is widely recognized as one of the most important early female archaeologists. She was the first woman to be named a professor at Cambridge University in

England. There, she held the Disney Chair of Archaeology from 1939 until 1952. This is a very distinguished professorship that has nothing to do with Walt Disney, but rather was established back in about 1851 by a man named John Disney.

In any event, Dorothy Garrod's specialty was the Paleolithic period or the Old Stone Age. This period covers much of what we've been talking about—from about 2.6 million years ago, all the way down to about 12,000 years ago. Her first excavation at Mount Carmel was in Kebara Cave, which she briefly dug in 1928. She then moved on and spent five years, from 1929–1934, excavating two other caves. The more famous one is known as Tabun Cave; the other is known as el-Wad. She was able to show that the two caves were occupied pretty much continuously for about 500,000 years. Tabun Cave was occupied first, from about 500,000 years ago until 40,000 years ago. The occupation of el-Wad begins just before Tabun is abandoned, about 45,000 years ago.

Within Tabun Cave, there is a burial of a Neanderthal woman, dating to about 120,000 years ago. While the skull indicates that her brain was about the same size as ours today, she had no real chin and a very low forehead, which means she probably looked a lot like Hollywood's depictions of Neanderthals.

There are also burials from nearby Skhul Cave. However, these burials, and there's about 14 of them in all, are what are called anatomically modern people—that is, *Homo sapiens sapiens*. These have generated much discussion among scholars, who include this evidence to support the fact that Neanderthals and modern humans lived side by side for a time.

From 1982–1989, Harvard archaeologist Ofer Bar-Yosef returned to Kebara Cave, where Garrod had dug in 1928. There, he and his team found a Neanderthal burial—an adult male who lived about 60,000 years ago. Nicknamed Moshe, he may be the most complete Neanderthal skeleton that we've found to date. It caused a great deal of excitement when he was discovered because even though Moshe's head was missing, there were bones from his throat that indicated he was probably capable of speech.

Even closer to us in time, but up in France and Spain, are other caves with evidence for Neanderthals and other hominid inhabitants. These, though, have cave paintings, for which they are rightfully famous. We'll take a brief look at three of these: Chauvet and Lascaux in France and Altamira in Spain. Chauvet is the oldest of these three; it dates back to at least 30,000 B.C., if not 6 or 7,000 years even earlier; then comes Lascaux at approximately 15,000 B.C., and then Altamira at about 12,000 B.C.

The story of Lascaux's discovery is well known. Four teenage boys and their dog, whose name was Robot for some reason, came upon the cave in 1940. They were walking on a hill above the town of Montignac near Bordeaux in southern France, and they decided to explore a hole that they found—reportedly because their dog started digging in it, and they thought it might contain buried treasure. We now know that it did contain buried treasure, but it was a treasure trove of art, not the treasure of gold that the boys were originally hoping for.

The cave is about 650 feet long, with at least 600 paintings, and another 1500 engravings on the walls. Interestingly, when Willard Libby was first experimenting with the technique of radiocarbon dating back in 1947, one of the first trials of the new method was done on a piece of charcoal that had been found at Lascaux. In part as a result of the new technique, the cave is now generally dated to about 17,000 years ago, or 15,000 B.C. The current entrance, and possibly the original entrance as well, leads into the huge Hall of Bulls, which has four huge bulls more than five meters in length painted on the cave wall. To be exact, these are actually aurochs, a now-extinct species of wild cattle. There are also smaller horses and tiny deer painted here.

From the Hall of Bulls, you can proceed straight ahead into the Axial Gallery. This area has paintings of cattle, deer, and horses; including the so-called Chinese horses, which are not Chinese but are called that nevertheless. However, if you turn to the right instead of going into the Axial Gallery, you're in a passageway that has almost 400 more engravings, mostly of horses. And then if you go right again, you're in the Great Apse. That has another 1,000 or more engravings on its walls. Lascaux also features the

Chamber of the Felines, which has six large felines among dozens of other engravings.

The cave was never really excavated, but it was simply prepared for tourism and was opened up to the public in 1948. However, having more than 100,000 annual visitors quickly began to take its toll on the paintings. By 1963, the cave was closed to the public, and only small groups were let in from then on. Problems still abound, though. In 2000, after the installation of a new air-conditioning system, fungus began to grow on the walls and the images. And in 2006, black mold began to grow on them as well. The damage is probably irreparable, which is why a replica of the cave has been built nearby, and the public can visit that instead.

The paintings in the cave at Altamira, in northern Spain, have also undergone similar problems as a result of too many tourists. This was discovered by a hunter in 1868 and was then visited by a local landowner. In 1876, he found it; and then two years later, having been inspired by a show about Paleolithic art in Paris, he returned to the cave with his eight-year-old daughter Maria. She spotted the paintings on the cave while he was busy excavating the cave floor, looking for tools and other artifacts. His subsequent announcement of the discovery in 1880 was met with disbelief by the scholarly establishment. And it was only decades later, long after his death, that the scholars admitted that he had been correct all along.

The paintings in the cave are usually dated towards the end of the Magdalenian period during the Paleolithic—that is, about 12,000 B.C., at the time of the end of the last Ice Age. Some, though, argue they could be a great deal earlier. But they're certainly not any more recent than about 12,000 B.C. because a rockslide sealed closed the entrance to the cave at that time. The cave itself is about 300 meters long, with the usual passages and chambers that we've come to expect in such caves. Of the animals that are painted or engraved on the walls, the most famous are those on the Polychrome Ceiling, which include a herd of bison, plus a couple of horses, a deer, and possibly other animals.

In 1979, Altamira was closed to the general public because of fears that the same thing would happen as had happened at Lascaux. But then it was reopened, with a quota of visitors limited to less than 10,000 per year. It closed again in 2002, and an exact replica of the cave was built nearby, which reportedly has attracted up to a quarter of a million people per year. By 2014, small groups of visitors were again being allowed to enter the actual cave. But in March 2015, scientists advised that it should be closed to visitors again. Their suggestion was ignored, and instead, five randomly selected visitors were being allowed in for 37 minutes once a week—which seems rather a strange compromise, to be honest.

Chauvet is the oldest of our three caves, but it's also the most recently discovered. It's located in the Ardèche region of southern France. The huge cave, which may be as much as 400 meters long and cover more than 8,000 square meters, was first discovered and explored in late December of 1994 by Jean-Marie Chauvet and a small group of colleagues. Chauvet has also been brought to life by a 3-D movie produced by famed director Werner Herzog, which was released in 2011. Nearly 4,000 artifacts and animal bones have been found so far, as well as 1,000 images on the walls. The drawings and paintings in here are simply exquisite; they include some of the earliest and best-preserved cave art in the world, depicting at least 13 different species—which range from lions, horses, and woolly rhinos to owls, mammoths, bears, and other animals.

Discussions as to their date have been rather heated. On one side of the dispute, they place the age during the Gravettian period several thousand years later. But the generally-accepted dates from radiocarbon analysis conducted on different samples over the years put most of them in the Aurignacian Period—that is, between 30,000 and 32,000 years before present. The cave was then abandoned for several thousand years before being reoccupied during the Gravettian Period, between 25,000 and 27,000 years before present. And that is the time when dozens more paintings were added.

There's also a child's footprint that has been preserved on the soft clay floor of the cave, which probably dates from this second period of occupation. However, even these dates have been pushed further back, as DNA and radiocarbon tests on the skeletons of the cave bears that have been found inside confirm that they date between 37,000 and 29,000 years ago. Several thousand years later, a rockslide closed off the cave entrance so that nobody, and no animals, could enter after that.

It was not an accidental discovery, though. Jean-Marie Chauvet was a park ranger working for France's Ministry of Culture and was actively out looking for such caves. This particular cave is located high up on a limestone cliff above the former route of the Ardèche River. It's very close to a natural limestone bridge called the Pont d'Arc. Although the original entrance to the cave had been closed by the rockslide, members of Chauvet's group noticed cold air coming from a small opening on the cliff face.

The smallest member of the group, a woman named Éliette Brunel, climbed in after they had removed a few rocks to enlarge the opening. The others quickly followed her in and used a chain ladder that they had brought to descend a deep 30-foot shaft. They found themselves in a huge cavern, with stalagmites and stalactites everywhere. They noticed animal bones on the floor and then the first few paintings on the walls. Brunel yelled out, "They've been here"—meaning Paleolithic cave painters.

There is some dispute about exactly who was with Chauvet that day and who was brought there by him soon afterward, as well as whether he was even the first to notice the small initial opening. But these first intrepid explorers inside the cave saw hundreds of drawings and paintings—some huge and some fairly small; some isolated and others painted as a group, overlapping as needed. They had seen enough. They quickly alerted the authorities, who sent Jean Clottes—a specialist in cave paintings who was also a scientific advisor to the Ministry of Culture. Clottes declared it to be one of the great discoveries of the 20th century.

Clottes assembled a team of specialists who have been studying the Chauvet cave paintings since 1996. In all that time, the cave has remained closed to the public in order to avoid the kinds of problems caused by opening Lascaux and Altamira to tourists. In fact, even the research team only enters the Chauvet cave twice a year, for a few weeks in the spring and another few weeks in the fall. At all other times, a four-foot-tall locked steel door at its entrance protects it.

There are a number of different parts to the cave. The original entrance chamber, which is now sealed off from the outside by the ancient rockslide, leads into a huge area named the Brunel Chamber—for Éliette Brunel, the first person who enter the cave in 22,000 years or so. From here you go into the Chamber of the Bear Hollows, which has lots of evidence for occupation by cave bears, including hollows that they dug into the soft clay floor.

Two other galleries can be reached from the bears' chamber. One is a fairly short gallery called the Cactus Gallery. This contains the first painting seen by Chauvet and his group—a small red mammoth painted on a rock. This was the painting that Éliette Brunel was looking at when she called out, "They've been here!" The other Gallery is much larger and leads to additional galleries and chambers beyond. This is known as the Red Panels Gallery since most of the paintings found here are in a series of panels on the eastern wall and are primarily painted in red.

From the Red Panels Gallery you can go to the left—that is, west—and enter the Candle Gallery. This is the beginning of the second part of the cave system. From the Candle Gallery, you enter the Hillaire Chamber; named after Christian Hillaire, who was the third member of the original trio who discovered the cave. This is about 30 meters in diameter—so about 100 feet wide—with a ceiling that's nearly as high. There are lots of wall paintings drawings in here. Some of them are overlapping, probably meaning that they were created at different points in time. A natural calcite coating also covers a number of them, meaning that there's no way that these are fakes, in case anyone was wondering.

From the Hillaire Chamber, there are two choices. If you continue heading west, the Skull Chamber is next. Here, there is a bear skull that was very carefully placed long, long ago on a stone that had fallen from the ceiling. Beyond the Skull Chamber is the final gallery in this direction, the Gallery of the Crosshatching, where a large horse is drawn on the rock. However, if you continue north from the Hillaire Chamber instead of going west, you enter the Megaloceros Chamber. There are drawings of several rhinoceroses, but it gets its name from a drawing of a megaloceros, which is an extinct type of giant deer with huge antlers. The largest member of the megaloceros genus stood far taller than an average human and is known variously as the Irish Elk, Irish Deer, or simply the Giant Elk.

From the Megaloceros Chamber or Gallery, you proceed into the so-called End Chamber, in which some of the finest images are found. These include bison, rhinoceroses, mammoths, and large cats. There are so many here that they make up more than a third of all the images in the entire cave. One of the highlights of the End Chamber is a group of 16 lions hunting a herd of bison. In this, and many other cases throughout the whole cave, the artist or artists used features in the rock itself to make it look like the animals were moving and alive.

On one side, it's possible to go from the End Chamber into the Sacristy, which has drawings of a horse, a big bison, a large cat, and a rhinoceros on the wall and lots and lots of animal prints in the soft clay floor. At this point, you reach the end of the cave system, at least as it's currently known.

In late April 2015, a replica of the Chauvet cave opened up nearby. It cost 55 million Euros to build—that's approximately $63 million—but it allows the general public to finally see the amazing images painted on the walls and rocks of the actual cave. Each of the images is an exact replica of the original, created by using 3-D models, digital images, and other techniques, ranging from scientific to artistic. The original limestone walls are now reproduced in concrete; the stalagmites and stalactites have been recreated in resin. Reportedly, the results are stunning, and it's now on my bucket list to visit.

What I find extremely interesting is that all three of these caves are now essentially closed off to the public, but the replicas that have been built at each of them are either attracting or have the potential to attract, more visitors than the originals ever handled. For example, even at its height, Altamira cave had about 150,000 annual visitors, but now the replica is reporting up to 250,000 annual visitors. Perhaps this is incentive to create more such replicas, just as has been done with King Tut's tomb in Egypt now. Far from Disney-fying the site—or altering it irrevocably like Sir Arthur Evans did at Knossos—creating such identical replicas may allow many more members of the general public to enjoy these ancient wonders while still leaving the originals relatively untouched and able to be further studied by scientists.

Prehistoric archaeology is unique in allowing us to glimpse the earliest times in hominid and human history, ranging from the three individuals who left their footprints in the ash at Laetoli in Tanzania several million years ago, to more recent times when our direct ancestors were busy painting on the walls of caves in France and Spain. It's a fast-moving field of research, with more discoveries made every year, and I for one cannot wait to hear what's going to be found next.

Lecture 7: Göbekli Tepe, Çatalhöyük, and Jericho

In this lecture, we'll explore three sites from the Neolithic period: Göbekli Tepe, Jericho, and Çatalhöyük. The Neolithic period, or New Stone Age, started about 12,000 years ago, in about 10,000 B.C., in the ancient Near East. The period is often associated with the term *Neolithic Revolution* because it saw the beginning of a completely new way of life. Not only did stone tools change, but plants and animals were domesticated for the first time. However, we are still in the process of learning about the Neolithic. As we will see, much remains to be found at Göbekli Tepe, Jericho, and Çatalhöyük, which will undoubtedly change our understanding of the Neolithic period.

Göbekli Tepe

- Göbekli Tepe is a site in modern Turkey that dates back nearly 11,000 years ago, to about 9600 B.C. This date puts it in the pre-pottery Neolithic period—the first 4,000 years or so of the Neolithic, before pottery as we know it had been invented. Göbekli Tepe appears to be one of the oldest pre-pottery Neolithic sites with evidence for religious beliefs.

- Göbekli Tepe is located on the northern edge of the Fertile Crescent, an arc of sites that runs from the top of the Persian Gulf across to where Turkey meets Syria and down the Mediterranean coast to Egypt. Göbekli Tepe seems to be one of the earliest sites from this period. In fact, it seems to have been inhabited just before the domestication of plants and animals.

- Göbekli Tepe has the oldest known examples of monumental architecture in the ancient Near East. So far, archaeologists have uncovered at least five stone circles of various sizes, one of which is 65 feet across. According to the German archaeologist Klaus Schmidt, there are at least 16 other stone circles still buried, which he detected using remote-sensing techniques.

- Each of the circles that has been excavated so far contains a number of standing stones, including two large T-shaped stones in the middle, with smaller standing stones around them. The larger stones can be up to 16 feet tall.

- Most of the standing stones have figures or scenes carved on them, including pictures of lizards, scorpions, bulls, lions, vultures, and possibly dogs or wolves, in addition to other species. Some of these images may even be pictographs, that is, images that tell a story.

- It is not at all clear what the inhabitants of Göbekli Tepe were trying to do at this site, but Schmidt was convinced that it was a holy place, perhaps the earliest with architecture deliberately built by humans.

- It has long been thought that humans were able to settle down because of the domestication of plants and animals, but such sites as Göbekli Tepe might indicate the opposite. It may be that because so many people were gathered at this site—creating the stone rings, carving the standing stones, and so on—that greater supplies of food were needed, beyond what the usual hunting and gathering methods could supply. For this reason, Göbekli Tepe is considered an extremely important site; it may shed light on the earliest practice of religion.

Jericho
- Jericho is located in the West Bank, in the region of Israel and the Palestinian Territories. It is familiar to many because of the biblical story concerning Joshua and the Israelites, who invaded Canaan at the end of the Exodus from Egypt. Jericho is located in an oasis situated in the middle of what is otherwise a desert. The water supply allows for drinking and irrigation, enabling people to survive and even flourish here.

- From 1930 to 1936, a British archaeologist named John Garstang conducted excavations at Jericho and identified one of the layers within the mound as the city captured by Joshua and the Israelites. However, his conclusion came under fire; it was suggested that he had misdated the pottery found in the level and, therefore, had misinterpreted his findings.

- Eventually, Garstang invited archaeologist Kathleen Kenyon to reexamine the pottery that he had found. She returned to Jericho in 1952 and began her own series of excavations, which lasted until 1958. The stratigraphy at the site, documenting four different levels and periods of occupation, turned out to be more complicated than expected. Her drawings of the sections that she excavated show a tangled mess of walls, floors, destructions, and other archaeological remains.

- Kenyon also found evidence, particularly more pottery, indicating that the destruction found by Garstang actually dated to 1,000 years before the time of Joshua; the remains of that city were from the Early Bronze Age, not the Late Bronze Age. Moreover, Kenyon believed that the city had already been abandoned by the middle of the 2nd millennium B.C. and would have been deserted, if not completely in ruins, by the time that Joshua and the Israelites invaded the region. Not everyone accepts her findings, though, and a debate continues to this day about whether or not there is archaeological evidence for Joshua's destruction of Jericho.

- Perhaps the most important find made by Kenyon is the Jericho Tower, which dates to about 7500 B.C. This is about 2,000 years after the Göbekli Tepe remains but is still in the pre-pottery Neolithic period. Jericho at that time probably had a population of about 2,000 to 3,000 people. It was protected by a thick stone wall, as well as the 26-foot-tall tower, giving rise to the notion that Jericho is the first known walled town. However, the actual use of the tower is a matter of dispute among archaeologists.

- The inhabitants of Jericho buried their dead under the floors of their houses during this period. Kenyon found almost 300 burials, but what was especially strange was what the inhabitants did with the skulls of their dead during the second half of this period, which lasted down to about 6000 B.C.

- During this time at Jericho, and at about a dozen other sites elsewhere in the Near East, the inhabitants would remove the skull from the rest of the skeleton, presumably after the body had decayed enough to allow the removal of the skull easily. They would also remove the lower jaw, then plaster the rest of the skull with clay. In essence, they were basically restoring the flesh of the face with clay.

- They would also put seashells, especially cowrie shells, where the eyes had once been, thereby creating a lifelike appearance. Frequently, they would then place the skulls in a prominent place, such as in the living room of their homes. It is generally thought that this practice reflects some sort of ancestor worship, but we cannot know for certain.

• More recently, a joint Italian and Palestinian team of archaeologists excavated again at Jericho, from 1997 to 2000. They found additional interesting information, including evidence for a large lower city dating to the Middle Bronze Age, but their work came to a halt when tensions in the region made it unsafe to continue.

Çatalhöyük

• Çatalhöyük, in modern-day Turkey, dates slightly later than Jericho, flourishing from 6500 to 5600 B.C. Excavations at the site first began in the early 1960s under the direction of James Mellaart, a British archaeologist. He uncovered about 160 houses belonging to a village with a population between 3,000 and 8,000.

• These houses are all interconnected, with party walls serving two houses at a time. All the walls are made of mudbrick, but none of the houses has either doors or windows. There are also no streets or alleyways between the houses. It is believed that the inhabitants used ladders to climb up to the roofs of the homes and to get down into the interior. A possible explanation for this unusual arrangement comes from a wall painting depicting a large animal

Wall paintings at Çatalhöyük seem to indicate that large wild animals roamed the area outside the village, which may explain the fact that ladders were used to access homes, rather than doors.

being hunted by a group of much smaller humans. It may be that the lack of access to the homes served to protect the villagers from possible predators.

- In addition to this and other hunting scenes, Mellaart found a number of other wall paintings during his excavations. One shows large-scale men running, clad only in loincloths. Another has a pleasing geometric pattern above a number of white hands on a red background. A number of the paintings show bulls, and clay sculptures of bulls' heads or horns have been found in some of the rooms.
  - One wall painting seems to depict a landscape, perhaps the view that inhabitants would have seen when gazing out from the village in the direction of a large mountain in the distance. This large mountain is actually a volcano and may have been the source for all the obsidian found in the region.

- An additional scene shows large birds that look like vultures that seem to be attacking a human figure who is lying prone. This has led some scholars to hypothesize that dead bodies may have occasionally been left out in the open deliberately, so that the flesh would be consumed by carnivores before the skeletal remains were buried.

- Ian Hodder of Stanford University renewed excavations of Çatalhöyük in 1993. Before coming to Stanford, Hodder had been a professor at Cambridge University, where he initiated *post-processual archaeology*.
  - Processual archaeology was developed by Lewis Binford in the 1960s in an effort to make archaeology more explanatory and scientific, rather than merely descriptive. Binford wanted archaeologists to use scientific processes and try to develop universal laws or generalizations to explain their findings.

  - In the 1980s, the movement known as post-processual archaeology, or post-processualism, emerged in reaction Binford. Ian Hodder and others rejected, at least to an extent, Binford's reliance on science, which they said "dehumanized" archaeology. Post-processualism maintains that we can't understand the past unless we try to understand people and their possible motivations.

- In addition to some fairly typical figures of animals, figurines of women have also been found at Çatalhöyük. The women are usually seated and have rather voluptuous proportions. They fit into a category of female figurines that are found across Europe from this particular time period. Marija Gimbutas, who was a professor at UCLA, saw these as mother goddess figurines, meant to symbolize fertility and motherhood, but we don't actually know what the figurines represent.

Suggested Reading

Balter, *The Goddess and the Bull.*

Hodder, *The Leopard's Tale.*

Kelly and Thomas, *Archaeology.*

Kenyon, *Digging Up Jericho.*

Questions to Consider

1. What do you think Göbekli Tepe was used for?

2. How would you interpret all the bull representations at Çatalhöyük?

Lecture 7 Transcript
Göbekli Tepe, Çatalhöyük, and Jericho

Some sites make headlines around the world when they are discovered. Some sites attract outlandish theories like flies to honey. And some sites do both. Such is the case with Göbekli Tepe, a site in modern Turkey that dates back more than 11,000 years ago, to about 9600 B.C. According to various accounts, it was discovered in 1983 by a farmer, who found a carved stone in his field and took it to the local museum. However, the University of Chicago had previously conducted an archaeological survey back in the 1960s and had already dismissed the site as a probable medieval cemetery, because of all the broken slabs of stones that they saw, which they thought were possible tombstones. So, not much was made of the farmer's discovery, at least initially.

In 1993, Klaus Schmidt, a German archaeologist, saw the carved stone that the farmer had found, and began investigations two years later in 1995. Actual excavations didn't begin until 2007. Within just a few years, the site was already making headlines and became the focus of outlandish theories, including being featured on an episode of *Ancient Aliens* in 2010. Schmidt, who was not happy about the unwanted attention, led the excavations until his unexpected and untimely death from a heart attack while swimming in July 2014.

So, what is Göbekli Tepe? Well, to put it simply, it appears to be one of the oldest pre-pottery Neolithic sites with evidence for religious beliefs that has ever been found. The Neolithic Period, or New Stone Age from the Greek *neos* meaning "new" and *lithos* meaning "stone," started about 12,000 years ago, so about 10,000 B.C in the ancient Near East. During the first part of this period, which lasted for about 4,000 years, pottery as we know it hadn't yet been invented, so it is called the pre-pottery Neolithic period.

We usually talk about the Neolithic Revolution when we are discussing this period because it sees the beginning of a whole new way of life. Not only do stone tools change, which is why we call this the New Stone Age in the first place, but this is when we see the first domestication of plants and animals, including wheat and barley, sheep and goats, and so on. There is an arc of sites, running from the top of the Persian Gulf up across to where Turkey meets Syria and then down the Mediterranean coast all the way to Egypt, where evidence for the earliest domestication has been found. The area is collectively known as the Fertile Crescent to archaeologists.

There are a wide variety of theories about why agriculture and domestication of plants and animals began in this region in the Neolithic period, including suggestions about possible climate change, but this isn't the place or the time to go into those. What's important for us is that Göbekli Tepe is located on the northern edge of the Fertile Crescent, and it seems to be one of the earliest sites from this time period. In fact, it seems to have been inhabited just before the inhabitants learned the art of domestication because the thousands of animal bones that have now been recovered and studied indicate the inhabitants were hunting and eating wild game, primarily gazelles and birds.

Göbekli Tepe has the oldest known examples of monumental architecture in the ancient Near East. So far archaeologists have uncovered at least five stone circles of various sizes—one of them is 65 feet across. According to Klaus Schmidt, there are at least 16 other stone circles still buried, which he detected using remote sensing techniques such as ground-penetrating radar. Each of the circles that have been excavated so far contains a number of standing stones within them, including two large T-shaped stones in the middle, with smaller standing stones around them. The larger stones can be up to 16 or even 18 feet tall.

Most of the standing stones have figures or scenes carved on them, including pictures of animals, which has excited the interest of a lot of people, ranging from professional archaeologists to the general public to those with far-out theories. The animals include lizards, scorpions, bulls, lions, vultures, and possible dogs or wolves, in addition to other species. Some of them might even be pictographs—that is, images that tell a story—although this novel suggestion was only first offered during the summer of 2015.

It is not at all clear what the inhabitants of Göbekli Tepe were trying to do here, but Schmidt was convinced that it was a holy place, perhaps the earliest with architecture deliberately built by humans. In 2008, the *Smithsonian* magazine published an article wondering whether this is the world's first known temple, and in 2011, *National Geographic* published an article that suggested the urge to worship sparked civilization.

In that *National Geographic* article, the author pointed out that the builders of Göbekli Tepe were able to cut, shape, and transport 16-ton stones hundreds of feet despite having no wheels or beasts of burden. He also pointed out that they were living in a world that did not yet have writing, metal, or pottery.

Now, it has long been thought that humans were able to settle down because of the invention of the domestication of plants and animals, but sites like Göbekli Tepe might actually indicate the opposite. It might well be that because so many people were gathered at a site like this, creating the stone rings, carving the standing stones, and so on, that they needed to figure out a way to feed them all if the usual hunting and gathering methods couldn't sustain them. So, Göbekli Tepe is an extremely important site, but the archaeological investigations have really only just begun. We'll see more from this site in the coming years, as the excavations continue under the direction of a new chief archaeologist.

But, I should also mention what Göbekli Tepe is not. It's not the Garden of Eden, and Schmidt never claimed that it was, despite some newspaper accounts that said he did. It also is not an ancient site related to Watchers or ancient Nephilim from the Bible, or to a global catastrophe that some think took place after the end of the last ice age, as was claimed in a book published in 2014.

It is, plain and simple, one of the most interesting sites currently being investigated by archaeologists. It may shed light on the earliest practice of religion, and it will definitely shed light on the period when humans began to settle down and domesticate plants and animals. In that regard, it joins two other sites that are extremely fascinating in both regards, which we shall now take a look at now: Çatalhöyük, in modern-day Turkey, and Jericho, now located in the West Bank, in the region of Israel and the Palestinian Territories.

If we turn to Jericho first, this is a site that is probably familiar to many of you because of the biblical story concerning Joshua and the Israelites. They invaded Canaan at the end of the Exodus from Egypt according to the Bible. There's a whole kettle of fish involved with the archaeology of that story, but in fact, that's what led to the discovery of Neolithic Jericho.

Jericho is located in an oasis situated in the middle of what is otherwise forlorn desert. The water supply allows for plentiful drinking as well as irrigation. This allowed people to survive and even flourish here. From 1930 until about 1936, a well-known British archaeologist named John Garstang conducted excavations at Jericho. As part of his interpretation of what he found, he identified one of the layers within the mound as the city that was captured by Joshua and the Israelites. However, his suggestion came under fire, and it was suggested that he had misdated the pottery in that level, and therefore he had misinterpreted everything.

He eventually invited Kathleen Kenyon, who was the daughter of the Director of the British Museum and a respected archaeologist in her own right, to come and reexamine the pottery that he had found. She eventually decided that there wasn't enough evidence to make a clear decision and that what she needed to do more excavating at the site. By the way, that's actually a very common decision for archaeologists to make.

So, she went back to Jericho in 1952 and began her own series of excavations, which lasted until 1958. The stratigraphy at the site, documenting four different levels and periods of occupation turned out to be far more complicated than expected. Her drawings of the sections that she made, after she had excavated through an entire part of the mound, show a tangled mess of walls, floors, destructions, and other archaeological remains.

However, she found evidence, particularly more pottery, that indicated to her, and to much of the scholarly world, that the destruction found by Garstang actually dated to a thousand years before the time of Joshua—the remains of that city were from the Early Bronze Age, not the Late Bronze Age. Moreover, it looked to her as if the city had already been abandoned by the middle of the second millennium B.C. and that it would have been deserted and empty, if not completely in ruins, by the time that Joshua and the Israelites invaded the region. Not everyone accepts her findings, though, and so a debate continues to this day about whether we have archaeological evidence for Joshua destroying Jericho or not.

In any case, while Kenyon was digging at Jericho, she also found Neolithic levels that included walls, buildings, and tombs, and it's these that I want to focus on today. Perhaps the most important, and certainly most famous, find that she made is the so-called Jericho Tower, which dates to about 7500 B.C. This is about 2,000 years after the Göbekli Tepe remains that we just looked at, but it's still in the Pre-pottery Neolithic period. In fact, it's in the first half of this period, referred to as the Pre-pottery Neolithic A, or PPNA for short.

Jericho at that time probably had a population of about 2–3,000 people at most. It was protected by a thick stone wall as well as the 26-foot-tall tower, giving rise to the notion found in much archaeological literature that Jericho is the first known walled town. However, the actual use of the tower is a matter of dispute among archaeologists, with some saying that it served a more social function or even an astronomical purpose. Suffice it to say, the jury is still out though it could certainly have served several functions at the same time.

The inhabitants of Jericho buried their dead under the floors of their houses during this period. Kenyon found almost 300 burials, but what was especially strange was what the inhabitants of Jericho did with the skulls of their dead during the second half of this period, in the PPNB phase, which lasted down to about 6000 B.C.

During this time at Jericho, and at about a dozen other sites elsewhere in the Near East as well, the inhabitants would remove the skull from the rest of the skeleton, presumably, after the body had decayed enough to allow the removal of the skull easily, rather than trying to cut it off. They would also remove the lower jaw and then plastered the rest of the skull. In essence, they were basically restoring the flesh of the face. They would also put seashells, especially cowrie shells, where the eyes had once been, thereby creating a lifelike appearance. And then they would frequently place the skulls in a prominent place, such as in the living room of their house.

It's generally thought that this reflects some sort of ancestor worship, but we can't know for certain because they didn't leave any records telling us why they did this. It is a bit weird, and creepy, at least in my opinion, to think of the head of your Uncle Fred, or even your own deceased parental unit, sitting in the corner of your living room, watching everything you do. And yet, I have a painting of my late mother in our dining room, so that's not so far removed, is it?

When the artist Damien Hirst produced his own version of such a skull, I showed the images side by side to my students—a skull from Jericho and the Damien Hirst skull that he created in 2007. We agreed that they were somewhat similar, but the one that Damien Hirst made was probably a bit more costly because he created it by using 8,600 flawless diamonds as well as platinum. The materials alone cost 14 million British pounds, that's almost 22 million U.S. dollars; it was offered for sale at the bargain price of 50 million British pounds.

Most recently, a joint Italian and Palestinian team of archaeologists excavated again at Jericho, for four seasons from 1997–2000. They found additional interesting information, including evidence for a large lower city dated to the Middle Bronze Age, but their work came to a halt when tensions in the region made it unsafe to continue.

The last site that I want to discuss in this lecture has also just produced two plaster skulls of the sort found at Jericho, but it's better known for other things. Dating slightly later than Jericho, and flourishing between 6500–5600 B.C., during the PPNB period, this is the site of Çatalhöyük in modern-day Turkey.

Excavations at the site first began in the early 1960s, under the direction of James Mellaart, a British archaeologist. He uncovered about 160 houses belonging to an amazing village or small town, which had a population that was anywhere from about 3,000–8,000 people at any one given time. The houses were all interconnected, with party walls serving two houses at a time. All of the walls are made of mud brick, but the very strange thing is none of them have either doors or windows—no doors, no windows. There's also no streets and no alleyways between the houses because they're all connected.

Now I assume that some of you are thinking the same thing that I thought when I first heard about their site. If there are no windows and no doors and no access from streets or alleyways, how on earth were you supposed to get into your own house? The answer, we think, is ladders. Ladders to get up onto the roof of the house and then ladders to get down into the interior of the house. This has to be the explanation because it's clear that the people did have access to the interior of their houses. But I think you'll agree that this is a rather unusual living arrangement. What could possibly have prompted them to build the houses in this way?

The answer, I think, is made clear by the discovery of a wall painting that decorated one of the houses. The painting depicts a scene of a very large animal, possibly with horns, that is being hunted by a group of much smaller humans together with a few horses. I presume that the artist had a little bit of a problem with perspective, because otherwise this animal, which looks a lot like a wild pig or probably even a bull, has got to be monstrously huge. Even if it wasn't as big in reality as it looks in this picture, it still is an indication that there were large wild animals roaming around in the area outside this village. Undoubtedly, the villagers were afraid of these wild animals and tried to protect themselves from them. I think that's why they had no doors or windows, so the animals could not get in that way. By using ladders, which the animals presumably can't climb, the inhabitants were able to ensure their survival, at least from unwanted predators at night. I can't think of any other explanation that works as well, though if you think so or think of any, please let me know.

Mellaart found this painting during his excavations in the 1960s, but unfortunately, he left it unprotected from the elements, so it's not in very good shape now. He found a lot of other wall paintings as well, including one with large-scale men shown running, clad only in loincloths. Another has a rather pleasing geometric pattern above and then a number of white hands on a red background below. The hands remind me of the paintings that I used to do in kindergarten, where I would either trace around my own hand on a piece of paper and then color it in or actually put my hand in the paint and stick it on the paper. They've done somewhat the same thing here, in white on red.

Other paintings seem to show additional hunting scenes, including one in which lots of little men are surrounding a rather large deer or antelope or some other similar animal with large horns. These hunting scenes, many of which are in the same room within a single house, all have in common that the animals are depicted much larger than the human beings who are apparently hunting them. Again, I would suspect that this is simply an indication of the importance of the animals that they are hunting, rather than the fact that they were actually really, really huge.

On the other hand, the inhabitants do seem to have had a bit of a fixation with bulls. In addition to the paintings showing bulls, there are also what we call plastic, or three-dimensional, sculptures found in some of the rooms. These are primarily clay bulls' heads, complete with horns, or often just the horns themselves.

We've got no clue why they were so fascinated by these bulls. The later Minoans, who lived on the island of Crete in the Aegean about 4000 years later, during the Bronze Age, also had a fixation with bulls. There are some theories that the original settlers of Crete came from ancient Anatolia, but the time span is just too great to try to link the Neolithic bulls of Çatalhöyük with the Bronze Age bulls of Knossos, even if it is tempting.

There is also another wall painting that seems to depict a landscape. In fact, it seems to be the view that one sees when gazing out from the village in the direction of a large mountain that rises in the distance. This large mountain is actually a volcano, which may have been the source for all of the obsidian that's found in the region. There are lots of little squares shown in front of the mountain in the wall painting. This may be the artist trying to depict his or her village in the foreground; in other words, Çatalhöyük itself. It also may be the case that the volcano is supposed to actually be erupting in the picture; at least, that is what one team of scholars has suggested.

I should mention that there is an additional scene in which large winged birds that look like vultures seem to be attacking a human figure who's lying prone. This has led some scholars to hypothesize that dead bodies may have occasionally been left out in the open rather deliberately so that the flesh would be consumed by carnivores before the skeletal remains were buried.

In fact, Mellaart, and now his successor at the site, Ian Hodder of Stanford University, found a number of burials underneath the floor of the houses, just like Kathleen Kenyon found at Jericho. It's difficult to tell whether they were defleshed before burial here though the articulated skeletons in at least some of the burials indicate that those were still fully intact when placed in the grave.

Hodder brought all sorts of new ideas with him when he began the renewed excavations at the site in 1993, including basic ones like putting a huge roof over the excavation area, to protect what they were finding rather than leaving everything exposed to the elements like Mellaart had done. He also implemented new approaches to raising funds for the excavations, including affiliation with a large local bank, much like the naming of a football or baseball stadium in the United States. He also got support from major sponsors like IBM, Pepsi, British Airways, and Shell, which is virtually unheard of at other sites—though I must say that it isn't a bad idea at all. He was also involved in the staging of a fashion show in Istanbul in 1997 and again at the 2010 World Expo in Shanghai, which involved building a large replica of Çatalhöyük so that models could emerge from it before proceeding to strut along a catwalk in their Neolithic-inspired outfits.

Hodder had previously been known more for his theoretical proposals regarding archaeology. Before coming to Stanford, he had been a professor at Cambridge University in England. There, he had initiated what we call post-processual archaeology, which I'll take just a minute to explain here.

It used to be that archaeologists only studied monuments, lists of kings, types of pottery, and things like that, mostly just using what we call thick description to talk about them—that is, simply describing them, as one would describe a painting hanging in an art gallery or a statue in a museum. However, starting in the 1960s, an American archaeologist named Lewis Binford developed what's called processual archaeology frequently referred to just as new archaeology. He wanted to make archaeology into more of a science—more anthropological, as it were. In this, he was continuing the trend started by other American archaeologists in the late 1950s. They became famous for saying, "Archaeology is anthropology or it is nothing."

Binford wanted archaeology to try to explain things, not just to describe them. So, rather than just enumerating what and who, he also wanted archaeologists to describe how and why. He wanted archaeologists to come up with universal laws or generalizations to explain things like Einstein had done for physics. He also wanted them to use scientific processes and be absolutely neutral and objective in their discussions. This was quite different from what previous archaeologists had been doing.

Binford was extremely influential, especially in the 1960s and 1970s, and he and his students spread the message far and wide. It was mostly Americans who took to it, however. The Europeans were not quite as enthralled by it, and by the 1980s, a movement began in reaction to it.

This is what is known as post-processual archaeology, or post-processualism. Among the leaders was, and still is, Ian Hodder. Hodder and others rejected, at least to some extent, Binford's reliance on science. They said that he had essentially dehumanized archaeology and that you couldn't understand the past unless you tried to understand the people and their possible motivations, including the fact that there are multiple voices from the past, including women and minorities in addition to famous dead men like Alexander the Great and Julius Caesar. Hodder is well known for having stated, basically as a reply to Binford, something like "Archaeology is archaeology and archaeology is history—but archaeology is not anthropology." Ironically, Hodder is now in the Anthropology department at Stanford.

Anyway, the post-processualists rejected much of Binford's teachings. They said that there simply aren't any universal laws governing human behavior and that it was ridiculous to try and search for them. They also argued that there shouldn't be as much use of explicit scientific methods because archaeology is not a hard science as my chemistry and physics buddies at GW remind me *ad nauseum* whenever we go to lunch. Hodder and his followers said that trying to pretend to be objective and neutral in our discussions and interpretations was, basically, absurd. Post-processualism is still very much around today but has led to some problems, including being a little too open to amateurs since it holds that everything is relative and open to interpretation, even potentially by non-experts.

In fact, this has led to some interesting things at Çatalhöyük itself, where New Age and Mother Goddess devotees visit the site, not only because of Hodder's perceived openness to their alternative hypotheses but also because of some of the figurines that have been found here.

In addition to some fairly typical figures of animals, probably of sheep, goats, and cattle, which could be just children's toys or could be objects of worship—it's impossible to tell—there are also figurines of women. The women are usually seated and have rather voluptuous proportions. They fit into a category of female figurines that are really only found in this particular time period but are found all across Europe, as far south as Turkey, including here at Çatalhöyük. Marija Gimbutas, who was a professor at UCLA, saw these as Mother Goddess figurines, meant to symbolize fertility, motherhood, and so on.

However, it is not actually clear what these figurines represent at all. While in all likelihood, some do represent some aspect of fertility or motherhood, it's not clear whether it is the goddess who is being depicted and for what reason. Would the owner of the figurine have been a woman who wanted to get pregnant or one who was giving thanks for having been pregnant? Or was it none of the above? Some of the figurines show the woman seated on what looks very much like a throne, including one where she appears to have an animal skin tied around her shoulders. To me, this indicates that it might be a depiction of a queen or a priestess, rather than the goddess herself. Gimbutas's theories are by no means universally accepted, but Çatalhöyük is nevertheless on the itinerary of many Mother Goddess tours.

In any event, I think we can all agree that the Neolithic is an extremely interesting period, even if one judges it just on the basis of the three sites that we've talked about in this lecture. It was clearly an amazing time of transformation, but it's also clear that we're still in the process of learning about it. The finds made at Göbekli Tepe from the mid-1990s until today, as well as those being made at Çatalhöyük during the same period, and those at Jericho in the late 1990s, indicate that there is much more still to be found, and it will undoubtedly change our understanding of the Neolithic period.

Lecture

8   Pyramids, Mummies, and Hieroglyphics

Everyone seems to be fascinated by the ancient Egyptians and knows a little something about them, especially about pyramids, mummies, and hieroglyphics. Or do they? In fact, the amount of misinformation people seem to have about ancient Egypt is astounding. It's not true, for example, that the pyramids were built by the Israelites or, for that matter, by aliens. In this lecture, then, we'll look at three popular topics related to ancient Egypt—pyramids, mummies, and hieroglyphics—to help us sift through the often-dubious claims made about them.

Geography of Egypt

- Egypt is split into two parts: The Nile and the area immediately on either side of it is one part, and the desert is the other. The Egyptians referred to these two parts as the Red Land for the desert and the Black Land for the land on either side of the Nile, so-called because of the life-giving silt that was deposited during the annual flooding of the river.

- Egypt is also split another way, with Lower Egypt in the north and Upper Egypt in the south. This division results from the fact that the Nile flows from south to north, rather than from north to south. It eventually empties into the Mediterranean Sea via the delta region, where the once-large river splits into many smaller tributaries.

- Upper and Lower Egypt were first unified sometime around 3000 B.C. by a man known variously as Menes or Narmer. An artifact called the Narmer Palette may depict this unification. Found in 1897, the object looks somewhat like an artist's palette, but we don't know whether it was actually used for that purpose. It has long been suggested that the images on the palette are intended to show the unification of Upper and Lower Egypt under Narmer, although not all scholars agree with this interpretation.

The Decipherment of Hieroglyphics

- To understand the decipherment of hieroglyphics, we must go back to 1799, a year or so after Napoleon and his troops had invaded Egypt as part of the campaign to capture the Near East. The French troops were in the village of Rosetta, in the Delta region, when they discovered an inscription that turned out to date from 196 B.C. It had been written to honor the pharaoh Ptolemy V and was in three different scripts: Egyptian hieroglyphics at the top; demotic—essentially, Egyptian cursive or handwriting—in the middle; and Greek on the bottom.

- Using this trilingual inscription, a brilliant French scholar named Jean-François Champollion was able to crack the code of Egyptian hieroglyphics. He did so in part by identifying two royal names, Ptolemy and Cleopatra, in the Greek text. Using this as a basis, he looked for repetition in the Egyptian hieroglyphics and was eventually able to use this as the key to his decipherment.
    o With Champollion's work, it suddenly became clear that all the pretty pictures painted on tomb walls and inscribed elsewhere were, in fact, texts containing the biographies of nobles.

    o It also turned out that the signs could be read in various ways. For instance, a hieroglyph could be a word sign and stand for the item being pictured, such as a bird or a bull; it could stand for a single sound, such as the first letter of the word for that animal; it could be a syllabic sign representing a combination of consonants; or it could be used as a determinative to tell how the word next to it should be read.

- Although many of the inscriptions we have today have survived because they were carved into stone, the Egyptians frequently wrote on sheets of papyrus, using black and red ink created from carbon and other materials. One text often found written on papyrus, as well as on tomb walls, is the Book of the Dead, or the Book of Going Forth by Day. This manual held the answers to questions people would be asked before being allowed to enter the afterworld.

Mummification

- In Egypt, staying in the underworld entailed keeping the physical body intact, even long after a person had died. This requirement resulted in the development of mummification.

- The first step in mummification was to place the body into a type of desiccating salt called *natron* and leave it there for 70 days. The inner organs were removed by means of a slit cut up the side of the body and placed in canopic jars. Then, sweet-smelling herbs and spices would be stuffed into the body cavity, and the slit would be sewn up.

- The heart would be left in the body because the ancient Egyptians thought it was the center of intelligence and would be needed in the afterlife. The brain was not understood and was simply discarded.

Mastabas and Pyramids

- In addition to mummifying the body, ancient Egyptians also had to protect the mummy from the elements. That's why, before about 3000 B.C., we find *mastabas*, or low benches made out of mudbricks, placed above graves. Even if a sandstorm hit the cemetery and all the sand was swept away, the *mastaba* would remain in place and the mummy would not be exposed to the elements or scavengers. The idea of the *mastaba* may have been what led to the pyramids several centuries later.

- It seems to have been Djoser (or Zozer), a pharaoh who lived during the 3rd Dynasty (just after 2700 B.C.), who first asked Imhotep, his vizier, to create a majestic burial place. Thus, the Step Pyramid was constructed, the first pyramid ever built in Egypt.
    - If you look at the Step Pyramid, it appears that Imhotep simply placed about six *mastabas* one on top of the other, decreasing in size toward the top, so that he ended up with a pyramid built in stages or steps.

- It was just a short hop from that Step Pyramid to the huge, smooth-sided pyramids that we know from outside of Cairo today.

- How exactly the pyramids were built is still a matter of debate. The workers may have used blocks, tackles, and pulleys, or they might have pulled the blocks into place via earthen ramps that ran in a spiral around the pyramid.

- The pyramids were not built in isolation but were usually part of a much larger funerary complex that also contained ceremonial courts, religious shrines, and other buildings, all dedicated to keeping the king's memory alive. This is the case at Giza, outside of modern-day Cairo, where the three greatest Egyptian pyramids were built.
  - These three pyramids date to the 4th Dynasty, the so-called Pyramid Age, during the Old Kingdom. They were built one after other by a father-son-grandson combination named Khufu, Khafre, and Menkaure, or as the later Greeks called them, Cheops, Chephren, and Mycerinus.

  - The first one, built by Khufu, is the earliest and largest and is known today as the Great Pyramid. The second pyramid, built by Khafre, is the one to which the Sphinx probably belongs, because the Sphinx sits at what was originally the entrance to the funerary complex for Khafre. The third one is also the smallest, built by Menkaure.

- The Great Pyramid probably took 10 to 20 years to build, but it probably wasn't built by slaves, as most people think. In fact, Herodotus tells us that it took 100,000 people working in four shifts per year to build such a pyramid. The general thinking today is that the workforce probably consisted of peasants, farmers, and other members of the lower classes who worked for pay during the off season, after the harvest had been brought in.

- The number of stone blocks used in each pyramid was tremendous. For example, the Great Pyramid was originally probably about 480 feet tall and about 755 feet on each side. There are 2.3 million blocks in the Great Pyramid, some of them weighing several tons. Originally, the pyramid would have been finished off with an outer casing of white limestone, but those limestone blocks are long gone, with many of them reused in later buildings.

- Within the Great Pyramid is a series of passageways and chambers. These are still much debated, but it seems that the original entrance and passageway led down to a chamber where the king would have been buried underneath the ground. However, it is possible that this customary plan was changed, because another passageway leads upward, to what is called the Grand Gallery and the King's Chamber, in which a large granite sarcophagus is still in place.

- As mentioned, the Sphinx stands at the entrance to the second pyramid, the one built by Khafre. It dates to about 2550 B.C. It sits in one of the quarries from which the Egyptians got the blocks for the pyramids, but it was left because the core of the body was "rotten"; that is, the stone wasn't good enough to be used as building material. Thus, the core was shaped to look like a body, and blocks were added to form the paws, as well as the head and face.
    - In about 1400 B.C., the pharaoh Thutmose IV left an inscription claiming that, when he was still a young prince, he had fallen asleep in the shadow of the Sphinx, which was buried up to its neck in sand. In a dream, the Sphinx told Thutmose that if he removed the sand, the Sphinx would make him king of Egypt.

    - He excavated the sand away, fixed the blocks where they were crumbling, and when he eventually became king, left what is now known as the Sphinx Dream Stele between its paws, where modern Egyptologists found it.

Although Napoleon's troops used the Sphinx for target practice, it's not true that they shot off its nose; the nose may have been removed by a Muslim ruler in 1378 A.D. because the Egyptian peasants were treating the Sphinx as a pagan idol.

Suggested Reading

Bard, *An Introduction to the Archaeology of Ancient Egypt.*

Fagan, *The Rape of the Nile.*

Wilkinson, *The Rise and Fall of Ancient Egypt.*

Questions to Consider

1. Do you agree that building pyramids can be viewed as the equivalent of large-scale public works projects today in terms of pumping money back into the economy?

2. Why are we so fascinated today by the ancient Egyptians?

Lecture 8 Transcript
Pyramids, Mummies, and Hieroglyphics

Egyptology is one of the most discussed topics in archaeology, so we definitely have to talk about it in this course. Everyone seems to be fascinated by the ancient Egyptians, and they all think they know a little something about them, especially pyramids, and mummies, and hieroglyphics. But do they actually? The amount of misinformation about ancient Egypt that's floating around, especially on the Internet these days, is absolutely astounding.

Every year I and my colleagues have to correct misunderstandings. "No, the Israelites did not build the pyramids; the pyramids were already hundreds of years old before the Israelites ever got to Egypt"—every year we're barraged by questions after any one of the numerous television shows airs, that claims the pyramids were built by aliens or that the Sphinx is 10,000 years old, or some other nonsense dreamed up by amateur enthusiasts, if I can use that term.

So let's discuss those three highly popular topics—pyramids, mummies, and hieroglyphics—so that you will be in a better position to sift through the often-dubious claims that are made about them.

And let's begin by taking a quick look at a map of Egypt. You can see right away that its split into two parts: the Nile and the area immediately on either side of it is one part, and the desert is another part entirely. The Egyptians referred to these two parts as the Red Land and the Black Land—the Red Land is the desert, for obvious reasons, the Black Land is the land on either side of the Nile, and it's called that because of the life-giving silt that is deposited during the annual flood, and that was caused by rain and snow far to the south.

But Egypt is also split another way, with Lower Egypt in the north and Upper Egypt in the south. This is because the Nile River flows from south to north, rather than from north to south. It eventually empties out into the

Mediterranean Sea via the Delta region, where the once-big river splits into many smaller tributaries.

Upper and Lower Egypt, were first unified sometime about 3000 B.C., by a man known variously as Menes or Narmer. It has been suggested that these names belong to the same guy, with one name being his real name and the other being his throne name—just like the Pope takes a new name when he becomes Pope—but it's also conceivable that it took more than one person to unify Egypt or that it happened more than once in those early days.

We do have one artifact from Egypt that may depict the unification. Found in 1897, it's known as the Narmer Palette—first because Narmer's name is written on both sides of the object, and second because it does look a bit like an artist's palette. Whether it was actually used as a palette or not, what's important for us are the depictions upon it, because it's long been suggested that these are intended to show the unification of Upper and Lower Egypt under Narmer, but not all scholars agree with this interpretation.

Now, Narmer's Palette was found fairly early in the history of Egyptology. But in order to see the actual origins of Egyptology, we have to go even further back and take a look at some of the first archaeologists who worked in Egypt. Actually, the first ones often weren't really Egyptologists or, at least, didn't originally intend to be.

Take Belzoni for example—Giovanni Battista Belzoni, who was born in 1778. He was a strong man in a circus, he was 6 feet 6 inches tall and able to lift 12 men at a time, but he could also be considered an engineer of sorts. He first went over to Egypt in 1815 to show the Ottoman ruler a new plan for drawing water out of the Nile, but he ended up becoming one of the first Egyptologists. Now, I use that term loosely, though, because Belzoni is remembered more for tomb robbing and collecting mummies than he is for any actual science or archaeology.

Karl Lepsius and Auguste Mariette, on the other hand, can rightly be considered giants in Egyptology, even if they weren't physically as large as Belzoni. Lepsius was a Prussian Egyptologist, who led an expedition to Egypt in 1842. Their mission was to record as many monuments as they could, which they did astonishingly well. The resulting 12 huge volumes of drawings and illustrations were published over a 10-year period from 1849 to 1859, it was called *Monuments of Egypt and Ethiopia*. Now, the volumes of written material that went with them took another 40 years or more to be published and didn't see the light of day until more than a decade after Lepsius himself had died. Now, taken as a whole, the volumes of texts and plates are considered by many to be the foundations of modern Egyptology.

Auguste Mariette, who was born in France in 1821, started digging in Egypt in about 1850. Eight years later, he was appointed the first Director of Antiquities in Egypt. Among other things, he built the first national museum, and the collection still forms the basis of the Egyptian Museum in Cairo today.

Lepsius and Mariette were able to establish their careers in part because of an event that had taken place by 1823 when they were both still just children. This is one of the most famous events in Egyptology—it's the decipherment of Egyptian hieroglyphics.

In order to understand how this took place, we must first go back to 1799 that's a year or so after Napoleon and his troops had invaded Egypt. The French troops were in the village of Rosetta, in the Delta region, they were rebuilding a fort, digging foxholes, things like that—the story actually differs. But in the process, they found an inscription that turned out to date from 196 B.C. It had been written to honor Ptolemy V—an Egyptian pharaoh who otherwise is not all that memorable. But it's extremely important because the text of the inscription is written in three different scripts. At the top, the text is written in Egyptian hieroglyphics. In the middle, the same text is written again, but, this time, called demotic—essentially Egyptian cursive or handwriting. And, the bottom third of the stone has the inscription written once again, but this time in Greek.

Using this tri-lingual inscription, a brilliant French scholar named Jean-François Champollion was able to crack the code of Egyptian hieroglyphics. He did it in part by reading the Greek version, which wasn't a problem, and realizing that two royal names appeared again and again: Ptolemy and Cleopatra. Using this as a basis, he looked for repetition in the

Egyptian hieroglyphics and was eventually able to use this as the key to his decipherment. Now, Champollion wasn't the only scholar working on this; a British linguist named Thomas Young very nearly beat him to the translation. But, it's Champollion who gets the credit for doing so, in 1823, that was just 24 years after the inscription had been found.

It suddenly became clear that all of the pretty pictures that were painted on the walls of the tombs of nobles and inscribed elsewhere were, in fact, long inscriptions containing their biographies, lifetime achievements and so on. One set of hieroglyphs that appeared frequently in these contexts is now known to be the symbols for eternity, which of course makes sense in a tomb setting.

It also turned out that the hieroglyphics could be read in various directions—you just have to see which way the figures are facing and then be consistent in your reading—the figures always face towards the beginning of the line. The signs could also be read in various ways. For instance, a hieroglyph could be a word-sign and stand for the item being pictured, like a bird or a bull or whatever, or it could stand for a single sound, like of the first letter of the word for that animal, or it could be a syllabic sign representing a combination of consonants, or it could be used as a determinative to tell you how to read the word next to it. Now, it's no wonder that not many people knew how to read and write in ancient Egypt—probably only about one percent of the population. Scribes had a respected position at the royal court, and it's quite possible that even the king and the queen didn't know how to read or write.

While many of the inscriptions that we have today have survived because they're carved into stone, the Egyptians frequently wrote on sheets of papyrus, which was their version of paper. They used ink created from carbon and other materials. The ink could be black, or it could be red, often with both colors used in the same manuscript. In those cases, the word written in red might be the first word of the new sentence, so you knew where one sentence ended, and another one began because there's no punctuation as we know it. Red ink could also mark the beginning of a spell, or even just a title or a heading, depending upon the context and the need.

One thing that we frequently find written on papyrus, but also on the walls of tombs of wealthy people, is the Book of the Dead. This is also known as the Book of Going Forth by Day, and it's essentially a manual to help you get into the afterlife right after you had died, because it contains the answers to the questions that you would be asked before you're allowed to enter the afterworld—it is, essentially, a cheat sheet. This went hand in hand with the weighing of the heart ceremony, during which your heart is placed on one scale, and a feather is placed on the other scale, to see if you had lived a good and just life. If they weighed the same, you passed. If they didn't, you didn't.

Now, once you were in the afterworld, you probably wanted to stay there, but this entailed keeping your physical body intact, even long after you had died. So, two things developed. One was the process of mummification. The other was the creation of mastabas, or benches, that were made out of mud brick, they were used to protect the burial place. Many scholars suspect that these were the distant ancestors, or the predecessors, of the pyramids. So, let's look at the two processes one at a time.

First, mummification. Now, how many of you know how to mummify a body? How many of you have had kids that have tried to mummify something? And I'm not kidding; this is a frequent school project, usually done in elementary school, it often involving chickens, rather than your family pet, which is fortunate unless, of course, your family pet happens to be a chicken.

Now, we actually know quite a bit about mummification, in part because we have a rather detailed description from the Greek historian Herodotus, he traveled to Egypt during the 5th century B.C. and learned about the process.

Now, I'm not actually sure that I'd recommend trying this at home, but basically, what you need to do is to put the body into a type of desiccating salt called natron and then you leave it there for 70 days. The natron basically wicks the moisture out of the body and helps to mummify it. But you also need to remove a number of the inner organs. That means you'll have to make a slit up the side of the body and then reach in to remove the stomach, and the upper intestines, the lower intestines, the lungs, and the liver. These are all placed in what we call canopic jars. That's the modern name for them because they were first identified by early Egyptologists, who thought they were associated with the Greek myth of Canopus, a Mycenaean warrior who was bitten by a snake and died while visiting Egypt.

Canopic jars were essential equipment for the tomb. Each set could be different, but during the New Kingdom, the lids of the jars depicted the four sons of Horus, who guarded the organs. The stomach and the upper intestines would go into one jar that had a jackal head for a lid. The lower intestines were placed in one that had a falcon head for a lid. The lungs would go into a baboon-headed jar, and the liver would go into a jar that had a lid shaped like a human head. Then, sweet smelling herbs and spices would be stuffed into the body cavity where the organs had been, and the slit in the side of the body would be sewn up again.

However, the heart would be left in place within the body, because the ancient Egyptians thought that the heart was the center of intelligence and would be needed in the afterlife. The brain, on the other hand, was not understood and was simply discarded. But, there were two ways to get the brain out. Now, are any of you about to eat? If so, you might want to pause this temporarily, and come back after your meal—you'll see why in just a moment.

OK, so one way to remove the brain is simply to take a long piece of wire, with the end bent into a hook shape. This was shoved up the dead person's nose until the bent end was up in the brain cavity, and then it was quickly pulled out, bringing the brain with it. Now, if not all the brain came out the first time, you repeated the process until you had gotten all of the brain out. The other way: The other way to do it was to tilt the person's head back and put drops into their nose like nose drops. The drops, though, were the equivalent of something like hydrochloric acid, so when the drops ran up into the brain cavity, they would melt the brain. When the head was tilted back down again, the gray gooey mess would simply run out the person's nose, and voila. The brain cavity was now empty, but you had a disgusting mess on your hands.

Now, the precise method that the Egyptians used is still debated, even in scientific articles, but in 2012, an object identified as a brain-removal tool was found in the skull of a 2,500-year-old mummy. It was probably used for both liquefying and removing the brain, or so researchers think.

Now the embalming: The embalming was done out of sight of the family members, and that was probably a good idea because accidents sometimes did happen. One story involves a woman whose cheeks had sunken because of the embalming process. She was a priestess from the 21st Dynasty, so she lived and died sometime in the 10th century B.C., or about 3,000 years ago. Now, the embalmers had stuffed her cheeks with cotton pads, perhaps in an effort to make her appear more lifelike, which seems to have been the custom at the time. However, they put in too much and at some point both of her cheeks simply ripped off. Of course, once again, she didn't get to stay in the afterlife because her body had not remained intact, but nobody knew that because they sewed everything back on and nobody found it out until the mummy was unwrapped thousands of years later.

So, mummifying the body was one thing that the ancient Egyptians did, but they also had to protect the mummy from the elements. That's why, before about 3000 B.C., we find mastabas or low benches made out of mud bricks, placed above the grave into which the mummy was placed. That way, even if a sandstorm hit the cemetery and all of the sand was swept away, the mastaba would remain in the place, and the mummy wouldn't be exposed to the elements, or to the pecking beak of a bird or the jaws of a hyena or some other such scavenger.

And this may have been what eventually led to the pyramids, several centuries later. Now, we're not certain, of course, exactly what triggered the idea of building the first pyramids, but it had nothing to do with ancient aliens. There were a number of early attempts to build pyramids before the successful measurements were identified, so we have things like the Bent Pyramid, in which we can see some of the early experiments and the failures.

But, it seems to have been Djoser (or Zozer), a pharaoh who lived during the 3rd Dynasty, in the years just after 2700 B.C., who was first responsible for asking Imhotep, his vizier, to create something a bit more majestic as his burial place. And so, the Step Pyramid was constructed, which we identify as the first pyramid ever to really be built in Egypt. By the way, Imhotep seems to have also been Djoser's personal physician as well as his architect, and he's later hailed as the Father of Egyptian medicine, and he's then eventually deified into a god of healing and, even later was linked to the Greek god Asclepius.

Now, if you look at the Step Pyramid, it appears that Imhotep simply took about six mastabas and put them one on top of another, decreasing in size as you get to the top, so he ended up with a pyramid built in stages or steps. It's just a short hop from that Step Pyramid to the huge smooth-sided pyramids that we know from outside of Cairo today because all you really had to do was to fill in the missing parts and smooth out the sides.

Of course, there's a lot more to it than that, and it's still very much a matter of debate as to how exactly the pharaohs built the pyramids. I personally favor the idea of blocks and tackles and pulleys, just like you would hoist up heavy stones today, but I also like the idea of pulling the blocks up into place via earthen ramps that ran in a spiral around the pyramid. If that method was used, probably the last thing that you would do after putting the final blocks into place at the top would be to dismantle the earthen ramps that would have been surrounding your pyramid at that point.

But there's all sorts of other theories out there, and in fact, a student once told me of another professor who told his class with a straight face that the blocks were maneuvered into place using telepathy. I never did find out who it was, and so to this day, I don't know whether he seriously believed that or if he was just trying to see which of the students were really listening instead of sleeping in class.

The other thing to keep in mind, though, is that such big pyramids were not built in isolation; they were normally part of a much larger funerary complex, which also contained things like ceremonial courts, religious shrines, and other buildings, all dedicated to keeping the king's memory alive. So, we do have a funerary complex for Djoser, of which the Step Pyramid is just one part. We have the same thing at Giza, outside of modern-day Cairo, where the three greatest Egyptian pyramids were built.

These three pyramids date to the 4th Dynasty, the so-called Pyramid Age during the Old Kingdom Period. They were built one after another, by a father-son-grandson combination called Khufu, Khafre, and Menkaure, or—as the later Greeks called them—Cheops, Chephren, and Mycerinus. The first one, built by Khufu—or Cheops—is the earliest and largest, so today it's known as the Great Pyramid.

The second pyramid, the one built by Khafre—or Chephren—is the one to which the Sphinx probably belongs because the Sphinx sits at what was originally the entrance to the funerary complex for Khafre.

The third one is also the smallest, built by Menkaure—or Mycerinus. Going inside this pyramid was probably the most claustrophobic experience of my life. My shoulders brushed the sides of the corridor on both sides, and I had to bend my head to walk without hitting the roof of the passageway. I've actually heard rumors of people getting stuck in there and that one time the entire Nebraska football team had to be extracted one player at a time—I think that was just a joke going around at one of the Egyptology conferences.

The Great Pyramid is the one that everybody talks about. It probably took 10–20 years to build, but it probably also wasn't built by slaves, as most people think. In fact, Herodotus tells us that it took a 100,000 people working in four shifts per year to build such a pyramid. But it's not clear whether Herodotus meant that there were 25,000 people at a time, for a total of 100,000 people, or if there were 100,000 people at a time, for a total of 400,000. Either way, that's a lot of people.

Now, there's no way that there were that many slaves working on such a long project. The general thinking today is that the workforce probably consisted of peasants, farmers, and other members of the lower classes who were working for pay during the offseason after the harvest had been brought in. If that's the case, then these pyramids were essentially great public works projects, like FDR did in the United States during the 1930s, because building them would have pumped an incredible amount of money back into the economy.

Now, it's clear that a huge workforce was needed, though, because the number of stone blocks used in each pyramid was tremendous. For example, the Great Pyramid was originally probably about 480 feet tall and about 755 feet on each side. I often ask people to guess how many blocks that it took to build the Great Pyramid. So, what do you think? Think there was 10,000 blocks in the pyramid? 50,000? 100,000? Actually, there are 2.3 million blocks in the Great Pyramid, some of them weighing several tons. The whole pyramid is estimated to weigh almost 6 million tons. Now, originally it would have been finished off with an outer casing of white limestone, but those limestone blocks are now long gone, many of them have been reused in later buildings both in Cairo itself and in the villages surrounding the pyramids.

Within the Great Pyramid are a series of passageways and chambers. These are still much debated, but it seems that the original entrance and passageway led down to a chamber where the king would have been buried underneath the ground level, as per usual. However, it's possible the plan was changed, because there's another passageway that leads upwards, to what's called the Grand Gallery and then to the King's Chamber, and in there a large granite sarcophagus is still in place.

There's also two narrow shafts leading up from the King's Chamber to either side of the pyramid. These used to be, and sometimes still are, referred to as air shafts, though now some attribute a more realistic, or ritualistic purpose to them. They've been put to good use, though, in recent years because when it was noticed that the crush of tourists inside the pyramid was creating problems, air conditioners or extractor fans were placed in the shafts, to pull the moist air out and pull in the dry desert air. So, if you're in the Great Pyramid, and you think that you hear air conditioners, you're not hearing things, they really are air conditioners.

As for the Sphinx, well, as I said, it stands at the entrance to the second pyramid complex, the one built by Khafre, and Egyptologists have noticed the resemblance of its face to statues of Khafre. It's not 10,000 years old, rather dates to about 2550 B.C. It sits in one of the quarries from which the Egyptians got the blocks for the pyramids, but it was left because the core of the body was rotten—that is, it's stone that wasn't good enough to be used as building material. So, the core was shaped to look like a body, and then blocks were added to form the paws as well as the head and the face.

Now, the Sphinx had already been excavated once in antiquity, because the Pharaoh Thutmose IV left an inscription that says that when he was a young prince, he had fallen asleep in the shadow of the Sphinx, which was buried up to its neck in sand at the time. This would have been about 1400 B.C. In a dream, the Sphinx told him that if he removed the sand, the Sphinx would make him king over Egypt. So, he excavated the sand away, fixed the blocks where they were crumbling, and, when he eventually became king, he left what is now known as the Sphinx Dream Stele between its paws, where modern Egyptologists then found it.

And, to end this lecture now, with a bit of trivia, let me put to rest the legend that the nose of the Sphinx is gone because Napoleon's troops shot it off in 1798 or 1799 because that's simply not true. Now, his troops did use the Sphinx for target practice, but the nose was already long gone by that point. According to an Arab historian, who was writing in the 15th century, a Sufi Muslim ruler hacked off the nose back in 1378 because the Egyptian peasants were making offerings to the Sphinx and treating it as a pagan idol.

Well, I hope this excursion into the world of ancient Egypt has shed some light on the remarkable achievements of this great civilization. And especially when it comes to pyramids, mummies, and hieroglyphics, I hope that you are feeling better situated now to judge some of the claims that are made about them, whether online, on TV, or by well-meaning neighbors.

Lecture 9

King Tut's Tomb

On November 26, 1922, Howard Carter peered into the tomb of King Tutankhamen for the very first time. In fact, it was the first time that anyone had looked into the tomb in more than 3,000 years. Everywhere in the room, there was the glint of gold. Carter and his benefactor, Lord Carnarvon, had finally found the tomb for which they had been searching, right underneath where they had been pitching their tents for the past five or six years. In this lecture, we'll discuss their amazing discovery in the Valley of the Kings.

The Search for Tut's Tomb
- The story of the discovery of King Tut's tomb opens in about 1907. Howard Carter was already a well-known Egyptologist at the time, but he was out of a job when Lord Carnarvon first approached him. Carnarvon had been ordered by his doctor to spend his winters in Egypt rather than England and sought out Carter to do some digging during his time there.

- Carter and Carnarvon spent about 10 years digging in various locations in Egypt. Then, in 1917, they settled on the idea of looking in the Valley of the Kings for the missing tomb of King Tut. Tut had come to the throne of Egypt in about 1330 B.C., when he was only about eight years old. Ten years later, he died unexpectedly and was buried in the Valley of the Kings, but his tomb had never been located.

- It was in this valley, located across the river from the modern town of Luxor, that most of the New Kingdom pharaohs of Egypt were buried.
  - Much earlier, during the Old Kingdom period in the 3rd millennium B.C., Egyptian kings had begun the practice of constructing pyramids for their tombs. Pyramid building continued into the early 2nd millennium B.C., but pyramids were easy targets for tomb robbers.

- By the New Kingdom period, beginning with the 18th Dynasty in about 1500 B.C., pharaohs were buried in tombs dug into the hillsides in the Valley of the Kings. Most of those tombs were also found and robbed in antiquity, but a few had eluded discovery, including King Tut's tomb.

- Carter and Carnarvon spent five years searching the valley for Tut's tomb but with no real luck. Eventually Carnarvon began to run out of money, interest, or both and informed Carter that they would have to stop. Carter asked for one more season of funding, realizing that there was only one place remaining in the Valley of the Kings where they had not yet looked: their campsite. Carter ordered his men to begin digging there, and within just a few days, they found the first steps leading down to Tut's tomb.

Inside the Tomb
- Carter followed the steps to the tomb entrance and saw the seals stamped into the clay by the necropolis guards near the top of the door. He immediately stopped digging and summoned Carnarvon, who was in England at the time. Carter promised that he would wait to open the tomb until Carnarvon arrived. In the meantime, Carter also alerted the world media. But what Carter failed to mention to anyone was the fact that he could see that the tomb had been broken into in antiquity. For all he knew, it might be empty.

- When Carnarvon arrived in Egypt two weeks later, Carter and the workmen began excavating where they had left off. When they cleared the rest of the entrance, they realized that they had found Tut's tomb; seals with his cartouche could be plainly seen on the door below the seals of the necropolis guards that Carter had seen previously.

- When Carter and Carnarvon opened the first door to the tomb on November 23, all they could see was a rubble-filled passageway. It took three days to clear the corridor; they finally reached the door to the first room, now known as the antechamber, on November 26.

A cartouche is an oval that contains hieroglyphics representing a monarch's name.

According to Carter, when Carnarvon asked him if he could see anything inside, he replied, "Yes, wonderful things."

- The first room held at least one disassembled chariot; along with several beds, some with sides in the shapes of animals; chairs; stools; boxes; and other items. An annex behind this first room contained even more grave goods, as did another small room off the burial chamber, usually called the Treasury. It included a statue of the jackal-headed god Anubis and four canopic jars that should have held King Tut's internal organs.

- Finds in the Treasury included a statue of the Tut harpoon fishing, made of ebony overlaid with gold; a vessel of alabaster or calcite that may have served as a lamp; inlaid pieces of furniture; jewelry; and an unguent jar in the shape of a lion that probably held some sort of perfumed oil.

The Burial Chamber

- There were so many artifacts stuffed into the tomb that it took Carter almost three full months to catalogue enough of the grave goods in the other rooms and remove them so that he could enter the burial chamber. That didn't happen until February 1923. And it was not until almost a year after that, in January 1924, that he was able to reach the sarcophagus of the king.

- The burial chamber contained four shrines, one within the other, surrounding the sarcophagus. The first two outer coffins were of wood, with gold leaf on them, but the third coffin was of solid gold, weighing nearly 250 pounds. It reportedly took eight men to carry it out of the tomb! Of course, the gold mask covering Tut's actual mummy, which is probably the best-known piece from the tomb, was also of solid gold, inlaid with lapis lazuli and blue glass.
    - The three coffins and the gold mask do not all look the same; in fact, it seems that at least one of the coffins was originally made for another recipient, quite possibly Queen Hatshepsut, rather than Tut.

    - This may also have been the case for a number of other artifacts found in the tomb that bear traces of other royal names. It may be that Tut's sudden death resulted in some haste in gathering the grave goods.

The King Himself

- It was not an easy task for Carter to get King Tut out of his coffin because a thick layer of bitumen (tar) had been poured over the mummy's legs, below where the gold mask ended. Carter used a crowbar to no avail, though he may have broken a few of Tut's bones in the process of trying. He even lit a fire underneath the coffin in an effort to melt the tar.
    - In the end, Carter was able to remove the mummy from the coffin and extract it from the gold mask. An X-ray taken sometime soon afterward shows the bones of a young man, confirming that Tut was probably between 18 and 22 when he died. A bone sliver within the brain casing was thought for a

long while to have been the cause of Tut's death, but now that is more usually thought to have been a byproduct of Carter's efforts to get Tut out of the coffin.

  o The broken bones, however, are more debated. Carter may have caused some of them, but a CT scan done in 2005 indicated that Tut may have suffered a compound fracture of one of his leg bones, perhaps leading to an infection and death. After the study appeared, many believed that he had perhaps fallen from his chariot and broken his leg. Such a scenario would put to rest speculation that he was murdered.

- Also in 2005, three teams of forensic anthropologists were given the task of trying to re-create what Tut might have looked like before he died. Another set of about 2,000 CT scans done in 2014 resulted in a "virtual autopsy" that concluded that Tut had buck teeth, a club foot, and various genetic disorders and had perhaps suffered or died from malaria.

- DNA testing on Tut's mummy has also shed light on the question of his parentage, strongly indicating that Akhenaten was the father of the boy king. However, the debate continues about his mother, who may have either been Akhenaten's sister or his more famous wife, Nefertiti.

King Tut and Akhenaten
- A number of other mysteries still surround King Tut and his tomb. Principal among these is the question of the tremendous number of grave goods that were buried with him in the various chambers of the tomb.

- Both Egyptologists and members of the public have wondered at this display of extravagant wealth. If all this was buried with a young man who ruled for only 10 years, what must have been in the tomb of such a ruler as Ramses II, who was pharaoh for decades?

- Some scholars, however, believe that Tut's tomb might have been the exception rather than the rule. Although he ruled for only 10 years, he is the pharaoh who undid all the reforms of his father, Akhenaten, who is perhaps better known as the heretic pharaoh.

- Akhenaten had outlawed the worship of Egypt's numerous gods and goddesses, with the exception of the god Aten, represented by the disk of the sun. The temples of all those deities were ordered closed, and their treasuries were confiscated by Akhenaten.

- It is sometimes suggested that Akhenaten was, in this way, responsible for the invention of monotheism. However, this was not monotheism as we understand it because the ordinary Egyptian was not allowed to worship Aten directly. Instead, he or she had to worship Akhenaten, who then prayed to Aten on behalf of all

One reason that King Tut's tomb was full of such rich grave goods may be the times in which he lived; when he came to the throne in about 1330 B.C., Egypt was at the height of its power and wealth.

others. Thus, for the ordinary Egyptian, there were effectively two gods: Akhenaten and Aten.

- It also seems likely that Akhenaten's decree was not motivated by religion but, instead, was a calculated political move that ensured the pharaoh more power, control, and wealth.
  - Some of the priests, especially those of the god Amun, had been getting more powerful and richer. In outlawing the gods and goddesses, closing the temples, and confiscating the treasuries, all while making himself the main spokesman to and from Aten, Akhenaten flipped the tables.

  - He increased his wealth and his political and religious control even as he decreased the power and wealth of his competitors. He was already the head of the army and the head of the government; now, he was the head of the religion, as well.

- King Tut undid all of Akhenaten's religious reforms, allowed the worship of all the traditional gods and goddesses to resume, and restored the priests to power. With his early death, the newly restored priests may have filled his tomb with grave goods as thanks for what he had done for them while he was alive.

Suggested Reading

Hawass, *Tutankhamun and the Golden Age of the Pharaohs*.

Reeves, *The Complete Tutankhamun*.

Reeves and Wilkinson, *The Complete Valley of the Kings*.

Questions to Consider

1. How and why do you think Tut died at such a young age?

2. Is there anything left to find in the Valley of the Kings now?

Lecture 9 Transcript: King Tut's Tomb

On November 26th, 1922, Howard Carter peered into the tomb of King Tut for the very first time. In fact, it was the first time that anyone had looked into the tomb in more than 3,000 years. He squinted, trying to see through the small opening that they had made, without burning off his eyebrows from the candle that he was holding. He found himself looking into a room crammed from floor to ceiling with all kinds of objects, including items of gold; everywhere there was the glint of gold. The Earl of Carnarvon, who had underwritten the cost of the dig but who was much shorter than Carter, tugged on Carter's coat and then jumped up and down with impatience. "What do you see?" he demanded. "What do you see?" Carter answered, "I see wonderful things."

At least, that's the official story that is usually told. There are different accounts as to what Carter may or may not have actually said at that precise moment, but the important fact is this: They had finally found the tomb they'd been searching for. And they had found it right underneath where they'd been pitching their tents for the past five or six years. The tomb hadn't been found before because it had been buried under a layer of rock chips when Ramses VI's tomb was constructed nearby during the 20th Dynasty.

So, on that day in late November 1922, it was Howard Carter, the Egyptologist, and his benefactor George Herbert, the 5th Earl of Carnarvon better known as simply Lord Carnarvon, who first opened the tomb of the boy king Tutankhamen. They were in the Valley of the Kings in Egypt, across the river from modern-day Luxor. They weren't alone, though; there were dozens of members of the world media in attendance and the opening of the tomb was front-page news around the globe.

Excavation of the nearly unlooted tomb took fully 10 years while a fascinated world watched. The tomb goods that were removed and recorded are now on display in the museum in Cairo; some of them are occasionally sent around the world on tour, where crowds of thousands see them in city after city. In fact, I still distinctly remember playing hooky from high school in 1978, with my parents' express permission because we went to see the original King Tut exhibit when it came to the Los Angeles County Museum of Art.

More recently, I've also seen the newer show when it was in Chicago and Philadelphia in 2006 and 2007 and then again a show in New York City in 2010, mostly because I was asked by GW, my university, to lead alumni groups through it. I always agree, because I never turn down an opportunity to see these amazing items. And, of course, I always go to see the objects on display in the Cairo Museum whenever I'm there, which isn't nearly often enough.

I've also visited the actual tomb in the Valley of the Kings. My first time was on a long weekend visit back in 1985. I was digging at a site way up north in the Nile Delta. My primary memories are of being hot, thirsty, and a little surprised at how small the tomb was.

Today, so many tourists visit that a new replica of the tomb has been created right next to the real one; and the real one will be closed off because of the unintentional damage being caused by the hordes of admirers.

The death of Lord Carnarvon soon after the opening of the tomb also led to the idea of the mummy's curse that's so beloved by Hollywood. An enterprising journalist had created the story of an inscription carved above the entrance to the tomb, which threatened death to anyone who entered. In fact, there wasn't any such inscription, but when Carnarvon died—of blood poisoning caused when he accidentally cut open a mosquito bite while shaving—the story seemed to be confirmed. And so after that, whenever anyone associated with the tomb and its opening died, it was reported in the media. Even the death of their pets was reported. But Carter himself lived on until 1939, so if there was a curse, it had difficulty finding him for quite a while.

But, let's backtrack for a moment and start at the beginning of the story, which opens in about 1907. Carter was already a well-known Egyptologist at the time but was out of a job when Carnarvon first approached him, because of a fight with a French tourist sometime earlier. Carnarvon had been ordered by his doctor to spend his winters in Egypt rather than in England. He had punctured his lung in an automobile accident when he had rolled his car going around a curve at the unheard of speed of 20 miles an hour.

By the way, Carnarvon's ancestral home in England was at Highclere Castle. Highclere is still owned by the Carnarvon family. It used to be primarily known for its collection of Egyptian antiquities that Lord Carnarvon had acquired, but today it is perhaps more famous as the setting for the TV series "Downton Abbey."

To while away the time in Egypt, Carnarvon hired Carter. This wasn't unusual; other wealthy Americans and British nobles hired their own pet egyptologists as well. The two of them, Carter and Carnarvon, spent about 10 years digging in various locations in Egypt. Then, in 1917, they settled upon the idea of looking in the Valley of the Kings for the missing tomb of King Tut. Tut had come to the throne of Egypt in about 1330 B.C. when he was only eight years old or so. Ten years later, he died unexpectedly and was buried in the Valley of the Kings, but his tomb had never been located.

It was in this valley, located across the river from the modern town of Luxor, that most of the New Kingdom pharaohs of Egypt were buried. Much earlier, during the Old Kingdom period in the 3rd millennium B.C., Egyptian kings had begun the practice of constructing pyramids in which they were buried. Pyramid building continued into the early second millennium B.C., though not on as grand a scale. But it was too easy for tomb robbers to locate and ransack the burials of the kings who were in the pyramids.

So, by the New Kingdom Period, beginning about 1500 B.C., the pharaohs were buried in tombs that were dug into the hillsides in the Valley of the Kings. Most of those tombs were found and robbed in antiquity anyway, but a few had eluded discovery, and King Tut's tomb was one of those.

Carter and Carnarvon spent five years searching the Valley for Tut's tomb, but with no real luck. It was dry, hot, dusty, and fairly thankless work though every so often their team found something of enough interest to keep them going for a while longer, like a small pit dug into the rock that contained a few items from the 18th or 19th Dynasty.

Eventually, Carnarvon began to run out of either money or interest, or both, and he informed Carter that they would have to stop. Carter asked for just one more season of funding, realizing that there was only one place remaining in the entire Valley of the Kings where they had not yet looked. Because it seems they had been setting up their camp in the same place within the valley each year, so now Carter ordered his men to dig there instead of camping. Within just a few days, they found the first of the steps leading down to Tut's tomb.

I've always used this story as a lesson at my own excavations. For instance, at Tel Kabri, we have a storage container that we keep at the site to hold our tools and equipment. It's the size of a railroad car, so it's pretty big and can only be moved using a large truck. So, whenever we decide to put it somewhere each season, I always joke that we should then dig right there, because of what happened to Carter. One time we did decide to move it and did dig there instead. We found good stuff, but not a royal tomb.

In any event, after Carter found the steps leading down to the tomb in early November 1922, he followed them down to the tomb entrance, and he saw the seals stamped into the clay by the necropolis guards near the top of the door. He immediately stopped digging and sent a telegram to Carnarvon, who was still in England at that point, and he instructed him to come over immediately. Carter said that he would wait to open the tomb until Carnarvon was able to arrive. In the meantime, Carter also alerted the world media, so that by the time they did open the tomb in late November, journalists and photographers from around the world surrounded them.

However, what Carter failed to mention to Carnarvon, but which kept him up at night right up until they opened the tomb, was that he could see that it had been broken into in antiquity. He could see where a hole had been cut at least once, and then resealed with the stamps and seals of the necropolis guards, so, for all he knew, when it finally came time to open the tomb, it might be completely empty.

When Carnarvon finally arrived in Egypt two weeks later, Carter and the workmen began excavating where they had left off. When they cleared the rest of the entrance, they realized that they had found Tut's tomb because seals with his cartouche could now be plainly seen on the door, below the seals of the necropolis guards that Carter had seen previously. A cartouche, by the way, is an oval that contains hieroglyphics representing the king's name.

When Carter and Carnarvon opened the first door to the tomb on November 23rd, all they could see was a rubble-filled passageway. It took three days to clear the corridor and so it was only on November 26th that they were able to reach the door into the first room, now known as the antechamber. That, at least, to me, explains why Carter said—probably with much relief in his voice—that he saw wonderful things when he peered into the opening that they had made and saw a room full of objects, rather than a completely empty room. He later elaborated upon the scene in his book, writing:

> At first, I could see nothing, the hot air escaping from the chamber causing the candle flame to flicker, but presently, as my eyes grew accustomed to the light, details of the room within emerged slowly from the mist, strange animals, statues, and gold—everywhere the glint of gold. For the moment, I was struck dumb with amazement, and when Lord Carnarvon, unable to stand the suspense any longer, inquired anxiously, "Can you see anything," it was all I could do to get out the words, "Yes, wonderful things."

As a side note, I should mention that when Carter and his team were clearing out the rubble that filled the long entrance corridor, they reportedly came across the remains of a handkerchief in which were five gold rings. Carter believed that one set of tomb robbers had dropped them in their haste to exit the tomb, perhaps when they were discovered.

The penalty for robbing a royal tomb in antiquity was death, usually by impalement on a sharp stake driven into the ground, so it wouldn't be surprising if Carter was correct that this is how the handkerchief and gold rings ended up in the entrance corridor. It would also explain why the first room was in such disarray, with objects strewn about the place as if somebody had ransacked and burgled it because indeed they had. The interior rooms, which the tomb robbers did not reach, were found to be in a much greater state of order than that first room.

Within this first room, though, were all sorts of wonderful things indeed. At least, one disassembled chariot was in there, along with several beds, some with sides in the shapes of animals. There were also chairs, stools, boxes, and other things. Some of the boxes were filled with various items, including one that contained pairs of fresh underwear—I tell my students that Tut's mother must have packed that one.

An annex behind this first room contained even more grave goods, as did another small room off of the burial chamber. That one is usually called the Treasury. It included a great statue of the jackal-headed god Anubis and four canopic jars that should have held King Tut's internal organs, or, at least, some of them, like his intestines and lungs.

Some of my favorite objects come from these rooms. Among them is a statue of the boy-king harpoon fishing. This is made of ebony wood overlaid with gold. It is so realistic that you can even see that he's got a bit of a tummy, very much like the portrayals of Akhenaten, the pharaoh who ruled just before him.

There is also a vessel of alabaster or calcite that may have served as a lamp, which has an engraving of a lion attacking a bull. The lid has a lion or panther or similar animal lying down with its tongue hanging out, as if it is panting, and King Tut's cartouche carved into its body. There are other alabaster or calcite lamps and bowls as well, some with Tut's cartouche on them and some without, including some very, very elaborate ones.

There are also, of course, inlaid pieces of furniture and lots and lots of jewelry, but my absolute favorite piece is an unguent jar, which probably would have held some sort of perfumed oil. It's in the shape of a lion standing on his hind legs, with his right arm or perhaps I should say his right front leg upraised and his tongue sticking out. After we saw the first King Tut show in 1978, my family basically adopted this piece as our hereditary emblem, much as other families have a family crest or something similar.

Thus, forever afterward, my mother would always greet me after an absence, like when I was away at college for a semester, with her right arm up and her tongue sticking out. I now do the same for my kids. I actually also mention it in my GW classes on occasion. So every so often now a student will pass me on the sidewalk; they'll be holding up their right hand and sticking out their tongue at me. I take this as a gesture of affection and respect, of course, rather than taking umbrage, though it does cause others in the vicinity to do a double-take sometimes.

The burial chamber itself contained some astonishing things, including a huge gilded shrine. It's actually four shrines, one within the other, which surrounded the sarcophagus of the king. But there were so many artifacts stuffed into the tomb that it took Carter almost three full months to catalog enough of the grave goods in the other rooms and then remove them so that he could enter the actual burial chamber. That didn't happen until February 1923. And, it wasn't until almost a year after that, in January 1924, that he was able to reach the actual sarcophagus and remove the granite lid. Only then, nearly 14 months after he had first entered the tomb, could Carter be sure that he had found King Tut, for there he was, interred inside three coffins—one inside the other—and with a gold death mask still in place.

The first two outer coffins were of wood, with gold leaf on them, but the innermost third coffin was of solid gold, weighing nearly 250 pounds. It reportedly took eight men to carry it out of the tomb. And, of course, the gold mask covering Tut's actual mummy, which is probably the best-known piece from the tomb, was also of solid gold, inlaid with lapis lazuli and blue glass.

The three coffins and the gold mask don't all look the same, and it seems that at least one of the coffins had been originally made for another recipient, quite possibly Hatshepsut, rather than Tut. This may also have been the case for a number of the artifacts found within the tomb because some bear traces of other royal names, and it might be that Tut's sudden death resulted in some haste with which the grave goods were given over and placed within the tomb.

It wasn't an easy task for Carter to get King Tut out of his coffin because a thick layer of bitumen—or tar—had been poured over the mummy's legs, below where the gold mask ended. Carter used a crowbar to no avail though he may have broken a few of Tut's bones in the process of trying. He even lit a fire underneath the coffin, in an effort to heat up and then melt the tar, so that he could get the mummy out. It is very rare to see pictures of the mummy still in the coffin, but there is, at least, one that shows Carter staring into the coffin alongside a workman, with the mummy, gold mask, and bitumen-covered legs all still firmly in place.

In the end, Carter was able to remove the mummy from the coffin and extract it from the gold mask. An x-ray was taken sometime soon after, and it shows the bones of a young man, confirming that Tut was probably between 18 and 22 years old when he died. A bone sliver within the brain casing was thought for a long while to have been the cause of Tut's death, but now that is more usually thought to have been a by-product of Carter's efforts to get Tut out of the coffin. The broken bones, on the other hand, are more debated.

Carter may have caused some of the broken bones, but a CT-scan study done in 2005 by a team led by Zahi Hawass, former National Geographic Explorer-in-Residence, indicated that Tut might have suffered a compound fracture of one of his leg bones, perhaps leading to an infection and then to his death. After the study appeared, there was much speculation that maybe he had fallen from his chariot, and broken his leg in that way. Such a scenario would put to rest speculation centering on the possibility that he maybe was murdered. That's the thesis of a number of books and articles, mostly by amateur Egyptologists, including at least one written by professional detectives along the lines of a murder mystery.

That same year, in 2005, forensic anthropologists got into the act as well. Three teams were given the task of trying to recreate what Tut might have looked like before he died. The French team's efforts looked a lot like you'd expect from looking at the death mask while the Egyptian team has him looking quite heavy-set. The third team, consisting of Americans, was the only team who had no idea whose head it was that they were attempting to reconstruct—they did it blind, as it is called, and ended up with an individual who looks completely different from any of the other recreations. The French reconstruction ended up on the cover of the June 2005 issue of National Geographic magazine. And in fact, I think we've got a copy of that around here. Give me a moment, I think it's back here. Yes, here it is. Here is the reconstruction that ended up on the cover of National Geographic magazine back then.

Another set of about 2,000 CT-scans done in 2014 resulted in a virtual autopsy that concluded that Tut had buck teeth, a club foot, various genetic disorders, and perhaps suffered from or died from malaria. DNA testing on Tut's mummy has also shed light on the question of his parents. Although it has long been assumed that Akhenaten was Tut's father, but many have wondered about this because ancient inscriptions show Akhenaten only in the company of his wife and daughters, but no son. But DNA studies published in 2010 strongly indicate that Akhenaten was indeed the father of the boy king though the debate continues about his mother. She might have either been Akhenaten's sister or his more famous wife, Nefertiti.

There are a number of other mysteries that still surround King Tut and his tomb. Principal among these is the tremendous number of grave goods that were buried with him, in the various chambers of his tomb—in fact, an article published by egyptologist Nicholas Reeves in August 2015 and reported in National Geographic News suggested that there might still be other chambers left to find, including a whole section of the tomb that might also contain the body of Queen Nefertiti. Even as I was writing this lecture, researchers were preparing to conduct remote sensing scans to look for these hidden chambers.

Egyptologists and members of the general public alike have wondered at this display of extravagant wealth in King Tut's tomb. This has led more than one person to suggest that, if this much was buried with a kid who ruled for only 10 years, think just how much was buried with someone like Ramses II, who ruled for decades? If only his tomb, and virtually all of the others in the Valley of the Kings, hadn't been looted long ago we would know better.

However, I—and some others—have a different suggestion. I wonder if Tut's tomb might not have been an exception rather than the rule. Although he did only rule for 10 years, he is the pharaoh, who undid all of the reforms of his father Akhenaten, who is perhaps better known as the heretic pharaoh.

Akhenaten had outlawed the worship of Egypt's numerous gods and goddesses, with the single exception of the god Aten, who's represented by the disk of the sun. Note that Aten is not the sun, that's Ra or Re, but is rather the outside rim, or disk, of the sun. With the outlawing of all of the other gods and goddesses, the temples of those deities were all ordered closed as well, and their treasuries were confiscated by Akhenaten.

It is sometimes suggested that Akhenaten was, therefore, responsible for the invention of monotheism. but this was not monotheism as we understand it because the ordinary Egyptian was not allowed to worship Aten directly. Instead, he or she had to worship Akhenaten, who then prayed to Aten on behalf of all the others. The equivalent today perhaps would be as if we were all supposed to pray to the Pope, who then prays on behalf of everyone else. For the ordinary Egyptian, therefore, there were effectively two gods: Akhenaten and Aten. This is not monotheism, at least as I understand it.

I also think that the outlawing of the other gods and goddesses was not necessarily done out of a sense of a religious revolution, or even anything close to it. Instead, it might have been a calculated political move, which ensured more power, more control, and more wealth for Akhenaten as a result. Some of the priests had been getting more and more powerful, and more and more rich, especially the priests of the god Amun. In outlawing the gods and goddesses, closing the temples, and confiscating the treasuries, all while making himself the main spokesman for Aten, Akhenaten flipped the tables. He increased his wealth and his political and religious control even as he decreased the power and wealth of his competitors. He was already the head of the army and the head of the government; now he's also the head of the religion as well. Rather than being a religious firebrand, I think Akhenaten might have been just an extremely savvy politician and leader.

In any event, King Tut, whose name was originally Tutankhaten but who changed it to Tutankhamen, undid all of Akhenaten's religious reforms. He allowed the worship of all the traditional gods and goddesses to resume, and he restored the priests to power. I suspect that his early death led those newly restored priests to fill his tomb with grave goods as thanks for what he had done for them while he was alive. In other words, the unbelievable wealth in Tut's tomb may have been fairly unique, and it may not be the case that

Ramses II's tomb would have been even more unbelievable if we had found it unlooted. But, we don't have any other unlooted royal tombs that we can compare to Tut's at the moment; it's only when, or if, we find another one that we'll actually know if Tut's tomb goods are the rule or the exception.

It may also be that Tut's tomb was full of such rich grave goods because of the times in which he lived. When he came to the throne about 1330 B.C., Egypt was at the height of its power. It was a Great Power among the Great Powers of the day. Tut's father and grandfather, Akhenaten and Amenhotep III, had ruled over an empire that extended up the coast into Canaan, modern-day Israel, Lebanon, and Syria and they were in direct and continuous contact with all of the other major rulers of the day.

We know this from an archive of letters that was found in 1887 at Akhenaten's capital city, now called Tell el-Amarna. The Amarna Letters, as they are called, include royal correspondence that discusses marriages and huge dowries, among other things. Amenhotep III and Akhenaten both married foreign princesses, some from as far away as Babylon in what is now Iraq. The list of gifts that were sent as part of the dowries went on, in some cases, for several pages—or rather, for several clay tablets because the letters were inscribed on clay.

Tut was part of this fabulous world. Some of the letters in the Amarna archive are thought to have been sent to him or are copies of letters sent by him to the foreign kings. Therefore, the amount of wealth found in his tomb should not be surprising, even if it's not related to the changes that he made in Egyptian religion. Still, it would be exciting to find another unlooted royal tomb in Egypt and to be able to compare the grave goods. And, if it turns out that Nefertiti really is buried in a hidden section of Tut's tomb, or even in a tomb located somewhere nearby, it will be fascinating to see what was buried with her.

Lecture 10
How Do You Excavate at a Site?

In this lecture, we'll look at a fundamental question of archaeology: How do you excavate at a site? This question actually involves two issues: (1) How do you, as a team member, physically excavate at a site? (2) How do you, as a dig director, attack an ancient site as part of a concerted plan? The first question is easier to answer; although you won't be an expert right away, you could probably learn how to dig in about 15 minutes. The second question, however, is much more difficult. How do you plan to excavate a site, then execute your strategy as a dig director? We'll talk about both of these questions in this lecture.

Archaeological Tools
- The archaeologist Israel Finkelstein has been known to say, "Used properly, a pick [pickaxe] can be the most delicate instrument on the tell." In fact, pickaxes are used for almost every kind of archaeological work. You can use one to dig quickly but carefully through a certain number of centimeters of dirt, or you can use it to straighten up the balks, that is, the interior sides of the 5-by-5 square in which you're digging. The secret to using a pickaxe correctly is not to raise it higher than your hips and to let the pick head drop down into the soil because of its own weight, rather than raising it above your head and swinging wildly.

- Another important tool is a trowel, preferably a Marshalltown trowel (in America) or a WHS trowel (in Europe). If you're going on a dig, bring your own trowel rather than depending on the tools provided at the dig, which may be cheap brands. You might also want to bring your own *pastiche*, a small hand pick. Dustpans, brushes, and measuring tapes will all be provided by the dig.

- Some archaeologists also carry a set of dental tools, which are useful if you're excavating something very delicate, such as a skeleton.

Common Finds and Systems

- If you're excavating at a site in the Mediterranean, you will probably find broken pieces of pottery with almost every trowel of dirt. These are called *sherds*. Because pottery is not biodegradable once it's fired, you'll find either whole pots or many pieces from broken vessels. Remember, these are the types of pieces that you also found while surveying, which marked the existence and location of a site; now you are finding them still in context, within the site itself.

- You'll also find animal bones, dirt, and rocks. Some of these rocks are random finds; others are parts of walls and buildings. Before you throw any rocks away, keep in mind this archaeological maxim: One rock is a rock; two rocks is a feature; three rocks is a wall; and four rocks is a palace. Of course, that's not always the case, but

Discerning the difference between a random rock and one that's part of a wall or building can be tricky; excavators need to be careful to avoid discarding pieces of structure.

you should be aware that if you start coming across rocks that are in a line, that's probably not accidental. Also, be aware that small rocks and pottery sherds may resemble each other. It can take some time to learn to tell the difference, but you can always asked a more experienced team member.

- Many sites use a color-coded bucket system. For instance, you might put dirt in black buckets, pottery in orange buckets, and animal bones in green buckets. Every so often, the black buckets are emptied at a dump site.

- As you're digging, if you see a change in the color of the soil or the texture of whatever it is you're digging through, stop and alert somebody before continuing to dig, because you might be going through a floor or some other important feature. Your supervisor will probably have you change buckets, just in case the change you noted represents an actual change back in antiquity, such as a new level within the mound. If this is the case, you'll also see that change in the balks when you look at the stratigraphy.

- Another important rule is to never pull anything out of the ground when it first starts appearing as you dig. It is more important to know where the bottom of an object is than where its top is, because it may be resting on a floor, for instance. You need to know the context of the object. If you come across something, tell your square or area supervisor. Then, continue digging until the object, and whatever other objects might be related to it, are sitting as if they are on top of your dining room table.
  - Only when you are able to simply pick them up and take them away should you begin to think about removing any objects.

  - But before you do that, if the objects are significant enough, the supervisors will probably want to photograph and perhaps even draw them while they are still *in situ* ("in place").

A Team Member's Day
- A normal workday for archaeologists on a dig begins by 5:00 am. You'll dig until 8:30 am, then stop to have breakfast. The digging continues until 1:00 pm, when everyone piles on to the bus and heads back to wherever you're staying for lunch and an afternoon rest.

- You then reconvene at 4:00 pm, at which point you may wash pottery or animal bones, enter data into the computer, or do whatever other task you might have been assigned. Dinner is usually served around 7:00, followed by a lecture at 8:00, because many people go on digs for college credit.

- The next day, you're out at the site by 5:00, and the whole routine begins again, usually for five or six days per week and anywhere from four to seven weeks per field season. Many of the volunteers at digs are college students, but you may also meet retired doctors, lawyers, nurses, schoolteachers, and others.

Acting as Site Director
- As site director, you immediately have some choices to make that will determine your first steps. For example, do you want to start with *selective digging*; that is, doing a few probes or test pits here and there to try to get a feel for the chronological sequence or extent of the site?
    - In that case, you'll probably want to conduct *vertical excavation* (digging deep in a few selected areas). This approach can be a good way to get an idea of the stratigraphy that you might encounter if you later decide to expand your excavations at the site.

    - However, you might instead want to conduct *horizontal excavation*, in which you expose one layer over the entire site, then record it, draw it, and photograph it.

- If you're doing vertical archaeology or even if you're just going reasonably deep while doing horizontal archaeology, you will see interesting stratigraphy in the side sections of your excavated squares. If you've excavated properly, then you should see a mirror reflection of any changes in soil color or texture in the balks of your area. For instance, one layer of the balk may be gray and black with ash, indicating a fire; another may be sandy, indicating a period of abandonment; still another may show the outlines of mudbricks from building walls.

- The complications of stratigraphy prompted Kathleen Kenyon and Mortimer Wheeler to create the Kenyon-Wheeler (or Wheeler-Kenyon) method of digging. You'll recall that this method involves excavating in 5-meter-by-5-meter squares, with a meter-wide balk in between the squares. This method not only gave Kenyon and Wheeler a record of what they had dug through, but it also enabled them to publish detailed drawings and photographs of the excavated sections for other archaeologists to study.

Organizing an Excavation

- An archaeological dig may have has many as 60 to 200 people, including excavation staff, such as area supervisors, square supervisors, and their assistants; specialists, such as botanists, geologists, and zoologists; and laboratory and other staff members, including artists and on-site conservators and pottery restorers. A dig also needs an administrator, who is basically the person who makes sure the dig has all the supplies it needs and runs any necessary errands.

- Of course, even before you put a team together, you first have to get permission to excavate at a site. This frequently involves drawing up a research plan and submitting it to agencies, including the government agency that will issue the permit to dig. That agency will want to know all the details, from how you plan to excavate to how you will conserve what you have found once the season is over.

- You'll also probably use the same research plan to raise money for your expedition. This will involve applying to such agencies as the National Science Foundation, the National Endowment for the Humanities, National Geographic, universities or museums, and private donors. Each of these groups will to want to know what you are looking for, what your larger research questions are, and exactly how you plan to spend the money.

- Unless you are fortunate enough to get a multiyear grant or a sponsor who will underwrite your entire dig for its duration, you'll probably have to scrounge for funding in between every field season. And it's not just for money to cover the work in the field; money is also required for the work that needs to be done afterward, including carbon-14 dating, petrographic analysis, pottery restoration, illustration of the objects you find, and so on. All these costs can add up to between $120,000 to $150,000 for a six-week season for a team of 60; a larger dig, with 90 to 120 team members, can easily cost $250,000.

- The best objects you find will go to a museum, but most of the material will go into bags and boxes and be stored at a local university or museum. You and your team will study that material during the months that you're not in the field. In fact, a six- or seven-week field season can yield enough material that it may take two years or more to properly study and publish it.

- As you may have surmised, archaeology is not always as romantic as it is portrayed in the movies. It usually involves dirt, sometimes blood, always sweat, and occasionally tears. However, the rewards are great, whether you are having a unique experience on your first dig, returning to a dig for the second time, or publishing the results of your dig. There is something majestic about an archaeological project with all the planning that is involved and all the hard work that so many people perform during the season. In a way, it's a bit like a symphony orchestra performing a major piece; it doesn't work unless everyone plays his or her part.

Suggested Reading

Catling, *Discovering the Past through Archaeology*.

———, *A Practical Handbook of Archaeology*.

Drewett, *Field Archaeology*.

Questions to Consider

1. It costs a great deal of money to excavate a site these days. Can you think of ways to keep the costs down while maintaining the quality of both the excavation and the analyses afterward?

2. Why might you not want to excavate 100 percent of a site even if you could do so?

Lecture 10 Transcript

How Do You Excavate at a Site?

So far in this course we've covered a lot of ground, if you'll pardon the pun, but we haven't really taken time to address one pretty fundamental question: How do you excavate at a site? So let's address that question now. And let's begin by noting that this question actually asks two things. First, how do you, as a team member, personally, physically, excavate at a site? And secondly, how do you, as a dig director, attack an ancient site as part of a large concerted plan?

The first question is easier to answer and, indeed, if we were actually at a site, I could teach you how to dig in about 15 minutes. On our first morning of digging, you won't be an expert right away, of course, and you'll probably hack your way through a plaster floor or two while you're at it, but I can have you up and running in about 15 minutes. On the other hand, planning how you're going to excavate a site and then executing your strategy as a dig director—well, that's an entirely different matter. So, let's talk about both in this lecture.

But, before we do anything else, let me discuss in some detail the tools that you'll be using and how to use them. Let's begin with the fact that you'll most likely be looking and using a pickaxe far more than you ever expected, at least if you're working somewhere in the Mediterranean region. My friend and colleague at the Megiddo excavations, Israel Finkelstein, has been known to say on many occasions, "Used properly, a pick can be the most delicate instrument on the tell." And, he's right. You can use a pick for anything and everything. You can dig quickly but carefully through a set number of centimeters of dirt, as in "OK, take this down another ten centimeters and then we'll see what you've got."

Or you can use the pick to straighten up the balks—that is, the interior sides of the five by five square in which you're digging, because the balks have to be completely vertical if you're going to get a clear picture of what you've already dug through. Balks are straightened out on a daily basis, or at least every few days, so that you can keep tabs on what you're doing, including whether you've accidentally dug through any plaster floors. The secret, though, even if you're digging through ten centimeters of fill or soil at a time, is not to raise the pick higher than about your hips, and then to let the pick head drop just down into the soil because of its own weight, rather than raising it above your head and swinging away wildly. If you start just whacking away, somebody's going to get hurt. In fact, at one dig I was on, one of the volunteers swung a pick rather erratically and knocked their kneecap out of position and halfway up their thigh, or close to it. That meant a full-length cast for the next six weeks or so, so please do be careful.

OK. Now, the rest of your tool kit will consist of a variety of different implements depending on what part of the world you're working in, but it will always include a trowel. But you can't just use any old trowel from your local hardware store. Marshalltown trowels or a WHS trowel are the preferred brands, depending upon whether you're American, in which case you'll use a Marshalltown like this one, or a British or European, in which case you'll probably use a WHS trowel and sneer at the Americans.

Now, you'll want your own, rather than depending upon whatever kind the dig provides, because they could get you a local cheap brand rather than a Marshalltown or a WHS. It'll cost you less than about $20, even if you spring for a fancy leather holster in which to carry it on your belt. I don't do that, by the way, but others find it useful.

You might also want to bring your own patiche, which is what we call a small hand pick in Israel. You can pick one up for about $60 from a couple of companies in the States. However, the dig will definitely provide these, and I really don't see the need to have your own. I don't have my own and I never have, though some members of the teams that I've been on wouldn't be caught dead without theirs hanging from their belt.

Dustpans, brushes, measuring tapes—these will be provided by the dig. The dustpans and brooms, along with the trowels and patiches, will be your instruments of daily use. Get to know them and to love them; they are your friends. I used to bring dental tools with me every summer as well. My dentist, who was totally into archaeology, used to save the broken ones for me and gave them to me during my annual visit for a checkup and cleaning.

However, dental tools are usually only used if you're excavating something very delicate, like a skeleton. I usually just leave my case of dental tools in the supply room of whatever dig I'm on, since I use them so infrequently.

So, what will you find? Well, if you're excavating at a site in the Mediterranean, you'll be finding broken pieces of pottery with almost every trowelful of dirt. We call these sherds. They're not shards, which is a common mistake: shards refers to glass; sherds refers to pottery. Since pottery is not biodegradable once it's fired, you'll either find whole pots or lots and lots of pieces from broken vessels. Now remember, these are the types of pieces that you'll also find while you're surveying, which mark the existence and location of a site. Now you're finding them still in context, within the site itself.

You'll also find animal bones, and plenty of dirt, and lots of rocks—lots and lots of rocks. Some of these rocks are just random; others, as it will eventually become clear, are parts of walls and buildings. The trick is to figure this out before you pick up a rock and throw it away. There's nothing worse than realizing that you've just thrown away half of a wall. That is a rookie mistake. Be aware that if you do start coming across rocks that are in a line, that's probably not accidental. Also, some of the very small rocks look a lot like pottery sherds, and some of the pottery sherds look a lot like little rocks. It'll take you a while to figure out the difference, so don't be afraid to ask.

Now, you're probably also going to be using a color-coded bucket system. For instance, if you're digging with us at Kabri, you're probably going to put your dirt in the black buckets, your pottery in the orange buckets, and the animal bones that you'll find into green or blue buckets. Now, every so often, when the black buckets all get filled up with dirt, you'll form a bucket line and you'll pass the buckets down the line to the dump where they'll be emptied out. Either that or you'll simply transfer the dirt from the buckets into wheelbarrows, and then trundle them to the same dump and empty them. Either way, you will grow your muscles and shed your pounds. We often say that we're probably marketing our digs the wrong way—they should be advertised as health and wellness clinics, where you'll lose weight and get into shape, at the same time as uncovering ancient remains.

Once you do start really digging, and finding things, you should follow the advice that I was given on my very first dig back when I was a sophomore in college. First of all, if you see a change in the color of the soil or the texture of whatever it is that you're digging through, stop; alert somebody before continuing to dig, because you might be going right through a floor or some other important feature. Your supervisor will probably have you change buckets, just in case the change that you noted represents an actual change back in antiquity, like an entirely new level within the mound. If this is the case, you'll also end up seeing that change in the balks—that is, the sides of your square—when you take a look at your stratigraphy. I'll show you an example of that in a moment.

Now, secondly, never—never ever ever ever never—yank anything out of the ground when it first starts appearing as you dig. It's more important to know where the bottom of an object is than where its top is, because it might be resting on a floor, for instance. You need to know the context of the object. So, if you come across something, first of all tell your square or area supervisor. Then, continue digging as you were until the object, or whatever other objects might be related to it, are sitting as if they're on top of your dining room table. Only when you're able to simply pick them up and take them away should you even begin to think about removing them. But, before you do so, if they're significant enough, the supervisors will probably want to photograph and perhaps even draw them while they are still *in situ*, which is Latin for "still in place."

You'll find pottery and other small objects every day while digging if you're in the Mediterranean region, but chances are you won't find much to really write home about all that often. So, don't go to a dig expecting to find gold, or jewelry, or buried treasure, tombs, or anything like that. You'll most likely be finding mundane objects like pottery and walls of buildings, but you'll still be the first person to touch those objects in hundreds, if not thousands, of years, which is a pretty neat feeling.

Now, I should also tell you that a normal workday for archaeologists on a dig, at least in most of the Mediterranean region, begins with you out at the site and digging by five am. You'll dig for a little more than three hours, until about eight-thirty, and then you'll get to stop for half an hour to have breakfast. Then, you'll keep digging until 11, at which time you'll stop for a 15-minute break, and that's when we usually have coffee, or fruit, or cookies. And then the digging continues until about one pm. At that point you'll all pile on the bus and head back to wherever you're staying for a big lunch, followed by a trip to the swimming pool or a long nap in your air-conditioned room, if you're lucky enough to be on a dig that actually has air-conditioning or a pool in the place where the team is staying.

You'll then reconvene at four pm, at which point you'll either wash all of the pottery that the team found that day and then leave it out in the sun to dry so the directors can look at it the next day and figure out what time period it comes from, or you might wash the fragmentary animal bones that were found, or enter data into the computer, or do whatever other task you might have been assigned. And that'll go on until about 6 pm or maybe a bit longer, then dinner's at 7, followed by a lecture at 8—since many people are doing this for college credit—and then socializing until the lights go out at about 10 pm.

And then you wake up at four-thirty am the next morning, you're out at the site by five, and the whole routine begins again, usually for five or six days per week, and anywhere from four to seven weeks per field season. The digs at Megiddo and at Kabri usually last for six or seven weeks, in June and July, because that's when most people are able to come as volunteer team members. Most of them are college students, but others are people from all walks of life, usually ticking off an item on their bucket list. So, we have retired doctors, lawyers, nurses, schoolteachers, and so on. The one thing that they all have in common is that they had always wanted to go on a dig.

OK, so that covers the basics of how team members physically excavate at a site. Now, let's say that the shoe is on the other foot and you're actually in a position to organize your own dig in order to excavate an ancient site. How do you do that? Well, right off the bat, you have a few choices to make, which will then determine your first steps. For example, do you just want to do what we call selective digging—that is, do a few probes or test pits here and there to try and get a feel for the chronological sequence or the extent of the site?

In that case, you'll probably want to excavate in just a few areas and do what we call vertical excavation. That's when you go down deep in just a few select areas. That can be a good way to get an idea of the stratigraphy that you're going to encounter if you later decide to expand your excavations at the site. So, this is what archaeologists from the University of Chicago ended up doing in one area at Megiddo back in the 1920s and '30s, where they went all the way down to bedrock. That's how we know that there are at least 20 major levels at the site going back 3000 B.C. or even more.

Now, you might instead want to do what we call horizontal excavation, which is where you expose one entire layer over the whole site; then you record it, draw it, and photograph it. This is often what's done at sites like Colonial Williamsburg in the United States. If you're doing vertical archaeology, or even if you're just going reasonably deep while doing horizontal archaeology, you're going to wind up with some nice stratigraphy in the side sections of your excavated squares. You'll remember from one of our previous lectures that it was the man with the best name in the history of archaeology, Sir William Matthew Flinders Petrie, who first really showed the importance of using stratigraphy while excavating at a multi-level site.

If you've excavated properly, including changing buckets, tags, bags, labels, and everything else every time you noted a change in the soil color or texture, then you should see a mirror reflection of all that in the balks of your area. So, for instance, when I was excavating as an area supervisor at Tell el-Maskhuta in Egypt back in the mid-1980s, I ended up with a square that went down about 20 feet, with spectacular balks on the interior sides. In these, we could clearly see huge differences in colors between the different layers. Some were grey and black with ash, from where there had been a fire; others were sandy as the day is long, from when the site had been abandoned for a period. In still other layers, we could clearly see the outlines of mudbricks from the walls of buildings that had once gone right through our area at different periods.

Another time, at Tel Kabri, we found what I can only describe as a gorgeous set of white plaster floors with dark brown layers of soil in between them. These were from different phases of the palace as it went through renovations over time, and the balks looked like an ice cream layer cake.

In Athens, they came up with a unique way of showing the stratigraphy that they had to dig through when building the new Metro system in time for the 2004 Olympics. In some of the Metro stations, the walls were left to show the dirt and the stratigraphy still in place, as if they were the balks for an ongoing archaeological excavation. You can clearly see the different layers of soil, as well as the partial walls of buildings, and drains, and even parts of a road, all of which they now have behind glass, so that you can see it but not touch it.

Now, the stratigraphy at a site can get extremely complicated, as Kathleen Kenyon found at Jericho and Mortimer Wheeler found in India, and that's why the two of them created what we call the Kenyon-Wheeler—or the Wheeler-Kenyon—method of digging in the first place. You'll recall that this method involves excavating in five-meter by five-meter squares, with a meter-wide balk in between the squares. This method not only gave them a record of what they had dug through, it also enabled them to publish detailed drawings and photographs of the excavated sections, and that way other archaeologists could see them too, and either agree or disagree with the conclusions that they had reached.

OK, now that we've talked a bit about the choice between horizontal and vertical excavation, what I'd like to do next is to walk you through the process of organizing an archaeological excavation, from initial concept to final publication. I get a lot of questions about various aspects of this; at cocktail parties, dinner parties, holiday gatherings, and so on. People are really curious and they ask things like, "What exactly is involved in getting permission to dig at a site?" "How do you raise the money to dig?" And, of course, the ultimate question, and my personal favorite, "Do you get to keep what you find?"

So, let's begin at the beginning. First of all, you have to realize that the director, or co-director, of an excavation must be many things in addition to being a competent archaeologist. As Brian Fagan has pointed out, you'll probably also need to be an accountant, a politician, a personnel manager, and—if you don't have the money to hire people to do it—perhaps also a doctor, a mechanic, and even a cook.

Now ideally, though, you'll have enough money not only to arrange for your team's food, but also to fix your cars and take people to the emergency room as needed, especially for bee and scorpion stings, but probably most often for dehydration—that's what we worry about the most. The motto on our digs is "Drink to excess!" But we mean water, not alcohol.

The real expenses, though, go for room and board for your team, and that includes the specialists who will either be there the whole time or will drop by as needed, and these could include botanists, geologists, zoologists, and other specialists. Then you'll need your actual excavation staff, otherwise you're not going to be able to dig or do much of anything at all. So, these include the area supervisors and the square supervisors out in the field, as well as their assistants, plus the laboratory and other staff, including the artists and the on-site conservators and the pottery restorers, who stay busy processing and recording the finds as they come in.

You'll probably also want to lay out the money to hire an administrator, which is a fancy title for somebody who runs all the errands and makes certain that the excavation has all the supplies that it needs, from specific items of food, to rope, buckets, tools, and all of the other things that you need on a dig.

Now, I consider this person to be absolutely essential. When I was first talking to my co-director about beginning the dig at Kabri, I told him that the one thing I didn't ever want to have to do myself is to buy toilet paper for the entire team—that was my one request. And, in fact, I managed to make it through the first six years of the project before I was sent on an emergency run to get toilet paper for the porta-potties that we had on site, because the administrator was off doing something even more essential. Now that's probably more information than you wanted to know, but my point is that no detail is too small to be considered when you have anywhere from 60–200 people working for you out in the hot sun for several weeks.

You may also need to hire a dig photographer unless you already have someone on the team who can double as that. In our case, at Tel Kabri, I'm the photographer, so I always bring my camera, plus the equipment that goes into each official picture: a meter stick for scale; a north arrow so that you can see where north is in the picture; and a photo board with removable letters so that you can create an instant sign with all of the information pertinent to each picture, including date, square number, and so on.

So, hold on a moment, I've actually got these with me here. Now let me give you a quick demonstration. I've got my camera, meter stick, the actual board; so I'm going to put the meter stick down here, parallel to the object; here's our photo board with the information; north arrow's going to go here because north is there. Now this actually is a little bit more dirty than I would like, so you'll have to forgive me—it would normally be very clean. And then come back, take off the lens cap, turn the camera on, and then get everything ready in position, and take your picture.

OK. So, of course, even before you put a team together, you first have to get permission to excavate at a site. This frequently involves drawing up a research plan and submitting it to several places. One will be the government agency that will actually issue you the permit to dig. That agency is going to want to know all the details, from how you plan to excavate, to how you'll do flotation to retrieve small seeds, to how you're going to conserve what you've found once your season is over. If you're successful in receiving a permit, you'll usually be the only ones with permission to dig at that site for as long as you continue to apply for the permits, but you'll probably also have to reapply every year. As long as you're doing a good job, and as long as you're publishing your results in a timely manner, you shouldn't have any problem getting the permit renewed each year.

Now, you'll also probably use the same research plan to raise money for your expedition. If you're American, this will involve applying to agencies like NSF—the National Science Foundation—or NEH—the National Endowment for the Humanities, and it could also involve applying to organizations like National Geographic, as well as to your own university or museum, and, of course, to private donors. Now, there's actually a catch-22 involved here, because usually you won't be granted a permit in the first place if you can't show that you've already got the money that you need, but you frequently can't get the money that you need unless you can show that you've already received your permit. The trick is to tell both sides that the other is going to be forthcoming momentarily.

Each of these groups is going to want to know what you are looking for, what your larger research questions are, and exactly how you plan to spend the money, often right down to the last nickel. And if you're successful in raising money, be sure to keep all of your receipts, because you're going to need to account for how you spent it, again down to the last nickel, shekel, or euro. Thus, if you don't have enough money to hire an accountant, you'll suddenly find that you've become the accountant, which is what has happened to me at Tel Kabri. I now wish that I had been a business minor as well as an archaeology major back in college.

Now, unless you're fortunate enough to get a multi-year grant, or a sponsor who will underwrite your entire dig for its duration, you'll probably going to be scrounging for funding in between every field season; it's a never-ending process. And it's not just for money to cover the work in the field, it's also money for the work that needs to be done afterward, including carbon-14 dating, petrographic analysis, restoration of the pottery that you find, and drawing all of the objects and many of the sherds that you discovered. In order to publish your results promptly, you'll obviously want to get the best people that you can for these things, but it can be expensive.

I don't mind telling you that it usually costs us between $120,000 and $150,000 for a six-week season at Tel Kabri, including everything from room and board for 60 people, to daily buses to and from the site, and all the other costs I just mentioned. A dig like Megiddo, which can have 90–120 team members for a seven-week season, easily costs a quarter of a million dollars without being extravagant at all. Thus, the quest for funding for the next season frequently begins almost as soon as the current season ends.

As for the ultimate question, "Do you get to keep what you find?" there's a very short answer: "No." The best stuff will go to a museum, but most of the material that you find will go into bags and boxes. It will be stored at the local university, or museum, or whatever place that you've arranged in advance, so that your people can come in and study the material during the months that you're not in the field. A six- or seven-week field season can yield enough material that it'll take you and your team two years or more to properly study and then publish it.

Now, one final note, as we conclude this lecture. As you may have surmised by now, archaeology is not always as romantic as it's portrayed, especially by Hollywood. It usually involves dirt, sometimes blood and blisters, always sweat, and occasionally tears. In addition, there are often two different worlds on an excavation. One is that of the volunteers and the regular team members, most of whom are having a once in a lifetime experience and some of whom are potential future professional archaeologists gaining more experience. The other is the world of the directors and the senior staff who are actually running the excavation and who are most likely having a much more stressful time than the volunteers.

However, the rewards are great, whether you're having a unique experience on your first dig, returning to a dig for the second time, or publishing the results of your dig. There's something majestic about an archaeological project, with all of the planning that's involved and all of the hard work that so many people perform during the season. In a way, it's a bit like a symphony orchestra performing a major piece; it doesn't work unless everyone plays his or her part.

Lecture 11

Discovering Mycenae and Knossos

Heinrich Schliemann, the "discoverer" of Troy, is frequently referred to as the father of Mycenaean archaeology. The reason for this is simple: After he excavated at the site of Hisarlik from 1870 to 1873 and announced to the world that he had found Troy, he decided to go looking for Mycenaean sites, specifically, those related to Agamemnon, Menelaus, Odysseus, and others. In this lecture, we'll follow Schliemann as he attempted to find the grave of Agamemnon, before turning to Sir Arthur Evans and his excavation at Knossos.

Excavation at Mycenae
- In 1876, Schliemann took a break from digging at Hisarlik and tried his hand at excavating Mycenae, the city in the Greek Peloponnese where Agamemnon had once ruled. Schliemann believed that he knew where to look for Agamemnon's grave because of some detective work he had done two years earlier.

- According to ancient Greek sources, Agamemnon had been murdered by his wife, Clytemnestra, and her lover, Aegisthus, after he returned home from 10 years of fighting at Troy. The men who were with him were killed, as well. Pausanias, a 2nd-century-A.D. traveler to the area, wrote that Agamemnon and his men were buried inside the city limits of Mycenae, but he didn't give a specific location for the graves.

- When he returned to Mycenae in early August 1876, Schliemann assigned a large team to work in an area just 40 feet inside the famous Lion Gate. Within two weeks, the men found a well-marked grave circle with five deep shafts marked at their top by fragmentary tombstones depicting warriors and hunting scenes. This is now known as Grave Circle A; another grave circle was later found further down the hill and is known as Grave Circle B.

- The shafts that Schliemann found led down to graves with multiple burials and tremendous numbers of objects, including swords, bronze daggers, objects of rock crystal and semiprecious stones, and an amazing number of gold and silver objects, including gold masks covering the faces of several of the dead men.

- However, it is now considered unlikely that these are the graves of Agamemnon and his men. Their deaths would have taken place sometime between 1250 and 1175 B.C.—if the original story is true—but the pottery and other objects in the graves date from 1600 to 1500 B.C., which means they are from a period 300 or 400 years earlier than the time of the Trojan War.

- In fact, it is now thought that these are the graves of one of the first dynasties to rule at Mycenae. The city rose to prominence around 1700 B.C., and these would have been dug within a century or two of that rise. However, at some point near the end of the Late Bronze Age, probably about 1250 B.C., the fortifications of the city were rebuilt to enclose a larger area than previously, which is when the Lion Gate was constructed. At that time, Grave Circle A was brought inside the walls, when it had previously been outside.

- The graves in Grave Circle B are slightly earlier but overlap with those found by Schliemann in Grave Circle A. They date to 1650 to 1550 B.C. and may be the first kings and queens to have ruled at Mycenae.

- There are also a few large beehive-shaped tombs, built from huge blocks of stone, known as *tholos tombs*. Several of them have names given to them in relatively modern times, including the Tomb of Clytemnestra and the Tomb of Agamemnon (also called the Treasury of Atreus). Given that these were built about 1250 B.C., Agamemnon could have been buried here, but these tombs were all found completely looted and empty.

- Schliemann excavated at Mycenae for only one season. Thus, it was left to later archaeologists to uncover the rest of the site.

- What was left of the palace at the top of the citadel has now been completely excavated. Its interior, and possibly the exterior, was covered with brightly colored plaster, with scenes of hunting and other activities garishly painted on the walls.

- The rooms around the palace had multiple purposes, ranging from what were probably residential quarters for the royal family to workrooms for the craftsmen. There was even what appears to have been a cult center, possibly where religious rituals took place.

• It is not clear why Mycenae came to an end soon after 1200 B.C., but it did, in the general calamity that ended the whole of the Late Bronze Age in this region. Mycenae is built directly over a

> There is no doubt that Mycenae was a wealthy city with international connections; objects imported from Italy, Egypt, Canaan, Cyprus, Turkey, and even as far away as Mesopotamia have been found there.

seismic fault line, and at least one earthquake, if not more, caused destruction during this period. Or it may have been drought and famine, followed perhaps by either internal revolt or external invasion, that finally brought down this once-great city.

Excavation at Knossos

- Partway across the Aegean on the island of Crete, Schliemann also tried to purchase land at a site that he thought might be the capital city of the legendary king Minos. Because the landowner refused to sell to him, it was left to another archaeologist, Sir Arthur Evans, to excavate the site and bring the other great Bronze Age Aegean civilization, the Minoans, to light, beginning in 1900. The city Evans excavated is known as Knossos.

- At Knossos, Evans found a civilization that was a little older than that of the Mycenaeans and had influenced them when they were on the rise. For instance, a number of the objects that Schliemann found in the shaft graves at Mycenae were either of Minoan manufacture or bore the stamp of Minoan influence.

- The Minoans (a name given by Evans to this people) flourished at the end of the 3rd millennium B.C. and through most of the 2nd millennium B.C. Around 1700 B.C., a major earthquake hit Knossos, but the inhabitants survived and rebuilt the palace. Probably sometime about 1350 B.C., the Mycenaeans from the Greek mainland seem to have invaded and taken over, bringing with them a new way of writing, new types of scenes for wall paintings, and a more militaristic way of life that lasted for about 150 years, until everything collapsed soon after 1200 B.C.

- Evans made amazing discoveries at Knossos, but he also made an error in reconstructing things as he went along. For example, based on the remains of staircases, he imagined that the main part of the palace had three stories. He therefore reconstructed part of the palace with three floors, and because he used cement and other permanent materials, it is nearly impossible to undo his reconstruction today. He may well have been correct in part but not in everything, which is why today, such reconstructions are generally not permitted.

- Evans and his team found a large, essentially open-air palace, with a huge central courtyard. It not only served as headquarters for the ruler but also as a center for redistribution of produce. Locals would bring their goods for storage, such as wheat, barley, wine, grapes, and so on, and the palace would redistribute them as needed.

- Two things about the site remain a mystery. One is the fact that there are no fortification walls around the palace at Knossos. Why weren't the people on Crete afraid of attack? Many theories have been put forward to explain this situation, but none has been completely satisfactory. The second mystery is who ruled at Knossos. It might have been a king or queen, priest or priestess, or the community.

- The interior walls of the palace were ablaze with color in the form of many wall paintings. From these, we can tell a fair amount about the Minoans, including their dress and hair styles. However, Evans's reconstructions of some frescoes were completely wrong, including those of the Dolphin Fresco and the Priest-King Fresco.

- The central court at Knossos was undoubtedly used for large ceremonies, but it also seems to have been the site of a rather unusual event, depicted in a small wall painting in one of the buildings. The painting shows three people—one male and two female—leaping over a bull. Other finds at Knossos suggest a similar event involving bull-leaping and, perhaps, rituals in which stone bulls' heads were deliberately smashed. This focus on bulls brings to mind the Greek myth of Theseus and the Minotaur.
    o According to the myth, in the Bronze Age, King Minos demanded a sacrifice each year to the Minotaur, the half-man/half-bull creature who lived in the basement labyrinth of the palace. Each year, the king of Athens had to send seven boys

The Dolphin Fresco at Knossos, reconstructed by Arthur Evans, should probably have only two dolphins, rather than five, and should be on the floor, not the wall.

In the painting of the bull leapers, the man is in midflight, while one woman is in front of the bull, grasping his horns, and the other is behind, perhaps ready to catch the man when he lands; it's also possible that all three are in the process of leaping over the bull.

and seven girls to King Minos, who then sent them down into the labyrinth; no one had ever emerged alive.

- One year, Theseus, the son of the king of Athens, volunteered to go, so that he could try to kill the Minotaur and put an end to the annual sacrifice. Once Theseus arrived in Knossos, he befriended Ariadne, the daughter of King Minos, who provided him with a sword and a ball of string. As he went through the maze, he unwound the string to help find his way back out. He then killed the Minotaur with the sword, retraced his steps, and emerged victorious.

- It's possible that the story was created by later occupants of the area to explain the ruins of the palace of Knossos and the stories they vaguely remembered about the Minoans and bulls. However, there might be another explanation of the myth entirely.

- In the early 1990s, a huge wall painting was found, depicting multiple bulls and numerous bull leapers in action in front of a maze or labyrinth. It is a painting that we would expect to find at Knossos, except that it's in the Nile Delta region of Egypt, at the site of Tell el-Dab'a. And it dates to somewhere between the 17th and 15th centuries B.C., that is, right in the middle of the 2nd millennium, during the Bronze Age.

- Thus, it may be that the myth of Theseus and the Minotaur is much earlier than anyone expected and was not invented later to explain the ruins of Knossos. But the fact that such a painting is in Egypt, with a Minoan motif created by Minoan artists using techniques that were quite different from those of the Egyptians, is even more interesting—showing direct contact between Egypt and Crete at the time.

Suggested Reading

Cline, ed., *The Oxford Handbook of the Bronze Age Aegean*.

Fitton, *Minoans*.

Schofield, *The Mycenaeans*.

Questions to Consider

1. What do you think the lions (or, rather, lionesses) on the Lion Gate at Mycenae represent?

2. Why do you think that there are no fortification walls at any of the Minoan palaces on Crete?

Lecture 11 Transcript
Discovering Mycenae and Knossos

Heinrich Schliemann, the discoverer of Troy, is frequently referred to as the father of Mycenaean archaeology. The reason is simple: after he excavated at the site of Hisarlik in Turkey from 1870 to 1873 and announced to the world that he had found Troy, not to mention Priam's Treasure, he decided to go looking for the other side, namely Agamemnon, Menelaus, Odysseus, and the other Mycenaeans who had supposedly fought for 10 years against the Trojans.

So, Schliemann took a break from digging at Hisarlik and tried his hand at excavating at Mycenae, the city in the Greek Peloponnese where Agamemnon, king among kings, had once ruled. It was a lot easier to find Mycenae than it had been to find Troy, mostly because the modern village still has the same name—Mykēnē in Greek—and the remains of the famous Lion Gate entrance to the ancient citadel were still partially visible, sticking up out of the ground.

The Lion Gate is one of my favorite places in the world—our family takes a picture of ourselves in front of it whenever we go there, which is every couple of years. So we have a photomontage of our life, from dating to marriage to kids and beyond, all in front of this great entrance to Mycenae. Now, it's still debated exactly what the lions on the gate mean—and actually they're lionesses, not lions. I personally think that they, and the column that stands between them, are most likely the heraldic crest of the ruling family, but I could be wrong.

In any event, when Schliemann arrived at Mycenae in 1876, he didn't have a permit to dig at the site, but that had never stopped him before—he didn't have one for Troy when he began digging there either. And, he thought he knew where to look for Agamemnon at the site because of some detective work that he had done two years earlier.

Now, the ancient Greek sources, from Homer down to the later 5th century B.C. plays written by Sophocles, and Aeschylus, and Euripides, said that

Agamemnon had been killed after he returned home from 10 years of fighting at Troy. He was murdered by his wife Clytemnestra and her lover Aegisthus, reportedly at the dinner table during a feast, according to Homer, but perhaps while taking a bath, according to later accounts. The men that came home with him were killed as well.

A later traveler to the site, a man named Pausanias who wrote about his travels all over Greece during the 2nd century A.D., wrote that Agamemnon and his men were buried inside the city limits of Mycenae. Pausanias doesn't actually give a specific location for the graves, so Schliemann had to use his powers of deduction, and here's what he did.

In February of 1874, working without a permit, Schliemann did some exploratory work at the site. He dug, as he put it, "34 shafts in different places, in order to sound the ground and to find out the place where I should have to dig for them." In other words, he was digging test pits at the site to determine where he should concentrate his efforts once the real excavation started. I actually find it quite impressive that he did that, because that's something that we still frequently do today. Now, several of the test pits produced interesting results, but the most important were two that he dug not far inside the Lion Gate. Here, he says, that he found an unsculptured slab resembling a tombstone in addition to other finds, including female idols and small figurines.

So that was 1874. When he returned to Mycenae in early August 1876, Schliemann had a team of 63 workmen. He put two-thirds of them to work in an area that was just 40 feet inside the Lion Gate, and they were instructed to dig a huge area that was 113 feet long by 113 feet wide. And, sure enough, within 2 weeks, after he had doubled the number of workmen to 125, they found a well-marked grave circle with 5 deep shafts marked at their top by fragmentary tombstones. Now, on the tombstones were warriors and hunting scenes. This is now known as Grave Circle A, because there's another grave circle further down the hill, and that was found in the 1950s and it's now called Grave Circle B.

The shafts that Schliemann found led down to graves with multiple burials, tremendous numbers of swords, and an amazing amount of gold and silver objects. Among these were gold masks that were covering the faces of several of the dead men. Now, Schliemann was so certain that he had found what he was looking for that he immediately sent a telegram to the king of Greece, George I, which read, "I have gazed upon the face of Agamemnon." The king immediately rushed to Mycenae, where Schliemann showed him a marvelous gold mask with a kingly face engraved upon it, complete with a mustache and a beard. That mask now hangs front and center in a display case in the National Archaeological Museum in Athens.

The only problem is that wasn't the mask at which Schliemann was gazing when he sent the telegram to the king. He had instead been looking at another mask of a much more cherubic and pleasant looking fellow, but when Schliemann found the more kingly looking mask before the Greek monarch arrived, he showed him the new one instead.

Now, the grave goods that Schliemann found in those tombs were absolutely amazing: marvelous pieces of work, including bronze daggers inlaid with hunting and wildlife scenes on the blades; and objects of rock crystal and semi-precious stones; and gold, gold, gold, something like 800 kilograms worth of gold objects all told.

However, it's now considered very unlikely that these are actually the graves of Agamemnon and his men, because their deaths would have taken place sometime between 1250 and 1175 B.C., if the story really did happen rather than being the stuff of legend. We now know that the pottery and the other objects in those graves date from 1600–1500 B.C., which means they're from a period 300 or 400 years earlier than the time of the Trojan War.

Schliemann probably suspected as much, because in his 1878 book on Mycenae, he says specifically that the fragmentary tombstones probably dated to the middle of the 2nd millennium B.C., and he even gives them a date of 1500 B.C. in the table of contents for chapter 4. So, he was actually pretty much dead-on in terms of the date for the tombs, even if he was completely wrong about the bodies that they contained. In fact, it's now thought that these are most likely the graves of one of the first dynasties to rule at Mycenae, since the city rose to prominence at about 1700 B.C., and these would have been dug within a century or two of that rise. At some point, though, near the end of the Late Bronze Age, probably about 1250 B.C., the fortifications of the city were rebuilt to enclose a larger area than previously, and that's when the Lion Gate was constructed. It was also at that time that Grave Circle A was brought inside the city walls, when it had been outside previously.

As I mentioned, there's also another grave circle—Grave Circle B—that was found farther down the hill, which today is right next to a parking lot. The graves there are slightly earlier but they overlap with the ones that Schliemann found in Grave Circle A. These other ones date to 1650–1550 B.C. and they may be the very first kings and queens to have ruled at Mycenae. A few years ago, forensic anthropologists made an attempt to reconstruct some of the faces of these individuals in Grave Circle B, with interesting results.

There are also a few very large beehive-shaped tombs, built from huge blocks of stone, which are known as tholos tombs. Several of them have names that have been given to them in relatively modern times, including the Tomb of Clytemnestra and the Tomb of Agamemnon, which, by the way, is also called the Treasury of Atreus. These were built about 1250 B.C., so if Agamemnon is buried anywhere, it could have been in these. However, they were all found completely looted and totally empty.

Now, Schliemann only excavated at Mycenae during that one brief season in 1876. The next year, he went looking for Ithaca and Odysseus' home and then, in 1878, he went back to Troy for several more seasons of digging.

So, it was left to later archaeologists to uncover the rest of the site of Mycenae, with most of them using much better excavation methods than Schliemann did. What was left of the palace at the very top of the citadel has now been completely excavated, and it turns out that its interior, and possibly the exterior as well, was covered with brightly colored plaster; scenes of hunting and other activities garishly painted in blues, and yellows, reds, and other colors on the walls. The king would have sat at one side of a large room, surrounded by such painted scenes while a large fire blazed away in a hearth that was set in the middle of the floor. It was dark in there, and smoky and probably damp as well. Mycenaean palaces, to me at least, seem to have been a bit claustrophobic, with few windows or other openings, and they focused inward rather than looking outward.

The rooms around the palace were used for a multitude of things, ranging from what were probably residential quarters for the royal family to workrooms for the craftsmen. There was even what appears to be a cult center, possibly where religious rituals took place. Some strange idols and figurines have been found in here, along with wall paintings as well.

Now, there is no doubt that Mycenae was a wealthy city with international connections. Objects imported from Italy, and Egypt, Canaan, Cyprus, Turkey, and even as far away as Mesopotamia have been found here. Some of the most interesting to me are fragments of Egyptian faience plaques with the cartouche of the pharaoh Amenhotep III on them. I think these might have been left by an official Egyptian embassy that was sent to Mycenae in the middle of the 14th century B.C.

In any event, late in the Bronze Age, possibly about 1250 B.C. when the Lion Gate was built, a well-constructed tunnel with steps of stone was built, leading down to a water source so that the inhabitants didn't have to venture outside in times of siege. And this might have been an indication that they could see trouble brewing in the near future.

It's not clear why the city came to an end soon after 1200 B.C., but it did, in the general calamity that ended the whole of the Late Bronze Age in this region. Mycenae is built directly over a seismic fault line, and at least one earthquake, if not more, caused destruction during this period. But it might have been drought and famine, followed perhaps by either internal revolt or external invasion that finally brought down this once great city. There are some later remains, including a Doric temple that was built at the very top of the citadel region, but Mycenae never regained its lost glory.

Now, partway across the Aegean on the island of Crete, Schliemann had also tried to purchase land at a site that he thought might be the capital city of the legendary King Minos. The landowner refused to sell it to him, so it was left to another archaeologist, Sir Arthur Evans, to excavate the site and bring the other great Bronze Age Aegean civilization, the Minoans, to light, sometime around 1900. The city that he excavated is known as Knossos.

Evans had been searching for this city for years, ever since he saw a few items for sale in the marketplace in Athens. Known as milk stones and sold to pregnant women for help during and after giving birth, these small pieces of semi-precious stones had strange figures and carvings on them. Evans eventually traced them back to Crete, to the very hill that Schliemann had tried unsuccessfully to buy. Evans had better luck; he purchased the land, and he began excavating.

There's a great picture of Evans with his workmen, standing at the site of Knossos. He's dressed all in white with a pith helmet on. I've often thought that that would be the way that I should dress while digging, but it's a hard choice between that and the full jacket-and-tie look that other people were excavating in at that time.

What Evans found at Knossos turned out to be a civilization that was a little older than the Mycenaeans and that had influenced them when they were growing up. For instance, a number of the objects that Schliemann found in the shaft graves at Mycenae were either of Minoan manufacture or bore the stamp of Minoan influence.

Now, when we refer to the Minoans, we're actually using the name that Evans gave to these people, because we don't know what they called themselves. They flourished at the end of the third millennium B.C. and then throughout most of the second millennium B.C., what we now call the Middle and Late Bronze Age in this region. Around 1700 B.C., a major earthquake hit Knossos but the inhabitants survived and they rebuilt the palace. And then, probably sometime about 1350 B.C., the Mycenaeans from the Greek mainland seem to have invaded and taken over. And they brought with them a new way of writing, new types of scenes for the wall paintings, and a more militaristic way of life which lasted for about a century and a half until everything collapsed soon after 1200 B.C.

Now, Evans found amazing things at Knossos, but he also made what I would consider to be a fatal error of reconstructing things as he went along.

Thus, he imagined that the main part of the palace had three stories, based upon the remains of staircases that he found. Therefore, he reconstructed part of the palace with three floors, and because he used cement and other permanent materials, it's nearly impossible to undo his reconstruction today. He may well have been correct in part, but not in everything, which is why today such reconstructions are generally not permitted. What we really need at these sites is something more along the lines of a theater, with the reconstructions exhibited as 3-D models that can be changed as needed.

What it seems that Evans and his team of workmen did find was a large, essentially open-air palace with a huge central courtyard. It was light; it was airy; it was integrated into the environment. It even had running water and a sewer system. In other words, it was a very advanced building, which not only served as headquarters for the ruler, but also as a center for redistribution. Locals would bring their goods in for storage, like wheat, barley, wine, grapes, and so on, and then the palace would redistribute them as needed. There is, in fact, an entire part of the palace which consists only of corridors packed with large storage jars, including some that are sunk into the ground in order, probably, to keep their contents cold.

Two things remain a mystery, however. One is the fact that there are absolutely no fortification walls around the palace at Knossos. Nor are there any at any of the other six or seven smaller palaces that are elsewhere on Crete at this time, despite occasional claims to the contrary. So, this is strange. Why weren't the people on Crete afraid of being attacked?

Now, much later, the Greek historian Thucydides says that the Minoans had a thalassocracy—that is, they ruled the sea with their navy. But that only explains why they might not have been worried about invasion by outsiders; it still doesn't explain why they weren't worried about an attack from just down the road. Now, there have been many theories put forward to explain this situation, but none has been completely satisfactory. I think the most likely hypothesis is that one single family was ruling all of Crete at that time, with the father at Knossos, sons at other palaces like Phaistos, cousins at still other palaces like Khaniá, and so on.

But that brings us to the second mystery, because we have no idea if it was a king who ruled at Knossos. It might have been a queen; it might have been a priest or a priestess; it might have been community rule—we just don't know. Evans did label one room the king's throne room and another one the queen's megaron, but those are just names that he assigned. Someone was in charge, but we're not sure who it was.

Among the objects brought to light by Evans are the extremely well known figurines of women holding snakes, which are usually called snake goddesses or snake priestesses. They're made out of ivory, which Evans found in many fragments, and had to be put back together. Unfortunately, as it turns out, only a few of these are actually real. The rest of them, including many that are in museums around the world today, are forgeries, probably made by the very men who put the real ones together.

Now, the interior walls of the palace were ablaze with color in the form of many wall paintings, and from these we can tell a fair amount about the Minoans. For instance, there's one woman depicted who's so beautiful that Evans dubbed her "La Parisienne," as if she were from Paris. She's shown with an elaborate hairdo, makeup, jewelry, and a dress of red, white, and blue. Other frescoes show similarly dressed women. Men are pictured also, usually dressed only in a kilt, and they wear also jewelry and possibly makeup in addition.

There are a few frescos where the reconstructions of Evans and the restorers are probably downright wrong. One is the well-known Dolphin Fresco; another is the most famous painting at the site, the Priest-King Fresco. In the Dolphin Fresco, Evans reconstructed a painting with five dolphins and a few flying fish on a wall in the area of the queen's megaron. The painting wasn't still on the wall of course; Evans found the fragments lying in the dirt in front of the wall. He only found fragments from two dolphins, but the area where he thought the painting had been was large enough that he needed to suggest that originally there had been five dolphins.

Occam's razor comes into play here, though—the simplest solution is probably the correct one. If Evans found fragments from two dolphins, then he can only state for certain that there were two dolphins there originally;

everything else is a hypothesis. And since the painting could have come from anywhere in the room, we can look around for other possibilities. As it turns out, there is a space on the floor that is just perfect for a painting with only two dolphins, and both the Minoans and the Mycenaeans are known to have painted their floors. So, I'm going to go with the suggestion that was made by a professor at Hunter College back in about 1986 and say that the Dolphin Fresco should only have two dolphins, rather than five, and that it should be on the floor, not on the wall.

The other painting that Evans got totally wrong is the Priest-King Fresco, which today is reproduced everywhere, from the covers of books to placemats to plaster replicas. Here, Evans and his restorers put together a man whom they called the Priest-King of Knossos. Note that this title implies that they were unsure who was ruling the city, just as we are still unsure today: a priest, a king, a priest-king. They have him walking towards the left side of the painting with his head and his legs facing to the left but his body frontally facing the viewer and twisted towards the right. His right arm is cocked up against his chest and his left arm goes off-screen to the right holding a rope, which they said was attached to a bull that conveniently isn't shown.

So, what's wrong with all this? Well, just about everything. First of all, the pieces apparently were found in three different rooms in the building, not all together in one. Why Evans thought they were from all the same painting is just beyond me. Secondly, the flesh of the figure is in two different colors: the head, which is facing left, is white; the chest, which is twisted right, is reddish-brown; and the legs, which are headed to the left, are also reddish-brown. Now, in Minoan art, they used conventions to depict males and females—males are always red or brown; females are always white or yellow.

In other words, we have three different figures here, which Evans put together as a single person. We've got a woman headed left, of which we have only her head; a man also headed left, from whom we have only his legs; and perhaps a young boy or a teenager headed right, for whom we have only the torso, with the right hand cocked up against the chest. Moreover, the pose of the torso looks an awful lot like the pose adopted by two boxing boys in a painting found on Santorini. So much for the Priest-King of Knossos.

Okay, let's now turn from Evans' reconstructed frescoes and have a quick look at the big central court at Knossos. This was undoubtedly used for all sorts of things as such big ceremonial areas are throughout the world and in all eras. But the court at Knossos seems to have been where a rather unusual practice took place, at least if we can believe what's pictured in a small wall painting in one of the buildings.

Here we see three people—one male and two female—leaping over a bull. Now, the man is in mid-flight, doing a somersault over the bull's back. One of the women is in front of the bull, grabbing his horns, perhaps to distract him; the other is behind the bull and looks poised to catch the man when he lands. It's also possible, though, that all three might be leaping over the bull. If so, one woman has just landed, the man is in the process, and the other woman is about to fling herself over. So, it's unclear which interpretation is the correct one, but either way this is like doing a routine on the pommel horse at the Olympics, except that the pommel horse is alive, has horns, and is trying to kill you. Apart from that, it's the same.

Excavators at Knossos also found an ivory figurine, which can only be part of a bull-leaping group, because the figure is obviously flying through the air. It's got pointed toes and outstretched arms, and there's no way it could stand upright—it has to be in midair. Beyond that, there are several bulls' heads made in stone that have been found at Knossos, some of which appear to have been deliberately smashed, maybe after a ritual. These stone heads were hollow, with holes at the nostrils, so that if they were filled with red wine, for instance, and then held at the proper angle, it would look like you were holding the head of a bull that had just been sacrificed to the gods and was still dripping blood.

So, it seems that the Minoans were perhaps doing some bull leaping in their central courtyard as well as some rituals involving bulls in or around the palace. This in turn brings to mind the Greek myth of Theseus and the Minotaur. Now, just to refresh your memory, let me give you the quick version of it.

Back in the Bronze Age, King Minos demanded a sacrifice each year to the Minotaur—that's the half-man, half-bull creature who's living in the basement below the palace at Knossos. The basement was a labyrinth from which nobody had ever gotten out alive. Now each year the king of Athens had to send seven young boys and seven young girls to King Minos, who then sent them down into the labyrinth. Well, one year, Theseus, the son of the king of Athens, volunteered to go so that he could try to kill the Minotaur and put an end to the annual sacrifice. His distraught father reluctantly agreed. Once he got to Knossos, Theseus befriended Ariadne, the daughter of King Minos. She provided him with a sword and a ball of string, and as he went through the maze, he unwound the ball of string so that he could find his way back out again, and when he got to the Minotaur, he pulled out the sword and cut off the Minotaur's head. He then retraced the steps and emerged victorious.

Now, I have long thought that there might be a kernel of truth at the basis of many of the Greek myths. In this case, I suspect that the story might have been created in an attempt by later occupants of the area to explain the ruins of the palace of Knossos, the stories that they vaguely remembered about them doing something with bulls, and especially the maze-like appearance of the ruined storage areas.

But I could be wrong, and there could be another explanation entirely. I say this because in the early 1990s, a huge wall painting was found, depicting multiple bulls and numerous bull leapers in action in front of what can only be described as a maze or a labyrinth. It's a painting that we would totally expect to find at Knossos, except that that's not where it is. It's not even in Crete. In fact, it's in the Nile Delta region of Egypt, at the site of Tell el-Dab'a, and it dates somewhere between the 17th and 15th centuries B.C.—that is, right in the middle of the 2nd millennium during the Bronze Age.

So it may be that the myth of Theseus and the Minotaur is much earlier than anybody expected, and it wasn't made up later to explain the ruins of Knossos. But the very fact that such a painting is in Egypt with a Minoan motif and probably created by Minoan artists using techniques that were quite different from those of the Egyptians at that time is to my mind even more interesting. The excavator of the painting supposed that perhaps a Minoan princess had been brought over for a dynastic marriage. I don't think it's necessary to have such an elaborate explanation, but certainly the presence of such a painting shows that Egypt and Crete were in direct contact back in the Bronze Age.

Now, we already knew that such connections existed based on other evidence, but it's very satisfying to find such a vivid corroboration of the international connections that were ongoing across the Aegean and Eastern Mediterranean more than 3,000 years ago.

Lecture 12 — Santorini, Akrotiri, and the Atlantis Myth

Nearly every year, the lost island of Atlantis is "found"—everywhere from the Bahamas to off the coast of Cyprus—but in fact, it may be that the island is in plain sight. Many archaeologists suspect that the kernel of truth underlying the myth of Atlantis is the volcanic eruption of the Greek island of Santorini in the middle of the 2nd millennium B.C. But even if that eruption is not what underlies the story of Atlantis, the excavation of the site of Akrotiri on Santorini has shed important light on the Bronze Age Aegean at a time when the Minoans were engaged in contact and trade with such places as Egypt and Canaan in the Eastern Mediterranean.

The Island of Santorini
- The island of Santorini is about 70 miles north of Crete by boat. The name Santorini is rather recent; the island was named that by the Venetians after Saint Irene. An older name, frequently used by archaeologists, is Thera; according to the Greek historian Herodotus, this name comes from a Spartan commander who was the leader of a colony established there during the 1st millennium B.C.

- Sometime during the mid-2nd millennium, most likely in either the 17th or 16th century B.C., the volcano on Santorini erupted, scattering ash and pumice primarily to the south and east. Archaeologists and geologists have found the pumice in excavations and at the bottom of lakes in places ranging from Crete to Egypt to Turkey.

- As a result of the eruption, the entire middle part of the island is gone, with only the outer part remaining as an incomplete circle of land. The caldera, which is hundreds of feet deep, was filled with water from the Aegean Sea. That, in turn, most likely created a tidal wave or tsunami that affected places as far away as Crete.

In the middle of the caldera of Santorini today are several small islands that have popped up in the last century as a result of ongoing volcanic activity.

Akrotiri

- Akrotiri is frequently called the Pompeii of the Aegean because the ancient town was buried under a deep ash layer by the volcanic eruption. The houses are still standing to the second story in some places, and it is as if life simply stopped in a single instant more than 3,500 years ago.

- However, it is clear from some of the remains found that the site may have been nearly abandoned by the time of the eruption. There are indications that a major earthquake or, perhaps, multiple earthquakes may have hit the island about a decade before the final destruction and that at least some of the inhabitants had tried to repair the damage. We know that earthquakes frequently precede eruptions, and the ancients may have known that, as well. Given that no human remains and only a few objects made out of precious materials have been found, it's possible that most of the inhabitants left the island before the final eruption.

- The Greek archaeologist Spyridon Marinatos directed the excavations of Akrotiri from 1967 until his death in 1974. The excavations continued after his death and are today led by the well-known archaeologist Christos Doumas. Even though the site has been continuously excavated for nearly 50 years at this point, it is estimated that only about 10 percent of the ancient town has been uncovered.

- In many places, a similar situation to that seen at Pompeii was encountered, in which the original wood or other organic material had decomposed, leaving an empty space in the now-hardened volcanic ash. Into these spaces, excavators have poured either

Volcanic ash filled every nook and cranny of the site of Akrotiri, but as a result, it preserved everything as it was at the time of the explosion, including pottery, storage jars, and furniture.

cement or plaster of Paris, which is then colored brown to imitate the original wood. In this way, the buildings remain preserved up to their second story, just as Marinatos and Doumas found them, and are still rendered safe for both tourists and archaeologists.

- The excavation techniques used at Akrotiri are standard, with digging done using trowels, pickaxes, and dental tools. There is not really any stratigraphy to speak of, because the excavators are simply digging straight down through a very deep ash layer that was all laid down at the same time.

- Quite a bit of pottery has been recovered during the excavations, as well as objects made of stone and other materials. Some of these, especially the pottery, are painted with marine scenes, featuring dolphins and octopi.

Wall Paintings of Akrotiri
- The wall paintings of Akrotiri are among the best preserved from the Bronze Age Aegean. One is the so-called Nilotic Fresco, which features a scene that might be depicting the Nile in Egypt. It has a leaping feline in it, which might be chasing a duck or goose. On both sides of the river or stream are what look like palm trees or, perhaps, papyrus plants. This painting was found in the West House along with several other frescoes that have nautical or, perhaps, non-Theran scenes, suggesting that the house belonged to a ship captain or someone who had traveled overseas.

- Another rather exotic-looking wall painting shows blue monkeys with white cheeks swinging from trees. A similar wall painting at Knossos also shows blue monkeys, and blue monkey figurines with yellow cheeks have been found at Mycenae and Tiryns on the Greek mainland. As it turns out, there is a particular species of monkey in Africa called a green guenon, whose fur ranges from blue to green and who have yellow or whitish cheeks. These monkeys were prized as pets by the pharaohs of New Kingdom Egypt, who occasionally sent them as gifts to rulers of other countries.

- Other paintings depict human figures. One shows two young boys who seem to be boxing. They wear what look like loin cloths and have shaved heads with clumps of hair hanging down in curls. Another painting shows a naked young man holding two long strings of fish that he has just caught. Other pictures show women engaged in a variety of activities, such as picking flowers.

- Also in the West House is a painting known as the Miniature Fresco or the Flotilla Fresco, which includes a number of fascinating details.
  - On one end of the scene, we see warriors marching off to battle. They are dressed like some of the warriors whom Homer describes in the *Iliad*, wearing boar-tusk helmets and carrying tower shields. Behind the warriors is a large building, with women standing on the roof, apparently waving goodbye.

  - There are also what look like herd animals and a herdsman in the distance, above the warriors; below them is a scene with a few boats and men who are sideways or upside-down, which is the way dead and drowning men were depicted. This is usually interpreted as a naval battle, though one archaeologist has suggested that it might be a scene of sacrifice.

  - The fresco continues with a flotilla scene, showing as many as a dozen or more ships departing a port on an island that may or may not be Santorini. The men are rowing across the sea, accompanied by cavorting dolphins, toward a second city.

Redating the Eruption
- Santorini has been at the forefront of a debate among Bronze Age Aegean archaeologists since about 1987, when a radical redating of the eruption was proposed. It used to be thought that the Santorini eruption took place in about 1450 B.C. It also used to be thought—and actually still is—that the eruption took place at a time when a certain style of pottery, known as Late Helladic

or Late Minoan Ib pottery, was in vogue. Thus, wherever LH/LM Ib pottery has been found, the level at that site has been dated to about 1450 B.C.

- However, as a result of new studies of radiocarbon data, as well as information based on ice core analysis and several other techniques, it was proposed that the eruption actually took place in or around 1628 B.C. Given that the eruption and LH/LM Ib pottery are still tied together, that means that any level at any site that has such pottery actually dates to the 17th century B.C., not the 15th century B.C. This became known as the High Chronology.

- Many archaeologists acknowledge that there are problems with radiocarbon dating; thus not everyone has accepted this change in chronology. Some are willing to accept a bit of a change but only pushing the date of the eruption back to 1550 B.C., rather than 1628 B.C.

- It's important to note that even when we have buildings, pottery, and other artifacts from a site and we have an idea of when that site was flourishing, we cannot always be certain about the absolute date.

The Legend of Atlantis

- The story of Atlantis comes to us from the Greek philosopher Plato. In two of his shorter works, the *Timaeus* and the *Critias*, Plato tells us about a place with awesome warriors who dared to fight against Athens, but whose home sank beneath the waves, never to be seen again. In the *Timaeus*, he writes, "There occurred violent earthquakes and floods; and in a single day and night of misfortune all your warlike men in a body sank into the earth, and the island of Atlantis in like manner disappeared in the depths of the sea."

- The initial story of Atlantis, according to Plato, was told by an Egyptian priest to a visiting Greek lawgiver named Solon sometime after 590 B.C.; the priest told Solon that the events had taken place 9,000 years before their time, though many today think that 900 years fits better, because that would put the events at about 1500 B.C., rather than in the Neolithic Age. The story was then handed down until it reached Plato sometime around the year 400 B.C.

- Plato also gives a detailed description of what Atlantis looked like, including that it was built of concentric and alternating rings of land and water, with specific measurements of various parts of the city and so on.
  - It's true that Plato uses the people and the island of Atlantis in these two short pieces to describe what he thinks the perfect city and society might look like, which means there is no reason to believe that we could actually find the island.

  - However, it's also true that the eruption of Santorini would have been both heard and felt as far away as Egypt. Egyptians would also have seen the cloud resulting from the eruption, and eventually, they would have seen pieces of pumice floating on the water and ending up on the northern shores.

  - Moreover, if the Minoans and the Cycladic islanders, from such places as Santorini, stopped coming to Egypt at least temporarily after the eruption, as seems quite likely to have happened, then to the Egyptians it would have seemed as if a great island empire had "disappeared in the depths of the sea … in a single day and night of misfortune."

Suggested Reading

Doumas, *Thera*.

Luce, *End of Atlantis*.

Marinatos, *Art and Religion in Thera*.

Questions to Consider

1. What (or where) do you think is being represented in the Miniature Fresco? What islands or port cities are shown? Could this be a visual depiction of an actual event?

2. Could the eruption of Santorini be the kernel of truth underlying the myth of Atlantis?

Lecture 12 Transcript: Santorini, Akrotiri, and the Atlantis Myth

One of the things that archaeologists must combat is the claims of pseudo-archaeologists. These are enthusiastic amateurs with little or no training in archaeology who go searching every year for things like Noah's Ark or the Ark of the Covenant and sites like Atlantis. They also include those who see aliens everywhere, or at least their influence at the Sphinx in Egypt or Neolithic sites like Göbekli Tepe in Turkey. It's gotten so bad that one of my favorite tongue-in-cheek axioms in archaeology has now been adapted to account for this: One stone is a stone; two stones is a feature; three stones is a wall; four stones is a building; five stones is a palace; six stones is a palace built by aliens.

Now, one of the favorite places for pseudo-archaeologists to search for is the lost island of Atlantis. It gets found nearly every year, in places from the Bahamas to off the coast of Cyprus, but none of these reported discoveries ever pans out. Personally, I think this is because the island is probably in plain sight and always had been. I, and many other archaeologists, suspect that the kernel of truth underlying the myth of Atlantis might be the volcanic eruption of the Greek island of Santorini in the middle of the second millennium B.C.

I'll explain why this is a good possibility towards the end of this lecture. But for now let me also say that, even if the eruption of the island is not what underlies the story of Atlantis, the excavation of the site of Akrotiri on Santorini has shed very interesting and important light upon the Bronze Age Aegean at a time when the Minoans were engaged in contact and trade with places like Egypt and Canaan in the Eastern Mediterranean. It's also long been one of my favorite places to visit ever since I went there in 1980. There's excellent archaeology to see; spectacular beaches with your choice of white, red, or black sand; great views of the sunset as you enjoy dinner in a seafood restaurant in the main town of Firá; and excellent wine grown in vineyards on the island itself.

So, let me locate us geographically before we go any further. If we head north from the island of Crete and travel about 70 miles by boat, we'll reach the island of Santorini. We can also get there now by flying from Athens or other points of origin, but the best way to get there, at least in my opinion, is by boat, because it's so dramatic when you sail in to the caldera—that is, the huge crater in the middle of the volcano.

Now, the name Santorini for the island is actually fairly recent; it was named that by the Venetians, after Saint Irene. An older name, frequently used by archaeologists, is Thera, which the Greek historian Herodotus says comes from the name of a Spartan commander named Theras who was the leader of a colony that was established there during the first millennium B.C. Even before that, the island was called Kalliste, meaning the beautiful one or the fair one, which Herodotus says was the name that the Phoenicians gave to the island. Now some suggest that the very first name of the island might have been Strongili, which translates as the Round One, and that makes a lot of sense, because it was originally circular in shape. It's actually a volcano and it's still active today.

Sometime during the mid-2nd millennium, most likely in either the 17th or the 16th century B.C., the volcano blew its top. It scattered ash and pumice primarily to the south and the east. The explosion is said to have been 4 or 5 times more powerful than the explosion of Krakatoa that took place in 1883. Archaeologists and geologists have found the pumice in excavations and at the bottom of lakes in places ranging from Crete to Egypt to Turkey.

Now, the entire middle part of the island is completely gone as a result, with only the outer part remaining as an incomplete circle of land. The circle is broken in two parts, which is where tons of water rushed in from the Aegean Sea to fill up the caldera, which is hundreds of feet deep. That in turn most likely created a tidal wave, or a tsunami, that affected places as far away as Crete. In the middle of the caldera today are several small islands that have popped up just in the last century as a result of the ongoing volcanic activity. Today, tourists can take a boat out to these little islands and hike on them, though the rocks are very hot and everything stinks of sulfur, with an odor like rotting eggs. I've gone once or twice over the years, but it's not my favorite thing to do, to be perfectly honest.

So, let's say that you've come by boat to Santorini and have arrived at the Old Port—that's as opposed to the New Port, which is not as interesting, or even the airport, which is even less interesting. Your boat ties up at the modern dock that's about 300 feet below the modern city of Firá. There are three ways of getting to the top and this—this is where your adventure begins. Now, the easiest way, and the least exciting, is to just take the cable car up to the top. If you're lugging suitcases, of course, you're going to have to do this, but otherwise it's not the most interesting way.

The second and the third ways involve negotiating a narrow road. It's essentially a paved path, which will take you up to the top via a series of switchbacks. Now, unless you're James Bond riding a motorcycle, your choices are to either walk up or to ride a donkey. I highly recommend riding the donkey, because otherwise you're going to be stepping in gifts that the donkeys have left behind, if you get my drift. On the other hand, if you're riding the donkeys, they have a distinct propensity for walking as close to the inside wall as possible and trying to scrape you off. Actually, now that I think about it, riding the cable car might not be such a bad idea after all.

In any event, once you've made it up to the main city, check into your hotel, and then proceed to the archaeological site of Akrotiri just as soon as you can. The site is now open once again, after having been closed for a number of years after the original protective roof collapsed and killed a British tourist in 2005.

Akrotiri, which is one of the most wonderful sites that I've ever visited, is frequently called the Pompeii of the Aegean because the ancient town was buried under a deep ash layer by the volcanic eruption. In fact, in some places on the island, the ash layer is so thick that it is quarried today for use in things like cement. The houses in Akrotiri are still standing to the second-story in some places, and it's as if life simply stopped in a single instant more than 3,500 years ago.

In fact, it's clear from some of the remains that have been found during the excavation that the site might have been nearly abandoned by the time of the final eruption. There are indications that a major earthquake, or perhaps multiple earthquakes, might have hit the island about a decade before the final destruction, and that at least some of the inhabitants had tried to repair the damage. We know that earthquakes frequently precede eruptions, and the ancients might have known that as well. Since no human remains and only a few objects made out of gold or other precious materials have yet been found despite nearly 50 years of excavation, I suspect that most of the inhabitants cleared out long before the final end, taking their most valuable and easily transportable belongings with them. However, they still left behind plenty of things for us to find.

Now, the Greek archaeologist Spyridon Marinatos gets credit for discovering the site, but it actually wasn't all that hard to find. A portion of the site was in a gully, down which water would flow every time it rained. That water had washed away much of the ash in that area, so that some pieces of the site could readily be seen. The excavations began in 1967.

However, Marinatos had wanted to start the excavations for nearly 30 years by that point, ever since he had published an article in the journal *Antiquity* back in 1939. In that article, he had suggested that the Minoan civilization on Crete had been brought to an end, or at least dramatically and adversely affected, by an eruption of Santorini at some point during the second millennium B.C. These days, we basically take this as a given, but in 1939 it was such a radical suggestion that the editors only agreed to publish the article if they were allowed to add a note at the beginning suggesting that he should undertake excavations in order to test his hypothesis.

At any rate, Marinatos directed the Akrotiri excavations from 1967 until his death in 1974. Rumors abound as to the cause of his death. The official verdict was that it was caused by a massive stroke, which resulted in him tumbling off the balk and into a trench, where he died, but I've also heard suggestions that he might have been pushed by an irate workman. At any rate, he's buried at the site, though again I'm told it took several efforts before a proper grave could be dug because they kept hitting remains from the ancient site. Marinatos made discoveries from the very first day that he began digging. The excavations continued after his death and are today led by the well-known archaeologist Christos Doumas. Even though the site has been continuously excavated for nearly 50 years at this point, it's estimated that only a small percentage of the ancient town has actually been uncovered.

Lecture 12 Transcript—Santorini, Akrotiri, and the Atlantis Myth

In many places, a similar situation to that seen at Pompeii was encountered, in which the original wood or other organic material had decomposed, leaving an empty space in the now-hardened volcanic ash. Into those spaces, excavators have either poured cement or plaster of Paris, which is then colored brown to imitate the original wood. In this way, the buildings remain preserved up to their second storey and sometimes beyond, just as Marinatos and Doumas found them, and yet are still rendered safe for both the tourists and the archaeologists who wander among them. In some places, if the ruins were painted white and blue, the ancient town would be virtually indistinguishable from one of the modern villages on the island.

The excavation techniques used at Akrotiri are the usual, with the digging done using trowels, pickaxes, and dental tools, depending upon the delicacy needed in each situation. There's not really much stratigraphy to speak of, since you're just digging straight down through a very deep ash layer that was all laid down at about the same time, but it's still time-consuming and detailed work that demands good knees, a strong back, and attention to detail.

The ash is everywhere, having gone into every nook and cranny of the site, but as a result, it's preserved everything just as it was at the time of the explosion. So, large storage jars still remain and can be excavated in place, though often tipped or fallen over from their original position, and other large artifacts, like wooden beds, can be carefully excavated and retrieved, sometimes using that plaster of Paris technique where they've disintegrated and left empty spaces in the ash. In some places, though, the weight of the ash collapsed things in the ancient town. I'm thinking here specifically of one staircase in which the stone slabs that formed the stairs cracked in half, most likely because of the weight of the ash that was on them, though it's also possible that the damage was caused by an associated earthquake which might have accompanied the eruption.

Now, quite a bit of pottery has been recovered during the excavations, as well as objects made out of stone and other materials. Some of these, especially the pottery, are painted with marine scenes, featuring dolphins and octopi. Others show nature scenes, including flowers, and leaves, and long-stemmed grass, and even flying birds that look a lot like the swallows that can still be seen on the island even today.

There are also wall paintings that adorn the rooms in some of the houses. One of these, which features papyrus plants in a naturalistic scene that covers all four walls of the room, also has two of these little swallows interacting, just like you can see outside the site today.

In fact, the wall paintings of Akrotiri are among the best preserved that we have from the Bronze Age Aegean, rivaling those found by Sir Arthur Evans at Knossos. One of my favorites is the so-called Nilotic Fresco, which features a scene that might be depicting the Nile River in Egypt. It's got a leaping feline in it that might be chasing a duck or goose that can be seen in front of it. On both sides of the river, or the stream, are what look like palm trees or perhaps papyrus plants. It was found in a house—the so-called West House—along with several other frescoes that have nautical or perhaps non-Theran scenes, so it's possible that the house belonged to a ship captain or to somebody who had traveled overseas.

Now, another rather exotic-looking wall painting shows monkeys swinging from trees and generally hanging about, as monkeys like to do. The only thing is these monkeys are blue, with white cheeks, which seems a little bit strange. And yet there's a similar wall painting at Knossos on Crete, which also shows blue monkeys. Now, I've done a little investigation into this topic, because of two little blue monkey figurines with yellow cheeks that were found at Mycenae and Tiryns on the Greek mainland. And it turns out that there is a particular species of monkey in Africa that's called a green guenon, whose fur can be a bluish-green color and who have yellow or whitish cheeks.

They're found in areas like Nubia and were prized as pets by the pharaohs of New Kingdom Egypt, who occasionally sent them as gifts to rulers in other countries. So, strange as it might seem, it looks like these paintings are actually correct in their representations of the monkeys, and that they may represent a group of monkeys that someone had either seen in Egypt, or might have actually been sent to either Santorini or Crete from Egypt.

One painting that seems a masterpiece to me shows two animals that look like ibexes, or wild goats, typically found on islands like Crete. These two in particular are painted with a single bold stroke that goes from the tip of the tail all the way up to the neck and then the head of the animal, with the other details then added in as bold lines as well. This just seems like masterful simplicity to me, which completely captures the two animals.

There are also a number of human figures depicted. One shows two young boys who seem to be boxing. They're almost naked, wearing only what look like loincloths, and they've got shaved heads with clumps of hair hanging down in curls. Where their hair is cut close to the scalp, it's shown as blue rather than black. Now, there's a painting of a slightly older boy, or rather a young man, who's shown completely naked and holding two long strings of fish that he has just caught. This painting shows even more of his hair shaved off and fewer of those tendrils or ringlets, so it's been suggested that the young boys had perhaps more and more of their hair shaved off each year, perhaps in a ritual, so that by the time they were in their late teens, they essentially had a crew cut. I like this idea, though I would certainly admit that there's no way we can actually prove it.

Other pictures show women engaged in a variety of activities, including a number that are picking flowers like crocuses and saffron. One of these looks just like my wife, and I used to tease her about that when we first got married. Some of these young women also have mostly shaved heads, just like the boys, so if there was some sort of age-related ceremony related to hair, it apparently extended to the young women as well as the men. Many of the women are wearing earrings or other jewelry, along with elaborate dresses, so we can easily try to reconstruct what they were wearing and adorning themselves with even though it was way back then.

Now, in the same house that has the Nilotic scene, the so-called West House, there's another painting, which is known as the Miniature Fresco or the Flotilla Fresco. This is another one of my favorites for a variety of reasons, including the amount of detail that we can see, along with the mystery of what location is actually being depicted. On one end of the scene, we can see warriors marching off to battle. They're dressed like some of the warriors that Homer describes in the *Iliad*—they're wearing boar's tusk helmets and carrying what are called tower shields. Those are shields that are so long that they cover the person from their neck all the way down to their lower legs. Behind the warriors is a large building, with women standing on the roof apparently waving goodbye to the warriors.

There are also what look like herd animals and a herdsman in the distance above them, but below them is a scene with a few boats and men who are sideways or upside-down, and that's the way to depict dead and drowning men. Now this is usually interpreted as a naval battle, though one archaeologist has suggested that it might be a scene of sacrifice. I tend to go with the naval battle interpretation, though I don't see anybody that they're fighting—we've just got the upside-down and sideways people.

But wait; there's more. The fresco continues with a flotilla scene, showing as many as a dozen or more ships departing from a port on an island that may or may not be Santorini, with the men then rowing their way across the sea accompanied by cavorting dolphins, until they reach a second city, at which point they tie up the ships and presumably disembark. Now this part of the fresco has been the topic of much discussion among archaeologists, with some focusing on the design and depiction of the ships and others focusing on where they might have begun their voyage and where they might have ended it. Suggestions include, as you might expect, that this is a voyage to and from Egypt, or a voyage to and from Anatolia—that is, Turkey—but other possibilities have been suggested as well.

Santorini has been at the forefront of a huge debate among Bronze Age Aegean archaeologists ever since about 1987. That was when a radical redating of the eruption was proposed. It used to be thought that the Santorini eruption took place in about 1450 B.C. It also used to be thought, and actually still is, that the eruption took place at a time when a certain style of pottery known as Late Helladic or Late Minoan Ib pottery was in vogue. Thus, whenever LH or LM Ib pottery as we call it has been found, that level at that site was dated to about 1450 B.C. But, as a result of new studies of radiocarbon dating, as well as information based on other analyses, it was proposed that the eruption actually took place in or around 1628 B.C., rather than 1450. Since the eruption and that type of pottery are still tied together, though, that means that any level at any site that has this LH/LM Ib pottery actually dates to the 17th century and not the 15th century. Raising it up this way, this became known as the high chronology.

Now, not all archaeologists are fans of radiocarbon dating, and still others acknowledge that there are problems with it, so not everybody has accepted this change in chronology. Some people are willing to accept a bit of a change, but only pushing the date of the eruption back to about 1550, rather than all the way back to 1628 B.C.

Sturt Manning, now of Cornell University, has been at the forefront of these discussions for nearly 25 years, since they first began. He has published numerous articles on the subject, as well as a book called *A Test of Time*. One of the articles was based on the discovery of a piece of wood from an olive tree that had been buried by ash during the eruption. The olive wood dates to about 1628 B.C.

So, for me, there's no question that the high chronology is correct, but the debate is ongoing. I'm highlighting this here to show you especially that, even when we have lots of buildings, and pottery, and other artifacts from a site, and even when we know relatively when it was flourishing, we can't always be certain about the absolute, or chronological, date. And to be honest, that's in part what makes it fun, though. If everything were cut and dried, it would be a lot more boring.

But, Santorini and Akrotiri are never boring, that's for sure, at least to my mind. In part that's because the discoveries made there are central to any discussions we have about international trade and contact that might have been ongoing between Greece, Egypt, and the Near East 3,500 years ago. But they're also not boring because of the possible connections to the legend of Atlantis.

Now, here's where I should tell you—if you haven't guessed it already by this point—that I do tend to believe that there is a kernel of truth lying at the bottom of many of the Greek myths and legends. So, I think something did happen to spark the stories about the Trojan War. I also think that the sporting events that took place in the palace at Knossos, like bull leaping, and the layout of the palace and its ruins, gave rise to the myth of Theseus and the Minotaur. And I also think that the eruption of Santorini may be the real event that underlies the whole story of Atlantis. Now here, I admit, I am dangerously close to being in the realm of the pseudo-archaeologist, hunting for what may be fictional places, but I'll tell you briefly why I believe what I do.

For those who don't recall, or need a bit of memory touch-up, let me remind you that the story of Atlantis comes to us courtesy of the Greek philosopher Plato. In two of his shorter works, the *Timaeus* and the *Critias*, Plato tells us about a place with awesome warriors who dared to fight against Athens, but whose home sank beneath the waves, never to be seen again. In the *Timaeus* Plato says specifically:

> There occurred violent earthquakes and floods; and in a single day and night of misfortune all your warlike men in a body sank into the earth, and the island of Atlantis in like manner disappeared into the depths of the sea.

Now, the initial story of Atlantis, Plato says, was told by an Egyptian priest to a visiting Greek lawgiver named Solon sometime after 590 B.C. The priest told Solon that the events had taken place 9,000 years before that time, though many people today think that 900 years fits better, because that puts the events back in about 1500 B.C., rather than back in the Neolithic Age. The story was then handed down by Solon to his son, and then to his son's son, and so on, until it reached Plato somewhere around the year 400 B.C.

Plato also gives a very detailed description of what Atlantis looked like, including that it was built of concentric and alternating rings of land and water, with specific measurements of various parts of the city and so on. But since his description of its location is pretty general, people have looked for it in all sorts of places, including, like I said at the beginning of this lecture, from the Bahamas to off the coast of Cyprus and everywhere in between.

Now, one could argue that since Plato is using the people and the island of Atlantis in these two short pieces in order to describe what he thinks the perfect city and the perfect society might look like, there's actually no reason to believe that we could go and find it—he may have just made it up. And I would agree with this to a certain extent.

However, I would also point out that the eruption of Santorini would have been both heard and felt as far away as Egypt. Egyptians would also have seen the cloud resulting from the eruption and eventually they would have seen pieces of pumice floating on the water and ending up on the northern shores. There's even been a suggestion by some scholars that a well-known Egyptian inscription called the Tempest Stele may be a contemporary account of what they saw and heard during and after the eruption.

Moreover, if the Minoans and the Cycladic islanders from places like Santorini stopped coming to Egypt at least temporarily after the eruption, as seems quite likely to have happened, then to the Egyptians it would have seemed as if a great island empire had "disappeared in the depths of the sea in a single day and night of misfortune." Indeed, from the point of view of those who had been living in Akrotiri and perhaps elsewhere on the island, their world had indeed come to an end in a single day and night of misfortune.

And so, while I'm not at all certain that we're ever going to find Noah's Ark, or the Ark of the Covenant, or the Holy Grail, I will gently suggest that, in this case, the eruption of Santorini might lie at the basis of our story of Atlantis. And even if it doesn't, the archaeological finds that have been made at the site of Akrotiri by Marinatos, Doumas, and others have shed wonderful light on the Bronze Age Aegean during the second millennium B.C., which I think is among the most fascinating time periods during human history.

Lecture 13

The Uluburun Shipwreck

The Uluburun shipwreck, which sank off the coast of southwestern Turkey around 1300 B.C., is one of the most important archaeological discoveries of all times. It was found with a full cargo of raw materials and finished goods that shed light on the international trade and relations that took place more than 3,000 years ago. The fact that it was found in 1982 by a 17-year-old sponge diver on his first season of diving and that archaeologists conducted more than 20,000 dives to explore it over the course of a decade without a major accident makes it an even more amazing story.

George Bass: The Father of Underwater Archaeology

- In 1959, while he was still a graduate student, George Bass did the first underwater excavation on what is now known as the Cape Gelidonya shipwreck. The Gelidonya shipwreck is actually located reasonably close to the Uluburun shipwreck, though of course, Bass didn't know that at the time. It also dates from almost the same time period, about 1200 B.C.

- On the Gelidonya wreck, Bass found artifacts indicating that this small ship had probably been "tramping" around the Mediterranean, that is, going from port to port and buying and selling goods as it went. It does not appear to have belonged to a wealthy merchant or a king but, more likely, to a private individual trying to earn a living. Among the objects that Bass retrieved were ingots of solid copper that are now called *oxhide ingots* because they are in the shape of a cow or ox hide that someone might hang on a wall or use as a rug.

- Based on the artifacts he excavated, Bass also identified the wreck as a Canaanite ship, possibly on its way to the Aegean. This went against the scholarly thinking of the day because it was generally thought that only the Minoans on Crete might have been sailing the seas. Thus, when Bass published his book on the shipwreck in 1967, it was met with derision and disdain in some scholarly quarters.

However, Bass was not only correct on all counts, but he was far ahead of his time in recognizing that others besides the Minoans had sailed the seas.

- In 1972, Bass founded the American Institute of Nautical Archaeology; the institute is now located at Texas A&M University and has dropped the "American" from its name to reflect the international nature of its work.

Discovery of the Uluburun Shipwreck

- In 1982, news of the discovery of an oxhide ingot by a young man diving off the coast of Turkey made its way to Bass's institute. The next summer, Bass and his colleagues conducted preliminary dives and identified artifacts that dated the wreck to the Late Bronze Age. They had found what is now known as the Uluburun shipwreck.

- Sponsored by National Geographic, the excavation of the Uluburun shipwreck began in earnest during the summer of 1984, under Bass's direction. The next year, in 1985, he turned the project over to Cemal Pulak. From then until 1994, excavations were conducted virtually every summer, with a team of professional archaeologists and eager graduate students. Collectively, the dove on the wreck more than 22,500 times in 10 years.

- The top part of the wreck was 140 feet below sea level, but it continued down to 170 feet. The front part of the 50-foot-long ship had broken off and plunged off a cliff or ledge; it has never been recovered.

- The divers removed their flippers when they got to the bottom to avoid accidentally excavating by swimming too close to the sand on the sea floor. Team members used vacuums and their hands to remove loose sand.

- Each part of the wreck and each of the objects found within it were meticulously mapped by the archaeologists. Bass claimed that their final plans were as accurate, within a matter of millimeters,

Work on the finds of the Uluburun shipwreck was done at Turkey's Bodrum Museum of Underwater Archaeology.

as any plan done at an archaeological site on land. The teams found so many objects that the final report is still being written and will take up several volumes when it is finally published. In the meantime, Bass and Pulak have published numerous preliminary reports and presented papers at many conferences. They were also featured in a cover story in the December 1987 issue of *National Geographic*.

- In order to dive on the wreck, the team lived all season long in wooden buildings that they constructed on the cliff face of the promontory into which the Uluburun ship had probably slammed before it sank more than 3,000 years ago. There was also some space on their dive boat, the *Virazon*, which was permanently moved directly above the shipwreck. Every morning, a man from the port town of Kas sailed out to bring them fresh water, food, and oxygen tanks.

History of the Ship

- The ship sank in about 1300 B.C., about 30 years after the time of King Tut in Egypt and perhaps a few decades before the time of the Trojan War. This date was arrived at through several independent methods.
    - First, a gold scarab of Queen Nefertiti was found. She ruled with Pharaoh Akhenaten sometime around 1350 B.C., which means that the ship cannot have sunk before that time.

    - Second, some of the wood from the hull of the ship was recovered, and the tree rings on some of these pieces can be counted and linked to the broader scheme of dendrochronology. The rings indicate that the last time the tree was growing before it was cut down was about 1320 B.C.

    - Third, the Mycenaean and Minoan pottery on board is of a style called Late Helladic IIIA2, which archaeologists date to the last part of the 14th century B.C.

- When the wreck was first found, the excavators thought that the ship had probably been sailing around the Eastern Mediterranean and Aegean regions in a counterclockwise direction. They envisioned it tramping as the Gelidonya ship would do a century later, but with a cargo that was much richer. Since then, other suggestions have been made, including the possibility that it carried cargo meant as a royal gift from one king to another, perhaps being sent from Egypt, Canaan, or Cyprus to Greece.
    - In every case, it is agreed that the ship was heading to Greece because, although there are objects on board that come from at least seven different cultures and that are clearly meant as cargo, the only objects from Greece are a number of Minoan and Mycenaean ceramic vessels that are used, rather than new,

and two personal seals that would have been worn by someone from the Aegean.

- ○ Thus, it is generally agreed that the ship was heading for the Aegean with a cargo of goods that was primarily from Egypt and the Near East. On its return trip or, perhaps, on the continuation of its trip counterclockwise around the region, it probably would have carried a full cargo of Mycenaean and Minoan goods, including ceramic vessels full of wine, olive oil, and perfume destined for Egypt, Canaan, and Cyprus.

- ○ Of course, it never made that return voyage because it sank at Uluburun. Interestingly, no bodies or partial skeletons have been recovered from the shipwreck. It may be that the survivors swam to shore or that their bodies fell victim to wildlife in the sea.

Finds on the Ship
- At the bottom of the ship and running the length of the hull were approximately 14 large stone anchors. These were used as ballast for most of the journey, but as one was needed, it was put to use. If one of the anchors got stuck on a rock or a reef, the sailors could simply cut the rope and let it go, then retrieve another one from the cargo hull.

- The main cargo was 350 oxhide ingots of 99 percent pure raw copper from Cyprus. All told, there was more than 10 tons of copper on board this one ship. The Uluburun shipwreck also contained more than a ton of tin, ranging from fragments of oxhide ingots, to a smaller type of ingot called a *bun ingot*, to plates and other vessels made of tin. The origin of the tin seems to have been the Badakhshan region of Afghanistan.

- Also on board was approximately 1 ton of terebinth resin, which was used as incense and for making perfume, among other things. The resin was stored in some of the 140 Canaanite storage jars that were on board. Other jars held glass beads and probably food, such as figs and dates.

- One jar held a small folding wooden tablet with ivory hinges, known as a *diptych*. It probably floated into the jar by accident after the ship sank. Inside the tablet, the two sides would have originally held wax, on which messages could be written. By the end of the excavations, two such tablets had been found, but the wax was gone in both.

- Other raw goods on the ship included approximately 175 bun ingots of raw glass; most were dark cobalt blue, but others were light blue or amber. When chemically analyzed, these ingots of raw glass matched objects of glass in both Egypt and Greece from this time period, indicating that all these regions probably got their raw glass from the same source, possibly in northern Syria or Egypt. The ship also carried raw ivory, including both elephant tusks and hippopotamus canines and incisors.

- Among the finished goods on board the ship were large jars filled with new pottery, such as plates, bowls, jugs, and oil lamps. At least three swords were found on board, probably personal possessions of the crewmembers. There were also arrowheads and spearheads, various bronze tools, fishhooks, and lead weights. A strange-looking stone item may be a mace from the Balkans. Also found were a few fancy drinking cups, made of faience and in zoomorphic shapes. These are usually identified as items used by royalty, which may support the idea that the ship was carrying a gift from one king to another.

- The gold scarab of Queen Nefertiti mentioned earlier was one of many pieces of jewelry, ranging from silver bracelets to gold pendants, found by Bass, Pulak, and their team members. The scarab is inscribed with Nefertiti's name in hieroglyphics: Neferneferuaten. However, she used this version of her name only during the first five years or so of her reign, when her husband, the heretic pharaoh Akhenaten, was outlawing the worship of all gods except Aten. This is an extremely rare find and one, as we have noted, that helps date the ship; it cannot have sunk before the scarab was made—prior to about 1348 B.C.

Suggested Reading

Bass, "Oldest Known Shipwreck Reveals Splendors of the Bronze Age."

Pulak, "The Uluburun Shipwreck."

———, "Shipwreck."

Questions to Consider

1. Considering how much the discovery of this single ship has affected our knowledge of the Late Bronze Age in the Aegean and eastern Mediterranean, how likely is it that additional discoveries will significantly alter our understanding of the region and area? In what ways might such discoveries change or enhance our understanding?

2. Why weren't any bodies found on board the Uluburun shipwreck?

Lecture 13 Transcript
The Uluburun Shipwreck

The Uluburun shipwreck, which sank off the coast of southwestern Turkey in about 1300 B.C., is one of the most important archaeological discoveries of all time. It was found with a full cargo of raw materials and finished goods that shed light on the international trade and the relations that were taking place more than 3,000 years ago. The fact that it was found in 1982 by a 17-year-old sponge diver on his very first season of diving ever, and that archaeologists conducted more than 20,000 dives over the course of a decade without a major accident reported, makes it an even more amazing story.

The shipwreck is also near and dear to my heart because I wrote my Ph.D. dissertation on the international trade and relations between Greece and Egypt and the Near East during the Late Bronze Age. So, visiting the site of this shipwreck, which is a physical embodiment of the international connections of that period, was like going on a pilgrimage for me. I went twice during the late 1980s, once to the site of the ship itself, off the Uluburun promontory, and once to Turkey's Bodrum Museum of Underwater Archaeology where they were working on the finds. Oh, and I also got engaged to my wife while en route to visit the shipwreck, which is another reason why I love it. Now, perhaps I should have actually put that first in my account.

But, the story is not about me; rather it's about George Bass, the father of underwater archaeology, and Cemal Pulak, who was first Bass's student and now is his colleague at the Institute of Nautical Archaeology at Texas A&M University.

But, I need to begin the story back in 1959, when George Bass was himself a graduate student at the University of Pennsylvania. According to one story, which may or may not be apocryphal, he was looking around for a dissertation topic when Rodney Young, the Curator of the Mediterranean Section of the Penn Museum, called him into his office. It seems that a shipwreck had been found off the coast of Turkey, and someone was needed to excavate it. Young thought that Bass was the perfect person to do it, but Bass protested that he didn't know how to dive. "I know," Young replied. "That's why I've made you an appointment at the YMCA to take scuba lessons. You begin this afternoon." Now, I have got no way to actually ascertain if that's a true story, but it sounds pretty plausible.

So, Bass went out and did the world's first underwater excavation on what is now known as the Cape Gelidonya shipwreck. That's why he's referred to as the father of underwater archaeology. Now, the Gelidonya shipwreck is actually located reasonably close to the Uluburun shipwreck, though of course Bass didn't know that at the time. And it actually dates from almost the same time period because Gelidonya went down about 1200 B.C.

Now, on the Gelidonya wreck, Bass found artifacts that indicated it had been a small ship and was probably tramping around the Mediterranean—that is, going from port to port, buying and selling goods as it went. It doesn't seem to have belonged to a wealthy merchant or a king—more likely it was a private individual just trying to earn a living. Now, among the objects that Bass retrieved were ingots of solid copper, what we now call oxhide ingots, because they're in the shape of a cow or ox hide that you might hang on a wall or use as a rug. These copper ingots each weighed about 60 pounds or so.

Now, this ship dated to the end of the Late Bronze Age. And since you make bronze by combining 90 percent copper and 10 percent tin, it would make sense if there were also raw tin on board, right? Well, that's precisely what Bass found. Unfortunately, most of the tin now looked more like toothpaste, rather than raw tin and some scholars doubted his identification.

He also identified the wreck, based on artifacts that he excavated, as a Canaanite ship possibly on its way to the Aegean. Now, this went very much against the scholarly thinking of the day, especially since it was generally thought that only the Minoans on Crete might have been sailing the seas—after all, Thucydides talks about the Minoan thalassocracy or their rule of the sea. And so, when Bass published his book on the Gelidonya shipwreck in 1967, it was met with derision and disdain in some scholarly quarters. However, Bass was not only correct on all counts, but he was far ahead of his time in recognizing that others—besides the Minoans—had been sailing the seas.

Now, according to the reports that I've heard, Bass swore that he would find another wreck at some point that would confirm his conclusions about the Gelidonya shipwreck.

In the meantime, he founded the American Institute of Nautical Archaeology in 1972, while he was still at the University of Pennsylvania, and then he moved with it to Texas A&M University in 1976, where it—and he—have remained ever since, though they long ago dropped the American from their name, to reflect the international nature of their work.

So, in 1980, the Institute purchased a boat, and they began doing underwater surveys, searching for other shipwrecks. But, underwater surveys can be long and time-consuming, especially back then in the 1980s, when you surveyed as if you were on land, by following long transects and recording what you saw.

At some point, they had the bright idea that they could simply visit the villages in which the Turkish sponge divers lived and describe to them what they were looking for. That way, they could enlist the help of a lot of people who were diving to the bottom of the sea on a daily basis anyway.

And sure enough, in 1982, the young sponge diver on his very first season ever, emerged from the water and told his captain that he had seen a metal biscuit with ears. And when he drew a picture of it, the captain recognized it as one of the oxhide ingots that the archaeologists had told him to keep an eye out for. He contacted the Institute, and that next summer Bass and his colleagues conducted preliminary dives and identified artifacts that dated the wreck to the Late Bronze Age. They had found what is now known as the Uluburun shipwreck.

So Bass was on his way towards excavating another wreck that would confirm his conclusions about the Gelidonya shipwreck. What he didn't recognize at the time was that the Uluburun shipwreck was far richer and far more important than what he had found previously. The importance of his discovery can be measured by the fact that just a few years later, in 1986, and long before the culmination of the excavations, Bass was given the Gold Medal Award for Distinguished Archaeological Achievement from the Archaeological Institute of America. That's the highest honor that his colleagues could bestow. Nobody was scoffing anymore.

Sponsored by National Geographic, the excavation of the Uluburun shipwreck began in earnest during the summer of 1984, under Bass's direction. The next year, in 1985, he turned over direction of the project to Cemal Pulak. And from then until 1994, excavations were conducted virtually every summer, with a team of professional archaeologists and eager graduate students. They dove on the wreck every day, with each of them diving two times per day, but only spending about 20 minutes on the bottom each time. Even with such short individual dives, they collectively worked for more than 6,600 hours excavating the ship during those 10 years, since they dove on it more than 22,000 times.

It turned out that the top part of the wreck was 140 feet below sea level, but it continued on down to 170 feet below the surface, and even then, the front part of the 50-foot-long ship had broken off and plunged off a cliff or a ledge, and it's never been recovered. Now, at that depth, working between 140 and 170 feet below the surface, Bass says that it feels like you've had two martinis before even beginning work, so they had to plan out every dive meticulously in advance. They also dove in pairs, using the buddy system, and had an ex-Navy SEAL overseeing their safety, which explains the lack of reported accidents even over the course of a decade.

They removed their flippers when they got to the bottom, so they wouldn't accidentally excavate by swimming too close to the sand on the sea bottom. Team members used vacuums to remove a lot of the loose sand, but then moved their hand in a bit of a continuous scooping motion when they had to remove the sand carefully, not waving it back and forth—that does nothing—but scooping it in one direction.

Each part of the wreck and each of the objects found within it was meticulously mapped by the archaeologists. Bass claimed that their final plans were as accurate, within a matter of millimeters, as any plan done at an archaeological site on land, and I believe him. It's hard enough to do that well on land; I can't even begin to imagine doing it at 140 feet below the surface and feeling like I've had a two-martini lunch.

In any event, they found so many objects that the final report is still being written and will take up several volumes when it's finally published. In the meantime, though, Bass and Pulak have published numerous preliminary reports and presented papers at many conferences, which have since been published. They were also featured in a cover story in the December 1987 issue of *National Geographic*, which remains one of my favorite all-time issues for just that reason.

Now, when that issue came out, back in 1987, I was working on my dissertation in Greece, so I first saw it for sale in the Brussels Airport, en route back to the United States for the winter holidays. I bought a copy on the spot, even though the newsstand charged me the exorbitant price of $10, which was more than I usually spent in a week on my graduate student stipend. I tell my students that now, every time I see a copy of that issue in a used bookstore for a dime or a quarter, I buy it—just to make the cost of that initial purchase and have it come down a bit when averaged out. I've probably got about two dozen copies of that issue by this point.

Anyway, in order to dive on the wreck, the team lived all season long in wooden buildings that they constructed on the cliff face of the promontory into which the Uluburun ship had probably slammed before it sank more than 3,000 years ago. There was also some space on board their dive ship, the *Virazon*, which was permanently moored directly above the shipwreck. In these accommodations, the team truly lived off the grid, several hours boat ride away from the nearest town or city.

Every morning, though, a man from the port town of Kas sailed out to bring them fresh water, food, and oxygen tanks. And that's how my wife and I got to the site when we visited in the late 1980s, by hitching a ride with him early one morning. It was an amazing journey, across a still, black sea at three am, with a complete lunar eclipse above us. We had gotten engaged the afternoon before, which made it even more special—truly a moment to treasure.

So, to put the wreck into chronological context, when it sank in about 1300 B.C., that was just about 30 years after the time of King Tut in Egypt and perhaps a few decades before the time of the Trojan War. As I've said, it's a microcosm of the international connections and trade that were going on at that time. We know when it sank because of several independent ways of dating this event. First, there's a gold scarab of Queen Nefertiti, which we'll talk about at greater length in a moment. She ruled with Pharaoh Akhenaten sometime around 1350 B.C., so the ship can't have sunk before that time.

Secondly, some of the wood from the hull of the ship was recovered. And the tree rings on some of the pieces can be counted and can be linked to the broader scheme of dendrochronology, as it's called. These indicate that the last rings, that is, the last time that the tree was growing before it was cut down was about 1320 B.C. So, again, the ship can't have gone down before then.

And, then third, the Mycenaean and Minoan pottery on board are of a style called Late Helladic IIIA2, which archaeologists date to the last part of the 14th century B.C. So, while it's possible that the ship sank a few years earlier, a date of about 1300 B.C. is undoubtedly in the ballpark.

Now, when the wreck was first found, the excavators thought that the Uluburun ship had most likely been going around and around the Eastern Mediterranean and Aegean regions, in a counterclockwise direction. They envisioned it going from port to port, perhaps tramping like the Gelidonya ship would do a century later, but with a cargo that was much, much richer.

Since then, other suggestions have been made, including the possibility that it was a cargo meant as a royal gift from one king to another, and that perhaps it was being sent from Egypt to Greece or from Canaan to Greece or even Cyprus to Greece. In every case, though, it's agreed that it was heading towards Greece because, although there are objects on board that come from at least seven different cultures and that are clearly meant as cargo, the only objects from Greece are those Minoan and Mycenaean ceramic vessels that are all used—rather than new—as well as two personal seals that would have been worn by somebody from the Aegean.

And so, it's generally agreed that the ship was probably headed for the Aegean, with a cargo of goods that was primarily from Egypt and the Near East. On its return trip, or perhaps on the continuation of its trip counterclockwise around the region, it probably would have carried a full cargo of Mycenaean and Minoan goods, including ceramic vessels full of wine, olive oil, and perfume destined for Egypt, Canaan, and Cyprus.

Of course, it never made that return voyage because it sank at Uluburun, perhaps one dark and stormy night. Interestingly, there haven't been any bodies recovered from this shipwreck or any partial skeletons at all. It might be that the survivors swam to shore or that their bodies fell victim to the fishes and other sea life while lying underwater for 3200 years.

So, just what was on the ship? As Howard Carter might have said—there were wonderful things. Let me run through the main parts of the cargo with you and let's see if you agree with me about just how spectacular it is. One thing's for sure—somebody lost a fortune when this ship went down.

First of all, at the bottom of everything, and running the length of the hull, were approximately 14 large stone anchors. These were used as ballast for most of the journey, but as each one was needed, they were put into use. That way, if one of the anchors got stuck on a rock or a reef, the sailors could simply cut the rope and let it go, and then retrieve another one from down in the cargo hull.

But the main cargo was oxhide ingots—99 percent pure raw copper from Cyprus. There were more than 350 of these ingots on board the ship, stacked row upon row in the hold. We have one letter that was written from the King of Cyprus to the King of Egypt just a little bit earlier, about 1350 B.C., in which he apologizes for sending only 200 copper ingots or talents, as he calls them. This ship shows that as many as 350 could be shipped at once during this time period.

Now, all told, there is more than 10 tons of copper on board this one ship. Some of the ingots were so corroded that the archaeologists had to essentially invent a new type of glue, which they injected into the remains of the ingot and then allowed it to harden for the entire year between excavation seasons.

And then they carefully picked up each one and floated them to the surface one at a time, before taking them back to the museum at Bodrum. There they were conserved and cleaned of the corrosion that had accumulated upon their surface.

And, remember that tin that Bass had found on the Gelidonya shipwreck—the stuff that looked like toothpaste? Well, the Uluburun ship vindicated him here as well, because it contained more than a ton of tin, this time in recognizable forms, ranging from fragments of oxhide ingots to another, smaller type of ingot that's called a bun ingot. There were also actual plates and other vessels made of tin. The tin had come a long way already because its origin seems to have been the Badakhshan region of Afghanistan.

Now, 10 tons of copper and 1 ton of tin will make 10 or 11 tons of bronze. Bass once estimated that this would have been enough to outfit an army of 300 soldiers with swords, shields, helmets, greaves, and other necessary accoutrements. Not only did somebody lose a fortune when this ship went down, but somebody might have also lost a war.

Now, there are other types of raw materials on board as well, including approximately a ton of terebinth resin. This was used as incense or for making perfume, among other things. It comes from the pistachio tree, and it's never been found in such quantities in one place before—at least as far as I know.

The resin was being carried in some of the so-called Canaanite storage jars, of which there were about 140 on board. These are just what they sound like—transportation and storage jars made in Canaan—that is, modern-day Israel, Lebanon, Syria. They could hold any number of things. On the Uluburun ship, they were found to contain not only the resin but also things like glass beads—thousands of them in some cases—as well as possibly food like figs and dates.

One jar held a small folding wooden tablet, with ivory hinges. It probably floated into the jar by accident after the ship sank. And inside the tablet, the two sides, which are recessed, would have originally held wax, possibly colored yellow by terebinth resin. On this wax would have been written some sort of message, for this is what we call a diptych or a wooden writing tablet. Homer talks about such a tablet in Book VI of the *Iliad*, when he mentions a tablet with baneful signs. Unfortunately, the wax in the Uluburun tablet is long gone—actually, by the end of the excavations, two other tablets had been found, but the wax was gone in both of those too. So, we don't know what was originally written there. It might have been the ship's itinerary. It could have been a manifest of the cargo. It could have been a message from one king to another. But, we'll never know.

There were also several other types of raw goods that were being transported on the ship. First, there were approximately 175 bun ingots of raw glass. Most of them were colored dark, cobalt blue, but others were light blue, and some were even an amber color. When they were analyzed chemically, these ingots of raw glass matched objects of glass in both Egypt and Greece from this time period, which indicated that everybody was getting their raw glass from the same source—probably up in northern Syria or maybe in Egypt, itself.

Secondly, there was raw ivory on board the ship, including both elephant tusks and hippopotamus canines and incisors. In fact, after these were discovered in the wreck, other scholars went back and re-examined ivory objects dating to the Late Bronze Age in various museums around the world. They had previously assumed that most were made from elephant ivory, but to their surprise, it seems that most are actually from hippo ivory. There was also ebony wood found as part of the cargo, which comes from Nubia.

Oh, and there was also the remains of a house mouse found, whose origins have been identified as Syrian, perhaps the coastal port of Ugarit. Although the little mouse was definitely a stowaway on board the ship, I should definitely mention him nonetheless.

And then there are all of the finished goods that were on board the ship as cargo. Principal among these was something rather unexpected. In among the remains that the archaeologists were excavating were large jars. Similar jars can be seen on the deck of Bronze Age ships like painted in scenes on the walls of high-ranking Egyptian nobles. It's always been assumed that these large jars were used to hold fresh water so that the crewmembers could drink from them.

But, when the archaeologists began to lift one up and put it into a net so it could be floated up to the surface, it tilted forward, and pottery began to spill out. And it was nice pottery—fresh, brand new, unused pottery. There were plates. There were dishes and bowls. There were big jugs. There were little juglets. There were oil lamps—all of them from Cyprus and Canaan. It seems like these jars or, at least, this one, in particular, were not used to hold drinking water after all, but were actually what we would call china barrels like used to pack and protect new pottery in transit.

There were also a couple of swords on board. One seems to be Canaanite, one is of Aegean type, and one seems to be Italian. I suspect that these are probably personal possessions of the crewmembers or the captain, but I can't be sure. There are also arrowheads and spearheads, as well as various bronze tools—all of which could either be personal possessions or they could be parts of the cargo. Fishhooks and lead weights too, those were undoubtedly, I think, used by the crewmembers to help them catch fresh fish during the voyage.

Speaking of which, the foodstuffs that have been identified from the Uluburun wreck include olives, almonds, figs, and pomegranates, in addition to fish. In other words, pretty much the same thing that a ship's crew would be eating today in that same area.

There's also a very strange-looking stone item, which is identified as a mace from the Balkans; I don't know what that's doing on board. And, there are a few fancy drinking cups, made of faience, which is this material halfway between pottery and glass. They're in zoomorphic shapes, like a ram's head. These are usually identified as items that are used by royalty. Royal drinking cups, which might support the idea that the ship was carrying a royal gift from one king to another. We know, from textual evidence, that rulers did exchange lavish gifts during this period, so it's not out of the question that we might be looking at one here, maybe sent from Egypt or Canaan to a Mycenaean king—maybe Agamemnon's ancestor at Mycenae. But again, we'll probably never know.

Now, among the items that could be construed as worthy of a king is a single gold cup. I have had the honor of holding this gold cup in my own two hands; it was much lighter than I expected it to be. But, although pretty, it's not actually of much use in determining anything about the ship or its origins or the date, because it's actually pretty generic. There is an iconic photograph, now found in almost every archaeological textbook, that was taken before the cup was removed from the seabed. Also, in the picture are a Canaanite jar, a flask made from tin, and a rather plain-looking Mycenaean kylix. When I ask my students what the most important object in the picture is, they invariably point to the gold cup. But this would be wrong. And I quote from the third Indiana Jones movie, telling them that they "have chosen…poorly." While the Canaanite jar is important for what it contained, and the flask is important because it's one of the few that we've got that's made from tin—it's actually the plain-looking Mycenaean vessel that's the most important piece in the picture, because that's one of the objects that helped us to date the wreck.

Speaking of dating the wreck, we can now return to the solid gold scarab of Queen Nefertiti that I mentioned earlier. It's one of many pieces of jewelry, ranging from silver bracelets to gold pendants that were found by Bass, Pulak, and their team members. One of the pendants is a marvelous piece of work, with granulated dots of gold creating a falcon or some other bird, clutching a snake in its claws. Another depicts a woman holding a gazelle in each hand. There's also cylinder seals from Mesopotamia, including one made from rock crystal with a gold cap on either end, and that would have been worn tied around your wrist or your neck.

Now of all the scarabs and the other small items that are engraved with Egyptian hieroglyphics, including one small piece of black stone that's inscribed, "Ptah, Lord of Truth," the most important is also one of the smallest. This is the gold scarab inscribed with Nefertiti's name in hieroglyphics: Neferneferuaten. However, this is a version of her name that she only used during the first five years or so of her reign, when her husband, the heretic Pharaoh Akhenaten, was literally condemning everything under the sun, except for Aten. This is an extremely rare find and one, as we've noted, that helps us to date the ship because the ship cannot have sunk before the scarab was made; that is prior to about 1348 B.C.

In closing, let me mention a small figurine. It's made of bronze but covered with gold foil on its head, shoulders, hands, and feet. It was found completely corroded, but it cleaned up nicely, as they say. The style of the figurine is typical of votive objects—that is, figurines created to express both religious devotion and the desire for divine protection. This might have been the protective deity on the ship. If that's the case, though, it didn't do its job very well because the ship sank. However, their bad luck was our good luck, because we're now able to study this ship and its cargo in its entirety, and to get a glimpse of what life was like during the international world of the Late Bronze Age more than 3,000 years ago.

Lecture 14: The Dead Sea Scrolls

The Dead Sea Scrolls are about 2,000 years old and constitute the oldest extant copies of the Hebrew Bible. The earliest of the scrolls dates to the 3rd century B.C., while the latest dates to the 1st century A.D. Most scholars believe that the scrolls were the library of a settlement called Qumran, whose members belonged to one of the three main groups of Jews at the time: the Essenes. The inhabitants of Qumran probably hid the scrolls during the First Jewish Revolt (66–70 A.D.), with the intent of retrieving them after the Romans had left. However, the revolt was put down, the settlement was abandoned, and the inhabitants never came back for the scrolls.

Discovery of the Scrolls

- The first few Dead Sea Scrolls were found in 1947 by three Bedouin boys who were tending their flocks of sheep and goats. The boys found 10 pottery jars in a cave. According to them, most of the jars were filled with dirt, but one had several rolled-up scrolls in it, made of leather. The boys took the scrolls but left the jars in the cave.

- According to the usual version of the story, several weeks later, after the boys' Bedouin group had made their way to the outskirts of Bethlehem, the scrolls were taken to the shop of a man named Kando. He sold antiquities but also made shoes and other leather goods. Kando purchased the scrolls, thinking that he could always make them into sandals if he couldn't sell them as antiquities. An alternative version of the story holds that Kando bought four scrolls, while another Bethlehem antiquities dealer named Salahi bought three others.

- News of the scrolls ultimately reached a scholar in Jerusalem named Eliezer Sukenik, who traveled to Bethlehem and purchased three scrolls. When Sukenik translated the scrolls, he was startled to find that one of them was a copy of the book of Isaiah from the Hebrew Bible. To his astonishment, it was nearly identical to another copy of

Isaiah from a synagogue in Cairo that was dated almost 1,000 years later, to the 10th century A.D.; it differed from the modern version by only some 13 minor variants, probably all the result of scribal errors.

- The other two scrolls Sukenik had are now known as the Thanksgiving Scroll, which recorded the hymns and prayers of thanks of the Qumran community, and the War Scroll, which described the community's anticipation of Armageddon—the final battle between good and evil. Indeed, the inhabitants of Qumran called themselves the Sons of Light and envisioned a battle against the Sons of Darkness. The War Scroll outlines how they were to act and live their lives, all while waiting and planning for this battle.

- Soon, four more scrolls appeared on the antiquities market. These were being sold by Archbishop Samuel, who was with the Syrian

The inhabitants of the community at Qumran may have been Essenes; according to ancient sources, the members of this Jewish group were celibate and lived almost like monks in a monastery.

Orthodox Monastery of St. Mark in Jerusalem. He had bought them from Kando, reportedly for $250. He offered them to Sukenik, but they were unable to reach an agreement.

- In January 1949, the archbishop smuggled the four scrolls into the United Sates, where they were secretly kept in a Syrian Orthodox church in New Jersey for several years. Then, on June 1, 1954, he placed an ad in *The Wall Street Journal*, offering the scrolls for sale. As it happened, Yigael Yadin, a preeminent Israeli archaeologist and the son of Sukenik, was in the United States at the time. The advertisement was brought to his attention, and with the help of a middleman, Yadin purchased the four scrolls for the State of Israel. These seven scrolls are now kept in the Shrine of the Book at the Israel Museum in Jerusalem.
    - Of the four scrolls that Yadin purchased from Archbishop Samuel, one was another copy of the book of Isaiah. Another is now known as the Manual of Discipline; it contains the rules and regulations for the Qumran community.

    - The third scroll was an important commentary on the book of Habakkuk from the Hebrew Bible. It presents us with three figures: the Teacher of Righteousness and his two opponents, the Wicked Priest and the Man of the Lie. None of these figures has been definitely identified, but some scholars have suggested that the Teacher of Righteousness might be James the Just, the brother of Jesus.

    - The fourth scroll is known as the Genesis Apocryphon. Written in Aramaic, this is an alternative version of the book of Genesis. The scroll records a conversation between Noah and his father, Lamech, that is not found in modern Bibles.

- News of these remarkable documents shook the world of biblical scholarship and set off a race to find more scrolls during the 1950s and 1960s. Ultimately, multiple copies of nearly every book from the Hebrew Bible were found (except for the book of Esther), along with numerous other scrolls that were not religious in nature.

The original seven scrolls found at Qumran are now reunited and housed in the Shrine of the Book in Jerusalem.

The Copper Scroll

- The third cave, discovered in 1952, contained a scroll written on sheets of copper, broken into two parts. This scroll is a treasure map—a detailed set of instructions for finding 64 treasures.

- Because the Copper Scroll could not be unrolled, it was cut into small sections using a high-speed saw. The cuts went through the middle of some of the letters, but on the whole, the technique worked, enabling the rolled-up scrolls to be laid flat.

- Most of the Copper Scroll is written in Hebrew, but there are also some Greek letters and what appear to be numbers. The directions to the treasures it provides are bizarre; for example: "In the ruin which is in the valley, pass under the steps leading to the East forty cubits ...: [There is] a chest of money and its total: the weight of seventeen talents. In the sepulchral monument, in the third course: one hundred gold ingots."

- The Copper Scroll continues in this fashion for column after column of text. Little wonder, it seems, that no one has ever found any of the treasures. If the treasures described were real, they were most likely the annual tithes that people sent to the Temple in Jerusalem; of course, during the First Jewish Revolt, it would not have been safe to send such tithes, and they might have been hidden.

Studying Scroll Fragments

- The scrolls found in cave 4 had all fallen from their shelves and disintegrated into a mass of fragments on the floor. The scrolls were in tens of thousands of pieces, some smaller than a fingernail. The original scholarly committee that was formed to piece the fragments together worked on them for more than 40 years, with few other scholars even allowed to see them. This created both ill will and conspiracy theories about what might be contained in the texts.

- In the early 1990s, however, it was revealed that photographs of the fragments had been taken at some point and were stored in a vault at the Huntington Museum Library in Los Angeles. In subsequent years, a new group of scholars was assembled to work on the fragments and publish their results. These scholars brought new backgrounds, approaches, and insights to the study of the scrolls. New techniques were also used on the scroll fragments, such as taking infrared photographs, which allowed for much clearer reading of some of the writing.

- Studying the Dead Sea Scrolls, ranging from the whole ones to the completely fragmentary, has since become a cottage industry within academia and has yielded some remarkable observations.

Other Finds in the Region

- Archaeologists found additional caves in the region of the Dead Sea during their various searches. Some of these also had remnants of scrolls and ancient writing, as well as other objects, but they are probably unrelated to the main body of the Dead Sea Scrolls.

- One of the best known discoveries is a cave in a *wadi* (canyon or valley) called Nahal Mishmar. In what is now known as the Cave of the Treasure, archaeologists found a tremendous hoard of about 400 copper objects dating to the Chalcolithic period (about 3500 B.C.). We have no idea what most of the objects were used for, but some of them resemble crowns and scepters.

- Two other caves are even more famous. They are in a *wadi* called Nahal Hever, about 25 miles south of Qumran, and are called the Cave of Horror and the Cave of Letters. Both had a Roman siege camp built on the top of the cliff directly above them. Both caves were first discovered in 1953 but were not truly excavated until 1960 and 1961.

- The Cave of Horror is so-called because of the grisly discoveries made there. Archaeologists found 40 skeletons in the cave, all dating to the time of the Second Jewish Revolt (the Bar Kokhba Revolt, 132–135 A.D.). The bodies found in this cave are thought to have been refugees or rebels who were unable to escape because of the Romans camped above them. They may well have starved to death.

- The Cave of Letters yielded rich finds from three different periods: the Chalcolithic; the 1st century A.D., perhaps during the time of the First Jewish Revolt; and the 2nd century A.D., that is, the time of the Second Jewish Revolt.
    - The cave has two narrow entrances, both leading into what is called Hall A. Here, archaeologists found a fragment from a scroll with part of the book of Psalms and a hoard of metal objects.

- o In another part of the cave, known as Hall C, the most important and grisly finds were made: a basket with human skulls in it, along with a skeleton wrapped in a blanket and a child buried in a box lined with leather; actual correspondence written by the leader of the Second Jewish Revolt, Bar Kokhba; and an archive of letters and other objects belonging to a woman named Babatha, also dating to the time of the Second Jewish Revolt.

- The discoveries in the Cave of the Treasure, the Cave of Horror, and the Cave of Letters contributed dramatic new material to the field of biblical archaeology. However, the discovery of the Dead Sea Scrolls completely revolutionized the field of biblical studies by shedding light on the Hebrew Bible according to actual texts that date more than 2,000 years ago.

Suggested Reading

Davies, Brooke, and Callaway, *The Complete World of the Dead Sea Scrolls*.

Magness, *The Archaeology of Qumran and the Dead Sea Scrolls*.

Vermes, *The Complete Dead Sea Scrolls in English*.

Questions to Consider

1. Do you think the Dead Sea Scrolls originally belonged to the library at Qumran, or are they more likely to have been brought from elsewhere, such as Jerusalem?

2. What do you think is the actual reason that none of the treasures mentioned in the Copper Scroll has been found?

Lecture 14 Transcript
The Dead Sea Scrolls

I have been fascinated by the Dead Sea Scrolls for as long as I can remember, and I think that holds true for a lot of other people as well. The Dead Sea Scrolls are the oldest copies of the Hebrew Bible that we've got at the moment. They're about 2,000 years old, more or less. We've got them because they were hidden by their owners in caves by the Dead Sea in what is now Israel; those owners, whose identity is disputed, never came back for them.

The first scrolls were discovered in 1947 by three young Bedouin boys who were herding their sheep and goats by the shore of the Dead Sea. In the years that followed, archaeologists and the Bedouin engaged in a race to discover more caves with additional scrolls, including multiple copies of nearly every book from the Hebrew Bible.

The earliest of these scrolls dates to the 3rd century B.C. while the latest dates to the 1st century A.D. They were all most likely hidden in the caves around the Dead Sea sometime during the First Jewish Revolt against Rome. That began in the year 66 and ended in the year 70 A.D.

The Dead Sea is the lowest place on Earth. It's about 1,300 feet below sea level, and although the Jordan River flows into it, there's no exit for the water. The only way out is through evaporation, and that leaves the salts and the minerals behind. So, the Dead Sea is one of the saltiest bodies of water on the planet, even more than the Great Salt Lake in Utah.

If you jump into the Dead Sea today, you'll float rather than sink, but beware if you've got any open cuts or if you rub your eyes with your hands while in the water because you will feel so much pain that you're going to be talking about it for years to come. Trust me, I know from personal experience. On the other hand, you can float in the water in a sitting position and read the paper from cover to cover without ever getting a drop of water on it.

So, it's in the caves found in the cliffs surrounding the western side of the Dead Sea that these scrolls were found. Although there is a lot of debate about the scrolls, the majority of scholars subscribe to a two-part theory: first, that the scrolls constituted the library of the nearby settlement called Qumran; and second, that the inhabitants of Qumran hid them in the caves, intending to retrieve them after the revolt was over and the Romans had left. But, the revolt was put down, the settlement was abandoned, and the inhabitants never came back for the scrolls. As I tell my students, I think that makes them the oldest overdue library books in the history of the world.

Now, we're not actually certain who lived at Qumran, though most scholars believe that it might have been the Essenes. The Essenes were one of the three main groups of Jews at the time. The others were the Sadducees and the Pharisees. We know a little bit about the Essenes from ancient authors, like Philo and Pliny the Elder, as well as and Josephus. We're told that they were celibate and that they didn't have any personal possessions, among other things—in other words, almost like monks in a monastery. Pliny places them near Ein Gedi, which is right in the area. And as a result, many scholars have thought for a long time that the Essenes are the people who wrote the Dead Sea Scrolls.

Now, as I said, the first of these scrolls, of which there are now more than 900, were found in 1947 by three young Bedouin boys, usually reported to have been cousins. They were out watering their flocks of sheep and goat at the nearby watering hole of Ras Feshka. One of the boys wandered away from the others, perhaps in search of a stray goat.

As boys all want to do, he picked up a stone, and he tried to throw it into a cave that he could see high up in the cliff. After several different attempts, one stone flew straight into the cave, and he heard a loud crash and a shattering of pottery. He immediately thought the same thing that we would all think in such an instance—gold. Well, okay, so maybe most of us wouldn't think of gold if we heard a pottery vessel shatter, but that's what he later said that he immediately thought.

Since darkness was falling, he went back to the temporary camp, and he told the other two boys what had happened. But when the boys investigated the cave the next day, they were disappointed that there was no gold to be found. Instead, as they said later, there were 10 jars in the cave, one of which was now broken. That was the one that was shattered by the stone that had been thrown the day before. According to them, most of the jars were filled with dirt, but one had several rolled up scrolls in it, made of leather. They took the scrolls but left the jars in the cave.

Now, the usual story that's told is that, several weeks later, after the boys' Bedouin group had made their way to the outskirts of Bethlehem, the scrolls were taken to the shop of a man named Kando. He sold antiquities, but he also made shoes and sandals and other leather goods. He bought the scrolls thinking that he could always make them into sandals if he couldn't actually sell them as antiquities. So it seems that's how close we came to having the oldest copies of the Bible currently in existence ending up being worn on somebody's feet.

Now, by the way, an alternate version of the story is that Kando bought four scrolls, while another Bethlehem antiquities dealer, a man named Salahi, bought three more. In any event, news of the scrolls reached a scholar in Jerusalem named Eliezer Sukenik. He traveled down to Bethlehem and bought three scrolls—either from Kando or from Salahi. He returned to Jerusalem literally hours before the 1948 war broke out.

Now when Sukenik translated the three scrolls, he was startled to find that one of them was a copy of the Book of Isaiah from the Old Testament or the Hebrew Bible. He was the first person to have read the scroll in 2,000 years. To his astonishment, it was nearly identical to another copy of Isaiah from a synagogue in Cairo that was dated almost 1,000 years later, to the 10th century A.D., and it differed from our version today only by 13 or so minor variants, probably all the results of scribal errors during all the copying that was done over the centuries.

Of the other two scrolls, one of them is called the Thanksgiving Scroll. I tell my students that this records the first Thanksgiving that the pilgrims had in the New World, when they shared their food with the Native Americans and had turkey, perhaps for the first time. It takes a minute or two to sink in and for them to start looking kind of quizzical, but before they can say anything,

I say, "Just kidding." Actually, the Thanksgiving Scroll is essentially the community's hymns and prayers of thanks—hence the name.

The final scroll is known as the War Scroll. This, to me, is the most interesting of the three because it records the fact that the inhabitants of Qumran, or whomever the scroll belonged to, were waiting for Armageddon—that is for a final battle between good and evil. They saw themselves as a fighting force, calling themselves the Sons of Light. And they said they would be fighting the Sons of Darkness. The scroll outlines how they were going to act and live their lives, all the while waiting for and planning for this battle. Of course, one could say that the battle never happened, but I would argue that at least for them, it did if one wants to call the Romans the Sons of Darkness in this instance.

Now, soon thereafter, four more scrolls appeared on the antiquities market. Archbishop Samuel, who was with the Syrian Orthodox Monastery of St. Mark in Jerusalem was selling these. He had bought them from Kando, reportedly for $250 at most. And then he offered them to Sukenik, but they were unable to reach an agreement.

So, what to do? Well, in January 1949, the Archbishop smuggled the four scrolls into the United Sates, where they were secretly kept in a Syrian Orthodox church in New Jersey for several years. And then, on June 1, 1954, he placed an ad in the Wall Street Journal, which read: "The Four Dead Sea Scrolls—Biblical Manuscripts dating back to at least 200 B.C. are for sale. This would be an ideal gift to an educational or religious institution by an individual or group. Box F 206, The Wall Street Journal."

Now, it just so happened that Yigael Yadin, a preeminent Israeli archaeologist, was in the United States at that time; he was lecturing at the Johns Hopkins University in Baltimore. The advertisement was brought to his attention and with the help of a middleman from New York, Yadin purchased the four scrolls for the State of Israel. However, the final price was a quarter of a million dollars total.

Thus, the seven scrolls were reunited. They're now kept at the Israel Museum in Jerusalem, in their own quarters known as the Shrine of the Book. But the story gets even better because Yigael Yadin had actually changed his original name at one point. His birth name was Yigael Sukenik—he was Eliezer Sukenik's son. So, the son was able to buy the scrolls that had eluded his father. That seems very fitting to me.

Of the four scrolls that Yadin purchased from Archbishop Samuel, one of them was another copy of the Book of Isaiah, in even better shape than the one that his father had purchased. Another one was a copy of what's now called the Manual of Discipline. It contains the rules and the regulations for the community to which it belonged, which most people assume is the settlement at Qumran.

The third scroll was a commentary on the Book of Habakkuk from the Hebrew Bible. Habbakuk was one of the minor prophets, and the book that is attributed to him is not very long, but this commentary is very important. It presents us with three figures—one is called the Teacher of Righteousness and his two opponents—they're called the Wicked Priest and the Man of the Lie. Now, none of these figures have been definitively identified, but some scholars have suggested that the Teacher of Righteousness might be James the Just—that is, James, brother of Jesus. Now, as you might imagine, this scroll has been the focus of a lot of scholarly debate over the years.

As for the fourth scroll that Yadin acquired, it's known as the Genesis Apocryphon. It's written in Aramaic, rather than Hebrew, and it's an alternate version of the Book of Genesis. It's different from the version that we have in our current bibles. I tease my students by telling them that in this version the unicorns actually got on Noah's Ark, rather than being left behind. I'm joking. In actuality, the scroll records a supposed conversation between Noah and his father Lamech, which is a conversation that we don't find in our bibles today.

News of these remarkable documents shook the world of biblical scholarship. It also set off a race between the archaeologists and the Bedouin, searching for more caves during the 1950s and the 1960s. And they found them, one after the other—at least 11 caves in all. By the time that they were done, they had found multiple copies of nearly every book from the Hebrew Bible, except for the Book of Esther. They also found numerous other scrolls that weren't religious in nature.

Of all the caves besides the first one, I think most people find the scrolls from the third and fourth caves the most interesting.

The third cave, in particular, contained a doozy of a scroll. It wasn't written on leather or any other type of parchment but on sheets of copper. Archaeologists found these in 1952, broken into two parts. You'll find it in the scholarly and popular literature referred to as the Copper Scroll.

And there's been a lot written about it because it's a treasure map. Plain and simple, no bones about it, it's a treasure map, like the kind a pirate would leave, with X marks the spot. Except that it's not an X in each case; instead, it's a detailed set of instructions to 64 different treasures. Let me explain.

When they first found the Copper Scroll, archaeologists couldn't unroll it by themselves. In fact, they couldn't unroll it using any means that they knew of, so they simply cut it up. And I mean that, quite literally. They took it to Manchester, England, where they cut it up into 23 small sections using a high-speed saw. The cuts went right through the middle of some of the letters, but on the whole, the technique worked, so that the rolled-up scrolls were now able to be laid flat—although they look like pieces in a jigsaw puzzle, but all approximately the same size and the shape.

Now, most of the Copper Scroll is written in Hebrew, but there are some Greek letters and what appear to be numbers as well. But it is the directions that are most bizarre and which explain, at least, to me, why none of the 64 treasures listed on the scroll have ever been located.

The first set of directions, for example, says:

> In the ruin which is in the valley, pass under the steps leading to the East forty cubits there's a chest of money and its total: the weight of 17 talents. In the sepulchral monument, in the third course 100 gold ingots. In the great cistern of the courtyard of the peristyle, in

a hollow in the floor covered with sediment, in front of the upper opening 900 talents.

But, which ruin? Which valley? Which cistern? And which peristyle? It's not clear at all which valley, monument, or cistern is meant.

The Copper Scroll continues on like this for column after column after column of text. And it's no wonder that nobody has ever found any of the treasures It's also not clear at all where the treasures came from or if they were even real. If they were real, then they were most likely the annual tithes that people were sending to the Temple in Jerusalem, except that during the First Jewish Revolt it wasn't safe to send such tithes, so they may have been hidden instead. Still, you'd think that if such was the case, then something would have been found long ago. That's why other scholars suggest that, in fact, they were found long ago, but back in antiquity—like soon after they were buried. At any rate, it remains a mystery that various amateur archaeologists try to solve from time to time without any luck.

Now there's also another scroll that was found by the Bedouin in Cave Number 11. It made its way to Kando's shop in Bethlehem and eventually came into Yigael Yadin's hands after the Six-Day War in 1967. The main part of it had been kept in a shoebox with other fragments in a smaller cigar box. When it was very carefully unrolled, and the various fragments were reattached, it turned out to be what is now known as the Temple Scroll. It's got very explicit details about the construction and the appearance of a Jewish temple that was never built, complete with regulations about sacrifices and various temple practices. Yadin eventually published the whole story of its acquisition, and the Scroll itself remains an object of intense study today.

It was Cave Number 4 though, where we got a real mess in the world of archaeology and scholarship because the scrolls found in that cave had all fallen from the shelves and had disintegrated into a mass of fragments on the floor. The original scrolls are now in tens of thousands of fragments, some smaller than a fingernail. The original scholarly committee that was formed to piece the fragments back together and to publish them worked on them for more than 40 years, with few other scholars even allowed to see them. This created all sorts of ill will, not to mention conspiracy theories about what might be contained in the texts that the scholars were painstakingly putting back together.

In the end, the bottleneck was broken from several different directions, almost all at once, in the late 1980s and early 1990s. One involved photographs, lots and lots of photographs of the scroll fragments. These were left at one scholar's front door by somebody who still remains anonymous. Another involved a professor and his graduate student who reconstructed what was on the scroll fragments by working from a set of index cards that they had been given. Each of the cards had a single word from a scroll on it, along with the word that appeared before it and the word that appeared after it in the original scroll. This is known as a compendium, and copies of them were given out by the scroll team to trusted scholars. The professor and his graduate student wrote a computer program that matched the cards up and reconstructed the original contents of the fragments with about 90 percent accuracy.

However, probably the most important revelation was that additional photographs of all of the fragments had been taken at one point, but unbeknownst to most people, they were being stored in a vault for safekeeping at the Huntington Museum Library in Los Angeles. Now once this fact was revealed, and the Huntington declared in 1991 that anyone could access microfilm copies of them—the floodgates were opened.

In subsequent years, a new group of scholars was assembled to work on the fragments, and volume after volume has now appeared in rapid succession. Some of the most interesting developments came about because women and Jews were among the new scholars working on the texts; the original team had been all men and all Christian. The new scholars brought new backgrounds, new approaches, and new insights to the study of the scrolls. New techniques were also used on the scroll fragments, like taking infrared photographs, which allowed for much clearer reading of some of the writing on the fragments.

Studying the Dead Sea Scrolls, ranging from the whole ones to the completely fragmentary, has become a cottage industry within academia. An immense number of publications have now appeared, from the most scholarly to the most popularizing. And the intense study has yielded some remarkable observations—for example, that the earliest fragment dates to the late 3rd century B.C. and is from the Book of Samuel.

Now, there's also another fragment from the Book of Samuel that contains a passage that's missing from our copies of the Bible. Here, in 1st Samuel 10–11, two paragraphs in a row begin with the same person's name—Nahash, king of the Ammonites. It seems most likely that, at one point, a scribe recopying the manuscript perhaps looked up after writing the first paragraph and then, when looking down again, saw the same man's name at the beginning of the second paragraph—thinking he had already copied that paragraph—he went on to the next one. In fact, he had only copied the first paragraph, not both. And so, our bibles were missing that second paragraph. Many versions of the Bible today, though, now have restored that missing paragraph on the basis of this discovery in the Dead Sea Scrolls.

Now, before we conclude this lesson, I should add that the archaeologists found additional caves in the region of the Dead Sea during their various searches. Some of these also had remnants of scrolls and ancient writing, as well as other objects, but they're probably unrelated to the main body of the Dead Sea Scrolls because the remains in them are from other periods.

One of the best known is a cave in a wadi, which is a canyon or a valley, called Nahal Mishmar. In what is now known as the Cave of the Treasure, archaeologists found a tremendous hoard of about 400 copper objects that date to the Chalcolithic period—that is about 3500 B.C. We've got no idea what most of the objects were used for, but some of them look like crowns and others look like scepters.

Two other caves are even more famous. They are in a wadi called Nahal Hever, which is about 25 miles south of Qumran. One of them is called the Cave of Horror. The other is the Cave of Letters. Both of them had a Roman siege camp built on top of the cliff directly above them and both of them are on such a steep slope that it's best to reach them now by very precarious rope ladders.

Now, both caves were first discovered in 1953 but weren't truly investigated and excavated until 1960 and 1961. Then they were part of an effort by teams led by four distinguished Israeli archaeologists, including Yigael Yadin.

Now, the first one, the Cave of Horror, is called that because of the grisly discoveries that the archaeologists made in there. They found 40 skeletons in the cave, all dating to the time of the Second Jewish Revolt—that's known as the Bar Kokhba Revolt. As we've seen, the first revolt ended in 70 A.D. with the destruction of Jerusalem and the Second Temple. The second revolt lasted from 132–135 A.D. and was similarly unsuccessful. The bodies found in this cave are thought to have been refugees or rebels who were unable to get out or escape from the cave because of the Romans who were camped directly above them—no doubt very deliberately. These people may well have starved to death, but we'll never know the real story of what happened in this Cave of Horror.

About the Cave of Letters, though, we now know an amazing amount. Yadin was in charge of exploring this cave in 1960 and 61. He wasn't expecting to find much new material because the cave had already been fairly thoroughly explored by archaeologists back in 1953. But, it turned out to be extremely rich, with finds from three different periods. One period was the Chalcolithic, again about 3500 B.C., just like the Cave of the Treasure. A second period was the 1st century A.D., perhaps during the time of the First Jewish Revolt, back when all of the scrolls had been hidden in the caves that were closer to Qumran. And the third period was the 2nd century A.D.—that is, the time of the Second Jewish Rebellion.

The cave has two narrow entrances, both leading into what we now call Hall A. In here, archaeologists found a fragment from a scroll with part of the Book of Psalms. They also found a hoard of metal objects that they located when they were using a metal detector. Now, from here, a narrow tunnel leads to Hall B, with a narrow passage leading from B further into the depths, but there's also a larger tunnel that connects Hall B to Hall C. And it's in Hall C that the most important and grisly finds were made. There's a basket with human skulls in it, found in a crevice along with a skeleton wrapped in a blanket and a child buried in a box lined with leather. There's also actual correspondence written by Bar Kokhba, the leader of the rebellion, and an archive of letters and other objects that belonged to a woman named Babatha. Those also date to the time of the Second Jewish Revolt.

It turned out that there were at least three men, eight women, and six children whose skeletons were found in Hall C within that cave. And the correspondence written by Bar Kokhba—that was on wooden slates all wrapped up in papyri—one of them read, "Simeon bar Kosiba, leader or prince over Israel." I'd been told the story that when Yadin went to the President of Israel to personally tell him of the discovery, he saluted and said, "Message from your predecessor, sir." I don't know if there is any truth to that story, but I like it.

And the material in Babatha's archive includes 35 papyrus rolls, which were mostly legal documents regarding property that she had inherited from her father and the guardianship of her son. The photographer who was there on the day that they were discovered later wrote,

> As Yadin checked to make sure that he had missed nothing, his hand touched a bundle of rags. And when he brought it out, he could see a hoard of papyrus rolls wrapped together, what we now call the Babatha archive, describing everyday life during the Bar Kosiba period. Thirty-five years later, I remember that wonderful and exciting experience as the greatest in my life as a photographer.

The discoveries in the Cave of the Treasure, the Cave of Horror, and the Cave of Letters contributed dramatic new material to the field of biblical archaeology. However, the discovery of the Dead Sea Scrolls absolutely revolutionized the field of biblical studies by shedding light on the Hebrew Bible according to actual texts that date back more than 2,000 years ago. For those who are interested, there's a book called *The Dead Sea Scrolls Bible*, which documents alternative readings found in the Dead Sea Scrolls by presenting them in footnotes attached to the traditional text of the Bible. It's absolutely fascinating

And in fact, for those who are really interested, all of the Dead Sea Scrolls, right down to the smallest fragments, have now been digitized and are online for anyone and everyone to access. They can be found at the Leon

Levy Dead Sea Scrolls Digital Library, which is sponsored by the Israel Antiquities Authority. And it's great fun to browse through them if you've got a few spare moments or a couple hours or even weeks or months. Just go to deadseascrolls.org.il and start your journey.

Well, as I said at the outset, the Dead Sea Scrolls have fascinated me for as long as I can remember. From their accidental discovery to the intrigue of their trade on the antiquities market, right through to the academic controversies they have ignited—all of these elements make the scrolls one of the most enthralling archaeological finds of the 20th century.

Lecture 15: The Myth of Masada?

The ancient site of Masada in Israel has been a tourist attraction since Yigael Yadin first excavated the top of the mountain in the mid-1960s. It is the second most popular tourist site in Israel after Jerusalem and was named a World Heritage Site by UNESCO in 2001. Overall, Yadin's excavations at Masada served as a milestone for archaeology in Israel, especially in terms of his use of multinational volunteers and numerous other aspects of the logistics of the operation. The excavations remain significant today for tourism and because they are at the heart of recent discussions regarding the nature of interpretations made by archaeologists.

Milestones in Archaeology

- The work conducted by Yigael Yadin at Masada from 1963 to 1965 was a milestone for archaeology in several ways. For example, Yadin was the first to use international volunteers to help dig the site. The sheer number of volunteers who took part—no fewer than 300 at any given moment—was also amazing.

- In addition, the logistics of running the dig were staggering. Helicopters were sometimes commandeered to fly tools and equipment to the top of the mound, though the more usual route was to carry everything up via the Roman siege ramp. In the case of heavier equipment, a cable system next to the ramp was used.

- And the excavation itself has become the stuff of legend. Yadin says that when they first began planning the excavation, they couldn't see any structures with a recognizable plan on top of Masada. The entire area, he says, was covered with "mounds of stone and rubble." In actuality, though, many of the buildings could be plainly seen in aerial photographs.

- By the time the excavations were finished, the archaeologists had discovered an elaborate site with two palaces, one on the northern end of the rock plateau and one on Masada's western side.

- In addition to the two palaces, Yadin's team found rooms and buildings that served as tanneries, workshops, and a synagogue. They also found numerous storage areas to hold food and other provisions, some of which had jars that still contained charred grain from the final destruction, and many cisterns for holding water.

  - Some of the walls were covered in plaster painted with colorful images, and a few of the floors were inlaid with mosaics featuring elaborate designs. Only fragments of these artworks remain.

- Yadin reconstructed some of the original buildings from fallen stones, including a large complex of storerooms in the northeastern part of the site. Here, just the lower portions of the walls were left, but the stones from higher up in the walls were all lying where they had fallen. Yadin and his team reconstructed the rooms and walls, which turned out to be 11 feet high.

- According to Yadin, his team also put "every grain of earth ... through a special sieve"; close to 50,000 cubic yards of dirt was sifted. This was the first time that every single bucket of dirt had been sifted at an excavation in Israel. As a result, the team found numerous small items that would probably otherwise have been missed, including hundreds of coins, pieces of pottery, and small items of jewelry. The coins allowed Yadin to date the remains very precisely, particularly the coins that had been made just a few years earlier, during the First Jewish Revolt.

- However, Yadin's excavations at Masada have also been the subject of much debate in recent years, especially over his interpretation of the remains and his use of them in reconstructing the ancient narrative of what happened at the site.
  - Masada serves as an example of how archaeologists use historical information to supplement what they find during their excavations and to flesh out the bare details provided by their discoveries.

○ In this case, Yadin made particular use of the writings of Flavius Josephus, the Jewish general who became a Roman historian and wrote two books about the Jews in the 1st century A.D.

The Siege at Masada
- Masada is located at the southern end of the Dead Sea, at the opposite end from Qumran. Here, the Romans mounted a siege against a small group of Jewish rebels in 73 A.D. Josephus is perhaps our main source for information about the siege, relating the story of a mass suicide by the Jewish defenders.

- In 66 A.D., in the First Jewish Revolt, the Jews in what is now Israel rose up against the Romans who were occupying their land. That revolt lasted until 70 A.D., at which point the Romans captured Jerusalem and burned most of it to the ground, including the Temple that had been built there by Herod the Great to replace the original one constructed by King Solomon.

- When the rebellion ended, a group of rebels managed to escape the destruction of Jerusalem and settled at Masada. Led by a man named Eleazar ben Yair, these were the Sicarii, or "dagger men." They took over the fortified buildings and palaces that Herod had built on top of Masada as a place of last refuge for himself and his family, should they ever need it.

- In his account of events at Masada, Josephus gets some details wrong, leading scholars to suspect that he wasn't there himself but used someone else's notes. Other details, however, are correct; for instance, Josephus describes the floors in some of the buildings that "were paved with stones of several colors" and the many pits that were cut into rock to serve as cisterns.

- The rebel group held out at Masada for three years, raiding the surrounding countryside, until the Romans decided to put an end to the final remnants of the rebellion.
    ○ According to Josephus, the Romans, led by General Flavius Silva, surrounded Masada with a wall that encircled the

mountain, with separate garrisons or fortresses built at spaced intervals to prevent escape.

- ○ Next, the Romans began constructing a long ramp of earth and stones, making use of a natural ridge that reached from the desert floor to within "300 cubits" of the top of Masada. Once the ramp was finished, siege engines, such as a battering ram, catapults, and ballistae, could be wheeled up its length and used against the walls of Masada.

- Again, according to Josephus, General Silva ordered the battering ram to be dragged up the ramp and set against the wall. The Romans expected that the great piece of pointed wood that formed the battering ram would allow them to breach the wall quickly.

After Yadin's excavations at Masada, the Israeli army held induction ceremonies there for new recruits, making them swear that "never again; never again" would they allow such a thing to happen.

- However, the Jewish defenders had created their own wall just inside, which was made of wood and earth so that it would be soft and yielding. This second wall, set up against the stone fortification wall, helped to absorb the blows of the battering ram. Thus, it took the Romans far longer than they expected to break through the outer wall. And when they did, they were faced with the thick inner wall.

- In the end, the Romans simply set fire to the wall, Josephus says, and made preparations to enter the city. However, by the time the flames had died down, night had fallen, and the Romans returned to their camps; they prepared to overrun the defenders in the morning.

- This brief respite from the Roman attack gave the Jewish defenders the time and opportunity to decide to kill themselves rather than be killed or taken prisoner by the Romans. Josephus says that Eleazar ben Yair, their leader, asked each family man to kill his own wife and children.

- The men then drew lots, choosing 10 of their number to kill all the others. One man was then selected to kill the remaining 9 and himself, thereby becoming the only person to technically commit suicide, which is against Jewish law. When the Romans entered the next morning, they were greeted by silence. Only when some women and children emerged from their hiding place in a cistern did they learn the truth of what had happened. According to Josephus, 960 people died that night.

- The story is quite dramatic and has reverberated down through the ages; however, Josephus's account has a number of flaws. For example, if the Romans had punched a hole in the wall even as night was falling, they would never have returned to their camp. It's much more likely that when the Romans breached the wall, they poured in and massacred the Jewish defenders. Josephus, writing later back in Rome and using notes from the commanding officers who were actually present, was probably asked to whitewash the whole affair, and he used his own experience of a mass suicide at a site called Jotapata in 67 A.D. to do so.

Interpreting the Finds at Masada

- As mentioned, Yadin's interpretation of the objects he found at Masada remains a matter of great debate. For instance, among the objects found were belt buckles, door keys, arrowheads, spoons, rings, and other items made of iron, in addition to a great deal of pottery and many coins. Yadin interpreted these as belonging to the Jewish defenders of Masada, and they may have, but some of these items might have belonged to the Roman besiegers or even to later inhabitants or squatters at the site.

- Yadin's team also found fragments of scrolls, including a fragment with text identical to one found in the caves at Qumran. This find led Yadin and many other scholars to wonder whether there was any connection between the defenders of Masada and the Essenes at Qumran.

- Perhaps most importantly, Yadin also found bodies at the site, though fewer than 30 in all. Twenty-five of these were in a cave near the top of the southern cliff face, and 3 others were found near a small bathhouse on the lower terrace of the northern palace. Yadin believed that these three—a man, a woman, and a child—formed a family group.
    - This belief has been the focus of much debate over the years, as have the pottery sherds with names written on them in ink that he found, including one that says "ben Yair." To Yadin, these bodies and the sherds confirmed Josephus's story and the existence of Eleazar ben Yair.

    - However, more recent forensic analysis indicates that the bodies Yadin wrote about were only a few years apart in age and couldn't possibly have been a family.

- Some scholars have reviled Yadin and others have revered him, but overall, his excavations in Israel were remarkable for their use of volunteers and their ingenuity in facing logistical challenges, as well as the discussions they sparked about the nature of archaeological interpretation.

Suggested Reading

Ben-Tor, *Back to Masada.*

Ben-Yehuda, *The Masada Myth.*

Yadin, *Masada.*

Questions to Consider

1. Do you think Yadin's personal beliefs influenced his interpretation of the finds at Masada?

2. What do you think actually happened that night on top of Masada—a mass suicide or a mass slaughter?

Lecture 15 Transcript

The Myth of Masada?

I think the first time that I climbed the mountain of Masada in Israel was back in 1971, more than 40 years ago. I definitely have a picture of my sister and me at the Dead Sea from that time, so it stands to reason that we would've climbed Masada as well. However, the first time that I can really be sure that I climbed Masada was about 5 years later, during the summer of 1976. I remember running up the Snake Path, and later claiming it had only taken me about 15 minutes to get to the top. I'm pretty sure that I must have been exaggerating, though, and it was probably more like about 45 minutes, because that's a pretty tough climb—it's more than a thousand feet straight up. Nowadays, I simply admit defeat before I even start and I just take the tram up the mountain. Once, back in 1994, I did walk up the Roman siege ramp from the other side of the mountain, so at least I can claim that I've gone up Masada in all three of the possible ways.

Masada's been a tourist attraction since Yigael Yadin first excavated the top of the mountain back in the 1960s. Hundreds of tourists a day now roam around the ruins on top of the mountain—half a million people visit every year. It's the second most popular tourist site in all of Israel after Jerusalem. It was named a World Heritage Site by UNESCO in 2001. Those who are valiant enough to begin climbing before dawn are rewarded with one of the most spectacular sunrises that they'll ever see in their lives. I certainly still remember the one that I saw back in 1976, as well as each of them that I've seen since.

The work that Yadin conducted at Masada over two excavation seasons—from October 1963 to May 1964 and then again November 1964 to April 1965—was a milestone for archaeology in several ways. For example, Yadin was the first to use international volunteers to help dig the site. In fact, he recruited participants by placing ads in newspapers, both in Israel and in England, and he wound up with volunteers from 28 different countries, according to his own account.

Nowadays it's rare for a dig in Israel not to have participants from all over the world, but at that point in time it was a novelty. The sheer numbers that took part is also amazing—Yadin claims to have had no fewer than 300 volunteers digging at Masada at any given moment during his excavations. These included volunteers from the Israel Defense Forces, as well as high school students and kibbutz members, in addition to the international participants.

The logistics of running the dig were also staggering. Archaeologists active today, who were graduate students at the time, talk about helicopters sometimes being commandeered to fly tools and equipment up to the top of the mound, although the more usual route was to carry everything up the side of the mound via the Roman siege ramp. In the case of heavier equipment, a cable system next to the ramp was also used. The actual tents in which the expedition members lived were pitched at the foot of this same Roman ramp for a variety of logistical reasons.

And the excavation itself, it's become the stuff of legend. Yadin says that when they first began planning the excavation, they couldn't see any structure with a recognizable plan on top of Masada. The entire area, he says, was covered with mounds of stone and rubble, so that they couldn't see the buildings for the stones. In actuality, though, many of the buildings could be quite plainly seen once they took aerial photographs, so that they knew where to dig in many cases.

By the time that they finished the excavations, they had discovered that it was an elaborate place with two palaces. One of these was at the northern end of the rock plateau; it has three levels going down the side of the cliff. The other palace was on Masada's western side. Now, in addition to the two palaces, Yadin's team found rooms and buildings that served as tanneries, workshops, and even as a synagogue. They also found numerous storage areas to hold food and other provisions, some of which had jars that still contained charred grain from the final destruction, and many cisterns for holding water, which we'll come back to in a minute.

Some of the walls were covered in plaster, and were painted with images in deep blues, and brilliant reds, yellow, and black. Of these, only fragments now remain. A few of the floors were inlaid with mosaics featuring elaborate designs like those found more commonly in Greece or Rome. Presumably artisans hired by Herod the Great created these, perhaps to emulate what he had seen in Rome when he traveled there back in 40 B.C. Again, though, only parts of these now remain.

One of the things that Yadin did was to reconstruct some of the original buildings from the fallen stones that they found. The best example of this at Masada was the large complex of storerooms that were in the northeastern part of the site. Here, just the lower part of the walls were left, but the stones from higher up in the walls were all lying right where they had fallen. Yadin and his team reconstructed the walls and the rooms, using every available stone to rebuild the walls, which turned out to be about 11 feet high. In order to show what they had done, and what they had reconstructed, they painted a black line to separate the lower part that they had excavated from the upper part that they had reconstructed, and this is still done at some sites in Israel today. For instance, you can see something similar at Megiddo when you walk through the Late Bronze Age gate and enter the ancient city.

They also, Yadin says, put every grain of earth through a special sieve. Close to 50,000 cubic yards of dirt was sifted. It was the first time that every single bucket of dirt had been sifted at an excavation in Israel. As a result, they found numerous small items that would probably otherwise have been missed. Yadin describes these as including hundreds of coins, pieces of pottery with inscriptions on them, and small pieces of jewelry like rings and beads. The fragments of inscribed pottery were especially significant for Yadin, as we'll see in a moment, but the coins also allowed him to date very precisely the remains that they were uncovering, particularly the coins that had been made just a few years before the destruction, during the First Jewish Revolt. These included coins from all five years of the Revolt, including several very rare ones from the very last year of the rebellion.

However, Yadin's excavations at Masada have also been the subject of much debate in recent years, especially over his interpretation of the remains and his use of them in reconstructing the ancient narrative of what happened at the site, which he published in one of the first excavation reports ever aimed at a popular audience. It was a large coffee-table book simply entitled

Masada. The actual, official publications of the results have taken up 8 additional volumes and the efforts of basically dozens of scholars working for decades, with the most recent volume appearing in 2007, more than 40 years after the original excavation had ended.

So, the story of Masada is actually more than just a story of the archaeological excavations. It's an example of how archaeologists also use historical information to supplement what they find during the excavations and to flesh out the bare details provided by the archaeological discoveries. In this case, Yadin made particular use of the writings of Flavius Josephus, the Jewish general turned Roman historian who wrote two books about the Jews in the 1st century A.D. But the relationship between archaeology and the historical record cuts both ways. In other words, since we can't be certain that Josephus' discussions are 100 percent accurate, we can use archaeology to either corroborate—or challenge—the ancient text.

Before we do that, though, let me put the site into its context. Masada is, as I just mentioned, located by the Dead Sea in Israel. In fact, it's at the southern end of the Dead Sea, at the opposite end from Qumran and most of the caves in which the Dead Sea Scrolls were found. Now, you'll recall that the Dead Sea is the lowest place on Earth—it's at about 1,300 feet below sea level. We're basically out in the middle of the desert here and it's blazing hot. In fact, it gets so hot that these days you aren't even allowed to begin climbing Masada after nine-thirty in the morning because there's too much chance of getting dehydrated during the ascent.

It was in this context that the Romans mounted a siege against a small group of Jewish rebels at Masada in 73 or 74 A.D. And Josephus is perhaps our main source for information about that siege. The story that he tells, of a mass suicide by the Jewish defenders, had long been known, and in fact Yadin was using the archaeology to try to corroborate the details that Josephus gives.

That story is briefly told. Back in 66 A.D., the First Jewish Rebellion had begun, in which the Jews in what is now Israel rose up against the Romans who were occupying their land. The revolt lasted until 70 A.D., at which point the Romans captured Jerusalem and burnt most of it to the ground, including the temple that had been built there by Herod the Great to replace the original one constructed by King Solomon. As you may know, the Neo-Babylonians had destroyed Solomon's Temple centuries earlier. It's said that both the First and the Second Temples, that is those built by Solomon and Herod, respectively, were destroyed on the same day of the year, which is today a Jewish day of mourning known as Tisha B'Av.

Now, when the rebellion ended, a group of rebels managed to escape the destruction of Jerusalem and they settled at Masada. Led by a man named Eleazar ben Yair, these were the Sicarii, or the Dagger Men. They took over the fortified buildings and the palaces that Herod had built on top of Masada as a place of last refuge for himself and his family should they ever need it.

In his account of what happened, though, Josephus gets some of the details wrong, so that we suspect that perhaps he wasn't ever there himself, but was actually using somebody else's notes. For instance, he said that Herod built a palace at the western ascent but inclined to its north side. In actuality, as I've just said, the archaeologists found two palaces, not one—at the west and the north—on top of Masada.

Some of the other details that Josephus gives, though, are quite correct. For instance, he describes the baths that had been built there, and the fact that the floors in some of the buildings were paved with stones of several colors, and that many pits were carved into the living rock to serve as cisterns. I've already mentioned the mosaics that Yadin found still partially intact on some of the floors, which must be what Josephus is referring to, but I should also emphasize the sheer size of some of the cisterns that were dug into the rock on top of Masada, because they were simply enormous. It's usually estimated that they could each hold as much as 200,000 gallons of water.

In any event, the rebel group held out for three years, raiding the surrounding countryside for food, until the Romans decided to put an end to them and the final remnants of the rebellion. Josephus tells us that the Romans, led by General Flavius Silva, surrounded Masada with a wall that went the entire way around the mountain on the desert floor, and there were separate garrisons or fortresses built at spaced intervals along the wall so that nobody could escape. Today, about eight of these fortresses can still be seen, especially when you're up on top of Masada and looking down at the surrounding countryside. One big one, larger than the rest, is especially visible, with the stone foundations of the walls still apparent today. Most of the others, though, can still be clearly seen as well.

Next, the Romans began constructing a long ramp built of earth and stone, making use of a natural ridge that reached from the desert floor to within 300 cubits of the top of Masada. Once the ramp was constructed, siege engines—like a battering ram, and catapults that could fling large stones, and ballistae that shot huge arrows—could be wheeled upon its length and used against the walls of Masada. Josephus notes:

> There was a tower made of the height of 60 cubits, and all over plated with iron, out of which the Romans threw darts and stones from the engines, and soon made those that fought from the walls of the place to retire, and would not let them lift up their heads above the works.

Today, full-size replicas of some of these siege engines can still be seen at the site, but they were left there after ABC filmed a mini-series about Masada that aired in 1981. Yadin and the other archaeologists uncovered other objects during their excavations in the 1960s that can still be seen at the site, including what look like catapult balls that were flung up by the Romans and possibly sling stones that were thrown back down by the Jewish defenders.

Then the real siege began. Josephus tells us that General Silva ordered the battering ram to be dragged up the ramp and set against the wall. Several men grabbed the rope that was tied to the great piece of pointed wood that formed the actual battering ram and they pulled it back, back, back. And when they let go, the ram smashed against the fortification wall with a huge crash. It wasn't going to be long before they had breached the wall.

However, the Jewish defenders had created their own wall just inside, which was made of wood and earth, so that it would be soft and yielding, as Josephus tells us. He says they laid down great beams of wood lengthwise, right next to the inside of the wall, then they did the same about 10 feet or so away, so that they had two large stacks of wooden beams. And in between the two stacks they poured earth, so that in the end they had an extremely thick wall with wood on both sides and an earthen core. This second wall, set up directly against the stone fortification wall, helped to absorb the blows of the battering ram by spreading the impact. So, it took the Romans far longer than they had expected to actually knock a hole in the wall. And, even when they did punch a hole in the outer wall, they were then still faced with this thick wood-and-earthen wall.

In the end, the Romans simply set fire to it—that's what Josephus says—and then they made preparations to enter the city. However, by the time the flames had died down, night had fallen and so Josephus tells us that the Romans returned to their camp for the night and prepared to overrun the defenders in the morning. And it's this brief respite from the Roman attack that provided the Jewish defenders the time and the opportunity to decide to kill themselves rather than to be killed or to be taken prisoner and enslaved by the Romans. Josephus says that Eleazar ben Yair, their leader, asked each family man to kill his own wife and children, declaring, "It is still in our power to die bravely, and in a state of freedom, which has not been the case of others, who were conquered unexpectedly."

The men then drew lots, choosing 10 of their number to kill all of the others. The 10 then drew lots themselves and selected one to kill the other 9, and he then killed himself, thereby becoming the only person to actually commit suicide, technically speaking, because that's against Jewish law. In effect, though, it was all a mass suicide and when the Romans entered the next morning, they were greeted by a vast silence. Only when two women and five children emerged from their hiding place in a cistern did the Romans learn the truth of what had happened, because the women told of Eleazar's speech, repeating it word for word. According to Josephus, 960 people died that night.

The story is pretty dramatic, and so it has reverberated down through the ages until the present day. In fact, after Yadin's excavations at the site, the Israeli army used to hold its induction ceremonies for new recruits up on top of Masada, making them swear at a dramatic nighttime ritual in front of a blazing bonfire that never again—never again would they allow such a thing to happen.

But there are problems with Josephus' stories, not least of which is the fact that if the women and the children really had been hiding in the cistern, there's no way that they would have been able to hear Eleazar ben Yair's speech so clearly that they were able to repeat it and Josephus could quote it word for word, as he does in his manuscript.

A larger problem is the fact that, if the Romans had punched a hole in the wall even as night was falling, they would never have returned to their camps for the evening. Roman military tactics at the time called for them to press the advantage whenever and wherever they had it, regardless of the time of day or night. So they would've gone straight through the breached and burning wall, leaving no time for ben Yair to make his speech, no time for the husbands to kill their wives and families, no time for the 10 men to kill the others, and no time for the last man to kill the other 9. In short, it could not have happened as Josephus has described it.

More likely what happened was exactly what we might have expected. When the Romans breached the wall, they poured in and massacred the Jewish defenders. It was not a mass suicide but a mass slaughter. Josephus, writing later back in Rome and using notes and daybooks from the commanding officers who were actually present, may have been asked to whitewash the whole thing. In fact, the story that he tells about the men killing their families, and 10 men—or 9 men—killing the others, and then one man killing the rest, is taken from his own experience.

Because several years earlier, in 67 A.D., during the actual rebellion, Josephus had been a Jewish general fighting the Romans at a place called Jotapata. They managed to hold off the Romans for 47 days, but in the end Josephus and 40 others took refuge in a cave where they decided to commit suicide, with each man killing another, rather than surrender. In the end, only Josephus was left alive with one other man, and he persuaded him to surrender. So, the story that Josephus tells us of what happened at Masada actually seems to be the story of what happened to Josephus at Jotapata.

So, it's with all of these Josephus-related problems in mind, ranging from the fact that he didn't know how many palaces were actually at the site to the story of the women and children hiding in the cistern while the rest of the people committed suicide, Yadin decided to go to back to Masada and excavate to see what he could find and either prove or disprove the story.

As I mentioned, what Yadin found remains a matter of great debate. Now, the objects themselves are not debated; the question lies in how these objects should be interpreted. For instance, among the objects that Yadin found were belt buckles, and door keys, arrowheads, spoons, rings, and other items made out of iron, in addition to lots and lots of pottery and all those coins that I mentioned earlier. Yadin interpreted these as belonging to the Jewish defenders of Masada, as indeed they might, but some might've belonged to the Roman besiegers or even to later inhabitants or squatters at the site.

They also found fragments of scrolls, including scraps from the Book of Psalms, one containing portions of Psalms 81–85 and another from the last chapter in the book, Psalm 150, which reads "Praise ye the Lord. Praise Him with the sound of the trumpet." There are also other very important but fragmentary texts, including a fragment from a scroll whose lines of text are identical to one found in the Dead Sea Scroll caves at Qumran. This led Yadin, as well as many other scholars since then, to wonder whether there was any connection between the defenders of Masada and the Essenes at Qumran.

And, perhaps most importantly, Yadin also found bodies at the site, though less than 30 in all, and certainly not anywhere near the 960 that Josephus reports. Some of them still had hair intact and leather sandals nearby. It's these that have generated the most debate in recent years. Twenty-five of them were in a cave near the top of the southern cliff face, and these were given a state funeral in 1969, but over Yadin's objections, since he said that they couldn't be sure whether they were the Jewish defenders of Masada, or the Roman attackers, or some other group of people perhaps from a different period altogether.

Three other bodies were found near a small bathhouse on the lower terrace of the Northern Palace. Amnon Ben-Tor, the current director of the excavations at Hazor, says that he was the one who excavated these three skeletons and that it was the most thrilling day in his professional life. In the book that he published, Yadin made the most out of these. Let me quote from what might be the most famous description in the book of these three bodies that were found by the bathhouse. Yadin wrote:

> When we came to clear the formidable pile of debris which covered the chambers of the small bathhouse, we were arrested by a find which is difficult to consider in archaeological terms, for such an experience is not normal in archaeological excavations. Even the veterans and the more cynical among us stood frozen, gazing in awe at what had been uncovered; for as we gazed, we relived the final and most tragic moments of the drama of Masada. On the steps leading to the cold-water pool and on the ground nearby were the remains of three skeletons. One was that of a man of about 20, perhaps one of the commanders of Masada. Not far off, also on the steps, was the skeleton of a young woman, with her scalp preserved intact because of the extreme dryness of the atmosphere. Her dark hair, beautifully plaited, looked as if it had just been freshly coiffeured. The third skeleton was of that of a child, and there could be no doubt that what our eyes beheld were the remains of some of the defenders of Masada.

Yadin believed that they had formed a family group who died in close proximity to each other. This has been the focus of much debate over the years, as have the pottery sherds with names written on them in ink that he found, including one that says "ben Yair." To Yadin, these bodies and the sherds confirmed Josephus' story and the existence of Eleazar ben Yair. However, more recent forensic analysis indicates that the so-called family group that Yadin wrote about were actually only a few years apart in age and couldn't possibly have been the family that Yadin described. The man was more likely about 22 years old, the woman was 18, and the child was a boy about 11 years old.

This list of problems, or of finds that could be interpreted in other ways, was pulled together in two books written by Nachman Ben-Yehuda, a sociologist at the Hebrew University in Jerusalem. The first is called *The Masada Myth* and the second is called *Sacrificing Truth*. He basically accuses Yadin of creating a nationalist narrative out of the remains that he found at Masada to help the young state of Israel create an identity for itself and its citizens based on archaeology.

Ben-Yehuda makes some good points, but Yadin has his stalwart defenders. In 2009, Amnon Ben-Tor, who is now the Yigael Yadin Professor of Archaeology at the Hebrew University of Jerusalem, published a spirited defense entitled *Back to Masada*. In it, Ben-Tor goes through the archaeology again, dismissing each of Ben Yehuda's points and basically confirming Yadin's interpretations and conclusions.

Now, regardless of whether you follow Ben-Yehuda or Ben-Tor in reviling or revering Yadin, Ben-Tor's concluding remarks in the book that he wrote in defense of Yadin, still ring true. As he said:

> Placing Masada on the scientific agenda on the one hand, and in the public consciousness as a tourist site on the other, are both the proper expression and a true monument to the two aspects of Yadin's personality: the scholar and the public figure.

Overall, Yadin's excavations at Masada served as a milestone for archaeology in Israel, especially in terms of its use of multinational volunteers and numerous other aspects of the logistics of the operation. They remain significant today for tourism of course, but also because they're at the heart of recent discussions regarding the nature of interpretations made by archaeologists, especially those who may or may not have an agenda above and beyond a simple reading of the data that they've uncovered.

It was no secret that Yadin's excavations elsewhere in Israel, such as at Hazor in the 1950s, were in part undertaken in the hope of reinforcing Jewish claims to the land by linking them to both the biblical narratives and other famous events, including the story that Josephus describes as taking part in Masada. How much his interpretations were influenced by such a desire is still a matter of debate today.

Lecture 16
Megiddo: Excavating Armageddon

Megiddo is a 70-foot-high manmade mound. Inside the mound are at least 20 separate cities, built one on top of another, with the earliest dating back 5,000 years ago and the most recent dating to about the time of Alexander the Great. Many famous people have fought at Megiddo or in the surrounding Jezreel Valley, from the pharaoh Thutmose III in 1479 B.C. to Deborah, Gideon, Saul, and other figures from the Bible. The Romans fought here, too, as did the Crusaders, Mamluks, Mongols, Napoleon, and General Allenby in World War I. But of all the battles fought at Megiddo, the most famous is still to come: the battle of Armageddon, mentioned in the Book of Revelation.

Gottlieb Schumacher's Excavations

- In Hebrew, *Har Megiddo* means the "mound" or "mountain" of Megiddo; in Greek, the word was originally written *Harmageddon*, but over time, the initial *H* was lost, and it became *Armageddon*. A man named Gottlieb Schumacher conducted the first excavations at Megiddo from 1903 to 1905. He was actually an engineer by training, but he used the archaeological excavation methods current in his day.

- One of those methods involved employing hundreds of workmen to dig a huge trench through the middle of the mound. This trench yielded a tomb from the Middle Bronze Age that held the bodies of a number of men and women, along with gold objects and other finery.

- Schumacher also found one of the most famous objects ever to be discovered at Megiddo, an oval seal about 1.5 inches wide made of a type of stone called jasper. It has a lion on it and the name "Shema, servant of Jeroboam." It's not clear which Jeroboam this is because there are two mentioned in the Bible. Unfortunately, the seal is now missing.

- Schumacher's workmen also missed or discarded things while they were digging, including stones from walls that they took apart. One of these stones turned out to have the cartouche of the Egyptian pharaoh Shoshenq on it, but the workmen didn't notice it. Later, the stone was recognized for what it was—part of a monumental inscription that probably stood about 10 feet high. It would have been erected at the site as a victory inscription after Shoshenq captured and occupied the city.

University of Chicago Excavations
- A team from the University of Chicago dug at Megiddo for approximately 15 years, from 1925 to 1939. This project was under the direction of James Henry Breasted, founder of the Oriental

The Jezreel Valley is a perfect place for a battlefield, which may explain why at least 34 battles have been fought there over the past 4,000 years, most for control of Megiddo or nearby areas.

Institute at the University of Chicago, with a series of field directors who included Clarence Fisher, Gordon Loud, and P. L. O. Guy.

- The Chicago expedition was at the forefront of a new type of archaeology that was more careful and scientific than the type practiced by Schumacher. Courtesy of Sir William Matthew Flinders Petrie, archaeologists now knew about stratigraphy and pottery seriation, that is, the changes in pottery styles over time; thus, they could tell one city from another and do more accurate dating.

- Funded with money from John D. Rockefeller, the Chicago team started out doing horizontal excavation, in which they exposed one layer over the entire site, recorded it, then picked it up and removed it all so that they could expose the next layer. This approach was used for two full layers before the team started to run out of money and switched to vertical excavation. In a few areas, the digging goes much deeper—all the way to bedrock in some cases—which is how we know that there are at least 20 cities within the mound.

- The Chicago team was still prone to use the biblical account to buttress their findings at the site. Thus, when they were excavating a series of structures that looked like stables for horses, they turned to the book of 1 Kings to help with their identification.
    - There, they found two passages that they thought were relevant, in 1 Kings 9 and 1 Kings 10, both of which mention construction ordered by King Solomon. Combining the passages, the Chicago team decided that Megiddo must have been one of Solomon's cities and that the structures were stables dating back the 10th century B.C. Still today, the tour guides refer to these structures as Solomon's Stables.

    - However, similar structures have been found at other sites. Although those at Megiddo may indeed be stables, it is also possible that they were used as storehouses, as barracks for soldiers, or even as a *suq*, or marketplace.

o Moreover, radiocarbon dating and pottery found within these structures now indicate that they are unlikely to have been built during the time of Solomon. They probably date to at least a century later.

Yigael Yadin's Excavations
- The next person to lead an excavation at Megiddo was Yigael Yadin, who went there for a few brief seasons in the 1960s and 1970s. One of the things that Yadin and his team uncovered were the foundations of what appeared to be a large structure that he called Palace 6000.

- Only the foundations were left because the building lay directly underneath the northern set of "stables" that the Chicago team had found. The large blocks from Palace 6000 had been reused in the later building to make the troughs in which to put food for the horses.

- Yadin believed that this palace, not the stables above it, had been built by Solomon, but he had no proof beyond the same biblical passages cited earlier and the fact that he thought the palace was built at the same time (in the 10th century B.C., during Solomon's rule) as a large entrance gate to the city itself.

- A later archaeologist, Israel Finkelstein, used pottery found at the site to date both the gate and the palace to the 9th century B.C., although this date is still debated.

Recent Excavations
- Finkelstein has been leading the new set of excavations at Megiddo since 1992, with a series of codirectors. This team re-excavated the area in which both Yadin's Palace 6000 and Chicago's "stables" were located.

- In the part of the site called Area H, the buildings now on the surface are two palaces that date to the Neo-Assyrian period (the 8th century B.C.). The Chicago team exposed them but didn't dig any deeper in the area. The recent team has excavated a *step trench* down the side of the mound here to get a glimpse into the history of the site. As of 2014, the team had reached back into the Middle Bronze Age, in the middle of the 2nd millennium B.C. Along the way, they encountered several layers of ash, burning, and other signs of destruction, marking the dramatic end of several of the cities that once occupied the site.

- Among the finds in this area of the site was a small ceramic jar, discovered completely intact but filled with earth. When the earth was removed, out came a cache of gold jewelry, including earrings and many small beads that had probably once been part of a necklace or bracelet. Stylistically, these all date to about the 11th century B.C. and undoubtedly belonged to a fairly wealthy woman.

- In another area, dating back to the 3rd millennium B.C. and the Early Bronze Age, is perhaps one of the largest temples ever found in the ancient Near East. It stretches across an area where a famous round altar is also located. Contrary to many of the tour guides' assertions, there was no child sacrifice done on this altar by the Canaanites.

- In Area K, one of the most interesting levels is a destruction level that seems to be from the late 10th or 9th century B,C. When it became clear that excavators were digging the remains of a house that had been destroyed, they used a technique known as *fine gridding*.
    - Here, the standard 5-meter squares are divided into 1-meter squares, allowing excavators to reconstruct the locations of their finds very precisely. Using this technique, excavators identified the function of each room of the house, from the kitchen to the living room to the bedroom. Several skeletons were found in the house, as well, including that of a woman and several children.

    - What caused the destruction of this level and of the house? Some thought that it might have been done by invaders, such as King David or some other group of Israelites; others suggested that this might have been the city that was destroyed or captured by the Egyptian pharaoh Shoshenq when he left his inscription at the site. Still others believe that the destruction was caused by an earthquake.

- Another area at Megiddo does have evidence of a battle but not from the time period that excavators initially expected. In a part of the site that the University of Chicago team had excavated in 1925 and 1926, a large number of bullet casings were found that were stamped with dates of 1948 or earlier. Modern excavators also noted that the rocks of the Neo-Assyrian buildings in this area had been moved to form foxholes and firing pits. It was not known, however, who had fired the bullets—Arabs or Israelis.
  - Mostly 8-millimeter bullets were found, which would have been fired from one or more machine guns, most likely placed in the firing pits. Excavators were able to narrow down the type of machine guns that would have been available in 1948 to three specific types, two of which were German and one of which was Czech. They didn't have access, however, to any of those types of machine guns to try a ballistic comparison.

  - Ultimately, the Bureau of Alcohol, Tobacco, and Firearms got involved in the question and helped identify the bullets as being shot from the Czech machine gun.

- In 2009, Israel Finkelstein was awarded a large grant from the European Union Research Council that allowed him to incorporate newer scientific advances into biblical archaeology. One of the places where he used these techniques was at Megiddo, where he brought in specialists to look at specific features, such as vegetative material found on floors after the buildings were abandoned. These types of studies are referred to as *microarchaeology* and are now being included in many excavations in Israel and elsewhere.

- The excavations at Megiddo are continuing, and recent work by one of the new codirectors, Matt Adams, has now identified the site of the Roman camp that was established next to the ancient mound in the 2nd century A.D. His excavations there are yielding interesting finds, including roof tiles and armor scales, in addition to walls and buildings.

Suggested Reading

Cline, *The Battles of Armageddon.*

Davies, *Megiddo.*

Silberman, Finkelstein, Ussishkin, and Halpern, "Digging at Armageddon."

Questions to Consider

1. Why have so many battles been fought in and around Megiddo?

2. If you could participate in the excavations at Megiddo, what would you most hope to find?

Lecture 16 Transcript

Megiddo: Excavating Armageddon

There is nothing quite like walking across the top of a multi-level mound like Megiddo to start you wondering what lies beneath your feet. It could be anything, or it could be nothing. I dug at Megiddo every other year from 1994–2014 and every time I walked onto the site that's the way I felt. Mostly it's a feeling of enchantment, but I have to admit that sometimes there's a bit of frustration mixed in. Not knowing what the next day, or even the next bucket, will bring is both a blessing and a curse.

In any event, walking up onto Megiddo is an adventure in and of itself, because it is a manmade mound that towers more than 70 feet high. Inside the mound are at least 20 separate cities, built one on top of another, with the earliest dating back more than 5,000 years ago and the most recent dates to just after the time of Alexander the Great.

Walking up to the top is a strenuous hike. It's not as steep as Masada, but it can leave even those who are in good shape panting for breath halfway up. But, that's a good place to stop, because that's right where the main gate to the city is, with a great view of the surrounding Jezreel Valley.

The valley is in the northern part of Israel, and it's shaped a bit like a triangle that's lying on its side—the tip is over by Haifa, on the Mediterranean Sea, while the broad base is over by the river Jordan. It's about 20 or 30 miles from east to west, but only between 3 and 7 miles from north to south. It's a perfect place for a battlefield, which may explain why at least 34 battles have been fought here over the past 4,000 years. Most were fought for control of Megiddo or nearby areas because Megiddo looms over the entire valley, through which ran the Via Maris—the road that is called the Way of the Sea and that led from Egypt up to Mesopotamia and back again. The Egyptian pharaoh Thutmose III once said that the capturing of Megiddo is like the capturing of a thousand cities.

Many famous people have fought at Megiddo or in the Jezreel Valley, from Thutmose III in 1479 B.C. to Deborah, Barak, Gideon, Saul, Jonathan, and

Josiah, all from the Bible. The Romans fought here too, as did the Crusaders, the Mamlukes, Mongols, Napoleon, and even General Allenby in World War I. Only Alexander the Great, of all the invaders of this region, didn't fight a battle at Megiddo because the area seems to have simply given in to him. But, of the battles at Megiddo, the most famous is still to come—the battle of Armageddon, which is mentioned in the Book of Revelation.

In fact, the very word Armageddon comes from Megiddo, because in Hebrew, "Har Megiddo" means the "mound" or "mountain" of Megiddo, and originally the word was written Harmageddon in Greek. But, it is easy to lose the initial H in Greek, which simply is a little apostrophe at the beginning of the word, so over time, it became "Armageddon."

Probably the two most well-known archaeological remains at the site are the water tunnel, which was dug 100 feet straight down and then 300 feet straight out, so the inhabitants could get to the external spring without being subject to attack by enemy forces. The other one is the so-called Solomon's Stables, which might not be stables and almost certainly, weren't built by Solomon. But, we'll get to that.

A man named Gottlieb Schumacher conducted the first excavations at Megiddo from 1903–1905. He was actually an engineer by training, rather than an archaeologist, but he employed the excavation methods current in his day.

And one of those methods involved employing hundreds of workmen to dig a whacking-great trench right through the middle of the mound, just like Heinrich Schliemann had done at Troy some 30 years earlier. He also dug smaller trenches at various other places on the top of the mound, but it's the huge trench that yielded some of the most interesting finds. These included a tomb from the Middle Bronze Age that held the bodies of a number of men and women, along with gold objects and other finery.

Schumacher thought that he had found the bodies of the ruling family of Megiddo from that period, and he may well have. Unfortunately, most of the objects can't be located now, and it's not even entirely clear where the tomb was found, so we can't exactly check his work.

He also found one of the most famous objects ever to be discovered at Megiddo, namely an oval seal about an inch and a half wide made of a type of stone called jasper. It has a lion on it and the name Shema, servant of Jeroboam. It's not clear which Jeroboam this is because there are two kings with that name mentioned in the Bible, but it's definitely one of them. Unfortunately, the seal is now also missing, because Schumacher sent it to Istanbul, as a gift to the Ottoman Sultan who ruled the area at that time, and nobody knows where it is now.

Schumacher's workmen also missed things while they were digging, and they threw them out on the back dirt pile, or they simply piled them by the sides of their trenches, in the case of stones from walls that they took apart. One of these stones turned out to have the cartouche of the Egyptian pharaoh Shoshenq on it, but the workmen didn't even notice it.

It was only when the next expedition to Megiddo began that the stone was recognized for what it was. It was part of a monumental inscription that probably stood about 10 feet high originally. It would have been erected at the site as a victory inscription after Shoshenq captured and then occupied the city. Years later, it was taken down and broken apart, and it was reused in a wall of a new building. This is where Schumacher's men would have found it, but since they missed it and simply piled it on the side, we don't know from which city or which level it comes. If we knew, it would be wonderful because we could then attach that city to a known person because Shoshenq is not only known from Egypt but may also be known in the Bible, where he is called Shishak.

In any case, it was left to a team from the University of Chicago to identify this stone, which they did on the very first day. They were collecting material to use in building the staff headquarters at the site. The Chicago team dug at Megiddo for about 15 years, from 1925–1939; their efforts were only halted by the outbreak of World War II.

The overall project was under the direction of James Henry Breasted, founder of the Oriental Institute at the University of Chicago. The Chicago expedition was at the forefront of a new type of archaeology, which was more careful and more scientific than the type practiced by Schumacher.

Courtesy of Sir William Matthew Flinders Petrie, they now knew about stratigraphy and about pottery seriation, that is, the changes in pottery styles over time so that they could tell one city from another and get a good idea of its date, at least relatively speaking.

Funded by money from John D. Rockefeller, the Chicago team started out doing what we call horizontal excavation, in which they tried to expose one entire layer over the entire site, then recorded it, drew it, photographed it, and then picked it up and removed, so that they could then expose the next layer down. They did that for the very top level or Stratum I as they called it; then also for Stratum II; and then they exposed Stratum III, which dates to the Neo-Assyrian period, or the 8th and 7th centuries B.C. And then they started to run out of money.

They, therefore, switched to vertical excavation for the rest of their time at the site, which is why tourists today see mostly Neo-Assyrian remains on the current surface, with a few areas that go much, much deeper—all the way to bedrock in some cases. And that's how we know that there are at least 20 cities one on top of another within the mound because they dug all the way to bedrock in what is now known as the Chicago Trench.

The Chicago team was also still prone to use the biblical account to buttress their findings at the site. So, when they were excavating a series of structures that looked a lot like stables for horses, they turned to the Book of 1 Kings to help with their identification. There they found two passages that they thought were relevant, in 1 Kings 9 and 1 Kings 10.

The first one reads, "And this is the account of the forced labor which King Solomon levied to build the house of the Lord and his own house and the Millo and the wall of Jerusalem and Hazor and Megiddo and Gezer." That's 1 Kings 9:15. The second passage reads, "And Solomon gathered together chariots and horsemen; he had 1,400 chariots and 12,000 horsemen, whom he stationed in the chariot cities and with the king in Jerusalem," 1 Kings 10:26.

Combining these two passages, the Chicago excavators decided that Megiddo must have been one of Solomon's chariot cities and that the structures were stables for horses dating back to the time of Solomon in the 10th century B.C. So, still today, the tour guides refer to these as Solomon's Stables.

Similar structures have been found at other sites, though. So, while it is quite likely that these at Megiddo are indeed stables, it's also possible that they were used as storehouses, or as barracks for soldiers, or even as a suq or marketplace. And moreover, radiocarbon dating and the pottery found within these structures at Megiddo now indicate that they're unlikely to have been built during the time of Solomon. They're much more likely to date to at least 100 years later, perhaps to the time of Ahab and Omri or even to the time of Jeroboam I or the II. Solomon's Stables at Megiddo might not be stables and are almost certainly not Solomon's.

The next person to lead an excavation at Megiddo was Yigael Yadin. He came to Megiddo for a few brief seasons in the 1960s and 1970s. One of the things that Yadin and his team uncovered were the foundations of what appeared to be a large palatial structure, which he called Palace 6000. Only the foundations were left because the building lay directly underneath the northern set of stables that the Chicago team had found.

The large blocks from Yadin's Palace 6000 had been reused in the later building to make the troughs in which to put the food, and perhaps the water, for the horses. It was this palace, Yadin thought that had been built by Solomon, not the later stables built directly above it. But he didn't have any proof for this either, except for the same biblical passages and the fact that he thought the palace was built at the same time as a large entrance gate to the city itself.

This large gate had six chambers, and it appeared very similar to one that Yadin had found previously at Hazor, and to another one that he had identified at Gezer. Using the same passage from the Bible that mentions Megiddo, Hazor, and Gezer as having been fortified by Solomon, Yadin assigned them all to the 10th century—that is, during the time that Solomon ruled.

However, this is not the way that archaeology is supposed to work. The gates and the associated buildings should be dated by the pottery that's found within them, not by biblical passages that may or may not be related to them. So, when Israel Finkelstein looked again at the pottery found by both the Chicago team and by Yadin, he said that it dated both the gate and the palace to the 9th century B.C., not to the 10th century and the time of Solomon. If he is correct, then neither of the levels that previous excavators have dated to the time of Solomon are actually from that time period. However, the details are still being debated, even 20 years after Finkelstein dramatically suggested altering the dating, so the jury is still out.

Speaking of Finkelstein, he has been leading the new sets of excavations at Megiddo since 1992, with a series of co-directors, including myself most recently. As I mentioned, I started digging with him at the site in 1994. I started as a volunteer team member, even though I already had 15 seasons of experience elsewhere because I wanted to be part of a large-scale expedition to a well-known site in Israel. I rose up through the ranks, and I essentially outlasted everybody else so that I was appointed co-director in 2012 and held that position until I retired from the project.

I was part of the team who were fortunate enough to re-excavate the area in which both Yadin's Palace 6000 and Chicago's northern stables were located so that I've got firsthand knowledge of the issues involved in their re-dating. I've also dug in most of the other areas at one point or another, so I can tell you now about those as well, for each area has its own points of interest.

For instance, in the part of the site that we call Area H, the buildings now on the surface are two palaces that date to the Neo-Assyrian period, in the 8th century B.C. The Chicago team exposed them but then didn't dig any deeper in the area. We have excavated what is called a step trench down the side of the mound here so that we can get a glimpse into the history of the site, just like Chicago did on the other side of the mound.

After the 2014 season, we had dug more than 20 feet down from where we had started back in 1994. We had reached back into the Middle Bronze Age, in the middle of the 2nd millennium B.C. Along the way, we encountered several layers of ash, burning, and other signs of destruction, which mark the dramatic end of several of the cities that once occupied the site.

Among our finds is a smallish ceramic jar, which we discovered completely intact in 2010. It was full to the brim with earth, so we sent it in to the conservation lab to be cleaned out and perhaps to try doing some organic residue analysis on it, to see what it had once held. But the lab was very busy with previous commitments, so the jar sat on a shelf for nearly a year before one of the conservators was able to look at it.

When she did finally begin to work on it, and started to carefully remove the earth inside it, out came a cache of gold jewelry, including eight small gold hoop earrings and one large ornate one, plus many small beads that had probably once been part of a necklace or bracelet. Stylistically, these all date to about the 11th century B.C. or so, if not a bit earlier, and undoubtedly belonged to a fairly wealthy woman who hid, or kept, them in the jar and never retrieved them for whatever reason. That was quite a surprise for the conservator, and for the members of the excavation.

In another area that dates back to the 3rd millennium B.C. and the Early Bronze Age, we may have one of the largest temples ever found in the ancient Near East. It stretches across the entire excavation area that we call Area J, which is also where the famous round altar is located. Contrary to many of the tour guides' assertions, there was no child sacrifice done on this round altar by the Canaanites. Our excavations yielded thousands of bones from here, though, but they were mostly from sheep and goats, but also from cattle, and even from lions, but there weren't any children.

Other areas where we dug at Megiddo were more off the beaten path, and they didn't get as much tourist traffic. One of these is Area K, where we are also digging on the side of the mound and are now down in Middle Bronze Age levels after starting back up in Neo-Assyrian levels.

Here, one of the most interesting levels is a destruction level that seems to be from the late 10th or 9th century B.C. When it became clear, back in 1998, that we were digging the remains of a house that had been destroyed, we employed a technique known as fine gridding to help us dig. To my knowledge, this was the first time it had been employed at the site, and it was introduced by Assaf Yasur-Landau—who later became co-director with me at the site of Tel Kabri, where we use it pretty much all the time.

The fine grid simply means that you take each square, which normally measures five meters by five meters, and you split it into smaller squares, each measuring one meter by one meter. If you then record which finds, including pottery fragments, come from each of these smaller squares, you can then reconstruct exactly what you found and where very precisely. So, we've been able to identify the function of each room of that house with a reasonable degree of precision, from the kitchen to the living room to the bedroom. Several skeletons were found in the house as well, including a woman and several children, most of them were in the region that we've identified as the kitchen area.

The big question for us, though, was what had caused the destruction of this level and of the house? Some thought that it might have been done by invaders, like perhaps King David or some other group of Israelites; others suggested that it might have been the city that was destroyed or captured by the Egyptian pharaoh Shoshenq when he left his inscription at the site.

Based on the data, though, I think that an earthquake caused the destruction. Now, I'll be the first to admit that it's frequently hard to tell a destruction caused by an earthquake from that caused by invaders, but in this case, a couple of things stand out to me. First is that the walls are leaning over, or tilting and some of them are no longer in a straight line like they once were. Second is that the bodies in the house are not accompanied by any arrowheads, or spears, or swords, or cut marks, or anything else indicating that they might have been killed by enemies or invaders. In short, I think Mother Nature caused this destruction though I can't prove it for sure.

In another area at Megiddo we do have evidence for a battle, but not from the time period that we initially expected. This too is an example of the curveballs that archaeology can throw at you when you least expect it.

In 2008, we began to clear away the underbrush from an area that the University of Chicago had excavated back in 1925 and 1926. Nobody had been in the area since, or so we thought. We had the photographs and the drawings that the Chicago archaeologists had made, and we knew that they had found rectangular buildings with small rooms that dated to the Neo-Assyrian period in the 8th century B.C.

But when we began clearing the area, we found that some of the rooms were now round, rather than rectangular. Moreover, in and around them, we found a number of bullet casings, that is, the spent remains of bullets that had been ejected from a gun, which we thought at first were the result of weekend hunters or somebody doing target practice. But as more and more of these cartridge cases came to light, we begin to realize that perhaps something else had taken place here. So, we began to collect them, as if they were archaeological artifacts, which indeed it turned out they were.

One of my students, Anthony Sutter, took a number of the cartridge cases back with him to the United States for study. When he cleaned off the back of the casings, he was able to read the letters and the numbers stamped into the metal, which is known as headstamps. These identify the maker of the bullets and the year in which they were made. I took back others and cleaned them off as well. All of them, both his and mine, either said 1948 or earlier. Not one of the several hundred that we looked at had a later date, and it quickly became clear that we were looking at the material remains of the battle that we knew had taken place at Megiddo back in 1948. In short, it became clear that we were doing what's called battlefield archaeology, which has been applied to the area of the Little Bighorn where Custer had his last stand and to areas in Europe dating to World War I and World War II.

It also became clear why some of the rectangular rooms originally excavated by Chicago were now round. Someone had moved the rocks of the Neo-Assyrian buildings in 1948 to form foxholes and firing pits in which to crouch and to fire machine guns towards the British police station, which is now a prison, that's located across the fields about a kilometer away.

The one thing we didn't know was who had created the foxholes and firing pits, and who had fired the bullets in battle. And this is where things took an unexpected turn, and it shows how archaeologists can turn to the most unexpected places to find their answers. While we never did find out for certain who had created the foxholes, we were able to figure out, within a reasonable degree of certainty, who had fired the bullets.

We knew that we had mostly 8-millimeter bullets that would have been fired from one or more machine guns. We had even been able to narrow down the type of machine guns that would have been available to shoot the bullets back in 1948. We had narrowed it down to three specific types, two of which were German machine guns, and one of which was a Czech machine gun. But then we were stuck. We didn't know anybody who had any of these types of machine guns, let alone all three types, and which still worked so that we might try a ballistic comparison.

It was only when I happened to mention our finds to the chairman of our Forensic Sciences department at George Washington University that the breakthrough occurred. He was intrigued enough by my account that he gave me the name of an adjunct instructor whose primary job was at the ATF—the Bureau of Alcohol, Tobacco, and Firearms. She, in turn, put me in touch with someone in the ATF who worked at a place where they keep more than 6,000 guns, from all time periods and places. When I mentioned to him the three types of machine guns that we thought our bullets could be from, he said, "Yep, we've got those." Fortunately, it also turned out that he had been an archaeology major as an undergraduate, so he was very interested in the challenging problem that I presented.

In the end, he fired all three types of machine guns while I got to watch. We then took those recently fired bullet casings and went back to the original woman whom I had first contacted. She put the new casings and the Megiddo casings side-by-side into a special microscope; first the ones from one of the German machine guns, and then those from the second, and then the ones fired by the Czech machine gun. The Czech ones matched up perfectly with ours from Megiddo, with the same type of firing pin impressions. We had a definite identification. We had solved the case: CSI Megiddo; a cold case from 1948. It was a spectacular moment. Anthony Sutter and I later coauthored an article about the whole topic, which was published in the *Journal of Military History*.

But, the excavations at Megiddo have also been at the forefront of scientific archaeology in another way. That's because Israel Finkelstein was awarded a large grant from the European Union Research Council in 2009. This allowed him to incorporate newer scientific advances into biblical archaeology. One of the places where he used these techniques was at Megiddo, where he brought in specialists to look at specific things, like the material found on floors after they were abandoned, which can yield information about the types of vegetation in the area and the length of time that the building was abandoned before it was reoccupied. These types of studies are referred to as micro-archaeology, and they're now being included in many excavations, both in Israel and elsewhere.

The excavations at Megiddo are currently continuing and recent work by one of the new co-directors, Matt Adams, has now identified the site of the Roman camp called Leggio that was established next to the ancient mound in the 2nd century A.D. His excavations there are yielding very interesting finds, including roof tiles and armor scales, in addition to walls and buildings.

Megiddo is an exciting site and one of the most important in the entire Near East. I think back now to the days when I would walk over the site in the chill of the early morning, wondering what lay beneath my feet. I still wonder about that and so, along with all of you, I'm going to be watching and waiting to see what else will be uncovered in future seasons at this site of Armageddon.

Lecture 17 The Canaanite Palace at Tel Kabri

Tel Kabri is an amazing site—the third or fourth largest in ancient Israel and the only site at which a Middle Bronze Age Canaanite palace, dating to almost 4,000 years ago, is easily accessible for archaeological excavation. However, much about Tel Kabri remains a mystery. No writing has been found at the site, including any tablets that might have documented trade with other areas. Archaeologists are also still trying to learn what caused the destruction or abandonment of the site after 300 years of profitable living—perhaps an earthquake or the drying up of water sources. Whatever it was, the site was forgotten so thoroughly that we now have no clue what its ancient name might have been.

Trial Excavation and Area Survey

- The palace at Tel Kabri was first discovered in the 1960s and excavated in the 1980s, but those initial excavations ended in 1993. In 2003, archaeologist Assaf Yasur-Landau of the University of Haifa conducted a small remote-sensing survey and had found indications that there was more to dig at Tel Kabri. The magnetometer and the electric conductivity tests indicated the probable presence of walls and floors, though it didn't indicate how far down they were.

- In 2005, a small team was assembled to conduct a trial excavation to see if the results of the remote sensing were accurate and if there were enough remains left at the site to merit a multi-season excavation. After about 10 days of digging, the archaeologists came upon walls and floors in the trenches. The remote sensing had been correct; there was architecture present. After that, the team quickly found enough material to justify a multi-season excavation.

- Before embarking on that, though, they decided to spend two summers surveying the region around the site, that is, much of the western Galilee north of Haifa, 'Akko, and Nahariya. The aim was to see the context for Tel Kabri, especially because previous excavations

Lecture 17—The Canaanite Palace at Tel Kabri 301

had shown that it was essentially a one-phase site, occupied only in the Middle Bronze Age, from about 1700 to 1500 B.C. The team wanted to know what else was around in the area at that time.

- Because numerous surveys had already been carried out in the area during the past 30 years or more, the researchers decided to simply revisit sites in the region that previous surveys had already identified as dating to the Middle Bronze Age. They rechecked the pottery at those sites and re-measured the scatters that had been found to see if any of the sites were larger or smaller than previously thought and if they could specifically identify when during the Middle Bronze Age they were occupied.

- Although there may well be other sites in the area that have not yet been found, Tel Kabri is probably one of the largest sites, if not the largest. It was probably the center of a polity of some sort—that is, a small kingdom or a large estate—during most of its existence, until it was suddenly destroyed or abandoned about 1500 B.C.

- In 2009, in another limited season, the archaeologists opened up a few trenches and were able to establish a good stratigraphic sequence and determine that the palace had probably been occupied for 250 or 300 years. They were also able to determine where they should dig when the full team came together in 2009.

Painted Plaster

- In 2009, excavations began in earnest. The archaeologists found the first fragments of painted plaster, which established that finds at the site would give them insight into the international connections and, perhaps, the economics of the ancient palace.

- The fragments of painted frescoes, which came from both wall paintings and a painted floor, were not the first to be found at the site. In fact, it was the earlier discoveries that had brought Kabri to the attention of the Bronze Age archaeological world in the late 1980s and early 1990s. The previous excavators had found an intact painted floor and more than 2,000 fragments from a wall painting that had been torn off the wall and reused as packing underneath a threshold during a renovation of the palace.

- Both the painted floor and the fragments of the wall painting were done in a technique that was not local to Canaan but was more usually found in the Bronze Age Aegean, such as at Knossos and Akrotiri.

- The painted floor had squares on it, inside of which were painted flowers, such as irises and crocuses. In all, it was a very Minoan-looking floor, more at home on Crete than in the Levant. Similarly, the 2,000 fragments from the wall painting looked more like the frescoes found at Akrotiri, though it is nearly impossible to reconstruct the original picture.

- Most of the fragments of Aegean-style painted plaster found in 2009 seem to be from another wall painting. Although it's not certain what is being portrayed, a few pieces that fit together may form the fin of a flying fish of the wing of a griffin.

The Orthostat Building

- In 2011, the excavators planned to begin digging outside of the palace to compare the inside and outside areas, but they discovered a structure to the west of where they had been digging that had not shown up with remote sensing. Here were the remains of what must have been a beautiful building, or set of rooms, with an entranceway, a large central room, and a smaller back room. The entranceway and the central room had a thick plaster floor. The smaller back room also had a plaster floor, but here, the plaster was laid on blocks made of beach stone that had been carved and placed flat before being plastered.

- These same sorts of stone blocks were also placed upright along the entire length of both the large central room and the smaller back room, just inside the walls on all sides. In each of the blocks was carved a small square dowel hole to enable a vertical rod to be inserted; onto these vertical rods were lowered flat slats of wood.

The end result was rather like Venetian blinds in a modern house, only here, the wooden slats covered up the rock face of the walls, thereby creating a "wooden" room.

- This was an expensive and time-consuming architectural feature. Such carved blocks, especially with dowel holes, are known as *orthostats*; thus, the structure was dubbed the Orthostat Building. Interestingly, although they are known from elsewhere in the ancient Near East, the best parallels for those found at Kabri are in the palaces and sites of Minoan Crete.

- It's not yet clear what this building was used for. It looks a bit like a tripartite temple, but if it was a temple, it wasn't still being used in that manner at the end of its existence, because nothing was found in it except for three smashed storage jars in the back room. Remains of animal bones in and around the building also suggest that it might have been a feasting hall.

The Wine Cellar

- Possible confirmation of that hypothesis may come from finds during the 2013 season, when excavators began to uncover the storerooms of the palace, immediately to the west of the Orthostat Building. Here, they found 40 jars, each 3 feet tall. Each would have held about 100 liters of liquid—or 4,000 liters in total—making this the largest wine cellar discovered from the ancient Near East!

- LiDAR was used as part of the recording at Kabri. LiDAR works somewhat like radar, using light from a laser to produce highly accurate measurements. It's mostly used from an airplane to see through overgrown jungles in Central America, but it can also be used on the ground as a quick and accurate way to measure and record an archaeological situation. In this case, LiDAR yielded a huge amount of data that researchers could later analyze, including the precise location of every jar, accurate to within about 3 millimeters.

- At the same time that archaeologists were excavating and recording the jars, other researchers were conducting organic residue analysis to see what each had held. This process entailed taking a sherd from near the bottom of each jar, then boiling it in a solution that allowed extraction of the residue that had seeped into each sherd when the jar was full. All the jars tested contained either tartaric acid or syringic acid or both, and both of these acids are commonly found in wine.

- The team conducting the organic residue analysis also found indications of numerous additives in the wine. For example, methyl syringate, which was present in many of the jars, usually comes from honey, which means that much of the wine would have been sweetened. Other additives included moronic acid, which comes mostly from the pistachio tree and was used as a resin; cineole acid, which probably comes from either juniper berries or mint; and cinnamic acid, which comes from something called storax and was used as a resin to either help preserve the wine or to coat the inside of the jars.

- Interestingly, the Kabri wine seems to match, at least to a certain degree, the types of wine that are described by a king of Mari named Yasmah-Adad, who lived at approximately this same time, in the 18th century B.C., on the banks of the Euphrates. This king seems to have participated in a "wine of the month" club in which he exchanged wines with a king of Carchemish. This means it's possible that the Kabri wine was shipped from Mesopotamia to Canaan, but it's more likely that it was locally produced.

- In terms of quantity, 4,000 liters of wine would be the equivalent of about 5,300 bottles today, yet it's not enough to consider this a distribution center. Instead, this is probably the king's personal supply, which would have lasted for about a year. However, excavation in 2015 revealed additional storerooms that may have held at least 16,000 liters of wine, or the equivalent of about 21,000 bottles. If that's the case, then the storerooms at Kabri probably represent more than just the king's private supply!

- Eventually, researchers hope to take samples for ancient DNA analysis to determine the type of grapes that were used in making the wine. If they know that and know the additives that were introduced during the production process, they might be able to re-create the wine.

- If, on the other hand, the jars turn out to have held olive oil, wheat, or some other commodity, then the researchers will finally be able to explore the economy of the palace and the ancient site of Kabri.

Suggested Reading

Cline and Yasur-Landau, "Your Career Is in Ruins."

———, "Aegeans in Israel."

Cline, Yasur-Landau, and Goshen, "New Fragments of Aegean-Style Painted Plaster from Tel Kabri, Israel."

Questions to Consider

1. Why would the Canaanite ruler at Kabri have wanted some of the walls of his palace decorated by Aegean artists?

2. Do you think it serves any purpose to try to re-create such items as ancient Canaanite wine?

Lecture 17 Transcript

The Canaanite Palace at Tel Kabri

Archaeology is not nearly as glamorous as it looks in Hollywood movies or television shows. For example, it can be tough to wake up at 4 am, which pretty much feels like the middle of the night. But when you arrive at the site in time to see the sunrise every morning that makes it a special occupation.

Every archaeological site is different, and every archaeological team has its own personality. I tend to remember the different seasons of excavation by what we discovered, the people that were there, the practical jokes that were played, and the surprises that were in store for us during the excavation.

For example, I can distinguish each of my seasons at Tel Kabri in Israel, where I've been excavating and co-directing the team since 2005 with my good friend Assaf Yasur-Landau of the University of Haifa. The first season was a trial exploration to see if a long-term project was merited, which it was. The next two seasons were surveys in the area so that we could put the site in context before beginning to really to excavate it. 2008 was another exploratory season. And then, 2009 produced painted wall frescoes, 2011 produced our Orthostat Building, 2013 was the discovery of our wine cellar, and in 2015, we discovered more storage rooms.

But one of my clearest memories is the very first day that I arrived at the site, back in 2005. I was jet-lagged; I had just flown directly from the United States, and I had driven straight up north for more than two hours. I was tired; I was hungry, and I was badly in need of a shower. And yet Assaf insisted on taking me straight to the site before doing anything else. To say that I was underwhelmed is putting it mildly. We drove into what seemed to be the middle of an avocado grove which in fact it was. We parked, and we got out of the car. "Where is the site?" I asked. "You're standing on it," came the answer. It turned out that the site was so large that it extended out of sight in all directions. The little bump that I had felt a few minutes before getting out of the car that was when the road led us over the now-destroyed mud brick ramparts that had protected the city thousands of years ago.

The actual site surprised me that day, and it's continued to surprise me to this day. It is an amazing site; it's the third or fourth largest in ancient Israel, and it's the only site at which a Middle Bronze Age Canaanite palace, dating to almost 4,000 years ago, is easily accessible for archaeological excavation.

The palace was first discovered back in the 1960s when workmen digging a ditch for a large pipe to bring water to the coastal communities of 'Akko and Nahariya went right through the thick plaster floor of the palace. Several young archaeologists, who later went on to become very well known, were running up and down next to the workmen, trying to limit the destruction at that time.

Later, in the 1980s, Aharon Kempinski of Tel Aviv University began a full-scale excavation at the site. He was joined by Wolf-Dietrich Niemeier, who was then of the University of Heidelberg. Their excavations lasted through 1993 and were only brought to a halt by Kempinski's untimely death in 1994. Assaf was a volunteer on the team that dug at the site in 1990, and he had sworn to come back someday to run his own dig at the site. He has now made that dream come true.

As for me, I began digging at Tel Kabri because of a 30-second conversation that I had with Assaf back in 2004. I was working at Megiddo that summer and was in charge of taking the team volunteers on a Saturday field trip down to the site of Ashkelon, which was a few hours to the south of us. When we got off the bus there, Assaf ran up to me. We had first gotten to know each other back at Megiddo in 1998 when he was an Area Supervisor there, but this summer he was digging at Ashkelon. Anyway, he ran up to me, and he said, "Hey, do you want to reopen Tel Kabri with me?" Now, even though I had never been there, Tel Kabri is a magic name in certain circles within Near Eastern archaeology, because of the fragments of wall frescoes that had been found by the previous excavators, so I immediately replied, "Sure." "OK," he says, "I'll be in touch." And with that, he ran off again, back to his area at the site, and so began our partnership, with a 30-second conversation. It has since lasted a beautiful decade, with no end in sight.

It transpired that Assaf had conducted a small remote sensing survey with a colleague of his in 2003, and he had found indications that there was more to dig at Tel Kabri. The magnetometer and the electric conductivity tests indicated the probable presence of walls and possibly floors, but it didn't tell him how far down they were.

So, in 2005, we assembled a small team and enough money to last us for four weeks of excavation. We were conducting what we called a trial excavation, to see if the results of the remote sensing were accurate and if there were enough remains at the site left to dig that might merit a multi-season excavation. As it turned out, there certainly were, but it took us a while to determine that.

When we started digging, we put our small team into a couple of different squares, each five meters by five meters, according to the standard Kenyon-Wheeler method of digging, and carefully positioned between the avocado trees, so that we wouldn't harm any of them. The first day yielded nothing, and so we sent our volunteers to the swimming pool for the afternoon because we had no pottery to wash. The second, that was the same thing. The third day, same thing, and for the entire rest of that first week, for that matter—nothing, absolutely nothing

Finally, on the 10th day or so, we came down upon walls and floors in all of our trenches at the same time. The remote sensing had been correct—there was architecture down there, but it hadn't been able to tell us how far down it was. After that, we quickly found enough material to convince us that a multi-season excavation at the site was indeed merited. Before we embarked on that, though, we decided to spend two summers surveying the entire region around the site—that is, much of the western Galilee north of Haifa, 'Akko, and Nahariya. We wanted to see the context for our site, especially since the previous excavations had shown that it was essentially a one-phase site, pretty much occupied only in the Middle Bronze Age, from about 1700–1500 B.C. We wanted to know what else was in the area at that same time.

We had an advantage in that we didn't have to actually start surveying from scratch because numerous surveys had already been carried out in the area during the past 30 years or more. So, instead of hiking around and doing transects as one usually does on preliminary surveys, we decided to simply revisit the sites in the region that previous surveys had already identified as dating to the Middle Bronze Age. We rechecked the pottery at those sites and we re-measured the scatters that we found so that we could see if any of the sites were larger or smaller than previously thought and if we could specifically identify when during the Middle Bronze Age they were occupied.

Although there may well be other sites that have not yet been found, we're pretty confident that we have one of the largest sites in the region, if not the largest. Kabri was probably the center of what we would call a polity of some sort—that is, a kingdom if you want to call it that, or a large estate at the very least—during most of its existence until it was suddenly either destroyed or abandoned about 1500 B.C. at the latest.

Having completed our survey, we were ready to begin excavating in 2008. However, not so fast. First, we wanted to establish where we should concentrate our efforts in 2009, so 2008 was another small initial season like we had had back in 2005. I was also technically participating full-time at the Megiddo excavations that summer. Those were located about 45 minutes away, so I had to run back and forth between the two sites on almost a daily basis.

In the end, with a few significant trenches opened up, we were able to get a good stratigraphic sequence established and to figure out that the palace was probably occupied for 250 or 300 years all told, from its beginning to its end. We were also able to figure out where we should dig when our full team came together in 2009.

So, that next summer we began in earnest, having already had two preliminary seasons of excavation and two seasons of survey under our belt. And it was during that summer when we found the first fragments of painted plaster, which established that we were going to have some good finds that would give us an insight into the international connections and perhaps the economics of the ancient palace.

The fragments of painted frescoes, which came from both wall paintings and a painted floor, were not the first to be found at the site. In fact, it was the earlier discoveries that had brought Kabri to the attention of the Bronze

Age archaeological world in the late 1980s and early 1990s. The previous excavators had found an intact painted floor and more than 2,000 fragments from a wall painting that had been torn off the wall and reused as packing underneath a threshold during a renovation of the palace.

Both the painted floor and the fragments of wall painting were done in a technique that was not local to Canaan, but rather it was more usually found in the Bronze Age Aegean, like at Knossos on Crete and at Akrotiri on the island of Santorini. The painted floor had squares on it, which were made by dipping a string into red paint and then pulling it straight very quickly while just barely touching the floor so that a completely straight line was created. Inside the squares were painted flowers, like irises and crocuses. In all, this is a very Minoan looking floor, more at home on Crete than in the Levant.

Similarly, the 2,000 fragments from a miniature wall painting looked more like the frescoes found at Akrotiri on Santorini, though it is nearly impossible to reconstruct the original picture—think of having a jigsaw puzzle with 2,000 pieces but not having the box cover, so that you don't know what the full painting is actually supposed to look like.

Anyway, in 2009, we found our own fragments of Aegean-style painted plaster. At least one appears to be from another painted floor—because it's so thick—but most of the rest, which are about 60 pieces in total, seem to be from another wall painting. We've got all sorts of colors—orange, red, yellow, brown, and black—but the largest and most interesting pieces have both blue and white paint on them, with black paint outlining the white. We're not yet certain what's being portrayed, but the few pieces that do fit together could be from the fin of a flying fish, which would be similar to a wall painting found on the island of Melos in the Aegean, or they could be from the wing of a griffin, which would be similar to a slightly later painting found at the site of Mycenae on the Greek mainland.

We found a few more fragments of painted plaster in 2011, but the real discovery that season was a building to the west of where we had been digging. We hadn't been expecting it because we had done some experimental remote sensing one day during the summer of 2010 and hadn't seen anything in that area. The remote sensing that we used wasn't really right for our area.

We had planned to begin digging outside of the palace so that we could do some palatial versus non-palatial comparisons. To our surprise, we found that we weren't yet outside the palace. Instead, we found the remains of what must have been a very beautiful building, or set of rooms, with an entranceway, a large central room, and a smaller back room. The entranceway and the central room had a very thick plaster floor. The smaller back room also had a plaster floor, but here the plaster was laid down upon gorgeous blocks made out of beach stone, which had been carved and then placed flat to make a floor, before being plastered.

These same sorts of stone blocks were also placed upright along the entire length of both the large central room and the smaller back room, just inside the walls on all sides. In each of the blocks was carved a small square dowel hole, so that a vertical rod could be inserted, and onto these vertical rods were probably lowered flat slats of wood, so that the end result was kind of like Venetian blinds in a modern house, only here the wooden slats covered up the rock face of the walls, thereby creating a wooden room.

This was a very expensive, and time-consuming, architectural feature. Such carved blocks, especially with dowel holes, are known as orthostats and so we have dubbed this the Orthostat Building. Interestingly, although they're known from elsewhere in the ancient Near East, the best parallels for our particular ones are found at the palaces and sites of Minoan Crete, which may not be surprising, considering the painted wall plaster fragments that we also have from our site.

It's not yet clear what this building was used for. To my mind, it looks a little bit like a tripartite temple—that is, with three rooms, of which the smallest one in the back would have been used for the holy of holies—but if it was ever used in that manner, it wasn't still being used as a temple at the end of its existence, because we didn't find anything in that back room except for three smashed storage jars. But we did find some interesting remains of animal bones in and around the building, which lead Assaf, in particular, to speculate that this might have been used as some sort of feasting hall.

Possible confirmation of that hypothesis might come from our finds during the 2013 season, when we began to uncover the storerooms of the palace, just to the west of the Orthostat Building. Again, these were unexpected, and again we were actually hoping that we were digging outside the palace so that we could start thinking finally about the non-palatial aspects of the economy at the site. Once again, though, we found ourselves still in the palace, but now quite happily in what turned out to be the oldest and largest wine cellar ever discovered from the ancient Near East. Here's how it happened.

We were digging during the first week of our season—this is back in June 2013—when we came down upon a large jar that we nicknamed Bessie. Bessie was completely intact, and still retained her original shape, but she was completely shattered and lying on her side, with the soil holding the pieces still in place. It took us almost two weeks to uncover her completely and to find out that she was lying on the plaster floor of the room. By that time, she had been joined by what turned out to be 39 of her friends—because we found a total of 40 jars, each of them three feet high, in that room and in the corridor just to the north of it. We thought each jar would have held about 50 liters of liquid, which means about 2,000 liters all told, but we've since been told by our conservator, after he put one of these back together in the laboratory, that each one actually would have held more than 100 liters, so that means that this one room would have held about 4,000 liters in all.

Of course, the problem that we faced was that by the time we realized how many jars there were, our six-week season was nearly half over and yet we needed to excavate them carefully as well as quickly. Now that we had exposed them, we couldn't just leave them there because they would have disintegrated during the winter rains. Also, we had so many team members that not everyone could fit into that one room all at the same time, but we were running a field school and needed to train everyone.

So we did something unusual, which Assaf, my partner in crime, dreamed up. Instead of just digging a normal day, from 5 am until 1 pm, we split the team into two. Half of the team dug during the usual hours and the other half dug from 2 pm until 7 pm. And, it worked. Everyone got experience digging up the jars, and we got all of them excavated and fully recorded before the end of the season, with each jar carefully packed in pieces within its own crate, nicely labeled for future study and everything.

One part of our recording involved using LiDAR, which stands for Light Detection and Ranging. LiDAR works something like radar, using light from a laser to produce highly accurate measurements. It's mostly used from an airplane to see through overgrown jungles in Central America, but it can also be used on the ground as a quick and accurate, although expensive, way to measure and record an archaeological situation. In just three short hours, the team that we had hired had taken all of the measurements, involving thousands of discrete points, and gave us a huge amount of data that we could later analyze, including the precise location of everything, accurate to within about three millimeters. It was absolutely amazing.

At the same time as we were excavating and recording them, our other partner, Andrew Koh of Brandeis University, was taking a piece of each jar in order to conduct organic residue analysis on it and to figure out what was actually in each jar. This entailed taking a sherd from near the bottom of each jar and then boiling it in a solution that allowed Andrew and his team to extract the residue that had seeped into each sherd back when the jar was full of whatever it had once held since the pottery is porous rather than watertight.

They then ran the extracts from the jars though a Gas Chromatography machine back at Brandeis and were able to determine what type of acids had once been in the jars. All of the jars that they tested—which were 32 out of the 40 because they left some untested for future comparisons—have turned out to have either tartaric acid or syringic acid or both in them. Tartaric and syringic acids are most commonly found in wine, with tartaric acid found in both red and white wine, and syringic acid found only in red wine, and so we have little doubt that this storage room and the jars within it once held wine, most of it was red, some was white. Of course, it is now long gone, except for the residue left in the fabric of the jars, but I'm almost always asked by people what it would have tasted like. Since we don't yet know for certain, I simply answer that it's got an earthy taste now, and I leave it at that.

But, in fact, the Organic Residue Analysis that Andrew and his team ran also indicated that there were numerous additives in the wine. This was documented by the additional molecular acids that they noted in their analyses of the extracts. For example, methyl syringate, which is present in many of the jars, usually comes from honey, which means that much of our wine will have been sweet, or at least sweetened a bit. We also have something called moronic acid, yes, there is such an acid. But moronic acid comes mostly from the pistachio tree and was used as a resin. There is also cineole acid that probably comes from either juniper berries or mint. And, we also have cinnamic acid, which doesn't come from cinnamon but rather from something called storax. It's used as a resin and was probably added to either help preserve our wine or to coat the inside of the jars.

Interestingly, our wine seems to match, at least to a certain extent, the types of wine that are described by a king of Mari named Yasmah-Adad, who lived at approximately this same time, back in the 18th century B.C., but he was on the banks of the Euphrates in what is now modern-day Syria. This king was apparently quite fond of wine, and he even seems to have participated in a wine of the month club in which he exchanged wines with a friend of his who was the king of Carchemish. In one of his letters, Yasmah-Adad describes his wine cellar as containing "One jar of strong wine, one jar of sweet wine, and eight jars of wine of second quality shipped together with three types of herbal aromatics: one kirippum-jar of oil of Cyprus, one kirippum-jar of oil of myrtle, and one kirippum-jar of oil of juniper."

These sound just like the types of additives found in our wine jars, and so it is possible that we have here in our palace wine that was shipped from Mesopotamia to Canaan nearly 4,000 years ago. More likely, though, is that ours is locally produced because the jars are all locally made and all of the ingredients were also available locally.

In terms of quantities, 4,000 liters of wine would be the equivalent of about 5,300 bottles of wine today, so this is quite a large amount found in this one room. And yet, it's not enough to consider this a distribution center. Instead, this is probably just the king's personal supply for himself, his family, and his officials; it probably would have lasted about a year.

But, when we returned for our season in 2015, we found more. We knew that we would, because our five-meter by five-meter excavation square that revealed the original store room back in 2013 had also uncovered a doorway and the first several feet of the next room, which was located just to the south. On that floor, the shattered remains of more jars were just as thick if not thicker than in the original room, so we knew that we were going to find more.

And, indeed, we did. This time, in 2015, we started with our double shifts right away, just three days into the first week, with half the team working from 5 am to 1 pm and the other half of the team working from 2 pm until 7 pm. This worked extremely well because nobody got too tired and we were able to get in far more hours of work than is normal on an excavation.

By the end of the second week, we had not only uncovered most of the jars in that new, southern, store room but had also found another doorway leading again to the south and into yet another store room that had still more jars in it, and then we found another doorway into another room—the fourth in a row, all of them with jars.

In the new southern rooms, the jars were not in nearly as good a shape as they had been in the first one for some reason. Maybe it's because of the irrigation under the avocado trees, some of the jars were reduced to mere smears of pottery in the dirt, others, though, were just as intact but shattered in place as the first ones that we had found.

Although these may very well also contain wine, at least judging from their similar shape, we are currently awaiting the results of the Organic Residue Analysis that will tell us what was in them. If they did all contain wine, and in the same quantities as in the first storeroom, then these rooms together may have held at least 16,000 liters of wine or the equivalent of about 21,000 bottles of our wine today. If that is the case, we're probably looking at more than just the king's private supply rooms.

We hope to also eventually take samples for ancient DNA analysis so that we can try to determine the type of grapes that were used in making the wine. If we know that, and also know the additives that were introduced during the production process, we might actually be able to try to recreate the wine. But, we don't yet know whether any of the ancient DNA was still preserved, so stay tuned.

If on the other hand, the jars turn out to have held olive oil, or wheat, or some other commodity, then we should be able to finally really begin talking about the economy of the palace and of the ancient site of Kabri.

We are also still waiting to find any sort of writing at the site, including any tablets that might have documented trade with nearby or foreign areas or even documenting the items coming in and going out of the palace. It may be that our people didn't use writing, for whatever reason, though I personally tend to doubt that.

We're also still trying to learn what caused the destruction, or simple abandonment, of the palace and the site. It's still not clear what happened or why, but after about 300 years of profitable living, the inhabitants simply left, never to return. There is no evidence of an enemy attack or anything like that, so it might have been an earthquake, or maybe the water sources temporarily dried up, or it might have been something else entirely.

Whatever it was, the site was forgotten so thoroughly that we have no clue at the moment what its ancient name might have been. Perhaps one day we'll find an inscription that tells us where we have been digging for the past decade, but for now, it remains a mystery lost in the mists of time.

Lecture 18 Petra, Palmyra, and Ebla

Petra, Palmyra, and Ebla are three amazing sites that have been excavated in Jordan and Syria. Built by the Nabataeans, Petra is a UNESCO World Heritage site, known for its buildings carved from living rock. Palmyra, another Nabataean site, is an oasis in the Syrian Desert. And Elba is a huge site, covering about 140 acres, with a history dating from the 3rd millennium B.C. to 1600 B.C. There are also many other sites in this region, including Jerash and Pella in Jordan and Mari and Ugarit in Syria. Unfortunately, conflict in the Middle East has resulted in destruction at some of these sites, reminding us of just how precious—and fragile—these fragments of the past can be.

Petra
- Petra is located in the Jordanian desert a few hours south from the modern capital city of Amman. Although there were earlier people in the area, the city rose to prominence with the Nabataeans beginning in the 4th century B.C. It flourished for more than 500 years, especially during the time when the Romans were in this area, from the early 2nd century A.D. on. Then, after an earthquake destroyed nearly half of Petra in the mid-4th century A.D. and a second one hit in the 6th century A.D., activity there came to a halt.

- The Nabataeans are still a bit mysterious to us, but Petra seems to have been the center of their confederation of cities, which were focused on controlling the lucrative trade across the Arabian Peninsula. They are known for their hydraulic engineering, among other things, which allowed them to bring water from the occasional flash floods in to Petra through a series of dams, canals, and cisterns.

- The Wadi Musa, usually called the Siq, is the way that most tourists enter Petra today. It's a narrow canyon that twists and turns through sheer rock towering above on both sides. This was probably a ceremonial entrance, rather than the main entrance to the city. The narrow canyon walls suddenly open up onto a huge open space in front of what is now called the Treasury, more formally known as the Khaznah.

- The Nabateans carved the Khaznah out of the cliff face, as they did with many other buildings and structures at Petra. It was probably built to serve as a tomb but is called the Treasury because of a local tradition that gold or other valuables were hidden in the large urn on the façade; however, the urn is solid stone.

- Heading into the heart of Petra, visitors pass along the Street of Façades, which are tombs carved into the cliff face. On the western side are the remains of the Roman theater, which could hold more than 8,000 people. A little further on are the so-called Royal Tombs, which are, again, carved into the cliff face. The original occupants

> In an Internet poll conducted in 2007, Petra was named one of the New Seven Wonders of the World, and indeed, the view of the Treasury as visitors exit the canyon is breathtaking.

of these tombs are debated; we don't even know if they were actually royal. The only tomb whose occupant may be known is that of Sextus Florentinus, who was the governor of the Roman province of Arabia in the 2nd century A.D.

- Along the Colonnaded Street, which gets its name from the columns lining it, is the so-called Great Temple. This might not be a temple at all but the major administrative building for the city.

- On the hill opposite is the Temple of the Winged Lions. It was probably built in the early 1st century A.D., then destroyed in an earthquake a little more than 300 years later. It was first found in 1973 using remote sensing and has been excavated by American teams ever since.

- In the nearby church, which is built over Nabataean and Roman ruins and dates to the 5th and 6th centuries A.D., mosaics were found. In 1993, while in the process of building a shelter to protect the mosaics and the remains of the church, archaeologists uncovered at least 140 carbonized papyrus scrolls.
    ○ Dating from the 6th century A.D., the scrolls had been caught in a fire that, ironically, preserved some of them, although most are now illegible.

    ○ Papyrologists have been able to read a few dozen of the scrolls and to determine that they are written in Greek. Most of them have to do with various economic matters, from real estate to marriages, inheritances, divisions of property, and so on, including a case involving stolen goods.

- From this part of Petra, visitors can proceed via a long stairway to the upper reaches of the site, the location of the huge temple known as the Monastery. Like the Treasury, the façade of the Monastery is carved into the living face of the rock. It is approximately 130 feet high, just like the Treasury, but 60 feet wider.

Palmyra

- Palmyra is considered by most archaeologists to be the second most famous Nabataean site. It is an oasis located deep in the Syrian Desert, to the northeast of Damascus. It is also a UNESCO World Heritage site.

- Known as Tadmor in antiquity, this city was active already during the Bronze Age in the 2nd millennium B.C. but had its heyday during the time of the Roman Empire, especially during the 1st through 3rd centuries A.D. It served as a major stop on the caravan routes leading across the desert, connecting the Roman Empire to India and China. Its architecture reflects foreign influences, especially Greco-Roman and Persian. However, the city rebelled against the Romans in the early 270s A.D. in what is known as the rebellion of Queen Zenobia. After putting down the revolt, the Romans destroyed Palmyra in 273 A.D. It was rebuilt but was never the same again.

- The first major excavations at the site, especially of the Roman period ruins, began in 1929, by French archaeologists. The remains they uncovered, including the Temple of Bel and the Agora (marketplace), are impressive, especially the parts that have been partially reconstructed. Swiss and Syrian archaeologists have also excavated there, but the most consistent presence has been that of Polish archaeologists, who were working right up until 2011, when they were forced to leave at the beginning of the civil war in Syria.

- Some of the archaeology at Palmyra is similar to that at Petra. Like Petra, Palmyra has a Roman theater that could seat thousands of people. It also has a long colonnaded street, running from the Temple of Bel at its eastern end to a huge funerary temple at the western end.

- A monumental arch stretches across this main street near its eastern end. The arch was built by the Roman emperor Septimius Severus around the year 200 A.D., possibly to celebrate his victory over the Parthians in Mesopotamia. At about the same time, a *tetrapylon*

On the columns of Palmyra's colonnaded street are small ledges, where statues of the donors who paid for the construction of the street were once placed.

(a type of Roman monument) was built at an intersection about halfway down the street. Of the four pylons now visible, one is original.

- In addition, there is a huge Temple to Bel, or Ba'al, who was originally a Canaanite god from the 2nd millennium B.C. The altar in the temple was consecrated in 32 A.D., but the temple as it looked until fairly recently was probably completed about 100 years later, in the 2nd century A.D. Unfortunately, this temple was destroyed by ISIS in late August 2015.

Elba

- Paolo Matthiae from the Sapienza University of Rome and his team have been excavating the ancient city of Ebla (modern Tell Mardikh) since 1964. The site is absolutely huge, covering about 140 acres. There is a huge lower city and a citadel—a higher mound—in the middle of the site. On the citadel are the royal palaces, administrative buildings, and so on.

- Four years after starting the excavation, Matthiae's team found a statue dedicated by a local man named Ibbit-Lim. In the inscription, this man said that he was the son of the king of Ebla. This was quite a revelation because previous scholars had thought that Ebla was located further north in Syria, not at Tell Mardikh. However, after further digging, the archaeologists confirmed that they had indeed found ancient Ebla. We now know that Ebla is an extremely important site, with a history dating from the 3rd millennium B.C. to its destruction in about 1600 B.C.

- In 1973, when Matthiae's team began to work on the earlier phase of occupation (dating from about 2400 to 2250 B.C.), they began to discover clay tablets that sparked a controversy.
    - There may be as many as 20,000 tablets in total, mostly dating between 2350 B.C. and 2250 B.C. (Early Bronze Age). The tablets made headlines when the initial decipherment by the original epigrapher of the expedition, Giovanni Pettinato, suggested that Sodom and Gomorrah were mentioned, as well as figures from the Bible, including Abraham, Israel, David, Ishmael, and others.

    - It subsequently turned out that the tablets said nothing of the sort. The mistake in interpretation had been made because the tablets were written in a previously unknown language, now called Eblaite, which made use of Sumerian cuneiform signs. Because he knew Sumerian, Pettinato thought he could read the text, but he ended up completely mistranslating it.

    - Although they contain no biblical references, the Ebla tablets are extremely important. They include lists of kings who ruled at Ebla, treaties, place names, evidence of international trade, and evidence for a scribal school. They also proved that Ebla was a major center, ruling over a kingdom no one previously knew had existed.

- A number of the palaces and buildings at Ebla were destroyed by fire, preserving the ruins and some of the artifacts within them. The smaller artifacts range from a human-headed bull figure made of gold and steatite to fragments of ivory that once adorned pieces of wooden furniture. There is also a fragment from the lid of a stone bowl that has the name of the Old Kingdom Egyptian pharaoh Pepi I inscribed on it, which implies some sort of connection, even if indirect, between Egypt and Ebla at some point.

- Matthiae and his team stopped digging at the site in 2011, because of the Syrian civil war. Since then, it has been looted mercilessly by soldiers and locals. Tunnels have been dug, burial caves full of skeletons have been ransacked, and incalculable harm has been done. It will only be when the current violence racking the country has been reduced and it is deemed safe to return to the area again that we will know the extent of the damage.

Suggested Reading

Amadasi and Schneider, *Petra*.

Matthiae, *Ebla*.

Smith, *Roman Palmyra*.

Questions to Consider

1. What can we do to help prevent the destruction of antiquities during wartime?

2. The excavation of Ebla yielded evidence for a kingdom or empire that we didn't previously know existed. Do you think there are other such ancient kingdoms or small empires still left to be discovered in the Middle East?

Lecture 18 Transcript   **Petra, Palmyra, and Ebla**

You've heard me say that Indiana Jones is not an accurate portrayal of a real archaeologist. I tell my students that every fall semester as well. What he does on screen is not what archaeologists do in real life. And yet, in the third film of the series, *Indiana Jones and the Last Crusade,* his character managed to bring a UNESCO World Heritage site to the attention of more people in the world than had ever known about it before. This is the site of Petra, located in the Jordanian desert a few hours' drive south from the modern capital city Amman.

In an internet poll conducted in 2007, Petra was named one of the new seven wonders of the world. It is also on many people's bucket list as a place to visit, with more going all the time, especially now that there are huge five-star hotels with air conditioning in which one can stay. I was able to cross this site off my bucket list many years ago when I was a young whippersnapper just 25 years old, but I didn't get to stay in an air-conditioned hotel at the time.

I was in graduate school back then, and I had taken the month of January 1985, in order to go on an excavation that was being run by the University of Missouri at a cemetery site about an hour north of Amman. At one point during the dig, we had a long weekend break, and so a small group of us drove down to Petra, which none of us had ever been to before. Just getting there was an adventure in those days. I won't give you the details, but let's just say that we made it there, barely, and leave it at that.

When we got there, there was basically no place to stay. The big hotels had not yet been built, and there weren't even any smaller hotels near the site. But we were armed with an official letter giving us permission to actually stay inside the site, at the dig house that was used by the American Expedition to Petra and other teams during their field seasons. Excavations at the site actually first started way back in 1929, and they're still ongoing today.

The American Expedition to Petra was led by Philip Hammond from the University of Utah. He had been excavating at the site on and off since the

1960s. Among his most important finds is a building that's known as the Temple of the Winged Lions, which we'll discuss in a few minutes. I was told long ago that Hammond, who died in 2008 and is usually described as a colorful character, used to ride a white horse around during his excavations. I've never been able to confirm that, but the rumors and stories persist to this day, so I suspect that there is some truth to that.

And indeed, we rode horses at Petra as well. Actually, maybe it was donkeys, now that I come to think of it. But anyway, we rode them into the site that day in January 1985, because that was the only way to get in, unless we wanted to walk, which we didn't. The first view at the site, after a half hour or more of riding down the Siq, or the canyon, is absolutely amazing. Anybody who has seen the Indiana Jones movie can attest to that, even if they haven't been to the site themselves. When we got to the dig house, and we unloaded all of our stuff for the long weekend, we were a little chagrined to find that there was no electricity and no running water. But that didn't faze us too much. We simply went without showers and went to bed when the sun went down for the few days that we were there. It was absolutely worth it because we were able to wake up very early, before the sun rose, and hike up to some of the higher monuments, like the Monastery.

So, anyway, Petra is a rather famous site. And although the Indiana Jones franchise certainly extended that fame, Westerners have been celebrating the site since the early 19th century. For example, John Burgon's 1845 poem entitled "Petra" describes the buildings as "from the rock as if by magic grown, / eternal, silent, beautiful, alone!" And it ends with the rather immortal line: "a rose-red city half as old as time." In fact, Burgon had never seen Petra himself. He wrote his poem based solely on descriptions that he had read about the site, especially a travel account published by John Lloyd Stephens a few years earlier before Stephens headed off to the Yucatán and his famous Mayan discoveries.

In fact, the cliff faces into which many of the remains at Petra are carved do turn rose-red at certain times of the day, but they also turn many other colors as well, depending on the angle of the sun and things like that. It's a veritable photographer's paradise, in addition to being a wonderful archaeological site.

Now it was the Nabataeans who were responsible for building this site. There were people in the area before them, perhaps as early as the 5th century B.C., but the city rose to prominence with the Nabataeans beginning in the 4th century B.C. It then continued to flourish for more than 500 years, including and especially during the time when the Romans were in this area, which was from the early 2nd century A.D. on. But then after an earthquake destroyed nearly half of Petra in the mid-4th century A.D. and a second one hit in the 6th century A.D., everything came to a halt—no more building activities, no more coins being minted, and so on.

The Nabataeans themselves are still a bit mysterious to us. But Petra seems to have been the center of their confederation of cities, which were focused on controlling the lucrative trade coming across the Arabian Peninsula, connecting Asia to Egypt, and so on. They're known for their hydraulic engineering, among other things, which allowed them to bring water from the occasional flash floods in to Petra through a series of dams, canals, and cisterns.

After the city itself was essentially abandoned later in the 7th century A.D., it was basically lost to history, and it was remembered only by the locals which were living in its immediate vicinity. It wasn't until 1812 that Petra was rediscovered by the Western world. That year, a Swiss explorer named Johann Burckhardt came through the area. He was dressed in Arab garments of the day, and he called himself Sheikh Ibrahim Ibn 'Abd Allah. In this getup, and with an excellent command of Arabic, he was able to travel throughout the Middle East from 1809 until he died from dysentery in 1817.

Others followed in his footsteps, including the first American—namely John Lloyd Stephens, who later gained fame as an explorer in Central America by bringing the Maya to the attention of the educated public—but that's not until 1841. That was still five years in the future when Stephens emulated Burckhardt in 1836 by dressing as a merchant from Cairo. He renamed himself Abdel Hasis, and he rode down the Wadi Musa into Petra.

The Wadi Musa is usually called the Siq. It's the way that most tourists enter Petra today, just like I did in 1985, and just like Stephens did a century and a half earlier. It's a very narrow canyon, which twists and turns through sheer rock, which towers above your head on both sides. If there is a flash flood, as happens upon occasion during the year, you're probably not going to survive it. You can walk down the Siq, but most people choose to ride horses or donkeys like I did.

However, do be aware that this was probably not the main entrance to the city, but rather more of a ceremonial entrance. The final view, featured on postcards and photographs everywhere, is absolutely breathtaking, because the narrow canyon walls suddenly open up onto a huge plaza or an open space in front of what we now call the Treasury, which is more formally known as the Khaznah. As Stephens later wrote:

> The first view of that superb façade produces an effect which could never pass away. Even now I see before me the façade of that temple; neither the Colosseum at Rome, grand and interesting as it is, nor the ruins of the Acropolis at Athens, nor the pyramids, nor the mighty temples of the Nile, are so often present in my memory.

The Khaznah was, of course, the focus of the Indiana Jones film. The Nabateans carved it out of the actual cliff face, as they did with many other buildings and structures at Petra. Don't believe the film, though; the interior rooms of the Khaznah, are actually very small, and there isn't space for too many people to be inside at any one time, even if they do include a penitent man. It was probably built to serve as a tomb and was never meant to hold many people. It's called the Treasury because of a local tradition that there was gold or other valuables hidden in the large urn on the façade, but the urn is solid stone—although it is now riddled with bullet marks from efforts to blast it apart and collect the treasure, that's not there.

If we head now into the heart of Petra, we pass along what's called the Street of Façades, which are actually tombs carved into the cliff face. Eventually, we come to the remains of the Roman Theater on the left-hand, or western, side. This could hold more than 8,000 people in 33 rows of seats. And then, a little further on, we come to the so-called Royal Tombs, which again are carved into the cliff face, but this time on the right-hand, or eastern, side. Now these require a bit of climbing to get to, and I should warn you that the original occupants of these tombs are actually debated. We don't even know if they were actually royal. Even the names don't help, because they're mostly modern designations, like the Urn Tomb, or the Silk Tomb, the Corinthian Tomb, and the Palace Tomb. The only tomb whose occupant may actually be known is the Tomb of Sextus Florentinus, who was the governor of the Roman province of Arabia in the 2nd century A.D.

Proceeding along the Colonnaded Street, which gets this name from the columns that are lining it, we eventually pass by the so-called Great Temple. But this might not be a temple at all. It's been called the Great Temple ever since 1921 or so. Some think that it might actually be the major administrative building for the city, but nobody knows for certain. There are elephant heads on the tops of some of the columns in this building, which are pretty cool.

Now on the hill opposite is the Temple of the Winged Lions that has, as you might already have suspected, statues of winged lions in it. It was probably built in the early 1st century A.D. and then was destroyed in an earthquake a little over 300 years later. It was first found in 1973, using remote sensing, and it's been excavated by American teams ever since.

In the nearby church, which is built over Nabataean and Roman ruins and dates very late, to the 5th and the 6th centuries A.D., mosaics were found, including one that depicts the various seasons. In 1993, while in the process of building a shelter to protect the mosaics and the remains of the church, archaeologists uncovered at least 140 carbonized papyrus scrolls within a room in the church.

Dating from the 6th century A.D., the scrolls had been caught in a fire that, ironically, ended up preserving some of them, although most are now illegible. Archaeologists—or rather, papyrologists, as they're known—have been able to read a few dozen of them and to determine that they're written in Greek. Most of them have to do with various economic matters, from real estate to marriages, inheritance, divisions of property, and so on, including one case that involves stolen goods.

Now from this part of Petra, you can proceed via a long stairway to the upper reaches of the site, where you'll find the huge temple that's known as the Monastery. It's every bit as monumental as the Treasury far below. Like the

Treasury, the façade of the Monastery is carved into the living face of the rock. It's about 130 feet high, just like the Treasury, but it's about 60 feet wider.

Now from here you have a commanding view over the entire area. Even though all the guidebooks say to climb up to the Monastery in the late afternoon, I would argue that the hour-long climb is best undertaken in the early morning, before it gets too hot. And if you make it to the top before sunrise, as I did during that visit in 1985, you'll be rewarded with an amazing vista as the sun appears over the horizon. And here you can stop and reflect on the long history of the region, and the amazing city that was lost for hundreds of years to the outside world before you start the descent back down.

About three years after my visit to Petra in Jordan, I had the opportunity to visit what most archaeologists consider to be the second most famous Nabataean site. This is the site of Palmyra, an oasis located deep in the Syrian Desert, to the northeast of Damascus. It's also a UNESCO World Heritage site; it got that designation in 1980.

Known as Tadmor in antiquity, this city was active already during the Bronze Age in the 2nd millennium B.C., but it had its real heyday during the time of the Roman Empire, especially during the 1st–3rd centuries A.D. It served as a major stop on the caravan routes leading across the desert, that connected the Roman Empire to India and even to far-away China. Its architecture reflects foreign influences, especially Greco-Roman and Persian; however, the city rebelled against the Romans in the early 270s A.D. in what is known as the rebellion of Queen Zenobia. After putting down the rebellion, the Roman emperor Aurelian destroyed the city in 273 A.D. It was rebuilt, but it was never the same again.

Now the first major excavations of the site, especially of the Roman period ruins, began in 1929, and they were done by French archaeologists. The remains that they uncovered, including the Temple of Bel and the Agora, or marketplace, are very impressive, especially the parts that have been partially reconstructed. Swiss archaeologists and Syrian archaeologists have also excavated there, but the most consistent presence has been Polish archaeologists, and they were excavating there right up until 2011 when they were forced to leave at the beginning of the civil war in Syria.

Palmyra suffered damage as a result of mortar fire and other actions during the war, especially in 2012 and 2013. It was also in the news in May and June of 2015, when the forces of ISIS overran the site, and then again two months later, in August, when they killed the former director of Palmyra Antiquities. They also blew up two of the most famous temples as well as other monuments at the site, which sparked a worldwide outcry against their actions.

In calmer and safer times, Palmyra is an amazing place to visit, especially at sunrise and sunset. I spent several wonderful days there as a tourist in 1988, while in Syria, doing research for my dissertation. Since I'm an amateur photographer as well as a professional archaeologist, I was in absolute heaven, and I took some photographs that are still among my favorites today.

Now in terms of the archaeology at Palmyra, some of it is similar to that at Petra, even though Petra is in a closed-off canyon and Palmyra is located in a wide-open desert oasis. Like Petra, Palmyra has a Roman theater that can seat thousands of people. It also has a colonnaded street, which in Palmyra's case is extremely long; it runs for more than a kilometer, from the Temple of Bel at its eastern end to a huge funerary temple at the western end.

On the columns, about two-thirds of the way up, are little ledges or pedestals where statues of people were once placed. These were the donors who had actually paid for the construction of the street and the colonnade. The inscriptions that are just below the statues include details about their names and their families. As you might imagine, we've learned quite a bit about the inhabitants of Palmyra from those inscriptions.

There's also a monumental triumphal arch that stretches across this main street near its eastern end. The arch was built by the Roman emperor Septimius Severus around the year 200 A.D., possibly to celebrate his victory over the Parthians in Mesopotamia, which is an area that's not too far away from Palmyra. At about the same time, a tetrapylon was built at an intersection about halfway down the street. Of the four pylons that are now visible, one of them is original; the others are made of concrete and were put up in 1963 by the Syrian Antiquities Department.

In addition, there is also a huge temple to Bel, or Ba'al, who was originally a Canaanite god from the 2nd millennium B.C. The altar in the temple was consecrated in 32 A.D., but the temple as it looked until fairly recently was probably completed about a hundred years later, in the 2nd century. Unfortunately, this is one of the temples that ISIS blew up in late August 2015, thereby destroying a beautiful monument that had been standing for nearly 2,000 years. They also destroyed the triumphal arch a few months later, in October 2015.

Finally, at the end of the 3rd century and the beginning of the 4th century A.D., the Roman emperor Diocletian built a camp for his soldiers at Palmyra, which has been a focal point of archaeological excavations. Oh, and then, in the 17th century A.D., a local Arab emir built a castle high up on the hill overlooking the city; that's still there today and is worth a visit, provided that the situation in Syria permits.

One final word about Queen Zenobia. She was married to the King of Palmyra, but he was assassinated in 267 A.D. Since their young son was only one-year-old, she assumed the throne as regent. Soon afterward, she initiated a revolt against Rome that lasted for five years or more. She became known as the Warrior Queen. Initially, she and her army had a great deal of success—they captured Egypt, they took over the rest of Syria and what today we would call Israel and Lebanon, and they even got portions of Turkey.

It was only in 273 A.D. that the Roman army crushed the Palmyrene army and put down her rebellion. Zenobia herself was taken to Rome as a prisoner and was marched through the streets in golden chains the following year as part of the triumphal parade that Aurelian, the Roman emperor, staged to celebrate his victory. Along with Boudicca, who led a revolt against the Romans in Britain two centuries earlier, back in 60 and 61 A.D., Zenobia is one of the best-known female leaders from antiquity.

Now before we leave Syria, I'd like to take you to one more fascinating archaeological site, which was making headlines around the world when I was a teenager in the 1970s. This is the ancient city of Ebla, modern Tell

Mardikh, where Paolo Matthiae from the Sapienza University of Rome and his team have been excavating since 1964.

The site is absolutely huge; it covers about 140 acres. Outlines of some of the major architectural features can be clearly seen, including the earthen ramparts that protect the city, and which you can now drive through in one place in order to gain entrance to the rest of the site. There's a huge lower city and then a citadel, a higher mound, right in the middle of the site. On the citadel are the royal palaces, the administrative buildings, and other things like that.

Four years after starting the excavation, Matthiae's team found a statue dedicated by a local man named Ibbit-Lim. In the inscription, this man said that he was the son of the king of Ebla. Now this was quite a revelation because previous scholars had thought that Ebla was located further north in Syria, not here at Tell Mardikh. But after further digging, they were able to confirm that they had indeed found ancient Ebla.

As it turns out, we now know—after 40 years of excavation—Ebla is an extremely important site with a long history dating all the way back to the 3rd millennium B.C., and continuing until it was destroyed in about the year 1600 B.C. Now granted, this is a lot earlier than both Palmyra and Petra, but I'm going to seize this opportunity to talk about it briefly now, especially since I was fortunate enough to visit it in person on the same trip to Syria in 1988, just after I was at Palmyra.

Now starting in 1964, Matthiae and his team spent the first nine years or so working on the part of the mound and the buildings that dated to the second part of its occupation, from about 2000–1600 B.C. They were interested in this period in part because it was the time of the Amorites, who are known from the Bible, and the time of Hammurabi of Babylon, who ruled just after 1800 B.C.

It was only after 1973 that Matthiae's team began to work on the earlier phase of occupation, which dates from about 2400–2250 B.C. or so. The very next year they made a discovery that catapulted Ebla, and themselves, into the history books. That was the year when they found the first clay tablets at the site. They found more in 1975 and still more in 1976.

There may be as many as 20,000 tablets in total, most of which were found in two small rooms within what's known as Palace G. They were still lying on the floor where they had fallen off of the shelves after those had collapsed. They burned, collapsed; the tablets came down. They mostly date between 2350 and 2250 B.C.—so we're back in the 3rd millennium B.C., which is what archaeologists call the Early Bronze Age.

When they were first found, these tablets made headlines around the world. Soon thereafter they made headlines again, and a controversy was ignited, because the initial decipherment by the original epigrapher of the expedition, Giovanni Pettinato, suggested that Sodom and Gomorrah were mentioned, as well as figures from the Bible, like Abraham, Israel, David, Ishmael, and so on.

It subsequently turned out that the tablets said nothing of the sort—no Sodom and Gomorrah, no Abraham, no Israel, no David, no Ishmael. The mistake in interpretation had been made because the tablets were written in a previously unknown language that we now call Eblaite. It made use of Sumerian cuneiform signs, and so Pettinato thought he could read it because he knew Sumerian, but he ended up accidentally mistranslating it.

Think about a text which is written in Spanish, and how you would translate it if you didn't realize that it was in Spanish, but you thought it was actually in English. Although the alphabet used for both is the same, the words and their meanings are completely different, right? That's sort of what happened to the Ebla texts before it was realized that they were written in a different language than had been originally assumed.

Subsequently, Pettinato cut off his ties with Matthiae, and also resigned from the international committee that Matthiae had appointed to translate and publish the tablets. But he continued to publish on them on his own, including several books, even though a new chief epigrapher, named Alfonso Archi had replaced him.

In fact, the Ebla tablets are extremely important, even though they don't contain any biblical references at all. They do include lists of kings who ruled at Ebla, also treaties, place names, evidence of international trade, and evidence for a scribal school where students learned how to read and write. They also proved that Ebla was a major center, ruling over a kingdom that we had no idea previously had even existed. This is an extremely good example where the textual evidence found by the archaeologists supplements and amplifies the other archaeological data that they've excavated over the years.

In terms of the archaeological data, a number of the palaces and buildings at Ebla were destroyed by fire, which again was terrible for them, but very good for the archaeologists, because it preserved the ruins and some of the artifacts within them. The smaller artifacts range from a human-headed bull figure made of gold and steatite to fragments of ivory that once adorned pieces of wooden furniture. The furniture is now long gone, and most of the ivory fragments were burnt black by the fire, but the fragments do survive and can be somewhat reconstructed. There's also a fragment from the lid of a stone bowl that has the name of the Old Kingdom Egyptian pharaoh Pepi I inscribed on it. This implies some sort of connection, even if maybe indirect, between Egypt and Ebla at some point.

Matthiae and his team stopped digging at the site in 2011 because of the Syrian civil war. Since then, it's been damaged and looted mercilessly—tunnels have been dug, burial caves full of skeletons have been ransacked with the bones thrown away, incalculable harm has been done. It will only be when the current violence racking the country has been reduced, and it's deemed safe to return to the area again, that we will actually know the extent of the looting and the damage.

Petra, Palmyra, and Ebla are just three of the amazing sites that have been excavated in Jordan and Syria. There are many others as well, including Jerash and Pella in Jordan and Mari and Ugarit in Syria. The tragic consequences of ongoing conflict in the Middle East should serve to remind us of just how precious and fragile these fragments of the past can be.

Lecture 19 How Are Artifacts Dated and Preserved?

Archaeologists are frequently asked three questions: how they date the objects they find, how ancient objects can still be preserved, and how much are ancient objects worth. The answer to the first question depends on the relative age of the site being excavated. In this lecture, we'll explore several dating techniques used by archaeologists, such as radiocarbon dating, thermoluminescence, and potassium-argon dating. We'll also look at what types of objects are commonly preserved from antiquity and the environments that contribute to their preservation. Finally, we'll close with the reason that responsible archaeologists don't answer the last question: the serious problem of looting antiquities.

Common Dating Methods

- Common methods used to date ancient objects include radiocarbon dating, thermoluminescence, and potassium-argon dating. These techniques are used to determine the *absolute date* of an object, in other words, its date in calendar years, such as 2015 A.D. or 1350 B.C. Because it's not always possible to determine an absolute date, archaeologists sometimes settle for a *relative date*. For example, an object that comes from level 3 at a site must be older than one from level 2, but we might not have an absolute date for either, especially at an early stage in excavation.

- The lab technique used to determine an object's absolute date depends on the relative age of the site being excavated. For instance, if you're trying to date a stone tool from Olduvai Gorge, you might use potassium-argon dating. This technique measures how much potassium is in the rock versus how much argon is in it, because potassium decays and becomes argon over time. Because it takes a very long time for this to happen, this method is best used when the object in question is between 200,000 and 5 million years old.

- Thermoluminescence might be used on certain objects found at sites with a "younger" relative age. Thermoluminescence can measure the absolute age of something made from clay, such as a storage pot, by measuring the amount of electromagnetic or ionizing radiation still in it. Specifically, this method can tell you how long it has been since the object was baked or fired in a kiln.

- A similar but newer and still experimental method is rehydroxylation, which measures the amount of water in a piece of pottery. When a piece of pottery is fired in a kiln, all the water in the clay is removed during the process. But as soon as the pottery is removed from the kiln and cools off, it begins to absorb water again from the atmosphere at a constant slow rate, regardless of the environment of the vessel. Thus, measuring the amount of water in a particular sherd can determine the last time it was fired and, thus, probably its age.

- A similar method, obsidian hydration, can been done with pieces of obsidian. Obsidian is volcanic glass that was highly prized in antiquity for its sharpness. It also absorbs water at a constant and well-defined rate once it is exposed to air; thus, measuring the amount of water in a particular piece of obsidian can date stone tools and other items.

- Probably the most commonly used dating method is radiocarbon dating, otherwise known as carbon-14 dating. This has a "plus-minus" factor, as in "1450 B.C. plus or minus 20 years"; thus, it is more useful for things that are at least several hundred (or several thousand) years old, rather than things that are relatively close to us in age.
    - The basic idea behind radiocarbon dating is that all living things ingest, either through breathing or eating, a radioactive isotope of carbon. This radioactive isotope, which is called C-14 and is constantly being created in the atmosphere as part of a natural process, combines with oxygen to form a radioactive version of carbon dioxide.

    - Plants incorporate C-14 into their systems during photosynthesis; animals and humans then get it by eating plants. When the plant, animal, or human dies and stops ingesting the radioactive carbon, then radioactive decay sets in. C-14 has a half-life of just over 5,700 years; that is, half of the original amount will have decayed and disappeared in a little more than 5,700 years.

  o By measuring the amount of C-14 that is in something that was once organic, we can figure out when it died (in the case of a human or animal), was cut down (in the case of a tree), or otherwise ceased to exist (as in short-lived plants and weeds). Thus, such items as human skeletons, animal bones, pieces of wood, and burnt seeds can be dated with this method.

  o However, there are some known problems with the technique, most of which are linked to the fact that the amount of C-14 in the atmosphere has not always been constant. Thus, calibration curves accounting for such fluctuations have been created, as have other means of correction.

- For large fragments of wood, such as a beam that was once used in a ceiling or as part of a ship, dendrochronology, or tree-ring dating, is used. This technique, of course, involves counting the rings that can be seen in the wood.

- Finally, another way to date something is as simple as noting what was found with it. For instance, if you are excavating a grave in Israel and find a coin in it minted by the Roman emperor Vespasian, you know that the grave cannot date from before his time. Thus, everything in the grave along with the coin should also be from about the same period (unless it was an heirloom at the time that it was buried, which happens).

Preserving Objects
- As mentioned at the beginning of the lecture, people often wonder how ancient things can still be saved. Why haven't they crumbled to dust?

- The answer is that many ancient things have crumbled to dust or have been otherwise destroyed. We probably have only a small percentage of what once existed. But inorganic materials, such as stone and metal, frequently survive. In addition to metal objects, clay objects or fragments of clay objects are often preserved because clay becomes non-biodegradable once it is fired in a kiln.

- Other items that are made of organic or perishable goods are not as durable, though, and it can be difficult to find such items as textiles or leather at most archaeological sites. However, these objects can survive in very dry conditions. In King Tut's tomb in Egypt, for example, all the wooden furniture, boxes, and chariots were found completely intact. The wooden boats buried by the pyramids have also survived for the same reason, as have so many mummy coffins and pieces of papyrus from ancient Egypt.

- Organic materials can also survive in waterlogged conditions. One small wooden writing tablet that dates back to the 8th century B.C. was found submerged in a well at the site of Nimrud in Iraq, and as mentioned, pieces of two more tablets were found in the Uluburun shipwreck. The so-called Bog People, who have been found in such places as Denmark and England, are also good examples of organic materials that have been preserved in a waterlogged environment.

- In addition, organic materials can survive in extremely cold conditions, such as sites in the Arctic, as well as mountains in Peru, Argentina, and Italy. For example, Ötzi the Iceman was found in the Alps in 1991, and the so-called Ice Maiden was discovered in Peru in 1995.

- Finally, organic materials also survive in areas with little or no oxygen. Obviously, such areas are pretty rare, but they exist in such places as deep in the Black Sea, below 200 meters (650 feet), where the water is very still and oxygen doesn't circulate to the bottom. Because there is really no oxygen, there is nothing alive even at the microscopic level that could do damage to artifacts.

Valuing Objects

- Every object is found in a *matrix*, the physical substance surrounding it, such as dirt, sand, mud, gravel, cement, or water. In addition to a

> **Matrix, Provenance, and Context**
>
> Matrix = Physical Surroundings
>
> Provenance = Physical Surroundings + Time
>
> Context = Physical Surroundings + Time + Associations

matrix, every object also has a *provenance*, or *provenience*. This is its position both vertically and horizontally at the site, that is, where it sits in time, as well as in space. If you're trying to figure out an object's absolute date in calendar years, you'll have to settle for a relative date in the beginning—before proceeding further—but this

The interpretation of an artifact's context helps us reconstruct the human behavior that led to it being deposited where it was found and can frequently help to determine the absolute date of the object.

is usually obvious; for instance, it's pretty clear if you're digging in Late Bronze Age levels or in Roman levels. Finally, every object has a *context*, which is the combination of its matrix, provenance, and the other things that are found in association with it.

- It is the context of an ancient object that is a large part of what makes it important. In fact, archaeologists estimate that ancient objects that have been ripped from their archaeological contexts and sold on the art market lose about 90 percent of their value, because so little information is now attached to them.

- Looting is nothing new; some of the Egyptian pharaoh's tombs were looted in antiquity. But we are now seeing an upsurge in looting worldwide, including in Afghanistan, Egypt, Iraq, Jordan, Syria, and even Peru.

- On a small scale, illegal digging for antiquities has always been a way of life in some areas and cultures, usually done by impoverished people hoping to supplement their meager incomes. But it now seems that wholesale looting operations have swung into action, including in Syria, where ISIS is reportedly sponsoring and participating in the antiquities trade, including looting entire sites and destroying parts of others, such as Nimrud and the Mosul Museum.

- When the Iraq Museum in Baghdad was looted, some of its most famous pieces were stolen. Many were returned or have been recovered, but others are still missing. Some ended up on eBay, until pressure mounted and such sales were forbidden.

- Subsequently, the looting went beyond the museum and extended to actual archaeological sites in Iraq, with reports of as many as 400 men armed with both shovels and machine guns illegally digging at sites across the country. At least one site, the ancient city of Umma, has been so thoroughly looted that all you can see in the photographs are looters' pits, rather than ancient buildings.

- Lawmakers in the United States have long been interested in stopping the trade in looted antiquities. In fact, one of the earliest laws concerned with antiquities was passed in 1906, specifically because of a huge trade in painted pots from the American Southwest. There are many other such laws on the books now, and additional pieces of legislation are being passed, not only about artifacts found in the United States but also for those found elsewhere and smuggled into this country.

Suggested Reading

Bogdanos, *Thieves of Baghdad*.

Taylor and Aitken, eds., *Chronometric Dating in Archaeology*.

Questions to Consider

1. Can you think of any other methods that might be useful in dating ancient artifacts?

2. Do you think purchasing antiquities, even in places where it is legal, contributes to looting?

Lecture 19 Transcript
How Are Artifacts Dated and Preserved?

One of the questions that I'm asked most often at social gatherings is, "How do you know how old the things are that you find?" Another one is, "How can things that old still be preserved? Why haven't they crumbled to dust?" And then there's a third question that usually arrives these days in an email or via a phone call. It goes something like, "This has been in our family for years" or "A friend just brought this home for me," followed by "How much is it worth?"

So let's address the first question first. How do we know how old something is? Well, there are a variety of dating methods that are now available to the archaeologist—and please, don't make any jokes about the dating habits of archaeologists; that's as old as the hills, so don't even go there. But, common methods then used to date ancient objects—and, again, no jokes please—include radiocarbon dating, thermoluminescence, and potassium-argon techniques. These are what we use to determine what we call the absolute date of an object—in other words, its date in calendar years, like 2015 A.D.; 1350 B.C. It's not always possible to do this, so sometimes we have to settle for what we call a relative date—that is, level three at your site lies below level two at your site and it's therefore older, but you might not have an absolute date for either of them, especially at an early stage in your excavations.

The actual lab technique that you're going to use to determine an object's absolute date depends upon the relative age of the site that you're excavating. For instance, if you're trying to date a stone tool from Olduvai Gorge, which is a crucial site for understanding human origins, you might use potassium-argon dating. This measures how much potassium is in the rock versus how much argon is in it, because potassium decays and becomes argon over time. But it takes a very long time for this to happen, so this method is best used when something's between about 200,000 and 5 million years old.

On the other hand, thermoluminescence might be used on certain objects found at sites with a younger relative age. Thermoluminescence can measure the absolute age of something made from clay, like a storage pot, and we do this by measuring the amount of electromagnetic or ionizing radiation that is still in it. Specifically, this can tell you how long it's been since the object was baked or fired in a kiln. Researchers have found that the object, if it's been heated up to above 450 degrees centigrade, it has to be that high or the technique won't work.

A similar but newer and still experimental method is something called rehydroxylation. This measures the amount of water that's in a piece of pottery. Now, I first heard about it in 2010 and thought it was pretty cool. It seems that when you fire a piece of pottery in a kiln, all of the water in the clay is removed during the process. As soon as the piece of pottery is removed, though, and it begins to cools off, it also begins to absorb water again from the atmosphere at a constant slow rate, regardless of the environment of the vessel or of the sherd if the vessel is broken. So, if you measure the amount of water in a particular sherd or a vessel, you can determine the last time that it was fired and thus, probably, its age.

Of course, there can be problems with this. I was told the story of the original researchers being given a brick and trying this method on it. Now, it was a medieval brick, but the results again and again said that it was only 65 years old according to this method, and of course that couldn't be right. They knew it had to be several hundred years old because it's a medieval brick. It eventually turned out that the brick had been on display, and that building in which it was had been bombed in World War II and had burnt to the ground.

The brick had been rescued from the ruins of the building, but the fire had reset its water content back to zero as of the 1940s, so this dating method was telling the researchers that the brick was only about 65 years old. Now, I don't know if that's actually a true story, but it does indicate to me that if you're using this method, you've got to be aware that the date you get is the date of its most recent firing, not necessarily its original firing.

Now you can do something similar with a piece of obsidian, and this is called obsidian hydration. Obsidian is a volcanic glass that was highly prized in antiquity for its sharpness, and in fact it's still used in some surgical scalpels today. It also absorbs water at a constant and well-defined rate once it's been exposed to air, so measuring the amount of water in a particular piece of obsidian can be used to date stone tools and other items that have been made from that material.

Probably the most commonly used dating method is radiocarbon dating, otherwise known as carbon-14 dating. This has a plus/minus factor, as in 1450 B.C. plus or minus 20 years, so it's not really useful for things that are relatively close to us in age, but rather for things that are at least several hundred years old, and several thousand years is even better. This is the method that I use most often in my own work.

The basic idea, invented by a scientist named Willard Libby who won a Nobel Prize for his work, is that all living things ingest, either through breathing or eating, a radioactive isotope of carbon while they're alive. This radioactive isotope, which is called C-14, is constantly being created in the atmosphere as part of a natural process, and it combines with oxygen to form a radioactive version of carbon dioxide. Now, you don't have to worry about it, nobody's ever died from it; it's just part of nature.

Plants incorporate this C-14 into their system during photosynthesis; animals and humans then get it by eating the plants. And when the plant, or the animal, or the human dies, and stops ingesting the radioactive carbon, then radioactive decay sets in. Now, carbon-14 has a half-life of just over 5,700 years—that is, half of the original amount will have decayed and disappeared in just a little over 5,700 years.

By measuring the amount of C-14 that is in something that was once organic, we can figure out when it died—that is, in the case of a human or an animal; or when it was chopped down, in the case of a tree that became a piece of wood; or otherwise ceased to exist, as in short-lived plants and weeds. So, we can radiocarbon date things like human skeletons, human bones, pieces of wood, and burnt seeds. Now, burnt seeds are especially good, because they usually had a very short shelf life before essentially ceasing to exist. Similarly, short-lived brushwood is very good, and that's what the Uluburun excavators used to help date their shipwreck. Radiocarbon dating is relatively cheap, usually costing $100 or maybe a little bit more per sample.

Now, there are some known problems with the technique, though, most of which are linked to the fact that the amount of carbon-14 in the atmosphere hasn't always been constant, but it's fluctuated over time. So, calibration curves accounting for such fluctuations have been created, as have other means of correction, and so radiocarbon dating has been one of the most frequently used methods to date ancient sites. We use it at both Kabri and Megiddo, the sites where I've been working for the past two decades.

If you find a large fragment of wood, like a beam that was once used in a ceiling or a wall or even as part of a ship, there is something else that you can do with it, besides radiocarbon dating. This is called dendrochronology, or tree-ring dating, since it involves counting the rings that you can see in the wood. Now, many of you have probably visited places like Yosemite or Sequoia National Park, where there is often a very large stump of a tree on display, and there are little markers attached to some of the rings, saying things like "1620; Plymouth Rock" or "1861; Start of the Civil War."

The rings in those trees have been fit into a known sequence that has been constructed painstakingly by scientists over the years, so that if you too have a piece of wood that's got visible rings, you might be able to fit it into the sequence and figure out when it dates to. Such a technique was also used on the Uluburun shipwreck found off of Turkey, because there were beams that were used in the hull that could be dated this way, in addition to doing carbon-14 dating on that short-lived brushwood.

Having said all of that, the other way to date something can be as simple as seeing what was found with it—that is, in association with it, or in the same context. For instance, if you're excavating a grave in Israel and you find a coin in it that was minted by the Roman emperor Vespasian, you know that the grave can't date from before his time. So, everything in the grave along with the coin should also be from about the same period, unless of course the coin was an heirloom at the time it was buried, which does happen sometimes. Similarly, if you find an Egyptian scarab with the cartouche of the pharaoh Amenhotep III on the floor of a room that you're excavating, you know that everything else on the floor probably dates to the 14th century B.C., which was when he was ruling Egypt.

At Kabri, for instance, on the floor of one of our rooms in the palace that we are excavating, we found a type of scarab that dates specifically to the Hyksos period, which is the 17th and 16th centuries B.C. So this gave us an indication of the date for that room, which was then confirmed by the radiocarbon dates that we got from some of the charcoal samples that we had submitted for analysis. And the excavators of the Uluburun shipwreck used no fewer than four different ways to date their ship. They did radiocarbon dating, which I mentioned. They did dendrochronology, which I mentioned. But they also looked at the type of Minoan and Mycenaean pottery on board, and they had a scarab of Nefertiti. All of those pointed to a relative date in the Late Bronze Age and an absolute date of about 1300 B.C. for the time when the boat sank.

Of course, if you're the excavation director and you have a playful team, you'll want to make sure that your team isn't pulling a prank on you. A favorite trick on some digs is pretending to find a gold coin that's actually a piece of gelt—that is, the chocolate coins covered in gold foil that are given out to kids at Hanukkah. If they wait too long and the chocolate starts melting in the sun, though, then the game is up.

So, now you know how I answer the frequently asked question, "How do archaeologists know how old things are?" The second question that I am often asked is, "How can things that old still be preserved? Why haven't they crumbled to dust?"

Now, the answer is that a lot of ancient things have crumbled to dust or have been otherwise destroyed; we've probably only got a small percentage of what once existed. But, inorganic materials like stone and metal frequently survive, though silver will turn purple in the ground, bronze will turn green, and so on. It's only gold that stays the exact same color. I've only found gold a few times in my career, but I've found a lot of bronze over the years. In fact, one of my favorite stories about finding a bronze object involves my very first overseas experience. This was at Tel Anafa in Israel, back in 1980, when I was a sophomore in college, and it was my first overseas excavation.

One day, about midmorning, after I had already been digging for a few hours, it was getting really hot and I was starting to get kind of worried about getting sunstroke. Just then, my little patiche, or my digging hammer, hit an object at such an angle that the object flew straight up in the air, turning over and over, before it then came back down and landed again. And while it was still in midair, I noticed that it was green, and I remember thinking—in a bit of a daze because of the heat, and with everything kind of in slow motion—I thought, "Hey, it's a petrified monkey's paw!" Now, already by the time it landed, though, I had come to my senses and thought, "What on Earth would a petrified monkey's paw be doing here?" So I knew it couldn't be that.

And sure enough, when I examined it closely, it turned out to be a bronze furniture piece in the shape of the Greek god Pan, the one with the horns on his head who goes around playing on the double pipes. It probably would've been attached to the end of a wooden arm of a chair, but only this bronze piece was left where I was digging. And it was green because the bronze had turned that color during the 2,000 years that the piece was lying in the ground, waiting for me to find it. Now, incidentally, 30 years later, I saw it on display in a museum at the University of Haifa, where it was on loan from the national museum in Jerusalem, which was pretty cool, and I of course took a selfie of myself with it.

Anyway, in addition to metal objects we often find clay objects or fragments of clay objects that have been preserved for millennia. That's because clay becomes non-biodegradable once it's fired as pottery or ceramics in a kiln. So, even if a jar shatters into ten, or a hundred, or a thousand pieces, most of those pieces still exist and can be found. Of course, there are some instances where things like irrigation water can turn pottery into just smears in the ground, as I just saw myself at Tel Kabri this past season, but on the whole, we find tremendous numbers of sherds every day on a dig.

Other items that are made of organic or perishable goods are not as durable, though, and it can be difficult to find things like textiles or leather sandals at most archaeological sites. It takes a special set of circumstances to preserve such items, but it does happen. They will survive most frequently in very dry conditions, like we find in King Tut's tomb in Egypt, where all of the wooden furniture and the boxes and the chariots were found still completely intact. And the wooden boats buried by the pyramids also have survived for the same reason, as have the mummy coffins and the pieces of papyrus from ancient Egypt.

Organic materials can also survive in waterlogged conditions. One small writing tablet that dates back to the 8th century B.C. was found submerged in a well at the site of Nimrud in Iraq, and pieces of 2 more were found on the Uluburun shipwreck, where they had been preserved 140 feet below the surface of the Mediterranean Sea for the last 3,300 years. And then there are the so-called Bog People, who have been found in places like Denmark and England. They are also good examples of organic materials that have been preserved in a waterlogged environment, if you want to think of human beings as being organic material, which of course they are.

Now, organic materials also survive in extremely cold conditions, like sites in the Arctic, as well as mountains in Peru, Argentina, and even Italy. And as long as we're still on the subject of human bodies, I can cite the examples of Ötzi the Iceman, who was found in the Alps in 1991, and the so-called Ice Maiden, who was discovered in Peru in 1995.

Finally, organic materials also survive in areas that have little or no oxygen. Obviously such areas are pretty rare, but they do exist in places like deep in the Black Sea for instance, below 200 meters, or below about 650 feet, where the water is very still and the oxygen doesn't circulate all the way to the bottom. Since there's really no oxygen, there's no reason for anything to disintegrate because there's nothing alive down there even at the microscopic level that could do damage to the artifacts.

So, for instance, when Bob Ballard sent a remotely operated vehicle down into the depths of the Black Sea back in 1999 on an expedition sponsored by National Geographic, and then again in 2007, he found amazing things. Now, you may know Ballard as the discoverer of the Titanic, but in archaeology he's perhaps better known for his discoveries in the Black Sea, including a Neolithic settlement, an ancient shoreline, and a beach that are now about 150 meters below the current surface of the sea, meaning the whole area probably flooded about 7,500 years ago.

Ballard has also found several shipwrecks from the Roman and Byzantine periods dating between 1,000 and 1,500 or more years ago, and in at least one of them, the wood of the boat is so well preserved that you can still see the tool marks on the individual pieces of wood from when they were building the boat. And one of the jars that they brought up still had the original beeswax sealing the top closed.

Okay, so we've been dealing with the second question that I get asked a lot, "How can very old things be preserved?" And in a moment I'm going to address the third and final question, "How much is it worth?" But to reach that third question, I'm going to take a little detour and introduce you to some important terms that will provide background for my answer. The first of those terms is matrix.

Every object is found in a matrix, and, no, that's not the movie starring Keanu Reeves, but it's rather the physical substance that surrounds the object. This could be dirt, sand, mud, gravel, cement, water, or anything else in which the object is sitting—or lying or resting or whatever—at the time that it's discovered. So, in the case of the Bog People, for instance, the matrix is the bog or the peat itself.

Now, in addition to a matrix, every object also has a provenance or provenience. This is its position both vertically and horizontally at the site—that is, where it sits in time as well as in space. If you're trying to figure out an object's absolute date, in calendar years, you'll have to settle for a relative date in the beginning before you go any further, but this is pretty obvious—for instance, it's clear if you're digging in Late Bronze Age levels or in Roman levels. But, as the final step, in addition to the matrix and the provenance, every object has a context. This is simply the combination of the matrix, the provenance, and the other things that are found in association with the object, like the other grave goods found in King Tut's tomb, for instance.

The way I tell it to my students is matrix equals physical surroundings; provenance equals physical surroundings plus time; and context equals physical surroundings plus time plus associations. So, it's actually not just where it is found that is an object's context, it's also how it got there, why it got there, what got there with it, and so on. The interpretation of an artifact's context will help us to reconstruct the human behavior that led to it being deposited where we found it. But it will also frequently allow you to determine the absolute date of the object.

Now, it's the context of each ancient object that is a large part of what makes it so important. So, if you show me a gold bracelet, the first thing I'm going to say is, "Wow, where did it come from? What was its context?" And if you don't know the answer, it loses most of its inherent value for me as an archaeologist, because it means that you don't know where it was found, or when it was found, or what other objects were found with it or anything about its findspot at all. So that's why an object that is looted and then sold on the art market is so sad for an archaeologist to see. An object that could potentially have told us a huge amount is now only being sold because some collector thinks it's pretty or wants something from ancient Egypt or Iraq.

Context is everything. In fact, archaeologists estimate that ancient objects that have been ripped from their archaeological contexts and sold on the art market have lost about 90% of their value because so little information is now attached to them. Similarly, fakes and forgeries can irretrievably affect our thought processes about the ancient world as well.

And that's why I almost always have the exact same answer to the third question that I'm most often asked, the one where someone sends me an email or calls me on the phone and says, "This has been in our family for years" or "A friend just brought this home for me. How much is it worth?" Actually, I won't even usually bother to reply, but if I do, I will say, "I have no idea how much it's worth," because: a) I can't be certain that it's real and not a fake; and b) even if it is real, I don't know its context, so I don't know where it was discovered and thus I can't figure out its value.

And by the way, even if you do know its context and can tell me where it was discovered, I'm also bound by the Code of Ethics of the Archaeological Institute of America not to contribute in any way to the trade in undocumented antiquities, and to refrain from activities that enhance the commercial value of such objects. So, to me, telling you what your object is worth would be doing exactly that, so I'd rather not.

Right now we are seeing the highest levels of looting worldwide that I think have ever been documented. Of course, looting is nothing new—some of the Egyptian pharaoh's tombs were looted in antiquity, perhaps even before the body was cold. But now we're seeing an upsurge worldwide, including Afghanistan, Egypt, Iraq, Jordan, Syria, and even around the world in Peru. Ancient sites are now pockmarked with looters' pits, creating landscapes that look more like moonscapes.

Now, on a small scale, illegal digging for antiquities has always been a way of life in some areas and cultures. It's usually done by impoverished folks hoping to supplement their meager income in some way. But now it looks like wholesale looting operations have swung into action, including in Syria, where ISIS—or Daesh or the Islamic State or whatever you want to call it— is reportedly sponsoring and actively participating in the antiquities trade, including looting entire sites and destroying parts of others, like Nimrud and the Mosul Museum.

I was part of a delegation of observers that went to Egypt in May 2011 after the January revolution of that year. We went to do some ground truthing in order to check to see if the looting pits that Dr. Sarah Parcak thought she had spotted in a satellite photograph really were looting pits. Now Sarah, who is a National Geographic Explorer, is known as the space archaeologist because she works using satellite photographs to search for ancient ruins. Ground truthing is what you do when you put your boots on the ground and physically go to the area to double-check what you think you've seen in those photographs. In this case, what she saw in the photographs and thought were looting pits, in fact really were looting pits. I know—I was there with her; I've got pictures of them.

In fact, looted Egyptian antiquities have shown up on eBay, just as looted Iraqi antiquities have. When the Iraq Museum in Baghdad was looted, some of the most famous pieces in the museum were stolen. Many were returned or have been recovered in the meantime, but others are still missing. Some ended up on eBay, where I and anybody else could see them, until pressure mounted and such sales were forbidden. One of my favorite stories, though, is of somebody who was trying to sell a stolen item, only when examined closely it turned out to be one of the replicas that had been sold in the museum store.

Subsequently, though, the looting went beyond the museum and extended to actual archaeological sites in Iraq, with reports of as many as 400 men armed with both shovels and machine guns illegally digging at sites across the country. At least one site, the ancient city known as Umma, has been so thoroughly looted that all you can see in the photographs are looters' pits rather than ancient buildings or anything else.

Lawmakers in the United States have long been interested in stopping the trade in looted antiquities. In fact, one of the earliest laws concerned with antiquities was passed in U.S. back in 1906, specifically because of a huge trade in painted pots from the U.S. Southwest. This was known as the Antiquities Act of 1906 and it was aimed at stopping or at least controlling the looting that was going on then in New Mexico, and Arizona, and elsewhere.

Now, there are many other such laws on the books now and additional pieces of legislation are being passed these days, not only about artifacts found in the U.S. but also for artifacts found elsewhere and being smuggled into the United States. For example, in 2015 the House of Representatives passed legislation that would make it illegal to sell artifacts that had been looted from Syria.

So, to sum up, of the three questions that I am asked most often, you now know some of the specifics as to how we are able to date the things that we find. You also now have a fairly good idea about what kinds of things are preserved best in the archaeological record and where. And, perhaps most importantly, you now know not to contact me asking how much something is worth, whether you've had it in your family for years or just acquired it. I take the problem of looting very seriously, and I wouldn't want to think that you had somehow inadvertently come by something that was ripped from its ancient context and that actually belongs in a museum.

Lecture 20 The Terracotta Army, Sutton Hoo, and Ötzi

Considering that many remains from the ancient world have simply vanished, perhaps we should consider ourselves lucky that we have as much as we do. Sometimes it is the absence of something, such as oxygen deep in the Black Sea, that contributes to the preservation of ancient ships. Other times, it is the presence of something, such as peat, that preserved the bog bodies in England and Denmark or ice, which preserved Ötzi in the Alps and the Ice Maiden in Peru. And sometimes we just get lucky and have something unexpectedly preserved or can reconstruct the original by working from the pattern of what has been left. We will discuss all these situations in this lecture.

The Terracotta Warriors

- In 1974, farmers digging a well in China's Shaanxi Province were the first to discover the famous terracotta army. The soldiers, horses, and chariots that make up this army were buried more than 2,000 years ago, in 210 B.C. They were meant to accompany the first emperor of China, Qin Shi Huang, into the afterlife.

- So far, Emperor Qin's terracotta warriors have been found in three large pits, with much more still to be uncovered. There are estimated to be between 6,000 and 8,000 warriors, as well as several hundred horses and perhaps dozens of chariots in these pits.

- About a mile from the pits is Emperor Qin's tomb, which has not yet been excavated, though its location is fairly obvious; the huge mound that covers it is about 140 feet tall.
    - According to the writings of the grand historian of China, which date to about a century after the death of the emperor, it took more than 700,000 men working for about 36 years to construct the tomb and probably the pits, as well.

    - The interior of the tomb is supposedly magnificent, with a three-dimensional map that includes flowing rivers made of mercury. However, it is also supposed to contain many traps for the unwary tomb robber.

- Someday, archaeologists will probably excavate the tomb, but in the meantime, the surrounding pits are amazing! The first pit to be discovered (pit 1) has about 6,000 terracotta warriors, all life-sized. They are standing in rows, as if at attention in a parade drill. Most of the paint that originally colored their faces, mustaches, beards, and uniforms is now gone, probably because of exposure to the air after they were excavated.

- Pit 2 has at least 1,000 more warriors, as well as horses and chariots. Pit 3 has fewer than 100 warriors, plus some horses and a chariot,

The terracotta warriors found in pits near Emperor Qin's tomb may have been constructed on site in a sort of assembly line, with the head, arms, legs, and bodies made separately, then attached.

but it also has some intact weapons. Some scholars have interpreted this last pit as possibly the headquarters for the army commanders, in part because the figures are taller and are drawn up in battle formation.

- Overall, each of the figures in these pits appears to be an individual, distinguished by facial hair or a uniform or by something he is holding, such as a spear, a sword, a shield, or a crossbow. In reality, though, it seems that there are only about eight different facial types, though there are as many as 25 different styles of mustaches and beards.

- Interest in the terracotta army has led to other discoveries in Shaanxi Province, including the tombs of a later emperor and his wife, buried with 10,000 to 1 million terracotta figures; pits near Qin's tomb that contained figures of acrobats, musicians, courtiers, and officials; and the tomb of Emperor Qin's grandmother.

Anglo-Saxon and Viking Ships
- The Sutton Hoo ship in Suffolk, England, is 27 meters long and was found in 1939. The ship probably dates to sometime between 620 and 650 A.D., during the Anglo-Saxon period. Interestingly, the wood of the ship is no longer present, yet we can see it perfectly. There are stains in the dirt where the wood has disintegrated, there are raised ridges running the width of the ship, and there are rusted iron nails that once held the pieces of wood together. What we've got is almost the shadow of the boat.
    - Most scholars think that the boat was buried with its owner, probably a warrior, a king, or a similar hero. However, no body has been found in the boat or anywhere near it. It's possible that the body and bones decomposed so much that they simply vanished. Another possibility is that there never was a body on the ship. If that's the case, then this is a *cenotaph*, that is, a monument to someone who is actually buried elsewhere.

    - Though it didn't yield a body, the Sutton Hoo ship proved to be a treasure trove in other respects. In the center of the boat

One of the objects in the Sutton Hoo ship that excited a great deal of interest was an iron helmet, complete with a face plate with holes for the eyes and both a nose and a mouth made of metal.

was what seems to be a ruined burial chamber, full of objects, including shoulder clasps made of gold and with enamel inlays, a solid gold belt buckle, and a metal lid with enamel inlays that was probably part of a purse.

- In 2011, a similar discovery was made on the western coast of Scotland. Here, in a burial that is probably about 1,000 years old, is what appears to be a Viking warrior entombed in his boat. The grave is 5 feet wide and about 17 feet long, which is just enough to hold the entire boat. Just as with the Sutton Hoo ship, the wood of this boat has also decayed and is now almost completely missing. There is no body here either, but in this case, archaeologists have found a few teeth and some fragments from the warrior's arm bone.

Bog People

- The so-called bog people have been uncovered in a variety of peat bogs in England and Europe. These once-swampy areas contain peat, which is a deposit of dead and decayed plant material. It can be used as fuel, as insulation for cottage roofs, and so on. The workers who dig in these peat bogs have occasionally found human remains that have been almost completely preserved because of the acidic conditions and the lack of oxygen in the bogs.

- One such body, known as Lindow Man, was found in northwestern England in 1984. The autopsy indicates that he was about 25 years old when he died. He had been hit twice on the head with a heavy object, then strangled by a thin cord, and finally, had his throat cut. He may have been murdered or ritually sacrificed. The man was killed about 2,000 years ago, sometime during the 1st or early 2nd century A.D.

- Another preserved body was found in 1950 by two men cutting peat in a bog in Denmark. Known as the Tollund Man, he dates to the 4th century B.C. In his case, we can see every detail of the leather cap that is still on his head and the belt that is around his waist, as well as the stubble on his face and the rope around his neck that was used to hang him. The man may have been murdered, sacrificed, or put to death because of a crime. He was probably about 40 years old at the time of his death.

Other Preserved Bodies
- In 1991, another ancient body was found, this time preserved in ice. Called Ötzi the Iceman, he has been the subject of much analysis and discussion since he was accidentally discovered by hikers in the Alps on the border between Austria and Italy. He died in about 3200 B.C.
    - When Ötzi died, his body was among some rocks that were in a gully or hollow. When a glacier crept down the hill, the ice pack went right over the rocks and his body, so that he was preserved under many feet of ice and snow for thousands of years.

    - Initially, hikers and police hacked the body out of the ice, causing damage to Ötzi and his belongings. More scientific archaeological excavations were subsequently carried out in 1992, which retrieved additional artifacts belonging to Ötzi, including his bearskin cap. Since then, detailed studies have been made of Ötzi and his belongings, including a complete workup of his DNA.

    - Scientists determined that Ötzi had brown hair and deep-set brown eyes, a beard, and sunken cheeks. He was probably about 5 feet, 2 inches tall and weighed about 110 pounds at the time of his death, which occurred when he was between 40 and 50 years old. His death must have been a murder because there is an arrowhead embedded in his back.

    - Among the possessions and equipment found were a number of fascinating objects that shed additional light on Ötzi and his environment and way of life. He had 14 arrows with iron tips and a kit to repair them, plus a quiver full of half-finished arrows; he also had a partly finished long bow, a dagger with a flint blade, and an axe with a copper blade. Archaeologists also recovered a firestarter kit and a bone needle. Ötzi had a backpack in which he carried many of these possessions.

- He was quite the well-dressed man, with three layers of clothing. Underneath everything, he wore undergarments made from goatskin. He had leggings made of fur, a coat of leather, and a grass cape, plus a hat made of fur from a brown bear. On his feet, he had leather shoes insulated with straw.

- Ötzi is not the only ancient person to have been found preserved by ice. In 1995, anthropologist Johan Reinhard found a mummy of a 12- to 14-year-old Inca female on Mount Ampato in Peru. She is occasionally called the Ice Maiden or Juanita. She had been buried more than 500 years ago and may have been an Inca sacrifice. Reinhard also found a boy and a girl mummy on Mount Ampato. One PBS television show estimated that there may be hundreds more such Inca children encased in what are now ice tombs on top of peaks in the Andes, where more than 115 Inca sacred ceremonial sites have been found.

- Surprisingly, mummies have also been found in China. What is unique about these is that they have Caucasoid or European features; they are buried with textiles that look similar to plaid; and their DNA suggests that they are of Western origin, with links to Mesopotamia, the Indus Valley, and possibly even Europe. These may be the remains of travelers along the Silk Road.

Suggested Reading

Aldhouse-Green, *Bog Bodies Uncovered*.

Portal, *The First Emperor*.

Spindler, *The Man in the Ice*.

Williams, *Treasures from Sutton Hoo*.

Questions to Consider

1. What do you think archaeologists will find inside Qin's mausoleum when it is excavated?

2. What do you think the boat at Sutton Hoo was used for; was it an actual burial or a cenotaph?

Lecture 20 Transcript: The Terracotta Army, Sutton Hoo, and Ötzi

Considering that many remains from the ancient world like scrolls have simply vanished, often because they're made of perishable materials, perhaps we should consider ourselves lucky that we have as much as we actually do. Occasionally we get extremely lucky when circumstances come together to preserve an ancient artifact or a person, or even an entire site, which usually would have perished long ago.

Sometimes it is the absence of something, like oxygen deep in the Black Sea, that contributes to the preservation of ancient ships and shorelines. But sometimes it is the presence of things like peat, which preserves the bog bodies found in England and Denmark, or the presence of ice, which has preserved both Ötzi in the Alps and the Ice Maiden in Peru. And sometimes we just get lucky, and we either have something unexpectedly preserved, like the Terracotta Warriors in China or can reconstruct the original by working from the pattern of what has been left, as is the case with the Anglo-Saxon boat found at Sutton Hoo in England and a Viking ship uncovered in Scotland. Let's discuss all of these fascinating finds.

Let's start in China's Shaanxi Province, where farmers digging a well in 1974 were the first to discover the famous Terracotta Army. The story is told that the men had been digging for hours when one of them hit what he thought was a rock. It turned out to be the head and body of a fully armed and life-size warrior, made from terracotta. In the decades that have gone by since then, thousands of such warriors, as well as terracotta horses and chariots, have been uncovered at the site by archaeologists. Together, they are commonly referred to as the Terracotta Army or the Terracotta Warriors.

These soldiers, horses, and chariots that make up the army were buried more than 2,000 years ago, in 210 B.C. They were meant to accompany the first Emperor of China, Qin Shi Huang into the afterlife. So far, Emperor Qin's terracotta warriors have been found in three large pits, with much more still remaining to be uncovered. There are estimated to be between 6,000 and 8,000 warriors, as well as several hundred horses, and perhaps a couple dozen chariots in these pits. They were constructed near Qin's mausoleum. There's actually a fourth pit as well, but it was found almost completely empty.

About a mile from the pits is Emperor Qin's tomb itself. It hasn't been excavated yet, though it's pretty obvious where it is, since the huge mound that covers it is about 140 feet tall. According to the writings of the Grand Historian of China, which date to about a century after the death of the Emperor, it took more than 700,000 men working for about 36 years to construct the tomb, and probably the pits as well. The interior of the tomb is supposedly magnificent, with a three-dimensional map that includes flowing rivers made of mercury. However, it's also supposed to contain all sorts of traps for the unwary tomb robber—the Grand Historian says specifically that craftsmen were ordered to fix up crossbows so that any thief breaking in would be shot.

Some day, archaeologists will probably excavate the tomb, but in the meantime, the surrounding pits are amazing enough. The first pit to be discovered, which is appropriately referred to as Pit No. 1, has about 6,000 terracotta warriors, all of them life-sized. They're standing in rows, as if at attention in a parade drill. They're quite spectacular, even though most of the paint that originally colored their faces, and their mustaches, their beards, and their uniforms is now gone—possibly because of a fire that seems to have affected much of the pit, but maybe also because of the type of soil in which they were buried, but most likely it's because of exposure to the air after they were excavated.

Pit No. 2 has, at least, a thousand more warriors, as well as more horses and more chariots. Pit No. 3 has less than a hundred warriors, plus some horses and a chariot, but it also has some intact weapons. Some scholars have interpreted this last pit as possibly the headquarters for the army commanders, in part because the figures there are taller and are drawn up in battle formation, but that is just a theory.

Overall, each of the figures in these pits appears to be an individual, distinguished by facial hair or a uniform, or even something that they're holding, like a spear, or a sword, a shield, or a crossbow. In reality, though, it seems that there are only about eight different facial types though there are as many as 25 different styles of mustaches and beards.

It looks now like the warriors were constructed as if they were on an assembly line, with the head, arms, legs, and body all made separately and then attached. There are areas in the pits where broken pieces can be seen, and even bodies that don't yet have the heads attached. This might indicate that they were being made right on site. It took skilled craftsmen to make these, obviously, and according to one report, the names of 85 different sculptors have been found on various parts of the figures.

In 2010, 114 additional warriors were discovered in Pit No. 1. Many of them were brightly painted, and our technology had increased enough since 1974 that this time the archaeologists were able to conserve the paint fast enough so that it stayed attached to the figures rather than flaking off. National Geographic subsequently featured some of these in an online article that was published in 2012.

Then, in 2014, researchers announced that they had discovered more about the colors that were once painted on the warriors, including the binding agent that helped the paint to adhere to the life-sized figures. It turns out that several layers of lacquer were placed on the terracotta, with a layer of polychrome or paint then applied on top of that. Within the polychrome was animal glue, and that helped bind the outer layer of paint to the layers of lacquer below.

Now, interest in the Terracotta Army has led to other discoveries in that province in China. In fact, about 25 miles from Emperor Qin's tomb, additional pits with different types of terracotta warriors were found in 1990, when a new airport was being built to handle the masses of tourists that had begun arriving. These warriors are associated with two tombs belonging to a later emperor and his wife. But they are solid rather than hollow like the warriors in Qin's pits and they're also much smaller—less than two feet high.

Oh, and they are also completely naked, with no arms. I imagine that originally they were draped with clothing and had arms inserted, perhaps of precious materials that were later robbed, but right now they look very, very strange. Estimates for the number of figures in the pits associated with these two tombs range from 10,000 to a million.

Other pits near Qin's tomb have also been excavated. They contained figures of acrobats and of musicians playing various instruments. There are also courtiers and officials, as well as what appears to be a miniature version of the imperial stables.

And in 2014, the tomb of Emperor Qin's grandmother was discovered and excavated. Within it were the skeletons of twelve real horses and the two carriages that they were originally pulling.

As for the mound containing Qin's tomb itself, well, it has not yet been excavated, as I've mentioned, in part because we're waiting for our technology to get even better. Some remote sensing has been done, and it indicates that there are chambers inside the tomb, but it's been hypothesized that the emperor's burial chamber could be as much as 100 feet below the top of the mound. Hopefully, someday we will see what lies within.

Let's turn now to an example of what we might call accidental preservation. This is the Sutton Hoo ship in Suffolk, England. It is 27 meters long and was found in 1939. The owner of the property on which it was found had invited an archaeologist named Basil Brown to excavate a large mound on her land. Within the mound, he discovered the remains of this ship.

There are many interesting things about the ship, which probably dates to sometime between 620 and 650 A.D., during the Anglo-Saxon period. Perhaps the most interesting is that the ship isn't actually there anymore, and yet you can see it perfectly well.

That is, the wood of the ship is completely gone, but it's very clear where it once was. There are stains in the dirt where the wood has disintegrated; there are raised ridges running the width of the ship, spaced just a few feet apart for its entire length; and there are rusted iron nails, which once held the pieces of wood together. What we've got is almost the shadow of the boat, or maybe its reflection, rather than the boat itself.

So, why bury a boat? Most people think that the boat was buried with its owner; that is, it served as a final resting place for a warrior, or a king, or someone else deserving of such an honor. However, there's no body in the boat, or anywhere near it—at least that has been found so far. That seems a bit strange: if this is a burial, where is the body? One possibility is that the body and the bones have decomposed so much that they've simply vanished, just like the wood of the ship. If so, they left no mark at all. That's the scenario that some people believe.

However, the other possibility is that there was never a body here. If that's the case, then this is what is known as a cenotaph—that is, a monument to someone who is actually buried elsewhere. A lot of war monuments today are basically cenotaphs, and it might be that the Sutton Hoo ship is an ancient war monument—perhaps a commemoration of a battle fought by Anglo-Saxons in this part of England.

But even if it didn't yield a body, the Sutton Hoo ship proved to be a treasure trove in other respects. In the center of the boat was what seems to be a ruined burial chamber, and it's full of objects. These include shoulder clasps made of gold and with enamel inlays, which were probably attached to a cloth tunic or a shirt that has perished. There is also a solid gold belt buckle with an intricate design that I would be quite happy to wear today. A metal lid with enamel inlays is all that remains of what was once probably a purse, with the cloth or the leather part now all gone.

One of the objects that has excited the most interest is an iron helmet, complete with a face plate with holes for the eyes and both a nose and a mouth made out of metal. Parts of it are overlaid with gold, as decoration. It must have been very expensive back in the day, which might be an indication that this is the burial, or the cenotaph, of someone quite wealthy. Of course, that's probably already a given, considering that not many people are actually buried with their boat.

There are also drinking horns, inlaid with fancy designs. These again indicate that this is no ordinary burial, and one can only imagine the parties and the celebrations at which these drinking horns were once used.

In 2011, a similar discovery was made on the western coast of Scotland. Here, in a burial that's probably about a thousand years old, is what appears to be a Viking warrior who is buried in his boat. The grave is five feet wide and about 17 feet long. However, just like the Sutton Hoo boat, the wood of this boat has also decayed and is now completely missing, apart from a few remnants here and there. But, again, the archaeologists found the iron rivets that had once held the boat together—about 200 of them—and they could easily see the shape of the boat because of the impression that it left in the earth.

There is actually no body left here either, but in this case, we do know for certain that there once was one, because the archaeologists found a couple teeth and some fragments from his arm bone. They also found the remains of his iron sword and parts of his shield, which had originally been placed on his chest. The boat also contained the Viking's spear, a bronze pin, and a bronze piece from what may have been a drinking horn.

But let's leave our bodyless boats and look at a few instances where an ancient body has been so completely preserved that in one case we can still see individual whiskers in his beard and the strands of the rope that's around his neck.

I am referring to the so-called bog people or bog bodies, which have been uncovered in various peat bogs in England and Europe. These once-swampy areas, sometimes called fens, contain peat that is a deposit of dead and decayed plant material, usually moss. It can be used as fuel, or even as insulation on cottage roofs. The workers who dig in these peat bogs have occasionally found human remains, which have been almost completely preserved because of the acidic conditions and the lack of oxygen in the bogs.

One such body, known as Lindow Man, was found in England in 1984, in the Lindow Moss bog located in northwestern England. The autopsy indicates that he was about 25 years old when he died. He had been hit twice on the head with a heavy object and then strangled by a thin cord, which also broke his neck. Finally, he also had his throat cut for good measure. He was probably murdered, but it is also possible that he was ritually sacrificed.

Either way, this is definitely what we would call a cold case because he was killed about 2,000 years ago, sometime during the 1st or early 2nd century A.D.

Because of the conditions of the bog, his skin and hair are very well preserved, including his beard and moustache. His fingernails are also so well preserved that we can tell they were manicured. Some of his internal organs are also preserved; and they contain parts of what was probably his last meal, including a piece of unleavened bread made out of wheat and barley that had been cooked over a fire.

Another preserved body was found back in 1950 by two men cutting peat in a bog in Denmark, not far from the town of Silkeborg. Known as the Tollund Man, he dates to the 4th century B.C., so he is about 500 years older than Lindow Man. In his case, you can see every detail of the leather cap that's still on his head and the belt that's around his waist, as well as the stubble on his face and the rope around his neck that was used to hang him.

The two men who found him thought that he was a murder victim, and he may well have been. But, again, his death occurred nearly 2,500 years ago, and it's unclear whether he was actually murdered or whether he was put to death, perhaps for a crime or as part of a ritual sacrifice. He was probably about 40 years old at the time of his death. Since his stomach and intestines are preserved, the archaeologists who were called in to examine him were able to do analyses and determine that his last meal had been some sort of porridge.

However, bogs are not the only places where bodies can be well preserved. In 1991, another body was found, this time, preserved in ice. This is Ötzi the Iceman, who has been the subject of much analysis and discussion since he was accidentally discovered by hikers in the Alps, right on the border between Austria and Italy.

Once again it was first thought that Ötzi was a murder victim, and so the police were called in. This was most definitely a cold case, since not only was Ötzi encased in ice, but it turns out that he had been lying there for more than 5,000 years. In fact, it now looks like Ötzi died in about 3,200 B.C., which is more than 600 years before the Pyramids in Egypt were built.

When Ötzi died, his body was among some rocks in a gully or hollow. When a glacier came sweeping, or perhaps creeping is a better word, down the hill, the ice pack went right over the rocks and his body, so that he was preserved under many feet of ice and snow for thousands of years. In 1991, though, a combination of very warm weather and a sandstorm in faraway North Africa that sent sand up into the atmosphere that eventually settled onto the ice above Ötzi and absorbed the sun's rays; they helped to melt the ice and expose Ötzi's head, his shoulders, and his upper body.

Enthusiastic hikers and then the police joined the original discoverers and hacked the rest of the body out of the ice, causing all sorts of damage to Ötzi as well as to his belongings, which lay scattered around him. Nevertheless, he emerged from the debacle fairly intact, or, at least, as best that one can from that sort of scenario. More scientific archaeological excavations were subsequently carried out in 1992, and those retrieved additional artifacts belonging to Ötzi, including his bearskin cap. Ever since then, detailed studies have been made of Ötzi and his belongings, including a complete workup of his DNA.

As you might imagine, Ötzi has turned out to be incredibly important. The scientific discoveries, which came one after the other, have been published in a series of prestigious journals, including the *Journal of Archaeological Science* and *The Lancet*, among others.

Among the discoveries that were made, scientists determined that Ötzi had brown hair and deep-set brown eyes, he had a beard, and he had sunken cheeks. He was probably about 5 foot 2 inches tall, and he weighed about 110 pounds at the time of his death, and that death occurred when he was between 40 and 50 years old. The isotopes in his tooth enamel indicate that he lived his whole life near where he died, within about a 60-kilometer radius and most likely in a nearby valley in Italy.

His lungs were blackened, probably from inhaling smoke from campfires, either inside caves or outdoors. He suffered from tooth decay, and we can tell that he had been ill several times in the months just before he died. Scientists and archaeologists were also able to analyze the contents of his intestines, including pollen found there and they were able to figure out the contents of his last meal, which included red deer meat, bread made from einkorn, and some plums. They were also able to determine that his second to last meal included ibex meat, cereals, and various other plants.

It was also discovered that Ötzi was indeed murdered, just as the police who were called in to the scene had first thought. It took 10 years before this could be proven, but then the evidence was eventually quite obvious. Even though it hadn't been noticed before, in 2001, an alert radiologist who was examining X-rays and CT scans that had been taken of Ötzi saw a foreign object embedded in his back, just below his left shoulder. It turned out to be an arrowhead, with a corresponding entry wound several inches below, which means whoever shot him was standing behind Ötzi and shooting upwards.

It was subsequently determined that the arrowhead had severed an artery, meaning that Ötzi probably bled to death. It also means that he was shot in the back, which implies murder rather than an accident, and the fact that he has a defensive cut on his hand also indicates that some sort of fight had taken place and that he might have been fleeing from the battle when he was fatally shot. The pollen that was examined indicates that all of this probably took place in late spring or the early summer of that year.

Among Ötzi's possessions and equipment were a number of fascinating objects that shed additional light on him and his environment as well as his way of life. He had 14 arrows with iron tips and a kit to repair them, plus a quiver that was full of half-finished arrows; he also had a partly-finished long bow; a dagger with a flint blade; and an axe with a copper blade. Archaeologists also discovered a firestarter kit; a birchbark container that had embers from his previous fire; and a bone needle. And Ötzi also had a backpack in which he carried most of these possessions.

He was quite the well-dressed man, as well, with three layers of clothing. Underneath everything, he had undergarments that were made from goatskin. He had leggings made of fur, a coat of leather, and a grass cape over it all, plus a hat made of fur from a brown bear. On his feet, he had leather shoes that were insulated with straw. In 2004, a professor in the Czech Republic made a pair of shoes just like them and then went hiking with them on. And he said he didn't get blisters and that they were more comfortable than his normal hiking shoes.

All of this has now been recreated in several places, including the South Tyrol Museum of Archaeology in northern Italy, which is currently Ötzi's home.

Ötzi also spawned a worldwide craze, especially after his initial discovery, though this has now died down a bit. Still, especially in the region where he was found, you can find Ötzi wine, Ötzi chocolate—think Easter egg bunnies but in the shape of Ötzi—and, most relevant of all, in my opinion, Ötzi ice cream.

But Ötzi is not the only ancient person to have been found on ice, as it were. In 1995, anthropologist Johan Reinhard who was subsequently a National Geographic Explorer-in-Residence found a mummy of a 12–14-year-old Inca female on Mount Ampato in Peru. She is occasionally called The Ice Maiden but is more usually simply referred to as Juanita.

Reinhard found her near the peak of the mountain, at a height of more than 6,000 meters above sea level. She had been buried more than 500 years ago. He had climbed the mountain to photograph a nearby volcano that was erupting, thinking that he could get a good picture from there. It didn't seem to be a likely place for an Inca sacrifice, and yet there she was, exposed to the elements because the ash from the volcano had melted some of the ice that had protected her. In his book called *The Ice Maiden*, Reinhard describes carrying her down the mountain in his backpack because she weighed only 80 pounds.

And, apparently, she is not the only such Inca mummy to be found, because others had been discovered too, including two more that Reinhard also found on Mount Ampato, a boy and a girl who were located a thousand feet below the summit, when he returned with a full team to explore the mountain systematically. Also, 40 years earlier, in 1954, an 8-year-old little boy was also found on a mountaintop in Chile, extremely well preserved. And it's possible that here are hundreds more such Inca children encased in what are now ice tombs in the Andes, where more than 115 Inca sacred ceremonial sites have been found.

There is also any number of mummies preserved around the world, with the most famous mummies being found in Egypt, of course. Perhaps the most surprising, though, are found in China, and so it seems fitting to end this lecture as we started it, in China.

These mummies, some of whom are as much as 4,000 years old, were first reported to the rest of the world by a professor of Chinese Studies at the University of Pennsylvania named Victor Mair. He spotted them in a museum in the city of Ürümqi, in a remote part of China north of Tibet. This is known as the Tarim Basin. He began to study them along with Professor Elizabeth Barber of Occidental College, in California. Mair and Barber have both published books about the mummies, which were extremely well preserved because of the very dry conditions of the desert environment where they were buried.

What is unique about the mummies is that, even though they are found in China, they have Caucasoid or European features; they're buried with textiles and cloth that looks a lot like plaid; and their DNA suggests that they are of western origin, with links to Mesopotamia, the Indus Valley, and possibly even Europe. I suppose we shouldn't be particularly surprised by this because the Silk Road is known to have run through the Tarim Basin, and, in fact, some of the mummies were brought to the United States in 2010, as part of a traveling exhibition on the Silk Route in antiquity.

So, what we have seen in this lecture is that occasionally we get lucky, and we have objects—and people—that usually would have disintegrated long ago but are left to us because of the matrix in which they were buried, such as peat bogs, or ice. Such is the case with the mummies from Peru to China, as it is with Ötzi and the bog people.

Other times it is not luck so much as it is the skill of the archaeologists and conservators who are working on the project. This is the case with the new discoveries of additional Terracotta Warriors, on which the original paint can now be found and retained, even after the figures have been exposed to air after their long burial. It's also the case with both the Sutton Hoo ship in England and the Viking ship in Scotland, which have left only shadows of their original form to be excavated carefully by archaeologists.

Lecture 21 Discovering the Maya

Thus far, we've been looking at Old World archaeology, that is, the archaeology of Greece, Rome, Egypt, and the Near East. In the next few lectures, however, we'll shift our attention to the New World, exploring such civilizations as the Maya, Inca, Moche, and others. We'll begin in this lecture with Maya civilization and the early explorations of John Lloyd Stephens and Frederick Catherwood.

Stephens and Catherwood

- The earliest discoveries of Maya ruins, at the site of Palenque in what is now southern Mexico, were already being made by 1750 A.D. However, the initial discovery of Palenque went almost unnoticed by the Western world until John Lloyd Stephens's accounts of his travels introduced it to a broad audience in 1841. His travels in Central America with the artist and architect Frederick Catherwood resulted in bestselling travel books.

- In 1839, Stephens and Catherwood set off with a goal of visiting three ancient Mesoamerican sites: Copán, Palenque, and Uxmal. Rather than doing much excavation at these sites, however, the two men explored, cleared away trees and underbrush, surveyed, and drew. But because of their subsequent accounts, they are generally considered to have brought the Maya to the attention of the external world, and in the process, they established the beginnings of what we now call New World archaeology.

- Stephens was an incredibly astute observer—someone who could compare and contrast what he had seen in the Old World with what he was now discovering in the New World. For example, based on his previous experiences traveling in the Middle East, he concluded—quite correctly—that such cities as Copán and Palenque were not built by Egyptians or, as a few had suggested, survivors of Atlantis but by the indigenous people of the area, the Maya.

- Stephens and Catherwood faithfully recorded the hieroglyphics that were engraved on monuments at Copán and elsewhere. Stephens was convinced that once they were decoded, these hieroglyphics would reveal the history of the Maya. In this, he was again correct. When the hieroglyphics engraved on the monuments were finally deciphered, they recorded the history of the Maya in all its gory detail.

- It took the concerted efforts of a number of individuals to crack the Maya writing system, including an Englishman named Sir Eric Thompson, a Russian-American scholar named Tatiana Proskouriakoff, and a Ukrainian scholar named Yuri Knorosov. Knorosov made the ultimate breakthrough in reading the texts by using a manuscript on the Maya written by the 16th-century Spanish bishop Diego de Landa. Although Landa's own understanding of Maya writing was misguided, his manuscript served as an essential key to Knorosov.

- Stephens and Catherwood spent a total of 13 days at Copán, during which time they found 14 inscribed standing stones, or stelae. Catherwood drew all of these, as well as a structure called Altar Q, a fairly small, box-shaped stone, with the names of rulers depicted four to a side. They also cleared the undergrowth from other ruins at Copán, including the Temple of the Hieroglyphic Stairway and the sacred ball court.

Tikal

- After a break in their travels, Stephens and Catherwood went in search of Palenque in April 1840. Along the way, they bypassed the chance to visit a site lost in the jungle that was probably what we now know to be Tikal.

- Had they gone to Tikal, they would have received credit for finding one of the largest Maya cities in the region, with a population of as many 100,000. It wasn't until 1848, about a decade after Stephens and Catherwood came through the area, that Tikal was properly discovered, at least in the eyes of the Western world.

George Stuart, a former National Geographic archaeologist, estimated that there may be another 10,000 buildings from periods before 200 A.D. still buried at Tikal.

- The University of Pennsylvania conducted the first large archaeological project at Tikal from 1956 to 1970. There are approximately 3,000 buildings still visible at the site, though many are still covered by the forest. They include temples and palaces, dating to the period from 200 to 900 A.D.

- There are six temple-pyramids at Tikal, including Temple 1, the Temple of the Grand Jaguar. This temple held the tomb of the great Maya ruler sometimes referred to as Lord Chocolate, who ruled Tikal for 52 years, on either side of 700 A.D. Within his grave were found pieces of jade, shell ornaments, and ceramic vessels originally filled with food and drink. There were also some unusual carved bones, with scenes that appear to be from a Maya creation story.

Stephens and Catherwood in Palenque

- Stephens and Catherwood reached Palenque in May 1840. They stayed at the site for three weeks, although again, they spent most of their time clearing away the jungle growth, rather than actually digging. Among the buildings they uncovered was what we now call the Temple of the Inscriptions, which stood on top of an 80-foot-tall stone pyramid. The temple is famous for three huge tablets with more than 600 hieroglyphics on them.

- Unbeknownst to the explorers, the 80-foot-tall pyramid on which the Temple of the Inscriptions stood also served as the burial place for Lord Pakal, who ruled at Palenque from 615 to 683 A.D. His tomb was not found until 1952, by a Mexican archaeologist named Alberto Ruz Lhuillier.
    - Lhuillier discovered an entrance to the Temple of the Inscriptions at the top of the pyramid. The entrance led to a stairway filled with rubble and, ultimately, Pakal's tomb, 80 feet below the top of the pyramid. It is now thought that the tomb was built first and the pyramid was constructed around it.

    - Pakal was found accompanied by the skeletons of six other people, who had apparently been sacrificed to accompany the ruler into the afterlife.

    - Pakal himself was laid to rest within a limestone coffin or sarcophagus that is 13 feet long. Within the coffin, Pakal's skeleton rested undisturbed, a jade mask still on his face, where it had been placed 1,300 years ago. An amazing number of additional jade objects were also found, including necklaces, ear ornaments, two statuettes, and more.

- Stephens and Catherwood found and described many other buildings at Palenque during the short time that they were there, including the Palace and the Temple of the Cross. There is also, as at so many Mesoamerican sites, a large ball court.

- Palenque has been a magnet for more recent explorers and archaeologists, as well, with discoveries of new buildings and burials from 1993 to 2000. Among the discoveries is the tomb of the Red Queen, which included a tremendous cache of grave goods in Temple XIII. This temple is close to Pakal's burial pyramid, and it has been suggested that the Red Queen may have been Pakal's wife.

Chichén Itzá

- Stephens and Catherwood made a second journey to the Yucatán region in October 1841. The highlight of this journey was their exploration of the site of Chichén Itzá. It wasn't until 1895, however, that a systematic exploration of the site was conducted by Edward Thompson. His excavations covered a period of 30 years and included dredging the sacred cenote, pulling up both artifacts and human remains.

- Chichén Itzá flourished later than most of the other Maya sites we have discussed, reaching its peak from 800 to 1200 A.D., in part because of the arrival of the Toltecs during the midpoint of this period.

- Stephens described the cenotes of the Yucatan as "immense circular holes, from sixty to two hundred feet in diameter, ... and having at the bottom a great body of water." There were two at Chichén Itzá; the larger one was in the middle of a thick forest. Stephens was well aware of the tradition that human victims had been thrown into it.

- During the dredging and exploration of the sacred cenote by Thompson and others, human remains were indeed found, including the skeletons of at least 50 victims. Objects of jade and gold disks were also found, as were copper bells and other items. It is clear that sacrifices of many different kinds were made at this cenote over the years—and not just by the Maya; many of the objects are of Toltec manufacture, dating to the last two centuries or so of occupation at the site (ca. 1000–1200 A.D.).

- A large number of buildings have been found at the site, including the Temple of the Jaguars, the Temple of the Warriors, the Pyramid of Kukulkan, and the Platform of Venus. Some of these, including the Temple of the Jaguars and the Temple of the Warriors, contain murals and scenes depicting the conquest of this area by the Toltecs.

- Also at the site is an astronomical observatory, a long stone rack featuring numerous skulls carved in stone, and a huge ball court. Many of these structures date from the time of the Toltec period at the site.

The Use of LiDAR in the New World

- As far as the future of Maya studies goes, one of the most exciting developments in recent years involves the use of LiDAR for mapping known sites, discovering new ones, and discovering

The stone skull rack at Chichén Itzá features numerous skulls carved in stone, undoubtedly to simulate the genuine article.

previously unknown buildings at known sites. The problem with many of these Maya sites is that the forest grew over them and hid them from the outside world for long periods.

- As we've said, LiDAR is a remote-sensing technology that works like radar but uses light from a laser to produce highly accurate measurements by bouncing the laser beams off the ground and, thereby, creating three-dimensional images using hundreds of thousands of data points. It's usually used from an airplane and is especially useful in Central America, because it can quite literally see through the trees in a jungle or rain forest and provide images of lost temples, buildings, and even cities that are completely overgrown.

- Probably the best-known example was the use of LiDAR to map the Maya city of Caracol in Belize in 2009. Using an advanced LiDAR system, a huge patch of what looked like jungle from above was shown to contain buildings, roads, and other parts of a massive city that was hidden from sight.

- However, what is still a mystery is why the Classic Maya civilization came to an end just after 900 A.D., with all or most of the great sites abandoned and subsequently lost to the rest of the world. A favorite suggestion has been that the Maya were unable to deal with a century-long drought, but this is by no means certain. Numerous other hypotheses have also been put forward, including explanations that involve overpopulation and deforestation. But for this mystery to be resolved once and for all, more investigation is definitely needed.

Suggested Reading

Coe, *The Maya*.

Koch, *John Lloyd Stephens and Frederick Catherwood*.

Stuart, *The Order of Days*.

Questions to Consider

1. Do you think that Stephens's background in the Middle East helped him to recognize that the Egyptians or people from Atlantis did not build the Maya cities?

2. If new cities or even simply buildings are now discovered through the use of LiDAR, should we excavate them or leave them for future archaeologists who might have better techniques?

Lecture 21 Transcript

Discovering the Maya

Now, I'll be the first to admit that my own career has been based in Old World archaeology—that is, Greece, Rome, Egypt, and the Near East. But the New World fascinates me as well, with civilizations like the Maya, the Inca, the Moche, and others. So let's turn our attention to the New World now and let's begin our exploration with Maya civilization in Central America.

Now, what I think most people don't realize is that the earliest discoveries of Maya ruins, at the site of Palenque in what is now southern Mexico, were already being made by 1750 A.D., at the same approximate time that the first excavations at Pompeii were beginning. But the initial discovery of Palenque went almost unnoticed by the Western world until John Lloyd Stephens introduced it to a broad reading audience in 1841. His travels in Central America with Frederick Catherwood, the wonderful artist and architect, resulted in best-selling travel books, including the one that I read when I was in junior high school, which was called *Incidents of Travel in Yucatán*.

Stephens was understandably upset by Europe's lack of attention to Palenque. He noted that:

> If a like discovery had been made in Italy, Greece, Egypt, or Asia, within the reach of European travel, it would have created an interest not inferior to the discovery of Herculaneum, or Pompeii, or the ruins of Paestum.

Stephens knew what he was talking about. A lawyer by the time he was 20, he didn't practice for long, but instead he began traveling across Europe and the Middle East, including in Greece, Turkey, Egypt, and Jordan. He published accounts of his journeys, which quickly became best-selling books. In fact, it was his description of Petra, where he was the first American to visit the ancient city, that prompted John Burgon to compose his famous poem that ends with the immortal words, "a rose-red city half as old as time."

Catherwood was several years older than Stephens, but having formed a friendship, the two men decided to explore Central America together. Specifically, they wanted to search for ruins belonging to the civilization that we now call the Maya. So in 1839 they set off from the United States with a goal of visiting three ancient Mesoamerican sites—Copán, Palenque, and Uxmal.

Now, Stephens and Catherwood were by no means the first outsiders to have visited the sites, and rather than doing much excavation, they explored, they cleared away trees and underbrush, they surveyed, and they drew. But because of the accounts that they subsequently published, they are generally considered to have brought the Maya to the attention of the external world. And, in the process, they established the beginnings of what we now call New World archaeology. Moreover, all of this was done 30 years before Heinrich Schliemann dug at Troy, 70 years before Hiram Bingham discovered Machu Picchu, and more than 80 years before Howard Carter discovered King Tut.

Now, Stephens was an incredibly astute observer, somebody who could compare and contrast what he had seen in the Old World with what he was now discovering in the New World. For example, based on his previous experiences traveling in the Middle East, he was able to conclude—quite correctly—that cities like Copán and Palenque were not built by Egyptians or survivors of Atlantis, both of which had been suggested previously, but rather that they had been built by the indigenous people of the area, the Maya. After comparing and contrasting the pyramids, the columns, and the sculptures that he saw at Copán to those of the Egyptians, he wrote specifically:

> Opposed as my idea to all previous speculations, I am inclined to think that the ruins were constructed by the races who occupied the country at the time of the invasion by the Spaniards, or of not very distant progenitors.

Furthermore, he and Catherwood faithfully recorded the hieroglyphics that were engraved on the monuments at Copán and elsewhere. And he was convinced that, once they were decoded, these hieroglyphics would reveal the history of the Maya.

And he was completely correct. When the hieroglyphics engraved on the monuments were indeed finally deciphered, they did turn out to record the history of the Maya in all of its gory detail. It took quite a long time, until just the past few decades actually, for us to be able to read the inscriptions fairly accurately. But now we know that the Maya were not quite as peaceful as has been previously thought, and that their history was as full of rivalries and wars as any other ancient civilization, whether in the Old World or the New World.

It took the concerted efforts of a number of individuals to crack the Maya writing system, including an Englishman named Sir Eric Thompson, a Russian-American scholar named Tatiana Proskouriakoff, and a Ukranian scholar named Yuri Knorosov. Thompson and Knorosov are usually described as bitter rivals, somewhat along the lines of Jean-François Champollion and Thomas Young when the French and British scholars were racing to see who would decipher Egyptian hieroglyphics first.

Thompson was the grand old man of Maya hieroglyphic studies, with a major volume published back in 1950, but Proskouriakoff was the first to show that hieroglyphics recorded historical dates and events, as well as identifying specific women in the texts, as opposed to simply the men. However, it's now recognized that it was Knorosov, working in Stalinist Russia during the Cold War, who made the ultimate breakthrough in reading the texts by making use of a manuscript on the Maya left to us by the 16th century Spanish Bishop Diego de Landa. Although Landa's own understanding of Maya writing was misguided, his manuscript served as an essential key to Knorosov. For that reason, Landa's text has been called the Rosetta Stone of Maya hieroglyphics.

Now, some of the most significant advances in reading Maya hieroglyphics have been made in the past few decades by an American named David Stuart. Born in 1965, he's the son of Mayanist George Stuart, who worked for the National Geographic Society for nearly 40 years. David had been accompanying his parents to Maya ruins since he was a three-year-old toddler. By the age of eight, he was working on the hieroglyphs. By age 10, he was shadowing and helping the great Maya epigrapher Linda Schele during her work at Palenque.

By the time that Stuart received his Ph.D. in 1995, he had already published 13 articles and monographs, which is absolutely unheard of. He's still the youngest person ever to be awarded a MacArthur Fellowship, which he received when he was only 18, and he's one of the few people to have won both a MacArthur and a Guggenheim fellowship. He is probably best known to the general public, though, for a book that he published in 2011 during the media frenzy about the supposed Maya prediction that the end of the world would happen in 2012. He successfully showed that the Maya had not actually said that the world was going to come to an end, and in fact it did not, as we all now know.

It's thanks to these individuals and a handful of others that John Lloyd Stephens' prediction came true. Maya hieroglyphics have finally been deciphered, and the history of Copán, as well as other Mayan sites, is indeed, as Stephens put it, graven on its monuments.

So we now know that at Copán, for instance, which is located in modern Honduras, that the Maya listed the names of 16 of their rulers, covering a period of about four centuries, from 427 A.D. until a little after 810 A.D. These are carved on Altar Q, a fairly small box-shaped stone. It's about six feet wide by six feet long and it stands four feet high. The rulers are depicted four to a side. The founding king of this dynasty was a man known as Great Sun Green Quetzal Macaw.

Stephens and Catherwood spent a total of 13 days at Copán, during which time they found 14 inscribed standing stones, or stelae as they're called in Greece and elsewhere back in the Old World. Catherwood drew all of these, as well as Altar Q, which Stephens had also found. Amazingly, Stephens had an inkling of what was depicted on Altar Q, because he describes the 16 individuals pictured and mentions his suspicion that the hieroglyphics on which they were seated probably gave their name and office, which indeed they do. He was also quite correct in suggesting that the hieroglyphics on the Altar "beyond doubt record some event in the history of the mysterious people who once inhabited the city." He was dead-on.

Stephens and Catherwood also cleared the undergrowth from other ruins at Copán, including the Temple of the Hieroglyphic Stairway and the sacred

Ball Court. The Hieroglyphic Stairway has 63 stairs climbing 75 feet up to the top of the temple, with at least 2,200 hieroglyphics decorating its length. It is one of the longest Maya texts known and it appears to be a dynastic record. It was started by the unlucky 13th king of Copán, who was later captured in battle and beheaded while fighting a rival kingdom. It was doubled in length and completed by the 15th ruler in the 8th century A.D., who also turned it into a strange bilingual text. The right-hand column contains Maya hieroglyphs; the left-hand column has imaginary Teotihuacan hieroglyphs, which have no real meaning as far as we can tell and are more decorative than anything else.

The ball court is one of the best examples of its kind ever found at a Maya site, although the rules of the game are still debated. Some say it was played a bit like soccer, since you couldn't touch the ball with your hands. Apparently you won if you got the ball through a small ring, but the game ended if the ball touched either the ground or anybody's hands. And, while the winners were often treated as heroes, some scholars have argued that the losers were sometimes put to death.

However, since Stephens and Catherwood were at the site for less than two weeks, it was left to others to continue the exploration and the excavations of Copán. These included a well-known amateur archaeologist named Alfred Maudslay, who arrived in the 1880s, and then a team from the Carnegie Institution in the 1930s.

After a break in their travels, Stephens and Catherwood went in search of Palenque in April 1840. Along the way, they had a chance to visit a site that was lost in the jungle, and that was probably what we now know as the major site of Tikal. Although they had heard rumors of its existence, and Stephens had actually figured out that they could allocate ten days to get there, map it, and get back, they opted instead to head for Palenque without further delay.

Had they gone to Tikal, they would've received credit for finding one of the largest Maya cities in the region, where as many as 100,000 Maya may have once lived. But it wasn't until 1848, about a decade after Stephens and Catherwood came through the area, that it was properly discovered, at least in the eyes of the Western world. Other archaeologists and explorers came through soon afterward, but it was more than a century before the University of Pennsylvania conducted the first large archaeological project at the site from 1956 until 1970.

And it turns out that there are approximately 3,000 different buildings still visible at the site, though many are still covered by the forest. They include temples and palaces dating to the period from about 200–900 A.D., with most of them being built during the final three centuries. George Stuart, the former *National Geographic* archaeologist, estimated that there might be another 10,000 buildings from earlier periods still buried at Tikal. It's now a national park, in addition to being named as a UNESCO World Heritage Site in 1979.

Now, there are six different temple-pyramids at Tikal, including Temple 1, which is called the Temple of the Grand Jaguar. Within this temple, the tomb of the great Maya ruler who built it was found in 1962. Sometimes referred to as Lord Chocolate, he ruled Tikal for 52 years, on either side of 700 A.D. Within his grave were found pieces of jade, shell ornaments, and ceramic vessels that were originally filled with food and drink. There were also some unusual carved bones, with scenes that appear to be from a Maya creation story. In addition to all of the buildings, there were also 10 reservoirs found at the site, which provided the city with its drinking water.

But Stephens and Catherwood were intent on reaching and then exploring Palenque, and so they bypassed what were probably the remains of Tikal, a fact that they no doubt later regretted.

As I mentioned, they were by no means the first to look for Palenque and, in fact, their entire journey to the region had been sparked by the brief accounts that they had read about that lost city, which had been translated into English from reports filed by various Spanish explorers. Several of the reports attributed the massive ruins to the Egyptians, but at least one concluded that Palenque had been built by people from Atlantis. As we've noted, Stephens went against such opinions when he declared that Palenque and the other ruins had actually been built by the indigenous Maya, seeing no reason to involve Egyptians, Atlanteans, or any other people from the Old World.

After a difficult journey, Stephens and Catherwood finally reached Palenque, in southern Mexico, in May 1840. They were able to spend three weeks at the site, exploring and sketching the ruins. Again, they spent most of their time clearing away the trees and the jungle growth rather than actually digging. Among the buildings that they uncovered in this way was what we now call the Temple of the Inscriptions that stood on top of an 80-foot-tall stone pyramid. The temple is justifiably famous for the 3 huge tablets with more than 600 hieroglyphics on them. This is the second largest inscription known from the Maya world. Stephens was certain that the hieroglyphics looked identical to the ones they had seen at Copán, so he had Catherwood copy them exactly, in case a future scholar could decipher them, which, of course, is exactly what eventually happened.

But, it wasn't as easy as it sounds. The description that Stephens gives of what they had to do first, so that Catherwood could do his drawings, gives us some idea of what was involved. He says:

> When we first saw them, the tablets were covered with a thick coat of green moss, and it was necessary to wash and scrape them, clear the lines with a stick, and scrub them thoroughly. On account of the darkness in the corridor from the thick shade of the trees growing before it, it was necessary to burn candles or torches, and to throw a strong light upon the stones while Mr. Catherwood was drawing.

Stephens also describes the various illnesses that they suffered during their trip, as well as the depredations caused by the mosquitoes that gave them malaria, the unpleasantness of the burrowing insects that laid eggs under their toenails, and so on.

At any rate, and unbeknownst to them, the 80-foot-tall pyramid on which the Temple of the Inscriptions stood also served as the burial place for Lord Pakal who ruled at Palenque for almost 70 years, from 615 until 683 A.D. But his tomb was not found until 1952—more than a century after Stephens and Catherwood had explored the site.

It was a Mexican archaeologist named Alberto Ruz Lhuillier who discovered the tomb. He became curious about a stone slab in the floor of the Temple of the Inscriptions at the very top of the pyramid. The slab also had a double row of circular depressions with stone plugs in them, which he figured were meant to help remove the slab. So he did exactly that; he removed the slab and he revealed a staircase completely filled with rubble that led down into the supporting pyramid. It took his team several years to clear the long stairwell, where they found Pakal's tomb 80 feet below where they had started. Essentially, the tomb was at ground level, but inside the pyramid. It is now thought that the tomb was built first and then the pyramid was constructed around it. Pakal was not alone, though; he was found accompanied by the skeletons of six other people who had apparently been sacrificed in order to accompany Pakal into the afterlife.

Pakal himself was laid to rest within a limestone coffin or a sarcophagus that's 13 feet long. It's got a complicated carving on its lid, which depicts Pakal descending to the underworld. At first, the archaeologists didn't realize that this was a lid on top of a coffin. Instead, they thought the whole thing was a solid stone altar, with the carving on the top of the altar. It was only when they drilled a small exploratory hole into the stone that they realized the whole thing was hollow, not solid, and that, in fact, it was a sarcophagus rather than an altar. Within the coffin, in which Pakal's skeleton still rested undisturbed, a jade mask was found still on his face, where it had been placed 1,300 years ago. An amazing number of additional jade objects were also found, including necklaces, ear ornaments, a diadem, and a ring; pectorals as well, plus wristlets, two statuettes, and a belt.

Stephens and Catherwood found and described many other buildings at Palenque during the short time that they were there, including the so-called Palace and the Temple of the Cross. There is also, as at so many Mesoamerican sites, a large ball court.

Palenque has been a magnet for more recent archaeologists and explorers as well, including discoveries of new buildings and burials from 1993–2000. Among the discoveries is the so-called Red Queen, who was found in 1994 with a tremendous cache of grave goods within an elaborate chamber in Temple XIII. This temple is close to Pakal's burial pyramid and it's been suggested that the Red Queen might have been Pakal's wife, who died about 10 years before he did. The Palenque Mapping Project was also busy at the site in 1998 through 2000, surveying and mapping the buildings, including some that were still hidden in the forest.

Returning, though, to Stephens and Catherwood. From Palenque they continued on to the third site on their list, called Uxmal, but soon thereafter they called a halt to their explorations because Catherwood became quite ill. In fact, they had both suffered terribly during the journey, including bouts of malaria for both of them. They had been gone for about 10 months and it was now time to go home to New York. They returned to the United States in July of 1840, where Stephens promptly published a 2-volume set of their adventures, complete with illustrations by Catherwood. It appeared in June of 1841 and had already sold 20,000 copies by that December at the relatively affordable price of 5 dollars for the 2-volume set.

As a result, they soon made plans to return for a second time to the Yucatán region, leaving in October 1841, just 4 months after the release of their book. This time they were gone for 8 months, eventually returning to the United States in June 1842, and with the volumes describing this second voyage appearing already by February 1843.

They began with a visit to Uxmal, where their previous visit had been cut short, and explored a few additional small sites as well. But the highlight of this second journey has to be their exploration of the site of Chichén Itzá, near the tip of the Yucatán peninsula.

Stephens and Catherwood visited in 1841–42, and Maudslay came to see it in 1886, but it wasn't until 1895 that Edward Thompson began exploring Chichén Itzá systematically. His excavations covered a period of 30 years, and they included dredging the sacred cenote and pulling up artifacts as well as human remains. It then took almost another century before it was named a UNESCO World Heritage Site in 1988.

Now, I've always been fascinated by Chichén Itzá—I was drawn to it like I was drawn to Pompeii and to Troy, which are the other two sites that I learned about at approximately the same time during my adolescence. We now know that it flourished later than most of the other Maya sites that we've just talked about. It reached its peak from 800–1200 A.D, in part because of the arrival of the Toltecs during the midpoint of this period.

Stephens described the cenotes of the Yucatán as immense circular holes, from sixty to two hundred feet in diameter, with broken, rocky, perpendicular sides from fifty to one hundred feet deep, and having at the bottom a great body of water. There were two of these at Chichén Itzá, of which he says one was "the largest and wildest we had seen." He describes it as being in the middle of a thick forest, with a mysterious influence pervading it. He was well aware of the tradition that human victims had been thrown into it and he identified one building right on the edge as perhaps the place from which the victims were thrown into the dark well beneath.

During the dredging and the exploration of this sacred cenote by Thompson and others, human remains were indeed found, including the skeletons of at least 50 victims: young women, men, and a number of children. Objects of jade and gold disks were also found, as were copper bells and other items. It's clear that sacrifices of many different kinds were made at this cenote over the years, and not just by the Maya, for many of the objects are of Toltec manufacture and date to the last two centuries of occupation at the site.

Stephens and Catherwood spent a total of 18 days at Chichén Itzá, hiring local workers to help them remove the trees, and the underbrush, and the other debris from a number of the other buildings at the site. There are, in fact, a great many such buildings, including the Temple of the Jaguars, the Temple of the Warriors, the Pyramid of Kukulkan, and the Platform of Venus. Some of these, including the Temple of the Jaguars and the Temple of the Warriors, contain murals and scenes depicting the conquest of this area by the Toltecs from Mexico led by Topiltzin Quetzalcoatl. The murals indicate that the invaders arrived by sea and first beat the Maya defenders, who came out to meet them in canoes, and then they fought a great battle against these same Maya and defeated them again.

There is also an astronomical observatory, as well as a long, stone skull rack featuring lots of skulls carved in stone, undoubtedly to simulate real ones. And there's a huge ball court, which is the largest in Mesoamerica and which

Stephens described at length. As it turned out, many of these structures date from the time of the Toltec period at the site, replacing or being built in addition to the earlier Maya structures.

Now, there are numerous other Maya cities, both large and small, which we could also describe, but these four—Copán, Tikal, Palenque, and Chichén Itzá—are fairly representative overall. As far as the future of Maya studies goes, though, one of the most exciting developments in recent years involves a technological breakthrough. This is the use of LiDAR for mapping known sites and discovering new ones, or even just discovering previously unknown buildings at known sites.

The best example: to map the Maya city of Caracol in Belize in 2009. Suddenly, with just an airplane flying over the area with an advanced LiDAR system for just four days, a huge patch of what looked like jungle from above was shown to contain buildings, roads, and other parts of a massive city that was hidden from sight. One researcher has said that, in the jungle, you can be as little as 600 feet from a large site and not even suspect that it might be there. Using LiDAR has the potential to change all of that, for not only can it help locate lost cities, but it can map the ones that we know in a matter of days or even hours, as compared to the weeks and months, or even years, that it usually takes. I wonder how Stephens and Catherwood would feel about that. I suspect most likely they would be pleased.

However, what is still a mystery is why the classic Maya civilization came to an end just after 900 A.D., with all or most of the great sites abandoned and subsequently overgrown and lost to the rest of the world. A favorite suggestion is that they were unable to deal with a century-long drought—that is, climate change—but this is by no means certain. Numerous other hypotheses have also been put forward, including explanations that involve overpopulation and deforestation. But for this mystery to be resolved once and for all, more investigation is definitely needed.

Lecture 22
The Nazca Lines, Sipán, and Machu Picchu

In terms of archaeology in South America, the Nazca Lines in Peru resonate with the general public more than almost anything else. These huge figures drawn in the dry desert soil—technically known as *geoglyphs*—include a spider, a dog, birds, monkeys, a tree, and what appears to be an ancient astronaut. Although they had been known since the 1920s, they became famous worldwide beginning in the 1960s with the publication of Erich von Däniken's *Chariots of the Gods*. In this lecture, we'll explore the Nazca Lines, along with the Moche culture and the royal tombs of Sipán and Machu Picchu.

The Nazca Lines

- In his book *Chariots of the Gods*, Erich von Däniken decided that ancient astronauts must have been responsible for the Nazca Lines in Peru, in part because of one strange figure that looks like an astronaut and in part because he identified some of the lines as "landing strips" for ancient aircraft or spaceships. Almost all archaeologists disagree with von Däniken's conclusions, but a considerable portion of the public seems to have taken his theories seriously.

- The Nazca Lines are located in the high desert of southern Peru, about 200 miles from Machu Picchu. Rather than being the handiwork of ancient astronauts, they were probably made by an indigenous group known as the Nazca. The Nazca lived in this area between 200 B.C. and 600 A.D., and their graves and other ancient settlement remains are located near the lines.

- This theory of the origin of the lines is in part backed up by the similarity of the lines with designs found on Nazca pottery, including designs of animals, birds, and humans in red, white, and black paint on the vessels. In addition, carbon-14 dating done on the wooden stakes that were found at the ends of some of the lines indicates a date of about 525 A.D., plus or minus 80 years (sometime between 445 A.D. and 605 A.D.), which matches well with the known date for the Nazca presence in this area.

- Interestingly, the Nazca may not be the first people to create such lines in this region. An earlier culture known as the Paracas, from which the Nazca might have evolved, also created geoglyphs in the desert just a bit further to the north, near the modern town of Palpa. These date hundreds of years earlier in some cases. They are mostly found on the sides of hills rather than on the desert floor and include enigmatic human figures, as well as more of the "landing strips" to which von Däniken refers.

- The Nazca Lines drawn in the desert are huge, and there are hundreds of them, ranging from simple lines that go for miles to complex and stylized depictions of creatures. The lines and pictures were created simply by removing the oxidized rocks that form the top layer in the desert and digging down about a foot to reveal the lighter-colored sand that lies underneath. By doing this as a series of narrow lines, either straight or curved, designers can develop the outline of whatever they are interested in depicting and can create a picture that is easily seen from above, even if it isn't always readily identifiable.
  o In fact, in some cases, it's not clear at all what is being portrayed. For example, one animal is definitely a monkey, but it has no eyes or nose and has four digits on one paw and five on the other.

  o In contrast, there is a very convincing—and rather scary—spider that is 150 feet long. One of its hind legs goes way out of the bounds of the picture, perhaps representing the silken thread to which the spider is attached.

- Many people have put forth theories about the Nazca Lines since they first were noticed in the 1920s. Most recently, a joint German-Peruvian expedition has been documenting and studying the geoglyphs in both the Nazca area and the Palpa region. These researchers have found the ruins of many Nazca villages, with glyphs near virtually every settlement.

The figure of the astronaut in the Nazca Lines is almost 100 feet tall, with a bubble head and large, owl-like eyes.

- These findings suggest that there is a long history of such glyphs in the region, with some superimposed on others. It is also now clear that the earliest lines were created on hillsides, where they could be seen from the plain below, rather than from the air.

- Even the more complex lines have now been shown to be single-line drawings; a person could start walking at a specific point and walk along the line without ever having to cross another line. Thus, it has been suggested that the lines were used in ceremonial processions.

The Moche Culture and the Royal Tombs of Sipán

- In 1987, a royal tomb dating to about 250 A.D. was found in the area of Sipán in northern Peru. This was where the Moche culture flourished from 100 to 800 A.D. The tomb was excavated by a Peruvian archaeologist named Walter Alva.
    - At the time, Alva had received a call from the local police station near Sipán. It seems that several tomb robbers had had a falling out after finding a wealthy tomb and were fighting over the objects they found. Rather ironically, one of them called the police for help. The police confiscated the objects and called Alva.

    - Alva was amazed at what the police showed him and took a team of archaeologists back to where the robbers said they had found the tomb, which turned out to be in a huge pyramid made of mudbricks.

    - Alva hoped that there might be other tombs in the area that the looters had missed; thus, he and his team began a proper excavation. Soon, they did indeed find several other tombs, including one that belonged to the Lord of Sipán. Objects from these tombs, especially the Lord of Sipán's, were the New World equivalent of finding King Tut's tomb in terms of sheer quantities of valuable objects.

    - Subsequently, much archaeology has been done at a variety of Moche sites in northern Peru. Additional graves were found in 2001, and yet another grave in 2006, this time of a warrior woman, all of which were published in *National Geographic*.

- The Lord of Sipán's tomb is basically a large room measuring about 5 meters by 5 meters. After entering, excavators first found the body of a man whose feet had been cut off, possibly to ensure that he would stay in the tomb to protect the occupants, rather than walking away in the afterlife.

- The Lord of Sipán himself was found in the middle of the chamber, with additional burials on all sides of him. Counting the man whose feet had been cut off, there may have been as many as 11 people in the tomb besides the lord himself.

- There was also a total of more than 450 objects buried in the tomb, many of precious metal. Among the most interesting of these objects is a set of ear ornaments that features what appears to be a three-dimensional representation of the Lord of Sipán himself, complete with a spear or scepter, shield, ear ornaments, and a necklace of what may be skulls. If the lord wore this set of ear ornaments as part of his outfit when he was dressed up, then he'd be wearing a miniature of himself.

- In addition, several *backflaps* were found in the tomb, made in silver, gold, and bronze/copper. These were worn, as the name suggests, as part of the backside of an outfit. On several of these, the so-called Decapitator God is pictured, standing on what looks like a row of skulls.

- As for who this important person in the tomb actually was, Moche specialists have suggested that he may have been the Warrior Priest, who is known from pictorial scenes found on Moche pots and painted on murals. One of the most famous themes in these scenes is the so-called sacrifice ceremony.
  - In this ceremony, sacrificial victims had their throats cut and their blood poured into goblets for priests and other participants to drink.

  - The Warrior Priest is always shown wearing such ornaments as a helmet and headdress, backflaps, and earrings and carrying a large goblet or scepter, just like the Lord of Sipán has in his tomb. If that is the case, then the scenes that are portrayed on the pottery and in the murals apparently represent real events and people.

Machu Picchu

- The city of Machu Picchu is located in the southern part of Peru, directly east from the region of the Nazca Lines. It was first built about 1450 A.D. and was abandoned less than a century later, around 1532 A.D., at the time of the Spanish Conquest. It was an Inca site, located about five days walk from Cuzco, which was the Inca capital at the time. However, its exact purpose and function are still debated. Was it a winter or summer residence for the Inca king, or was it some sort of astronomical observatory?

- Hiram Bingham, who was a professor at Yale, gets credit for the discovery of Machu Picchu, which was first brought to the attention of the world in 1911. He didn't really discover it, though; it was basically just shown to him by the locals, who had always known it was there. Bingham excavated at the site in 1912, 1914, and 1915, then began writing books and articles about his

Looking out over the site of Machu Picchu, you can clearly see that it is split into an upper and a lower town.

discoveries. He actually thought that Machu Picchu might have been the lost Inca city of Vilcabamba, but that is now thought to be located elsewhere.

- The site of Machu Picchu is spectacular, like few others in the world. It encompasses a residential district, presumably where the regular people lived, as well as what seems to be a royal district. There are also temples, warehouses, channels for water, and many agricultural terraces. Within the so-called Temple of the Sun, there is a massive tower known as the Torreon, which was possibly used as an observatory (but that is still debated).

- All these buildings were constructed using the standard Inca technique. The stones were cut and fitted together so well that there was no need to use any mortar to bind or seal them. Most of the doors and windows are neither square nor rectangular but, rather, trapezoidal. Obviously, this was a deliberate architectural feature, and some people have suggested that it was to help prevent the buildings from collapsing during an earthquake.

- After his excavations at Machu Picchu, Bingham brought many artifacts back to Yale, where they remained for the next 90 years. Most of the objects were not returned to Peru until 2012. The objects that were returned are now displayed in a museum and research center in Cuzco.

Suggested Reading

Adams, *Turn Right at Machu Picchu*.

Alva and Donnan, *Royal Tombs of Sipán*.

Hall, "Spirits in the Sand."

Questions to Consider

1. How would you interpret the Nazca Lines?

2. How can we stop looting at such sites as Sipán?

Lecture 22 Transcript
The Nazca Lines, Sipán, and Machu Picchu

In terms of archaeology in South America, the Nazca Lines in Peru resonate with the general public more than almost anything else. These huge figures drawn in the dry desert soil—technically known as geoglyphs—include a spider, a dog, birds, monkeys, a tree, and what appears to be an ancient astronaut. Although they've been known since the 1920s when airplanes first started flying over this area of Peru, they became famous worldwide beginning in the 1960s because of Erich von Däniken's book *Chariots of the Gods*. He argued that only people who could see them from the air could possibly have drawn the figures, because they can't really be recognized at ground level.

Von Däniken decided that ancient astronauts must have been responsible, in part because of that one strange figure that looks like an astronaut, and in part because he identified some of the lines seen both here and a bit further north as landing strips for ancient aircraft or spaceships. This is a conclusion with which I, and almost all archaeologists, completely disagree, and actually I can't think of a single archaeologist who agrees with him, but there must be some somewhere, so I don't want to be sued by him, I'll say almost all rather than simply all.

And yet, a considerable portion of the general public seems to have taken von Däniken's theories seriously, so much so that his books have sold millions of copies over the years. And in fact, in 2003, he even opened up a theme park in Switzerland called Mystery Park. One of the seven pavilions at the park was devoted to a display and a discussion of the Nazca Lines. Unfortunately for von Däniken, even though there was an initial burst of enthusiasm, attendance at the amusement park quickly dropped off and the park itself closed down in 2006.

In any event, the Nazca Lines are very real and they are well worth a visit, even if ancient astronauts did not build them. They were designated as a UNESCO World Heritage Site in 1994, and are therefore protected, so most tourists can't actually walk through the site. But you'll want to arrange for an airplane, or a helicopter, or even a hot air balloon to fly you over the lines, since they really are best seen from the air.

Now, these lines were in the news again in August 2014, when new images were spotted after sandstorms and high winds hit the area. They also made headlines around the world later that same year, in December of 2014, when Greenpeace volunteers laid out a huge message saying, "Time for Change! The Future is Renewable." The Greenpeace people came under heavy criticism for damaging the ancient site in their zeal to protect the future, which is, frankly, rather ironic.

The Nazca Lines are located in the high desert of southern Peru. They're about 200 miles away from Machu Picchu, and rather than being the handwork of ancient astronauts, archaeologists are pretty sure that they were made by an indigenous group known as the Nazca. The Nazca lived in this area between 200 B.C. and 600 A.D., and their graves and other ancient settlement remains are located near the lines.

Now, I say this in part because of the similarity with the designs found on Nazca pottery, which includes designs of animals, birds, and humans in red, white, and black paint on the vessels. And, in addition, carbon-14 dating that's been done on the wooden stakes that were found at the end of some of the lines indicate a date of about 525 A.D., plus or minus about 80 years—so somewhere between 445 A.D. and 605 A.D., which matches well for the known date of the Nazca presence in this area.

However, a little known fact is that they might not even be the first people to create such lines in this region. An earlier culture known as the Paracas, from which the Nazca might have evolved, also created geoglyphs in the desert just a bit further to the north near the modern town of Palpa. These date hundreds of years earlier in some cases. They're mostly found on the sides of hills rather than on the desert floor and they include enigmatic human figures as well as more of those landing strips to which von Däniken refers.

In any event, the Nazca Lines drawn in the desert are huge, and there are hundreds of them, ranging from simple lines that go for miles to very complex and stylized depictions of creatures. The lines and the pictures were created simply by removing the oxidized rocks that form the top layer here in the desert and digging down about a foot to reveal the lighter-colored sand that lies underneath. By doing this as a series of narrow lines, either straight or curved, you can create a picture that is very easily seen from above, even if you can't always identify it from the bottom or even from the air.

In fact, in some cases, it's not clear at all what's being portrayed. There's one animal, for instance, that looks a bit like a cross between a scared cat and some sort of weird dog. I think it's supposed to be a dog, but it's very cartoonish, with completely straight legs and only three or four digits on each foot.

Another one is most definitely a monkey, but it doesn't have any eyes, and it doesn't have a nose, and its got four digits on one hand but five on the other. Speaking of hands, one of the Nazca figures is simply called The Hands, though I actually do think it looks a little bit more like a monkey, but unfinished. It also doesn't have any eyes or nose, and its got four digits on one hand and five on the other.

And then there is a very convincing—and, frankly, rather scary—spider that's 150 feet long. One of its hind legs goes way out of the bounds of the picture, not to mention reality, and my guess is that this is supposed to represent the silken thread that the spider is attached to, but they've done it very strangely by making it an extension of one of the legs.

There's also a huge stylized tree and a large bird-like figure known as the Heron. Now, one of my personal favorites is a 300-foot-long hummingbird with a beak that's about the same length as its body. There's another bird that's known as the Condor, and a fourth bird that's called the Parrot, even though it doesn't look much like a parrot to me.

And then, then there's the Astronaut. He was created on the side of a hill, much like the early Paracas drawings that are further to the north. This is a figure that's almost 100 feet tall, with a bubblehead and big owl-like eyes. In fact, he is sometimes called the Owl-Man. One of his arms is pointing up and the other one's pointing down. Now, he doesn't look much like an astronaut to me, and there are many other reasonable explanations out there for what he might be doing, including perhaps holding a fishing net and wearing a traditional poncho.

In fact, a lot of people have made a lot of suggestions about the Nazca Lines since they were first noticed back in the 1920s. Theories to explain their existence range from von Däniken's ancient astronauts using the region as landing strips to more scientific and anthropological hypotheses that involve water and ceremonial aspects of both the Paracas and the Nazca cultures.

Most recently a joint German-Peruvian expedition has been documenting and studying the geoglyphs in both the Nazca area and the Palpa region to the north. They're finding the ruins of many Nazca villages, with glyphs near virtually every settlement. The findings suggest that there is a long history of such glyphs in the region, with some of them superimposed upon others. It's also now clear that the earliest of them were created on hillsides from where they could be seen from the plain below, rather than needing to be seen from up in the air.

Even the more complex ones, like the hummingbird, have now been shown to be what are called single-line drawings. That means that you can start walking at a specific point and walk along the line without ever having to cross another line, so it's quite possible that these were used as something like ceremonial processions, which has been suggested, but here we're invoking religion to explain something whose use is actually not completely clear to us. In any case, there's simply no need to invoke extraterrestrial visitors in order to explain the amazing creations of the past, whether it's the Nazca Lines or the Egyptian Pyramids. Trust me, our predecessors on this planet were advanced enough not to need outside assistance in such building projects.

Now, speaking of amazing, let's turn now to a discovery that was only made in 1987 and that turned my world upside down just a few years later. This was the discovery of a royal tomb that dates to about 250 A.D. which was found in the area of Sipán in northern Peru. This is where the Moche culture flourished from about 100–800 A.D. The tomb was excavated by a Peruvian archaeologist named Walter Alva.

Now, I have to admit that I had never heard of the Moche before the early 1990s, but they're now one of my favorite people from antiquity. At the time, we were living in Fresno, California. We had helped to turn the Fresno County Archaeological Society into a local chapter of the national Archaeological Institute of America. That's got more than 100 such local chapters around the U.S. Now, this is one of our professional organizations, and bringing archaeology to the general public is one of its core missions. I'm also part of their lecture series, which sends archaeologists on lecture tours around the U.S., so if you're interested, go ahead and look the AIA as well call it—the Archaeological Institute of America—up on the Web, and then join a local society if there's one near you.

Anyway, instead of having a lecture each and every month, our Fresno society used to have field trips once or twice a year, and in 1993 we rented an air-conditioned bus for fifty people and traveled about three hours down to Los Angles. There was an exhibit there on the Moche at the Fowler Museum at UCLA. The exhibit was called the "Royal Tombs of Sipán" and it absolutely blew me away. I had never seen so much gold in my life, except for the time back in the mid-'70s when I went to see the King Tut traveling exhibit. In fact, the objects from the tombs, especially one tomb that belongs to the Lord of Sipán, are the New World equivalent of finding King Tut, at least in terms of sheer quantities of valuable objects.

Subsequently, I read as much as I could about the Moche, absolutely amazed that I had never heard of them before. I knew about the Aztecs, Inca, and Maya, of course, but I had no idea about the Moche. Now, I felt a little bit better when I learned that they had been studied since the 1960s, but had only become known outside a small circle of New World archaeologists with the discovery of the first royal tomb in 1987. Subsequently, a lot of archaeology has been done at a variety of Moche sites in northern Peru. Additional graves were found in 2001, and yet another grave in 2006, this time of a warrior woman, all of which were published in *National Geographic*.

Anyway, back in 1987, Walter Alva got a call from the local police station near Sipán. It seems that the police had been called in because several tomb robbers had had a falling out after they found a wealthy tomb, and they were fighting over the objects that they found. Rather ironically, one of them called the police for help. The police promptly confiscated the objects and called Walter Alva, and when he arrived at the police station, one of the officers reached into a paper bag and then pulled out a small gold mask. Alva nearly fell off of his chair in surprise.

Now, he took a team of archaeologists back to where the robbers said that they had found the tomb. It turned out to be located in an absolutely huge pyramid made of mudbricks. The pyramid, which is one of several at the site, was so damaged by erosion and other mostly natural forces that it almost looked more like a natural mountain than something constructed by humans.

Alva hoped that there might be other tombs that the looters had missed, so he and his team began a proper excavation. And soon they did indeed find several more tombs, including one that *National Geographic* has called the New World's richest unlooted tomb. This is tomb number one, the tomb belonging to the Lord of Sipán.

In the tomb, which is basically a large room measuring about five meters by five meters, they first found the body of a man whose feet had been cut off. This was possibly to prevent him from walking away in the afterlife, so that he had to stay to protect the other occupants. He's buried in the upper right-hand corner of the burial chamber, a few feet above the rest of the bodies.

Now, the Lord of Sipán himself was found in the middle of the chamber, with additional burials on all sides of him. Counting the man whose feet had been cut off, there may have been as many as 11 people in the tomb besides the lord himself. There are three other adult men, an adult woman, three adolescent boys and three adolescent girls, plus one child.

And there were also a total of more than 450 objects buried in this one tomb. Many of them were of precious metal, including gold and silver. There are also many of copper or bronze that has now oxidized to a very pleasant green color. Among my favorites are necklaces that have beads in the shape of what look like peanuts, including one that's got silver peanuts on one side and gold peanuts on the other. In fact, I looked it up, and according to the National Peanut Board—and, yes, there really is such a thing—it's thought that the peanut plant might have originated in either Peru or Brazil, which

I definitely didn't know before. So, maybe they really are supposed to represent peanuts.

Now, there are also three pairs of ear ornaments, including one set with an animal inlaid on them who looks a little bit like Rudolph the Red-Nosed Reindeer, to be perfectly honest. Another set has a bird that looks like a cross between a duck and a pelican. Then a third set actually has what appears to be a three-dimensional representation of the Lord of Sipán himself, all dressed up and ready to go, complete with a spear or a scepter, a shield, his own ear ornaments, and a necklace of what looks like skulls that goes from shoulder to shoulder. If the lord wore this last set of ear ornaments as part of his outfit when he was all dressed up, he'd be wearing a miniature of himself, which is kind of cool to think about.

On his chest were found hundreds of tiny beads still in place. They formed a magnificent pectoral collar of green, brown, and white. These had to be painstakingly preserved and conserved. Often the way to recover these types of things intact is to put some sort of easily removable glue onto cloth, or cardboard, or some other material, and then to lay it on top of the beads while they're still in place. Then you allow the whole thing to dry, you lift it all up, the beads come with it, still in the original place and with the original design still intact, although now it's backwards. You can then transport it safely wherever you want, place it back down, dissolve the glue, and take the supporting material away, and voila—you've got the original pectoral collar with all of the beads still in place, but now safely out of the tomb and in a place where you can work on it some more and in peace.

Now, there was also a huge crescent-shaped helmet or headdress made of gold, with feathers that probably went with it, and also probably a faceplate made of gold to cover the lower part of the lord's face. And then there's a scepter or a goblet made out of gold. There are also several backflaps made in silver, gold, and either bronze or copper. These were worn, as the name suggests, as part of the backside of the outfit, most likely covering his rear end.

On several of these, the so-called Decapitator god is pictured standing on what looks like a row of skulls. This Decapitator god is found on other objects in the tomb as well. Although small, he's not a god that I would want to meet in a dark alleyway. Other representations, presumably of other gods, are equally ferocious looking, including some with open mouths and lots of sharp, pointy teeth. But there are also small gold beads in the shape of faces with inlaid blue eyes that aren't nearly as scary to look at.

As for whom this important person in the tomb actually was, Moche specialists have suggested that he might have been the Warrior Priest who is known from pictorial scenes that have been found on Moche pots and painted on Moche murals. One of the most famous themes is the so-called Sacrifice Ceremony. In this ceremony, sacrificial victims have their throats cut, their blood is poured or drained into goblets, and then the priests and the other participants drink it. The Warrior Priest is always shown wearing things like a helmet and a headdress, backflaps, ear ornaments, and carrying a large goblet or a scepter, just like the Lord of Sipán has in his tomb. If that's the case, then the scenes that are portrayed on the pottery and in the murals apparently represent real-life events and real people.

As I mentioned, there are numerous other Moche sites that have been investigated over the past several decades, which have yielded important artifacts and information. The tomb of the Lord of Sipán remains among the best known, however, which has unfortunately resulted in large-scale attempts at looting by would-be tomb robbers looking for another rich burial nearby. At least one aerial photograph shows the region by Sipán looking more like a moonscape, with pits dug absolutely everywhere. Well, obviously this is one of the areas of the world where we've got to be proactive in the future to prevent such looting activities.

Moving now a bit later in time to about 1500 A.D. and back down to the southern part of Peru directly east from the region of the Nazca Lines, I'd like to spend the last part of this lecture discussing the site of Machu Picchu. This was declared a UNESCO World Heritage Site in 1983.

Now, somehow I suspect that many of you have already been to Machu Picchu or at least have it on your bucket list as a place that you must visit. I fall into the bucket list category and I'm very envious of those of you who have already been there. In fact, I just finished reading a great book by Mark

Adams, which is called *Turn Right at Machu Picchu*. It's both really funny and very well written. In it, he not only gives an exciting history of the "discovery" of the city by Hiram Bingham—and I put that word, discovery, in quotes for the moment—but he also gives a firsthand account of what it's like to actually hike the Inca trail and visit the ruins today.

The city of Machu Picchu dates back to a little over 500 years ago. It was first built during the 15th century, actually about 1450 A.D., and it was abandoned less than 100 years later, about 1532, at the time of the Spanish conquest. It's an Inca site located about five days walk from Cuzco, which was the Inca capital at the time, but its exact purpose and its function are still debated. Was Machu Picchu simply a winter residence or a summer residence for the Inca king? Was it some sort of astronomical observatory or something else along those lines?

For myself, not being a specialist in this region, I'm happy to regard it as a royal residence with perhaps a few of the buildings having some sort of astronomical associations, but I think the jury is still out. In fact, I'm not sure we will ever find out for sure, but that doesn't stop people, whether they are scholars or educated laypeople, from speculating about it.

Hiram Bingham, who was a professor at Yale, gets credit for the discovery of Machu Picchu, which he brought to the attention of the world in 1911. He didn't really discover it, though, because he was basically just shown it by the locals, who had always known it was there. He might not have even been the first explorer to find it, but he claimed credit for it, just like Heinrich Schliemann had done at Mycenae about 40 years earlier when the locals took him to the ruins of the Lion Gate.

Now, Bingham returned to the site in 1912, sponsored by both *National Geographic* and Yale University, and he excavated there for about 4 months, even though he had no formal training as an archaeologist. In 1913, *National Geographic* devoted their entire April issue to Machu Picchu, and some see that issue, and the National Geographic Society's association with Bingham, as the beginning of its rise to the international prominence that it still enjoys today.

Lecture 22 Transcript—The Nazca Lines, Sipán, and Machu Picchu

Additional excavations took place in 1914 and 1915, and then Bingham began writing books and articles about his discoveries of which probably the most famous is a book called *Lost City of the Incas*, which was published in 1948. He actually thought that Machu Picchu might have been the lost Inca city of Vilcabamba, but now that's thought to be located somewhere else.

Anyway, the site of Machu Picchu is spectacular, like few others in the world. The views are quite literally breathtaking, and I say that in part because, at that altitude, it's genuinely hard to catch your breath. In fact, many tourists suffer from altitude sickness while they're there, which is not really what you want on your eagerly anticipated vacation.

Now, if you're looking out over the site itself, you can see that it's split into an upper town and a lower town. There's a residential district, presumably where the regular people lived. There's also what seems to be a royal district, possibly for the nobles or the royalty. And then there are the temples, the warehouses, the channels for water, and lots and lots of agricultural terraces. Within the so-called Temple of the Sun, there is also a massive tower known as the Torreon, which was possibly used as an observatory, but that's still debated. A large stone called the Intihuatana might be a ritual stone used to mark winter and summer solstices, but that's also debated.

All of these buildings were constructed using the standard, or classic, Inca technique. The stones were cut and fitted together so well that there wasn't any need to use any mortar to bind or seal them together. Most of the windows and doors, they're not square or rectangular, but they're actually trapezoid. Now, obviously this was a deliberate architectural feature and some people have suggested that it was to help the buildings from collapsing during an earthquake, which is an interesting idea.

Bingham brought a lot of artifacts back to Yale from Machu Picchu after his excavations at the site both in 1912 and in 1914–15. He was supposed to have them for only 18 months so that experts in the United States could study them. In fact, they remained at Yale for the next 90 years, and it was only when the wife of the Peruvian president, who was an anthropologist herself, began agitating for their return that anything was actually done about it. The first few objects were returned in 2006 and by 2012 pretty much all of the artifacts had been sent back to Peru, except for those that both sides agreed should stay at Yale for further study.

The objects that were returned are now displayed in a museum and a research center in Cuzco, where both local and foreign archaeologists and students can study them. They include ceramic bottles decorated with highly intricate designs, some of which would have been used to hold things like oil or perfume. One can be seen to have a human face on the long neck of the bottle, with what looks like a flounced skirt on the body of the vessel. Another is in the shape of a hand holding an elongated cup. There's also a pin for a shawl, which is made out of bone, and it features two birds facing each, as well as various pieces of jewelry and other metal objects, including ceremonial knives.

So, we'll end our survey of archaeology in Peru on that note. We've seen some amazing cultures, ranging from the Nazca to the Moche to the Inca, and we've covered several thousand years and hundreds of square miles of territory, from the deserts to the mountains. As an Old World archaeologist and someone whose specialty is the Late Bronze Age, I find these New World cultures that are so much closer to us in time to be very different from those that I usually study. And yet we can clearly see the rise and fall of distinctive civilizations, each occupying the same general region one after the other, here in the New World just like in the Old World. It seems that the cycle of history is not so different, whether you're studying the Moche or Mesopotamia, the Inca or the Indus Valley, the Nazca or the New Kingdom of Egypt.

Lecture 23 Archaeology in North America

In this lecture, we'll visit a few sites in North America. We'll move around quite a bit—ranging from the shores of South Carolina to the Pueblo ruins in the American Southwest, but this tour will accomplish two goals: First, it will deepen your appreciation for the rich archaeological heritage of North America. Second, it will give you an idea of how legislation has been used in the United States to preserve that distinctive heritage.

CSS *Hunley*

- The Confederate vessel *H. L. Hunley* was the first submarine to fire on a ship in North American waters. However, the *Hunley* didn't really fire its torpedo; rather, the torpedo was attached to a 16-foot-long metal spar at the front of the sub. The target ship was the USS *Housatonic*. In addition to sinking the *Housatonic*, the *Hunley* itself also promptly became the first submarine to sink in North American waters. The incident took place off Sullivan's Island, near Fort Sumter in Charleston Harbor, during the Civil War in February 1864.

- When the *Hunley* rammed the *Housatonic*, the torpedo was left inside the ship, as designed. It was long thought that the crew then backed off about 150 feet before detonating the torpedo via a wire. However, recent evidence indicates that they may have only been about 20 feet away, which means it may have been directly detonated. The Confederates also may not have figured on the concussion shock wave caused by the detonation, or the detonation may have knocked loose a latch on the forward conning tower.

- In any case, when the torpedo went off, the *Housatonic* sank, but so did the *Hunley*, in 30 feet of water and with all eight men on board. It was actually the third time that the *Hunley* had sunk and men had drowned as a result, but this time, it was lost for good, at least until 1995.

- The excavation of the *Hunley* was conducted under the Abandoned Shipwreck Act, which was signed into law in 1988. The act is meant to stop the looting of shipwrecks that sank in either state or federal waters. It gives authority to the federal government and to the state in which the wreck was found.

- The 40-foot-long sub was found on its side, at a 45-degree angle, sunken into the silt of the sea floor, 30 feet below the surface of the water. Raising it involved a feat of engineering, but once it was safely in the laboratory, excavation began almost immediately. The first human remains were soon found, as were scraps of textile, part of a belt, and a corked glass bottle. The matrix of silt had protected the remains from the currents and the seawater, while the relative lack of oxygen had preserved the bodies and other artifacts.

- Excavation and investigation of the *Hunley* has continued since 2000. By now, the complete skeletons and skulls of all eight men have been recovered. One of the crewmembers, Joseph Ridgaway, has been positively identified through a DNA match. Another, the commander, Lieutenant George E. Dixon, has been tentatively identified through a coin he kept with him as a good-luck charm and through a healed bullet wound.

Jamestown, Virginia

- Excavations at Jamestown, Virginia, have been under the direction of William Kelso since the 1990s and have been subsidized in part by the National Geographic Society. They are an excellent example of traditional excavation methodology now enhanced by cutting-edge technology.

- Jamestown was the first permanent settlement to be established by British colonists in what would later become the Commonwealth of Virginia. The settlement was begun in 1607 by about 100 men. Reinforcements, including some women, arrived a few years later. The settlement is probably most well-known to people today because of Pocahontas, the Native American woman who reportedly saved the life of Captain John Smith and later married a colonist named John Rolfe.

- The site of Jamestown had almost vanished over the centuries. The writings of Captain Smith and others, a small sketch of the site, and a single church tower dating from a later period led Kelso to determine where to place the first trenches. Within hours of beginning excavation, his team found the first artifacts and remains of buildings.

- Immediately, the excavators came up with weapons and armor, as well as pottery, glass, coins, and other artifacts dating to the 17th century. They also found a line of postholes, which was all that remained of the wooden protective palisade wall belonging to the original fort. The wooden posts had long since disintegrated, but the holes in the ground were still plainly visible.

- As the excavations continued, the team found the outline of the whole fort and the remains of five additional buildings. By 2007, the researchers had also found numerous graves and skeletons in a variety of places, ranging from an actual cemetery to single graves underneath the church. The skeletal remains indicated that the men had mostly died before the age of 25. The women didn't live much longer than that.

- Four skeletons in particular caught Kelso's interest. The four bodies had been found in November 2013 in an area of the church. In late July 2015, the media reported that the remains had been positively identified as belonging to some of the early leaders of the colony.
    - According to some of those media reports, the skeletons had been taken to the Smithsonian's National Museum of Natural History, where the world-famous forensic anthropologist Doug Owsley worked on them. He and his team were able to identify the Jamestown skeletons using a combination of forensic analysis and historical records.

- Owsley's team also did chemical testing to determine the diet and such factors as the level of lead in the bones. The results indicated that the dead people were most likely English and of high status, because of their high-protein diet and their exposure to pewter bowls and glazed pottery, both of which contain lead. Their high status, or at least their importance in the colony, was also indicated by the fact that their graves were found under the chancel of the church.

- Two of the four men, Captain Gabriel Archer and Reverend Robert Hunt, were from the original group that arrived in 1607. The other two, Sir Ferdinando Wainman and Captain William West, were from the group of reinforcements that arrived in 1610.

- Kelso and his team uncovered some other human bones in 2012 that they thought merited further investigation.
  - The bones included fragments from a mutilated and incomplete skull and a severed leg bone. Kelso found them in the cellar of a Jamestown house, in a context with the discarded bones of butchered horses and dogs. Owsley had previously found evidence that the settlers at Jamestown had practiced cannibalism on at least one occasion; thus, he was called to study the bones further.

  - Owsley identified the bones as belonging to an English girl who was about 14 years old. Based on a variety of evidence, Oswley, Kelso, and others concluded that she died during the so-called Starving Time—the bleak winter months of 1609 to 1610; they also think that the other colonists ate her after she died.

Kennewick Man

- Owsley was also responsible for examining the skeleton of the Kennewick Man. This skeleton has been the subject of debate since its discovery in 1996, near Kennewick, Washington. In particular, Kennewick Man has stoked the controversy surrounding the Native

American Graves Protection and Repatriation Act (NAGPRA) of 1990.

- NAGPRA required every federally funded American museum and similar institution to provide an inventory of their Native American artifacts, including human remains, funerary objects, grave goods, and so on. Each institution that had such artifacts or remains was required to determine if there were any living Native Americans who could claim a relationship with the inventoried objects. If so, then the institution was required to offer to repatriate the objects, whatever they were.

- Kennewick Man, who died about 8,500 years ago, was discovered in July 1996 and has been the subject of litigation almost since the moment he was found. Native American groups argued that he was

The ruins at Mesa Verde, which include the famous Cliff Palace, are now protected by U.S. law and designation as a UNESCO Heritage site.

Native American and should be repatriated to them, while a number of prominent scholars argued that the remains were too old to be related to any of the current Native American tribes and should be cared for by the federal government. The case was settled in 2002 and affirmed by an appeals court in 2004 in favor of the scholars, although it is still debated today.

Southwestern Sites

- Lawmakers in the United States have been passing legislation aimed at preserving ancient sites and antiquities for more than a century now. In fact, one of the earliest laws concerned with antiquities was passed during the presidency of Theodore Roosevelt, specifically because of a vast trade in looted painted pots and other antiquities from Anasazi sites in the American Southwest. This is known as the Antiquities Act of 1906.

- As a result of this legislation, protection was given to such sites as Chaco Canyon in New Mexico. This site has amazing Pueblo ruins built by the Anasazi, dating between 850 and 1250 A.D.

- Here are a number of *great houses*—huge structures with multiple rooms and multiple stories. One of the best examples is Pueblo Bonito, which had between 600 and 800 rooms and was five stories tall. It was built in stages between 850 and 1150 A.D. It covers three acres, and estimates of its population range from about 800 to several thousand.

- The Chacoan culture covered portions of New Mexico, Colorado, Utah, and Arizona. Imported goods that have been found, including seashells and copper bells, attest to trade with areas as far away as Mexico. It is, however, unclear why Chacoan culture disappeared by about 1200 A.D., though both drought and migration have been suggested, among other factors.

- Also in 1906, an act of Congress established Mesa Verde National Park in southwestern Colorado. Within the park are more Pueblo ruins, including nearly 5,000 sites that date between the 6th and 13th

centuries A.D. There are about 600 cliff dwellings here, running the gamut from small storage rooms to impressively large villages with as many as 150 rooms.

- Other laws followed, including the Historic Sites Act of 1935, which gave the National Park Service the right to identify, protect, and preserve cultural property, such as Native American sites or sites from the colonial era. Another important piece of legislation is the Archaeological Resources Protection Act, which protects archaeological sites on federal land. Such laws are designed to help, rather than hinder, archaeologists, and in fact, have created innumerable jobs in archaeology, as well as opportunities to volunteer on archaeological projects.

Colonial Williamsburg is one North American archaeological site that welcomes visitors and has occasional volunteer opportunities to help excavate at the site.

Suggested Reading

Fagan, *Chaco Canyon*.

Kelso, *Jamestown*.

Ragan, *The Hunley*.

Questions to Consider

1. Are you in favor of using forensic anthropology to try to reconstruct what the people in the *Hunley* or at Jamestown would have looked like?

2. Do you think the legislation passed in the United States regarding the protection of antiquities has been successful, or are there other actions we can take?

Lecture 23 Transcript

Archaeology in North America

It's time we visit a few sites in North America. We're going to be moving around quite a bit, ranging from the shores of South Carolina to the Pueblo ruins in the American Southwest, but I hope the tour will accomplish a couple of things. First, I hope it'll deepen your appreciation for the rich archaeological heritage of North America. And second, I want to give you an idea of how legislation has been used in the U.S. to preserve that distinctive heritage. So let's start in South Carolina.

My 16-year-old son Joshua is intensely interested in all things military, especially those pertaining to World War II. So last year, for spring vacation, we took him to Charleston, South Carolina, where there are three World War II ships docked, including the USS *Laffey*, which he was most interested in.

On the last day of our trip, while heading to the airport, we passed a bronze statue of a small submarine that I recognized as the Confederate sub called the *H. L. Hunley*, which was sitting outside the Charleston Museum. The *Hunley* was the first submarine to fire on a ship in North American waters. Well, fire is perhaps the wrong word, because the *Hunley* didn't so much actually fire its torpedo, but rather it had it attached to a 16-foot-long metal spar—kind of like a long harpoon—that was at the front of the sub. The target ship was the USS *Housatonic*, and as we'll see, in addition to sinking the *Housatonic*, the *Hunley* itself also promptly became the first submarine to sink in North American waters. It happened off of Sullivan's Island, near Fort Sumter in Charleston Harbor, during the Civil War back in 1864.

When the *Hunley* basically rammed the *Housatonic*, the torpedo was left inside the ship, as designed. It was long thought that the crew then backed off about 150 feet before detonating the torpedo with a wire. However, recent evidence indicates that they might have only been about 20 feet away, so it might have been directly detonated. The Confederates also might not have figured on the concussion shock wave caused by the detonation, or else the detonation might have knocked a latch on the forward conning tower loose, because it was found unsecured. In any case, when the torpedo went off, the *Housatonic* sank, but so did the *Hunley*, in 30 feet of water and with all 8 men still on board. It was actually the third time that the *Hunley* had sunk and that men had drowned as a result, but this time it was lost for good, at least until 1995.

Now the *Hunley* is an example of an excavation that was conducted under the Abandoned Shipwreck Act, which was signed into law in 1988. The act is meant to stop the looting of ships that sank in either state or federal waters. It gives authority to the federal government and to the state in which the wreck was found. So, the *Hunley* is in the jurisdiction of South Carolina, because the submarine was discovered in 1995, 7 years after the act was signed into law, and it wasn't raised for another 5 years after that, in 2000. The *Hunley*, though, technically belongs to the federal government and to the U.S. Navy, because it's considered a spoil of war. Credit for finding the sub is usually given to the novelist Clive Cussler and his team, although there are some who dispute his claim, but the point's moot because the state is responsible for it.

To exercise this responsibility, South Carolina established the Hunley Commission, which serves as the custodian of the sub, meaning that it negotiates the details concerning its recovery, curation, and exhibition. Today, you can see the original submarine on display in North Charleston. There, it's kept in a 90,000-gallon tank of freshwater in order to prevent additional corrosion.

The 40-foot-long sub was found on its side at a 45-degree angle. It was sunken into the silt of the sea floor 30 feet below the surface of the water. Raising it involved a lot of people and a neat feat of engineering, but once it was safely in the freshwater tank in the laboratory, excavation was able to begin almost immediately. It was subsidized in part by the National Geographic Society, which had representatives present at the historic occasion of the recovery back in 2000. The first human remains—three ribs—were found soon after, as were scraps of textile, part of a belt, and a corked glass bottle. It turned out that the matrix of silt had protected the remains from the currents and the seawater, while the relative lack of oxygen had preserved the bodies and the other artifacts.

Investigation of the *Hunley* has continued ever since. By now, the complete skeletons, including the skulls of all eight men, have been recovered. Every one of them was found still sitting at his post, meaning that death might have been fairly instantaneous or that they might have been incapacitated and drowned while still in place.

One of the crewmembers, Joseph Ridgaway of Talbot County, Maryland, has been positively identified through a DNA match that was made in 2004. Another, the commander, Lieutenant George E. Dixon, has been tentatively identified. He kept an engraved $20 gold coin with him at all times as a good luck charm. A young girl had given it to him—some reports say that it was his fiancée. It had saved his life earlier when he had been shot at the Battle of Shiloh in Tennessee.

The archaeologists who were excavating the *Hunley* found just such a coin near the remains of one of the crewmembers. The coin had a deep indentation from a bullet and was inscribed with the words "Shiloh; April 6, 1862; my life preserver. G.E.D." Later they found that the skeleton of that same crewmember had a healed bullet wound in the left upper thigh with pieces of lead from a bullet and flecks of gold from the coin still embedded in his femur. It's pretty clear that this must be Dixon's body. They also found his pocket watch, as well as a wallet, a bandana, matches, and tobacco pipes.

The *Hunley* is a good example of an underwater archaeological find that is protected in the U.S. through legislation. UNESCO has now also begun efforts to protect underwater finds around the world by passing the Convention on the Protection of the Underwater Cultural Heritage in 2009. This came into play in an interesting way 2 years later when the Smithsonian was planning an exhibit that would have displayed objects from an Arab wreck that sank in the Java Sea in the 9th century A.D.

The shipwreck contained priceless artifacts from the Chinese Tang dynasty, but it wasn't excavated by professional archaeologists. Rather, the artifacts were recovered by a private company and later sold to another company for a reported $32 million. So, three different archaeological associations, as well as several members of the Smithsonian's own internal research unit, protested the proposed exhibit, saying that the process by which the artifacts had been recovered was closer to looting than to proper archaeological excavation. And, in the end, in the face of the protest, the exhibit was cancelled before it ever even opened.

But now let's get back to the tour of our North American sites, and what I'd like to do next is to move up the east coast from South Carolina and turn to the excavations at Jamestown, Virginia. These excavations have been under the direction of William Kelso since the 1990s, and they've been subsidized in part by the National Geographic Society. They're an excellent example of traditional excavation methodology now enhanced by cutting edge technology. They're also an illustration of what happens when an excavator who has labored in relative obscurity for decades suddenly finds something that the media deems to be of interest, which is what happened with Kelso and Jamestown during the summer of 2015.

Jamestown was the first permanent settlement to be established by British colonists in what would later become the Commonwealth of Virginia. The settlement was begun in 1607 by about 100 men who had a very rough time during the first few years. Reinforcements, including some women, arrived a few years later. Now, it's probably most well known to people today because of Pocahontas, the Native American woman who reportedly saved the life of Captain John Smith and then married a colonist named John Rolfe.

The site of Jamestown had pretty much vanished over the centuries. Before Kelso began his excavations, he had only a little bit of information to work with, mostly gleaned from archives stored in a library. Using the writings of Captain Smith and other eyewitness accounts, as well as a small sketch of the site that was made by a Spanish spy, as well as a single church tower, Kelso determined where he should place the first trenches. His archaeological intuition was excellent and within hours of beginning their excavations, his team had found the first artifacts and the remains of buildings.

So, what did they find? Well, right away they came up with weapons and armor, as well as pottery, glass, coins, and other artifacts dating to the 17th century. They also found a line of postholes, which was all that remained of the wooden protective palisade wall that belonged to the original fort. The wooden posts had long since disintegrated but the holes in the ground that they had left were still plainly visible. And, as the excavations continued over the years, they found the outline of the whole fort, as well as the remains of five additional buildings, including the church, the governor's house, the barracks, and a workshop or trading post.

By 2007, when Kelso published a brief description of their findings, they had also found numerous graves and skeletons in a variety of places, ranging from an actual cemetery with more than 70 internments to single graves underneath the church. The skeletal remains indicated the men had mostly died before the age of 25, and the women didn't live much longer than that.

It was four skeletons in particular, though, that caught Kelso's interest. The four bodies had been found back in November 2013, in the area of the church where Pocahontas and John Rolfe were married. The skeletal material was not very well preserved, so the effort to identify them involved the use of cutting edge technology and a lot of work. But then, in late July 2015, the media reported, rather breathlessly, that the remains had been positively identified as belonging to some of the early leaders of the colony.

Now, according to some of these media reports, the skeletons had been taken to the Smithsonian's National Museum of Natural History where Doug Owsley worked on them. Owsley is world famous and he's worked on many such cases, including the skeletons from the *Hunley*. Owsley and his team were able to identify the Jamestown skeletons using a combination of forensic analysis and historical records. The historical records allowed them to determine who had died between January 1608, when the church was constructed, and 1617, when it fell into disrepair and was actually moved. The forensic analysis gave them the approximate age at death and the gender for the remains of the four skeletons.

They also did chemical testing to determine the diet and such things as the level of lead in the bones. The results indicated that the dead people were most likely English and of high status because of their high protein diet and their exposure to things like pewter bowls and glazed pottery, both of which contain lead. Their high status, or at least their importance in the colony, was also indicated by the fact that their graves were found under the chancel of the church rather than the unmarked graveyard that was located elsewhere.

And it turns out that all four were men. Two were from the original group that had arrived in 1607. These were Captain Gabriel Archer and the Reverend Robert Hunt. Archer had come to the New World looking for gold and silver before his death at about the age of 35 in either 1609 or 1610. Hunt was the first chaplain of the settlement and he died at the age of 39 after less than a full year at Jamestown. The other two men were from the group of reinforcements that arrived in 1610. These are Sir Ferdinando Wainman, who was about 34 years old when he died of disease just a few months after arriving, and his relative, Captain William West, who was killed by the Native Americans in 1610 when he was only about 25 years old.

Now, Owsley had also previously found evidence that the settlers at Jamestown had practiced cannibalism on at least one occasion. Kelso and his team had uncovered some human remains in 2012 that they thought were unusual and merited further investigation. The bones included fragments from a mutilated and incomplete skull, including teeth and the lower jar, as well as a severed leg bone, specifically a tibia. Kelso had found them in the cellar of a Jamestown house in a context with the discarded bones of butchered horses and dogs, which is a rather unusual and unexpected location to say the least. So, he called in Owsley to look at the remains.

Owsley identified the bones as belonging to an English girl who was about 14 years old, based on the development of her third molar and the growth stage of her shinbone. They nicknamed her Jane, and although they couldn't determine her cause of death, Owsley and his associates noticed that her bones exhibited unusual cut marks. As the Smithsonian news report stated, there were four shallow cuts on her forehead, which the forensic anthropologists identified, and I quote here, as "a failed first attempt to open up the skull." The back of her head was then hit with a hatchet or a cleaver in a series of blows. The last one split her head open, presumably providing access to her brain. They also noticed that the lower jaw, or the mandible, had punctures and sharp cut on its bottom and sides. These, they said, were the result of efforts to remove tissue from the face and the throat using a knife.

Based on this evidence, Owsley, Kelso, and the others concluded that Jane died during the so-called Starving Time, which was the bleak winter months of 1609 and 1610 when the colony was ravaged by hunger and disease. They also think that the other colonists ate Jane after she died.

The forensic scientists also created a reconstruction of her head using CAT scans and other technology. The reconstruction was on display for a while at the National Museum of Natural History in Washington, D.C., while the actual skeletal remains are presented at Historic Jamestowne, the educational tourist center that's operated by the Jamestown Rediscovery project.

Doug Owsley provides a nice connection that takes us from the east coast all the way across North America to Washington State. That's because Owsley was also responsible for examining the almost 9,000-year-old skeleton of the so-called Kennewick Man. This skeleton has been the subject of a great deal of debate since its discovery in 1996 near Kennewick, Washington, by the banks of the Columbia River. And in particular, Kennewick Man has stoked the controversy that has always surrounded NAGPRA, which is perhaps the best-known piece of archaeological legislation in the last several decades within the U.S.

NAGPRA stands for the Native American Graves Protection and Repatriation Act of 1990. This act required every federally funded American museum and similar institution to provide an inventory of their Native American artifacts, including human remains, funerary objects, grave goods, and so on. Each institution that had such artifacts or remains was required to determine if there were any living Native Americans who could claim a relationship with the inventoried objects. And, if so, the institution was required to offer to repatriate whatever it was.

These included things like Ishi's brain, which belonged to the last known Native American still living in the wilds of California. Ishi had emerged from hiding in 1911 and was an instant media sensation. Berkeley anthropologist Alfred Kroeber is perhaps best known with his work with Ishi, while Alfred's wife Theodora, also an anthropologist, published a very popular book about him called *Ishi in Two Worlds*.

When I was a kid growing up in San Francisco in the 1960s, I knew all about Ishi, in part because we used to play in the forest that was at the end of our street. Within that forest was a cave known as Ishi's Cave. Now whether or not he had actually ever lived in it, I have no idea, but I wouldn't be at all surprised, because Ishi also had a lot of interaction with a doctor named Saxton Pope, who was at UC San Francisco, and that was within easy walking distance of both our house and that cave. Pope was an avid bow-and-arrow hunter. He befriended Ishi, who taught Pope how he made bows and arrows, and Pope subsequently published a book in 1923 called *Hunting with the Bow & Arrow*, which is still highly regarded today.

In any event, after Ishi's death in 1916, his brain was sent to the Smithsonian, and it was still there in a sealed tank within a warehouse in Suitland, Maryland, when NAGPRA was passed in 1990. So, Ishi's brain was eventually repatriated and was reunited with his cremated remains in California.

Now, NAGPRA really came to the forefront when Kennewick Man was found by the Columbia River, supposedly by two college students who were wading in the river in July of 1996. The initial discovery was part of his skull, which was found about ten feet from shore. It was first thought he might have been a murder victim, and so the coroner and a local archaeologist named James Chatters searched for more parts, and they quickly turned up almost his entire skeleton. It turns out that he died about 8,500 years ago.

Kennewick Man has been the subject of litigation almost since the moment that he was first found. Native American groups argue that he was Native American and he should be repatriated to them. But many prominent scholars have countered that his remains are too old to be related to any of the current tribes, and therefore he should be cared for by the federal government because they were found on federal land. The case was settled in 2002 and was affirmed by an appeals court in 2004 in favor of the scholars. Though the bones are in the Burke Museum of Natural History and Culture in Seattle, Washington, they're not on display, but they are available for study.

But the case is still debated even today. On the one hand, in 2014, Doug Owsley released a 680-page report to which 65 different scholars and researchers had contributed findings, and they declared that Kennewick Man was not Native American and was more likely to be related to Polynesians or another Pacific people. On the other hand, in 2015, geneticists from the University of Copenhagen and elsewhere published an article that compared the DNA of Kennewick Man to that of other populations and concluded that he is more closely related to modern Native Americans than he is to anybody else. So, we'll see what happens next.

All of this comes back to the fact that lawmakers in the United States have been passing legislation aimed at preserving ancient sites and antiquities for more than a century now. In fact, one of the earliest laws concerned with antiquities was passed during the presidency of Theodore Roosevelt, specifically because of a huge trade in looted painted pots and other antiquities from the Anasazi sites in the U.S. Southwest. This is known as the Antiquities Act of 1906. It was aimed at controlling the looting from sites like Casa Grande in Arizona. Casa Grande dates to about A.D. 1350 and was being looted for its wooden beams and other ancient remains.

As a result of acts like that one, protection was given to additional sites like Chaco Canyon in New Mexico, which is a National Historical Park near Albuquerque. It's got amazing Pueblo ruins that were built by the Anasazi, which by the way is a Navajo word that's come to mean, simply, ancient ones. And those ruins date between 850 and 1250 A.D.

Here, there are a number of what are referred to as great houses. These are huge structures with multiple rooms and multiple stories. One of the best examples is Pueblo Bonito, which had between 600 and 800 rooms and was 5 stories tall in places. It was built in stages between 850 and 1150 A.D., and it covers 3 acres, but scholars are unclear how many people actually lived there—estimates range from about 800 to several thousand. And it's also not completely clear whether it was a ritual center or simply a thriving village. The Chacoan Culture, as it's now called, covered portions of New Mexico, Colorado, Utah, and Arizona. Imported goods that have been found, including seashells and copper bells, attest to trade from areas as far away as Mexico.

Now in 1906, the same year that the Antiquities Act was passed, an act of Congress also established Mesa Verde National Park in southwestern Colorado. Within the park are more Pueblo ruins, including nearly 5,000 sites that date between the 6th and the 13th centuries A.D. There are about

600 cliff dwellings here, which run the gamut from small storage rooms to impressively large villages with as many as 150 rooms. The ruins at Mesa Verde, which include the famous Cliff Palace, were named a UNESCO Heritage site in 1978, so they're now protected in two different ways: by U.S. law and by UNESCO designation. Other laws followed, including the Historic Sites Act of 1935 that gave the National Park Service the right to identify, protect, and preserve cultural property like Native American sites or sites from the colonial era. And that's why quite a few professional archaeologists today work for the National Park Service.

Some of the most important pieces of archaeological legislation have been passed just since 1979. These include the Archaeological Resources Protection Act, which is called ARPA, which protects archaeological sites on federal land. If you take artifacts from such a site, you can be fined up to $20,000 and be sent to jail for a year and you'll also have a felony on your record from then on.

However, this is aimed pretty much at professional looters. If you find like an arrowhead on the surface of the ground while hiking in a national forest or someplace similar, you're not going to be sent to jail. The problem with this act is that it covers only federal land, it doesn't cover private land, so some people run businesses excavating the sites that they have on their land, allowing the paying tourists to keep the artifacts that they find.

If you want to go on a legitimate excavation in the United States, there are plenty of opportunities. For instance, there's Crow Canyon Archaeological Center near Mesa Verde National Park. Here you can participate in a number of different archaeological programs that cover the Anasazi or Chacoan sites, whether alone or with your entire family. Several of my students have participated in these and have then gone on to excavate with me at my sites.

There are also, of course, any number of North American archaeological sites that you can simply visit, including Colonial Williamsburg and George Washington's Mount Vernon, both of which recreate the time period and are aimed at informing the interested visitor, and both also occasionally welcome volunteers to help excavate at the sites.

I would also suggest visiting Serpent Mound in Ohio, which is a National Historic Landmark. There's not really much archaeology there per se these days, but it's quite spectacular. It's what's known as an effigy mound, meaning that it is in the shape of an animal. In this case, it's a snake with a long curled tail. Although it is accepted as a construction built by one of the Native American groups who lived in the Ohio region, it's still not quite clear to when it dates. Various suggestions, including those based on radiocarbon dating, have ranged from 300 B.C., which would be the Adena culture, to 1100 A.D., which would be the Fort Ancient culture.

Okay, as promised, we've visited a number of North American sites in this lecture, and I hope that you've come away with a desire to explore this rich archaeological heritage more deeply. I've also deliberately tried to put this heritage into the context of the laws that we have in the United States, so that you can see how the legislation has affected everything from the discovery, to the excavation, to the preservation, conservation, and promotion of archaeological sites.

And I applaud these laws, because they're designed to help, rather than to hinder, archaeologists, and in fact, along the way, they have created innumerable jobs in archaeology, from the archaeologists working for the National Park Service to cultural resources management archaeologists, who often go in just ahead of the bulldozers on construction projects.

And for those of you who live in the U.S., if you want to volunteer to do some archaeology in the area where you live, it's relatively easy to find a project. You might consider contacting your local university and ask to speak to somebody in the Anthropology department. Or you might contact the Archaeological Institute of America or the Society for American Archaeology and ask them to put you in touch with somebody in your local region. Those of you outside the U.S. can contact your local university or your local archaeological organization to find out what's going on in your region.

In any case, I hope that I've helped you to see the wonderful diversity of the archaeological landscape of North America. No matter where on the continent you happen to be, there's bound to be something that's interesting in the dirt.

Lecture 24

From the Aztecs to Future Archaeology

Some of the most recent discoveries in New World archaeology have taken place at the site of Teotihuacan, about 50 kilometers northeast of Mexico City, and in downtown Mexico City itself. The discoveries in downtown Mexico City have revealed previously unknown remains of Tenochtitlan, the capital city of the people whom we usually call the Aztecs. The city flourished from about 1325 A.D. until its destruction by the Spanish conquistadors in 1521. Of course, it's always been known that the ancient site lies underneath Mexico City, because the Spaniards destroyed much of it before building their own city right on top of the ruins.

Tenochtitlan

- Tenochtitlan was originally built on an island in the middle of Lake Texcoco, with causeways connecting it to the mainland. The actual space available for living was expanded by creating *chinampas,* or floating gardens, which eventually became firmly enough anchored and covered with enough soil that houses and other structures could be built on them. It looks as if the city was then split into four quarters and may have housed as many as 250,000 people.

- Even though modern Mexico City covers the ancient city, buildings and artifacts are constantly being discovered during various construction projects that shed light on what used to be there.
  - For example, the great Calendar Stone was discovered in December 1790, when the Mexico City Cathedral was being repaired. This huge stone is almost 12 feet across and weighs about 24 tons. It may have been used as either a ceremonial basin or an altar. The face in the middle might be the Aztec deity of the sun, which is why some people call this the Sun Stone.

  - The Calendar Stone was probably originally located on or in the Great Temple, usually called the Templo Mayor. Portions of the Templo Mayor itself were originally found in the mid-1900s, with more accidentally discovered in 1978. Since then, several entire city blocks of houses and shops were torn down in the center of the city so that the archaeologists could investigate the remains.

- o The Templo Mayor is actually a double pyramid dedicated to two gods: Huitzilopochtli, who is one of the two main gods of the Aztecs, and Tlaloc, who is the rain/water god. In addition to the actual remains of the temple pyramid, the archaeologists found artifacts of gold and jade, plus many animal skeletons and a rack of human skulls carved in stone. They also found that the Aztecs had buried objects from previous Mesoamerican civilizations!

- In 2006, archaeologists found a stone altar depicting Tlaloc that dates to about 1450 A.D. They also uncovered a monolith—a stone slab—made of pinkish andesite. The monolith depicts the earth goddess Tlaltecuhtli, originally painted with ocher, red, blue, white, and black. It was found lying flat but would have stood 11 feet tall, unless it was meant to lie flat. It weighs 12 tons and dates to the last Aztec period, from 1487–1520. The team that discovered the monolith thought that it might still be in its original position, perhaps at the entrance to a chamber or even a tomb, even though it had broken into four large pieces.

- Two years later, in a stone-lined shaft located beside the monolith, the archaeologists began finding additional Aztec religious offerings, including sacrificial knives made of white flint; objects made of jaguar bone; and bars of copal, or incense. Beneath these, in a stone box, were the skeletons of two golden eagles, surrounded by 27 sacrificial knives. And beneath these were yet more offerings; by January 2009, the archaeologists had found six separate sets of offerings in this one deep pit, which reached 24 feet below street level.
  - o Back at the 8-foot-deep mark, the archaeologists found a second stone box, containing the skeleton of a dog or a wolf that had been buried with a collar made from jade beads. It also had turquoise plugs—like earrings—in its ears and bracelets with little gold bells around its ankles.

- The skeleton is also covered with seashells and other remains of marine life, such as clams and crabs. The lead excavator of the dig thinks that the six sets of offerings mark the Aztec cosmology or belief system. For example, the dog/wolf with the seashells would represent the first level of the underworld, "serving to guide its master's soul across a dangerous river."

Teotihuacan

- Teotihuacan actually predates Aztec civilization, although the Aztecs gave the city its name, which may mean the "birthplace of the gods." However, it's still a matter of debate about who actually lived there and what they called their city. It was inhabited from about 100 B.C. to about 650 A.D. and probably had a population of at least 25,000—perhaps even up to 150,000 people when it was at its largest. Teotihuacan influenced hundreds of other Mesoamerican communities during its period of greatness and served as a beacon for later civilizations.

- It used to be thought that the Toltecs built the site, but that doesn't seem to be accurate because the site is earlier than the time of the Toltecs. For the moment, the inhabitants are simply referred to as Teotihuacanos.

- The site is dominated by a long central avenue, called the Avenue of the Dead, along which pyramids and temples were built. These include the Pyramid of the Sun and the Pyramid of the Moon, as well as the Temple of the Feathered Serpent. This last temple probably dates to about 200 A.D. Beginning in the 1980s, a series of pits was found in front of the temple that contained the bodies of nearly 200 warriors, both male and female, as well as their attendants. All of them had their hands tied behind their backs and were obviously ceremonial victims.

- In 2003, a tunnel was detected, leading from one of the plazas near the edge of the city to the Temple of the Feathered Serpent. It has since been mapped using remote sensing devices.

- The tunnel is more than 330 feet long, ending at least 40 and perhaps as many as 60 feet directly below the temple. It was sealed up about 1,800 years ago, with at least six walls erected to block the tunnel at various points along its length.

- During their excavations in the tunnel, the archaeologists have found more than 70,000 ancient objects, including jewelry, pottery, obsidian blades, rubber balls, and hundreds of large conch shells from the Caribbean.

- At the bottom of the tunnel are three chambers and offerings that include four large figurines of green stone, remains of jaguars, jade statues, and significant quantities of liquid mercury, which may have represented an underworld river or lake. The area beyond has yet to be investigated.

The Temple of the Feathered Serpent gets its name from the heads of the feathered serpents that stick out from the façade of the building, which weigh up to 4 tons each.

- We're not sure why, but Teotihuacan was eventually abandoned, probably sometime in the 7th or 8th century A.D. Even so, the location of this site was never forgotten. We know, for example, that the Aztecs used to come to Teotihuacan and were well aware of the people who had once lived there. It is this idea of layers of civilization—that each culture is built on the culture that came before it—that is at the very heart of what archaeologists do.

"Future Archaeology"

- As a thought experiment, try to imagine what such structures as the Washington Zoo, the Smithsonian Museum, or even a Starbucks will look like in the next 200 or 2,000 years. As archaeologists, what would we find in their ruins? Would we identify them properly? And if we misidentified them, in what way would we do so?

- Of all these places, it seems most likely that Starbucks and McDonalds might potentially cause the most confusion. Specifically, there may be a good chance of misidentifying Starbucks as a religion, complete with a goddess wearing a crown. Although this seems like a joke, if enough relevant records do not survive, those could be the kind of interpretations made by future archaeologists.

- Future archaeology is interesting to think about, especially given that we spend so much time looking at previously vanished cultures and don't usually consider what our culture will look like to future archaeologists. Think, for instance, about the fact that so much of our interactions are now online. Most of those interactions will vanish without a trace or will be inaccessible to future archaeologists. What will they conclude about our rate of literacy, for instance?

- It is worthwhile thinking about the fact that our current culture may be wildly misinterpreted by future archaeologists and that we may occasionally or, perhaps, even often misinterpret the past. That is an occupational hazard, but usually, once enough data is found, we come to a scholarly consensus about the proper interpretation of a building, a site, or even a civilization.

Doing Future Archaeology

- The future of archaeology is likely to see continued advances in technology that will allow us to peer even more easily beneath the earth or beneath the tree canopies in Central and South America. Apart from LiDAR, most of the techniques that we are using, such as magnetometers, resistivity, and so on, are now decades old. It is time for new developments.

- For example, might it be possible to detect plaster or other specific materials through a layer of earth, just as we can now detect buried walls and ditches? Would it make sense to partner with gas and oil exploration companies to use new techniques that might allow us to peer deeper into the depths of a mound or to do so in a series of slices at specific depths?

- At the same time, it seems fairly safe to say that the actual process of physically digging— that is, excavating with picks, shovels, trowels, and dental tools—will continue as it has since the first days of archaeology. There are only a limited number of ways that we can use to dig without actually destroying the remains that we have come to study.

- In this course, we've gone from the earliest archaeologists to the most recent archaeological discoveries, from the first crude excavations at Herculaneum to the high-tech methods being used at Teotihuacan today. We've learned what it takes to find sites and what it takes to dig them. Yet we've only just literally scratched the surface, because archaeology never ceases to yield remarkable discoveries. Every year, we uncover a few more pieces in the puzzle of human history and are able to glimpse a little bit more of the past.

Suggested Reading

Draper, "Unburying the Aztec."

Macaulay, *Motel of the Mysteries*.

Weisman, *The World without Us*.

Questions to Consider

1. How do you think future archaeologists will interpret such places as museums or hotels if they don't actually recognize what they are?

2. Do you think more of downtown Mexico City should be excavated by archaeologists, or do we know enough about the Aztecs already?

Lecture 24 Transcript: From the Aztecs to Future Archaeology

Some of the most recent discoveries in New World archaeology have been taking place at the site of Teotihuacan, about 50 kilometers northeast of Mexico City, and in downtown Mexico City itself. Let's begin with the discoveries in downtown Mexico City, which culminated in a November 2010 story in *National Geographic* magazine. These have revealed previously unknown remains of Tenochtitlan, the capital city of the people that we usually call the Aztecs. In actuality, the Aztecs were composed of a number of different groups. Those who settled at Tenochtitlan called themselves the Mexica. The city flourished from about 1325 A.D. until its destruction by the Spanish conquistadors in 1521. Of course, it's always been known that the ancient site lies underneath Mexico City because the Spaniards destroyed much of it before building their own city right on top of the ruins.

Fortunately, the conquistadors left us maps, including one that was supposedly drawn by Hernán Cortés himself; these show what the city looked like before its destruction. So we know that it was originally built on an island in the middle of Lake Texcoco, with causeways connecting it to the mainland. The actual space available for living was expanded by creating *chinampas*, or floating gardens, which eventually became firmly enough anchored and covered with enough soil that houses and other structures could be built upon them. It looks like the city was then split into four quarters and it may have housed as many as 250,000 people. Even though the modern city covers the ancient city, buildings and artifacts are constantly being discovered during the various construction projects, and they shed light on what used to be there.

For example, the great Calendar Stone, which is often called the Sun Stone, was discovered in December 1790 when the Mexico City Cathedral was being repaired. This huge stone is almost 12 feet across, and it weighs about 24 tons. Now it's not quite clear what it was actually originally used for, but it might have been either a ceremonial basin or an altar. On it are pictorial depictions of the four periods that the Aztecs thought preceded their own time, which lasted a total of 2,028 years. The face in the middle could be the Aztec deity of the sun, which is why some people call this the Sun Stone.

The Calendar Stone was probably originally located on or in the Great Temple, which is often called the Templo Mayor. Portions of this temple were originally found in the mid-1900s, and more of it was accidentally discovered in 1978 when electric cables were being laid down in the area. As British archaeologist Paul Bahn notes, the excavation project that was subsequently undertaken was mammoth—several entire city blocks of houses and shops were torn down in the very center of the city so that the archaeologists could investigate the remains. An archaeologist with the wonderfully appropriate name of Eduardo Matos Moctezuma led the team.

The Templo Mayor is actually a double pyramid dedicated to two of the major Aztec gods. In addition to the actual remains of the temple pyramid, the archaeologists found artifacts of gold and jade, plus many animal skeletons, and also a rack of human skulls carved in stone. They also found that the Aztecs had buried objects from previous Mesoamerican civilizations.

In 2006, archaeologists found a stone altar depicting the rain or water god that dates to about 1450 A.D. They also uncovered a monolith, a stone slab, made of pinkish andesite. The monolith depicts the earth goddess. It was originally painted with ocher, red, blue, white, and black colors. It was found lying flat, but it probably would have stood about 11 feet tall, unless it was actually meant to lie flat. It weighs 12 tons, and it dates to the last Aztec period, from 1487 until 1520. The team that discovered the monolith thought that it might still be in its original position, perhaps at the entrance to a chamber or even a tomb, even though it had broken into four large pieces.

Now two years later, in a stone-lined shaft located right next to the monolith, the archaeologists began finding additional Aztec religious offerings, including sacrificial knives made of white flint, objects made of jaguar bone, and bars of copal or incense. Beneath these, in a stone box, were the skeletons of two golden eagles, surrounded by 27 sacrificial knives, most of which were dressed up in costumes as if the knives were gods and goddesses. And beneath these were yet more offerings. By January 2009, the archaeologists had found six separate sets of offerings in this one deep pit, which reached 24 feet below street level.

Now back up at the eight-foot-deep mark, the archaeologists had found a second stone box. This one contained the skeleton of a dog or a wolf that had been buried with a collar that was made from jade beads. It also had turquoise plugs, like earrings, in its ears, and it had bracelets with little gold bells around its ankles. The archaeologists promptly nicknamed it Aristo-Canine, like the Aristocats but with a dog.

The skeleton is also covered with seashells and other remains of marine life, like clams and crabs. The lead excavator of the dig, who bears the wonderfully alliterative name of Leonardo López Luján, thinks that the six sets of offerings mark the Aztec cosmology or their belief system. For example, the dog or wolf with the seashells would represent the first level of the underworld, serving to guide its master's soul across a dangerous river. That's what Robert Draper wrote in the National Geographic story that documented this amazing find. López Luján believes that he might be close to finding the tomb of one of the last and most feared Aztec emperors, who died in 1502 or 1503.

Let's leave Tenochtitlan and travel northeast to Teotihuacan, where amazing artifacts have been revealed just since 2003. That was the year when a secret tunnel that might lead to a royal tomb was first uncovered.

Now Teotihuacan actually predates Aztec civilization, although the Aztecs gave the city its name, which might mean the birthplace of the gods. It was declared a UNESCO World Heritage site back in 1987, and it's one of the most visited tourist sites in Mexico; however, it's still a matter of debate about who actually lived there and what they called their city. It was inhabited from about 100 B.C. to about 650 A.D., and it probably had a population of at least 25,000 but maybe as much as 150,000 when it was at its largest. In an interview that was published in October 2015, David Carrasco of Harvard University described it as the imperial Rome of Mesoamerica. By this, he means that Teotihuacan influenced hundreds of other Mesoamerican communities during its period of greatness and that it served as a beacon for later civilizations to hark back to.

Now it used to be thought that the Toltecs built the site because that's apparently what the later Aztecs told the Spaniards when they arrived, but that doesn't seem to have actually been factually accurate since the site is earlier than the time of the Toltecs. For the moment, the inhabitants are simply referred to as Teotihuacanos. In any event, the site is dominated by a long central avenue, which is called the Avenue of the Dead. It runs for about a mile and a half. Along it, pyramids and temples were built. These include the Pyramid of the Sun and the Pyramid of the Moon, as well as the Temple of the Feathered Serpent.

Now the Pyramid of the Sun is the largest of the buildings; it's more than 700 feet wide at the base and over 200 feet tall, and it's got a ceremonial cave right underneath it. The Pyramid of the Moon is not far behind in its size, and human remains were found here in excavations that began in 1998. These revealed a burial chamber with rich grave goods, which included pyrite mirrors and obsidian blades.

The Temple of the Feathered Serpent is the third largest building at the site. It gets its name from the heads of the feathered serpents that are sticking out from the façade of the building; these weigh up to four tons each. The building itself probably dates to about 200 A.D. Beginning in the 1980s, a series of pits was found in front of the temple; these contained the bodies of nearly 200 warriors, both male and female, as well as their attendants. All of them had their hands tied behind their backs and were obviously ceremonial victims, perhaps sacrificed at the time that the building was dedicated or during ceremonies that were held on various occasions.

In 2003, a tunnel was detected, which led from one of the plazas near the edge of the city to the Temple of the Feathered Serpent. It was found accidentally after heavy rains opened up a small hole that was about 80 feet away from the temple.

It was then mapped by archaeologists using remote-sensing devices, specifically radar. Led by the Mexican archaeologist Sergio Gómez, excavation's been going on ever since, using remote-controlled robots in some places and pure hand labor in others. The tunnel is more than 330 feet long, and it ends at least 40 and maybe as much as 60 feet directly below the temple. It was sealed up about 1,800 years ago, with at least six different walls erected to block the tunnel at various points along its length. During their meticulous excavations in the tunnel, the archaeologists have found more than 70,000 ancient objects, which include jewelry, pottery, obsidian blades, rubber balls like were used in the Mesoamerican ball games, and hundreds of large conch shells from the Caribbean.

Some reports say that the tunnel ceiling and walls are coated with a glittery powder, perhaps ground-up pyrite or a similar substance; that would have caused them to sparkle and shimmer in the light of torches. At the bottom of the tunnel are three chambers, and offerings that include four large figurines made out of green stone, as well as remains of jaguars, jade statuettes, and significant quantities of liquid mercury, which may have represented an underworld river or lake. The area that's beyond has yet to be investigated, and it could possibly hold the bodies of rulers of the city, perhaps from an early period in its history.

We're not sure why, but Teotihuacan was eventually abandoned, probably sometime in the 7th or the 8th century A.D. Even so, one thing that's interesting about this site is that its location was never forgotten, even after it had been lying in ruins for centuries. We know, for example, that the Aztecs used to come to Teotihuacan, and that they were well aware of the people that had once lived there. It is, like Nabonidus the Neo-Babylonian and Hesiod the Greek poet, another example of a people whom we'd consider ancient knowing that there had been other civilizations in the region before them.

And this idea of layers of civilization—the idea that each culture is in a very real sense built upon the cultures that came before it—this concept is at the very heart of what archaeologists do. As we dig down through layers of dirt, we're not just uncovering objects; we're uncovering our deep connection to the past. And, of course, someday we will be the past. Our civilization, our culture will be long gone, and future archaeologists will be uncovering their connections to us—civilization building upon civilization building upon civilization—that is an intriguing thought.

In fact, I find it so intriguing that I'd like to end this course not by looking back, but by looking forward into the future. And in doing so, I want to address two questions. One is the question of how archaeologists will actually do archaeology in the future—that is, what new tools and what new techniques will they be using.

The other is the question of how archaeologists will interpret us—that is, our society and our civilization—in the future. Let's look at this question first. I've been talking about future archaeology ever since I saw a television program that came out after Alan Weisman published his bestselling book *The World Without Us*. The program aired on the National Geographic Channel; it was called *Aftermath: Population Zero*. Like Weisman's book, *Aftermath* looked at what would happen to our cities and our monuments in the coming years if we humans ceased to exist.

So let me ask you: What do you think a team of archaeologists would find 200 years from now if all humans—besides the archaeologists themselves, I suppose—disappeared today? What about in 2,000 years? How would they interpret what they find, and how would they reconstruct our society?

Let's put ourselves in the shoes of those future archaeologists, and for simplicity's sake, let's just stay in the United States for this little thought experiment, rather than trying to also figure out what we would do in France, or England, Australia, or elsewhere.

Leaving aside all of the big administration buildings, the schools, the homes, highways, bridges, roads, airports, and so on, what do you think structures like the Washington Zoo or the Smithsonian Museums, or even Starbucks and McDonald's, what do you think they would look like in 200 or 2,000 years? What would we find in their ruins? Would we identify them properly—that is, would we know that they were once a zoo or a Starbucks? And if we misidentified them, in what way would we do so? What would we think they were?

So this is just an educated guess, of course, but I think the zoo might cause a bit of a problem unless we can still read the signs that were once posted everywhere. It would also depend upon whether all of the animals had managed to escape, in which case all of the cages would be found empty, or if they had been trapped inside and we found their skeletons. Now if we both found the skeletons and could read the signs, it'd be pretty obvious, but otherwise, it might not be.

Now the Smithsonian Museums, or any large museum for that matter, like the Met in New York or the Museum of Fine Arts in Boston, that's going to definitely throw us for a loop until we realize that we're excavating a museum. Any building that's got the Hope Diamond, and dinosaurs, and a large whale is sure to cause much confusion and discussion among those future archaeologists until they realize that they've been excavating the National Museum of Natural History.

Personally, though, I think it's going to be places like Starbucks and McDonald's that are potentially going to cause the most confusion. Specifically, I think there is a good chance of misidentifying Starbucks as a religion, complete with a goddess wearing a crown and with flowing locks pictured everywhere, and with her shrine or temple located on virtually every block or street corner. On the other hand, perhaps that's actually the case. The same thing could be said for McDonald's, except in this case the deity being worshipped has a known name, Ronald McDonald, who has red hair and unusually large feet, seems to wear makeup, and dresses in a bright yellow and red outfit. Or maybe we would conclude that these two stand at the head of a pantheon, like Zeus and Hera for the Greeks and Jupiter and Juno for the Romans.

Now I joke, and yet, if enough relevant records don't survive, those could be the kind of interpretations made by future archaeologists. Already when we're on excavations and we find something that we don't immediately understand, we half-jokingly call it cultic or religious.

Anyway, future archaeology is interesting to think about, especially since we spend so much time looking at previously vanished cultures and don't usually consider what our culture is going to look like to future archaeologists. Think, for instance, about the fact that so much of our interactions are now online. Most of those interactions will vanish without a trace or will be inaccessible to future archaeologists, so what are they going to conclude about our rate of literacy, for instance? And what will they think about the ubiquitous rectangular blobs of metal, plastic, glass, and circuitry that seem to be associated with every skeleton, including many that had one clutched in their hand?

Actually, this thought process was already undertaken back in 1979. David Macaulay published a great short illustrated book called *Motel of the Mysteries*. The premise of this book is this: Life in North America is basically extinguished in a single day in 1985; then in the year 4022, amateur archaeologist Howard Carson accidentally stumbles upon an ancient site, which turns out to be the Motel of the Mysteries. He then brings in a team to help him, including an assistant named Harriet Burton.

Obviously, Howard Carson is based on Howard Carter, and his assistant Harriet Burton is based on the real-life Harry Burton, who was an Egyptologist and the photographer during Carter's very real excavation of King Tut's tomb. David Macaulay has a lot of fun with references to the discovery of Tut's tomb, including the famous phrase that Carter, or rather Carson in this case, utters, namely that he sees "wonderful things." As it turns out, although he doesn't realize it, he has actually discovered rather not a tomb, although he does first think he found that, and he does find two skeletons, but rather we, the knowing reader, recognize he's actually found a motel room.

Now the misinterpretations of what they find are absolutely hysterical, or at least, I think they are since there are so many inside jokes. But it also illustrates what I just said a moment ago, that if we don't know what something is, we often think it might be religious. So in the so-called Outer Chamber, Macaulay's Howard Carson finds everything facing the Great Altar, including the body that's still lying on top of the Ceremonial Platform and is still holding in its hand the Sacred Communicator. Of course, we recognize these: the Great Altar is nothing other than a television set; the Ceremonial Platform is actually just a bed; and the Sacred Communicator, that's the remote control for the TV. And yet, in this setting, 2,000 years after the fact and with nothing else to go on, Howard Carson interprets all of this as religious.

Now Macaulay tops it all off, at least for me, by having Harriet Burton put on and very proudly wear the Sacred Headband and the Sacred Collar that were still in place on the Sacred Urn when they found them. She also wears the plastic ear ornaments as earrings and places the exquisite silver chain and pendant around her neck. The accompanying illustration makes it quite plain that she actually is wearing the toilet seat around her neck. Also, the strip of paper that says "sanitized for your protection" is around her head. It's two toothbrushes that are dangling from her ears. And the rubber stopper from the bathtub, that is her necklace. Even better, the drawing is a dead ringer for the famous photograph that Heinrich Schliemann took of his wife Sophia when she was wearing all of the jewelry from Priam's Treasure that he supposedly found at Troy.

So, again, this is what it might come down to when someone in the future excavates Starbucks, McDonald's, museums, zoos, and possibly even motels from our time. I leave it to you to imagine similar hysterical situations. But all humor aside, it is worthwhile to think about the fact that our current culture might be wildly misinterpreted by future archaeologists, and that we may occasionally, or perhaps even often, misinterpret the past ourselves. That's an occupational hazard, but usually, once enough data is found, we do come to a scholarly consensus about the proper interpretation of a building or a site or even an entire civilization.

Now, what about how archaeologists will actually do archaeology in the future—that is, what new tools and techniques will they be using? Of course, we have absolutely no way of knowing this, just as Heinrich Schliemann and Howard Carter could not have predicted the use of remote sensing techniques being employed at both Troy and in King Tut's tomb; however, I suspect that there will continue to be advances in technology, which will allow us to peer even more easily beneath the earth, or beneath the tree canopies in Central and South America, before we begin digging. For instance, I am absolutely convinced and have been saying for years, that there must be a better way to conduct remote sensing. Apart from LiDAR, most of the techniques that we're using—like magnetometers, resistivity, and so on—are now decades old. It is time for new advances.

I wonder, for instance, if it might be possible to detect things like plaster or other specific materials through a layer of earth, just like we can now detect buried walls and ditches. Would some of the techniques that are being used in airports, for example, to catch drug runners and explosives, maybe that equipment can be repurposed to detect other chemical compounds that would belong to artifacts still buried in the earth. And would it make sense to partner perhaps with gas and oil exploration companies to utilize new techniques that might allow us to peer deeper into the depths of a mound, or to do so in a series of slices at specific depths? I do think that we are ripe for another series of technological breakthroughs, but I think it's also a matter of talking to the right engineering people, perhaps—someone who would say, "Wait. You want to do what? Oh yeah, we can do that, no problem." So if there's anybody out there who has a great remote-sensing idea, or knows some new technology, feel free to contact me.

On the other hand, I also think that it's fairly safe to say that the actual process of physically digging—that is, digging with picks, shovels, trowels, and dental tools—will continue as it has since the very first days of archaeology. There are only a limited number of ways that one can dig carefully and yet quickly, without actually destroying the remains that you've come to study. Still I could be surprised because there may be some new digging techniques invented that I cannot even begin to imagine at the moment.

However, there's one thing that won't change, and that's why we dig in the first place. The 1953 novel *The Go-Between* by British author L. P. Hartley, which was made into a movie starring Julie Christie in 1971, has the famous opening line: "The past is a foreign country; they do things differently there." I couldn't agree more. We archaeologists are adventurers. We are explorers. That doesn't mean we are Indiana Jones or David Livingstone, but it does mean that we are exploring our own humanity, our own origins, and our own past. In part, I think that's why I like being an archaeologist so much: I'm part explorer, part traveler, and part observer of humanity. Along the way, I get to do some actual traveling, I meet fascinating people, and above all, I get to play in the dirt. In some ways, I guess, I never really left the nursery school sandpit.

But archaeologists shouldn't be the only ones responsible for taking care of the past because that responsibility lies with everybody. As Brian Fagan has said: "All of us, whether professional archaeologist, avocational fieldworker, casually interested traveler or basically uninterested citizen, we all share a common responsibility for the past. It's our collective cultural heritage."

He also gives a simple list of five things that we can all do to help preserve the past for the future: Treat all archaeological sites and artifacts as finite resources. Never collect artifacts for yourself or buy and sell them for personal gain. Adhere to all federal, state, local, and tribal laws relating to archaeological sites. Report all accidental archaeological discoveries. Avoid disturbing any archaeological site, and respect the sanctity of all burial sites.

So it's up to all of us to help maintain the archaeological sites that have already been discovered. And those of you who are interested can volunteer for a dig and help to bring to light additional sites that have yet to be uncovered.

I'd like to end on one final note. I think that archaeology holds a fascination for many people because it allows us to look back into human history, to get a glimpse of what life was like for other people and in other times. Sometimes we find that they were very similar to us; other times, we find out that they could be quite different. In this course, we've gone from the earliest archaeologists to the most recent archaeological discoveries, from the first crude excavations at Herculaneum to the high-tech methods being used at Teotihuacan today. We've learned what it takes to find sites and what it takes to dig them. And we've traveled around the world—from Ur in Mesopotamia to Shanxi Province in China, from Masada in Israel to the ancient town of Akrotiri in Greece, from Sutton Hoo in England to Machu Picchu in Peru. We've had forays into Spain and France, Italy and North America, Africa, Mexico, and Turkey. And yet, we've only just literally scratched the surface because archaeology never ceases to yield remarkable discoveries. Every year we uncover a few more pieces in the puzzle of human history and are able to glimpse a little bit more of the past.

On a personal note, I've enjoyed my career in archaeology so far, and although it has had its ups and downs, just like any other academic discipline, on the whole, I have no regrets in following the decision that I made when I was seven years old to become an archaeologist. My only regret is that, as I have climbed the ladder of seniority on excavations, I have spent less and less time actually digging and more time on administration and supervising. One of these days, perhaps I'll shed all pretenses at authority and simply jump back down into a trench, grab a pickaxe, and start digging. And I hope that perhaps you will come join me and grab a pickaxe too because I suspect that you, like me, would probably rather be digging.

Bibliography

Adams, Mark. *Turn Right at Machu Picchu: Rediscovering the Lost City One Step at a Time*. New York: Dutton, 2011. An enjoyable book in which the author physically retraces Hiram Bingham's route to Machu Picchu while also retelling the story of the discovery and the saga since then.

Aldhouse-Green, Miranda. *Bog Bodies Uncovered: Solving Europe's Ancient Mystery*. London: Thames and Hudson, 2015. Thorough discussion of the various bodies that have been discovered in bogs in both England and Europe.

Alva, Walter, and Christopher B. Donnan. *Royal Tombs of Sipán*. Los Angeles: UCLA Fowler Museum of Cultural History, 1993. Discussion of the Sipán tombs by two of the leading Moche specialists.

Amadasi, Maria G., and Eugenia E. Schneider. *Petra*. Translated by Lydia G. Cochrane. Chicago: University of Chicago Press, 2002. An accessible book on Petra; reasonably up-to-date and with fine photographs.

Atwood, Roger. "Beneath the Capital's Busy Streets, Archaeologists Are Discovering the Buried World of the Aztecs." *Archaeology* 67/4 (9 June 2014): 26–33. A compelling article about discoveries made in Mexico City that expand our understanding of ancient Tenochtitlan.

Bahn, Paul. G. *100 Great Archaeological Discoveries*. New York: Facts on File, 1995. Superb compilation of 100 interesting and important archaeological discoveries; other versions, with alternative titles, are also available

Balter, Michael. *The Goddess and the Bull: Çatalhöyük—An Archaeological Journey to the Dawn of Civilization*. Walnut Creek, CA: Left Coast Press, 2009. Interesting first-person account from the Çatalhöyük excavations by a science writer who makes observations about the team personnel, as well as their discoveries.

Barber, Elizabeth W. *The Mummies of Ürümchi*. New York: W. W. Norton & Company, 1999. A compelling account of the intriguing mummies found in the region of the Tarim Basin (Ürümchi), China.

Bard, Kathryn A. *An Introduction to the Archaeology of Ancient Egypt*. 2nd ed. New York: Wiley-Blackwell, 2015. A good, recent overview and introduction to the archaeology of ancient Egypt, by a noted and respected Egyptologist.

Bass, George F. "Oldest Known Shipwreck Reveals Splendors of the Bronze Age." *National Geographic* 172/6 (December 1987): 692–733. Classic article describing the discovery and contents of the Uluburun shipwreck, found off the coast of Turkey and dating to about 1300 B.C.

Beard, Mary. *The Fires of Vesuvius: Pompeii Lost and Found*. Cambridge, MA: Belknap Press, 2010. Description and discussion of Pompeii by one of the best classicists writing today.

Ben-Tor, Amnon. *Back to Masada*. Jerusalem: Israel Exploration Society, 2009. A spirited defense of Yigael Yadin's excavations, discoveries, and interpretations at Masada, by one of his former students, now a senior and respected archaeologist in his own right.

Ben-Yehuda, Nachman. *The Masada Myth: Collective Memory and Mythmaking in Israel*. Madison, WI: University of Wisconsin Press, 1995. The book that first called into question Yadin's interpretations of what he had found at Masada during his excavations in the 1960s.

Berry, Joanne. *The Complete Pompeii*. Reprint ed. London: Thames and Hudson, 2007. Everything you ever wanted to know about Pompeii, and more ….

Bogdanos, Matthew. *Thieves of Baghdad*. New York: Bloomsbury USA, 2005. A discussion of the looting of the Baghdad Museum, written by Matthew Bogdanos, who was tasked with putting together a team and recovering as many of the objects as possible.

Catling, Christopher. *Discovering the Past through Archaeology: The Science and Practice of Studying Excavation Materials and Ancient Sites.* London: Southwater, 2012. An extremely well-illustrated reference book on archaeology; useful for armchair archaeologists and beginning excavators, as well as those with more experience.

———. *A Practical Handbook of Archaeology: A Beginner's Guide to Unearthing the Past.* London: Lorenz Books, 2013. Just as the title indicates, this useful handbook is aimed specifically at beginners.

Ceram, C. W. *Gods, Graves and Scholars.* 2nd rev. ed. New York: Random House, 1967. The original book that introduced the ancient world to thousands of people since the second edition appeared in 1967; unfortunately, it has not been updated since then.

Christie, Agatha. *Murder in Mesopotamia: A Hercule Poirot Mystery.* Reprint ed. New York: William Morrow Paperbacks, 2011. Agatha Christie's first murder mystery, in which the first victim is rumored to have been patterned after Lady Katharine Woolley.

Cline, Eric H. *The Battles of Armageddon: Megiddo and the Jezreel Valley from the Bronze Age to the Nuclear Age.* Ann Arbor: University of Michigan Press, 2000. Discussion of the 34 major battles at Megiddo (biblical Armageddon) and in the Jezreel Valley from about 2000 B.C.E. to 2000 C.E.

———. *Biblical Archaeology: A Very Short Introduction.* New York: Oxford University Press, 2009. As the title says, this is a short—yet thorough—introduction to biblical archaeology, covering the history of the field, as well as some of the main sites and primary discoveries.

———. *The Trojan War: A Very Short Introduction.* New York: Oxford University Press, 2013. Again, as the title says, a short but thorough introduction to the Trojan War, covering the Greek version of events, the evidence from Hittite texts, and the archaeologists and archaeology of Hisarlik, thought to be the site of ancient Troy.

———, ed. *The Oxford Handbook of the Bronze Age Aegean*. Oxford: Oxford University Press, 2010. An edited volume on the Bronze Age Aegean containing 60 chapters written by 66 specialists on everything to do with that period and area; individual chapters include those on Mycenae, Knossos, and Akrotiri, as well as the Trojan War and the eruption of Thera/Santorini.

Cline, Eric H., and Assaf Yasur-Landau. "Your Career Is in Ruins: How to Start an Excavation in Five Not-So-Easy Steps." *Biblical Archaeology Review* 32/1 (2006): 34–37, 71. Fun and factual article on how the renewed excavations at Tel Kabri were begun.

———. "Aegeans in Israel: Minoan Frescoes at Tel Kabri." *Biblical Archaeology Review* 39/4 (2013): 37–44, 64, 66. A popularizing and readable article on the Aegean-style paintings at Kabri and elsewhere in the eastern Mediterranean.

Cline, Eric H., Assaf Yasur-Landau, and Nurith Goshen. "New Fragments of Aegean-Style Painted Plaster from Tel Kabri, Israel." *American Journal of Archaeology* 115/2 (2011): 245–261. Discussion of painted fresco fragments found at Kabri during the 2009 season, published in one of the leading archaeological journals.

Coe, Michael D. *The Maya*. 7th ed. New York: Thames and Hudson, 2005. Classic book on the Maya by a preeminent scholar.

Curtis, Gregory B. *The Cave Painters: Probing the Mysteries of the World's First Artists*. New York: Knopf, 2006. A highly regarded and eminently readable overview of the painted caves in southern France and northern Spain, such as Lascaux, Chauvet, and Altamira.

Davies, Graham I. *Megiddo*. Cambridge: Lutterworth Press, 1986. A small book—almost a guidebook—to the history and ruins of Megiddo; almost nothing else is available at the moment in book form.

Davies, Philip R., George J. Brooke, and Phillip R. Callaway. *The Complete World of the Dead Sea Scrolls*. London: Thames and Hudson, 2002. These three respected scholars describe the world of the Mediterranean and the ancient Near East at the time of the Dead Sea Scrolls.

de Rojas, José Luis. *Tenochtitlan: Capital of the Aztec Empire*. Gainesville: University Press of Florida, 2012. An up-to-date examination of what we know about the ruins of Tenochtitlan, currently buried underneath modern Mexico City.

Doumas, Christos G. *Thera: Pompeii of the Ancient Aegean: Excavations at Akrotiri, 1967–1979*. London: Thames and Hudson, 1983. An accessible book on the ruins found at Akrotiri on Santorini, written by the current director of excavations at the site.

Draper, Robert. "Unburying the Aztec." *National Geographic* 218/5 (November 2010): 110–135. A fabulous article on the discoveries being made in downtown Mexico City, with great photographs.

Drewett, Peter. *Field Archaeology: An Introduction*. 2nd ed. Boston: Routledge, 2011. A good introduction for beginners on how to conduct excavations and other aspects of field archaeology.

Ellis, Steven. *The Making of Pompeii: Studies in the History and Urban Development of an Ancient Town*. Portsmouth, RI: Journal of Roman Archaeology Supplemental Series, 2011. Written by the current director of the University of Cincinnati excavations at Pompeii, this is a scholarly examination of the city at the time of the eruption of Mount Vesuvius.

Fagan, Brian A. *The Rape of the Nile: Tomb Robbers, Tourists, and Archaeologists in Egypt*. Boulder, CO: Westview Press, 2004. Written by an archaeologist and master wordsmith, this is a wonderful overview of archaeology and archaeologists in Egypt.

———. *Chaco Canyon: Archaeologists Explore the Lives of an Ancient Society*. Oxford: Oxford University Press, 2005. In this book, Fagan brings the ruins of Chaco Canyon to life in a masterful exploration of the buildings and the people who once lived in them.

———. *Return to Babylon: Travelers, Archaeologists, and Monuments in Mesopotamia*. Rev. ed. Boulder, CO: University of Colorado Press, 2007. In this compelling volume, Fagan takes a look back at the early archaeologists and their discoveries in Mesopotamia.

———, ed. *The Great Archaeologists*. London: Thames and Hudson, 2014. Fagan has collected a series of brief vignettes on famous archaeologists, written by their students, close colleagues, or other archaeologists; well worth purchasing and reading time and again.

Fagan, Brian A., and Nadia Durrani. *In the Beginning: An Introduction to Archaeology*. 13th ed. Boston: Pearson, 2014. One of Fagan's bestselling textbooks, used in introductory courses across the United States, this is now in its 13th edition and has been updated with additions by Nadia Durrani, a British archaeologist.

Fash, William L. *Scribes, Warriors and Kings: The City of Copán and the Ancient Maya*. Rev. ed. London: Thames and Hudson, 2001. A look at the Maya through the lens of the city of Copán and its monuments, including information derived from the decipherment of Maya hieroglyphs.

Finkel, Irving. *The Ark before Noah: Decoding the Story of the Flood*. New York: Hodder & Stoughton, 2014. An account of Finkel's translation of a new tablet detailing the story of a great flood; in this version, the ark is round.

Fitton, J. Leslie. *Minoans*. London: British Museum Press, 2002. An accessible book on the Minoans of Crete, written by a respected scholar of the Bronze Age Aegean.

Hall, Stephen S. "Spirits in the Sand: The Ancient Nasca Lines of Peru Shed Their Secrets." *National Geographic* (March 2010): 56–79. An interesting article on the Nazca Lines, full of information and accompanied by gorgeous photographs.

Hawass, Zahi. *Tutankhamun and the Golden Age of the Pharaohs*. Washington, DC: National Geographic Society, 2005. One of the essential books on King Tut; written by the former Egyptian Director of Antiquities and National Geographic Explorer-in-Residence Zahi Hawass.

Hester, Thomas R., Harry J. Shafer, and Kenneth L. Feder. *Field Methods in Archaeology*. 7th ed. Walnut Creek, CA: Left Coast Press, 2009. A useful field manual, especially aimed at undergraduate and graduate students moving up the chain of command on excavations—those who are being asked to do more than just grab a trowel and excavate.

Hodder, Ian. *The Leopard's Tale: Revealing the Mysteries of Çatalhöyük*. London: Thames and Hudson, 2011. Written by the current director of the excavations at Çatalhöyük, this is an interesting inside look, including his own interpretations of what has been found at the site to date.

Howard, Philip. *Archaeological Surveying and Mapping: Recording and Depicting the Landscape*. New ed. Boston: Routledge, 2007. A useful guide to current archaeological surveying and mapping procedures; interesting to both practicing and armchair archaeologists.

Johanson, Donald, and Maitland Edey. *Lucy: The Beginnings of Humankind*. New York: Simon and Schuster, 1981. The classic book on Lucy, written by her discoverer, Donald Johanson.

Johanson, Donald, and Kate Wong. *Lucy's Legacy: The Quest for Human Origins*. New York: Broadway Books, 2010. The discoverer of Lucy, Donald Johanson, puts the find into a larger context, 30 years after his original book was published.

Kelly, Robert L., and David Hurst Thomas. *Archaeology*. 6th ed. New York: Wadsworth. 2013. Introductory classroom textbook with good discussions on all kinds of archaeological topics, including such discussions such as processualism versus post-processualism; use in conjunction with Fagan and Durrani (2014).

Kelso, William M. *Jamestown: The Buried Truth*. Charlottesville, VA: University of Virginia Press, 2008. Written by the excavator, this is a fascinating look at the finds at Jamestown, though new discoveries have been made since the publication of this book.

Kenyon, Kathleen M. *Digging Up Jericho*. London: Ernest Benn, 1957. A classic in the field, this is Kenyon's own story of her excavations at the site of Jericho.

Koch, Peter O. *John Lloyd Stephens and Frederick Catherwood: Pioneers of Mayan Archaeology*. Jefferson, NC: McFarland & Company, 2013. To be read alongside, or even in lieu of, the books by Stephens and Catherwood, Koch's account brings their adventures in Central America to life.

Krober, Theodora. *Ishi in Two Worlds: A Biography of the Last Wild Indian in North America*. 50th anniversary ed. Berkeley, CA: University of California Press, 2011. Another classic volume in the field, on Ishi, the last member of his California tribe. Written by the wife of Alfred Kroeber, who was an anthropologist in her own right and mother of the science fiction writer Ursula K. Le Guin.

Leach, Peter E. *The Surveying of Archaeological Sites*. London: Archetype Publications Ltd., 1992. Another useful guide, though a bit dated now, to archaeological surveying procedures.

Leakey, Mary D. *Olduvai Gorge: My Search for Early Man*. London: Collins, 1979. An autobiography of sorts, about Leakey's work in Olduvai Gorge.

Leakey, Richard E., and Roger Lewin. *Origins*. New York: E. P. Dutton, 1979. A standard volume owned by every practicing and wanna-be paleoanthropologist, this is Richard Leakey's take on the finds made by his family and other scholars.

Lloyd, Seton. *Foundations in the Dust: The Story of Mesopotamian Exploration*. London: Thames and Hudson, 1980. This volume by Seton Lloyd, a highly respected British archaeologist, is considered to be one of the most fundamental volumes ever written about early archaeology and archaeologists in Mesopotamia.

Luce, J. V. *End of Atlantis*. London: Thames and Hudson, 1969. J. V. Luce's short but classic masterpiece examines Plato's story of Atlantis and links it to the excavations at Akrotiri and the eruption of Santorini during the Bronze Age.

Macaulay, David. *Motel of the Mysteries*. Boston: Houghton Mifflin, 1979. In this oversized paperback, David Macaulay envisions the hilarious misinterpretations by a future archaeologist investigating the remains of a motel in the United States from the 1970s.

Magness, Jodi. *The Archaeology of Qumran and the Dead Sea Scrolls*. Grand Rapids, MI: William B. Eerdmans, 2002. Magness brings her knowledge and no-nonsense approach to the remains found at Qumran and the nearby caves that contained the Dead Sea Scrolls.

Mallory, J. P., and Victor H. Mair. *The Tarim Mummies: Ancient China and the Mystery of the Earliest Peoples from the West*. London: Thames and Hudson, 2000. Another compelling account of the intriguing mummies found in the region of the Tarim Basin (Ürümchi), China.

Mallowan, Agatha Christie. *Come, Tell Me How You Live: An Archaeological Memoir*. Reprint ed. New York: William Morrow Paperbacks, 2012. An autobiography of sorts from Agatha Christie, who was married to the archaeologist Max Mallowan. This book was written to answer questions from her friends concerning life on an excavation and in the Middle East in general.

Marinatos, Nanno. *Art and Religion in Thera: Reconstructing a Bronze Age Society*. Athens: D. & I. Mathioulakis, 1984. Written by the archaeologist daughter of Spyridon Marinatos, the discoverer of the site of Akrotiri on Santorini, this volume contains her thoughts on finds made at the site, especially the wall paintings found in many of the houses.

Matthiae, Paolo. *Ebla: An Empire Rediscovered*. Translated by Christopher Holme. Garden City, NY: Doubleday, 1981. The original volume written by the excavator of Ebla, this is another classic to be read and treasured by both professional and armchair archaeologists everywhere.

Owsley, Douglas W., and Richard L. Jantz, eds. *Kennewick Man: The Scientific Investigation of an Ancient American Skeleton.* (Peopling of the Americas Publications). College Station, TX: Texas A&M University Press, 2014. The final report—680 pages long and with contributions from more than 65 scholars and professionals—of the investigation into Kennewick Man.

Portal, Jane. *The First Emperor: China's Terracotta Army.* Cambridge, MA: Harvard University Press, 2007. A well-written and well-illustrated account of the terracotta army, from its discovery through the first 30 years of study; should be supplemented by recent finds made since 2007, including more warriors and insights into the paint used on them.

Pulak, Cemal. "The Uluburun Shipwreck: An Overview." *International Journal of Nautical Archaeology* 27 (1998): 188–224. A scholarly overview of the shipwreck and its cargo found at Uluburun, off the coast of Turkey, dating to about 1300 B.C. (Late Bronze Age); written by one of the directors of the project.

———. "Shipwreck: Recovering 3,000-Year-Old Cargo." *Archaeology Odyssey* 2/4 (Sept/Oct 1999): 18–29. An overview of the Uluburun shipwreck and its cargo, written for the general public by one of the directors of the project; nice photographs.

———. "Uluburun Shipwreck." In *The Oxford Handbook of the Bronze Age Aegean*, edited by Eric H. Cline, pp. 862–876. Oxford: Oxford University Press, 2010. The most up-to-date overview of the shipwreck and its cargo found at Uluburun, off the coast of Turkey, written by one of the directors of the project; meant for scholars and students but accessibly written for the general public, as well.

Ragan, Mark K. *The Hunley.* Orangeburg, SC: Sandlapper Publication Company, 2006. One of the most definitive volumes written about the *Hunley* and the excavations, by the resident historian of the recovery and excavation project.

Reeves, Nicholas. *The Complete Tutankhamun.* London: Thames and Hudson, 1990. The best book available on King Tut; written by a former curator at the British Museum and at Highclere Castle, the estate of the earl of Carnarvon.

Reeves, Nicholas, and Richard H. Wilkinson. *The Complete Valley of the Kings: Tombs and Treasures of Ancient Egypt's Royal Burial Site.* London: Thames and Hudson, 2002. The best volume available on the Valley of the Kings; written by Reeves, the former curator at the British Museum and at Highclere Castle, and Wilkinson, a well-respected Egyptologist at the University of Arizona.

Reinhard, Johan. *The Nazca Lines: A New Perspective on Their Origin and Meaning.* Lima: Los Pinos, 1988. One of Johan Reinhard's first books about archaeology in Peru; he was later named a National Geographic Explorer-in-Residence.

———. *The Ice Maiden: Inca Mummies, Mountain Gods, and Sacred Sites in the Andes.* Washington, DC: National Geographic Books, 2005. The story of the discovery that first propelled Reinhard to international fame, the Ice Maiden found on the slopes of Mount Ampato.

———. *Machu Picchu: Exploring an Ancient Sacred Center.* Los Angeles: Cotsen Institute of Archaeology, UCLA, 2007. In this volume, Reinhard turns his sights on Machu Picchu, investigating it from the viewpoint of an archaeologist working a full century after the original explorations of Hiram Bingham.

Roux, George. *Ancient Iraq.* New ed. New York: Penguin Books, 1992. A bit dated but still a classic, this book was originally compiled from a series of articles that the author wrote for *ARAMCO* magazine, then continuously updated; extremely readable.

Schofield, Louise. *The Mycenaeans.* Malibu, CA: J. Paul Getty Museum, 2007. An accessible and readable introduction to the Mycenaeans of Late Bronze Age mainland Greece, with a great deal of information and minimal use of jargon.

Silberman, Neil A., Israel Finkelstein, David Ussishkin, and Baruch Halpern. "Digging at Armageddon." *Archaeology* (November/December 1999): 32–39. An article by the three codirectors and an archaeological journalist on the first several seasons of the renewed excavations at Megiddo in Israel, which commenced in 1992 and ran every other year.

Smith, Andrew M. II. *Roman Palmyra: Identity, Community, and State Formation.* Oxford: Oxford University Press, 2013. An expert on Roman Palmyra, Smith presents here a full scholarly study of the city and its inhabitants; not an easy read but worth the effort.

Spindler, Konrad. *The Man in the Ice: The Discovery of a 5,000-Year-Old Body Reveals the Secrets of the Stone Age.* New York: Harmony Books, 1995. The Austrian archaeologist in charge of the overall studies of Ötzi the Iceman, Konrad Spindler, has provided the reader with the story of the initial discovery and the first several years of investigation. Much more is now known, but this volume provides the important initial details.

Strauss, Barry. *The Trojan War: A New History.* New York: Simon & Schuster, 2006. Interesting exploration of the Trojan War but with a rather different take on things; engaging, but more fictional narrative than straight facts in places.

Stuart, David. *The Order of Days: The Maya World and the Truth about 2012.* New York: Harmony Books, 2011. Written by David Stuart, the Maya specialist who is the youngest-ever winner of a MacArthur Genius Fellowship, this excellent book was meant to soothe the fears of those who thought the Maya had predicted an end to the world in 2012. Along the way, Stuart introduces the reader to the fascinating civilization of the Maya as a whole.

Stuart, David, and George E. Stuart. *Palenque: Eternal City of the Maya.* London: Thames and Hudson, 2008. Written by a father-and-son team of Maya specialists, this is an interesting exploration of the Maya city of Palenque.

Taylor, R. E., and Martin J. Aitken, eds. *Chronometric Dating in Archaeology*. London: Springer, 1997. This edited volume goes into great detail about the various dating methods available to archaeologists as of 1997; there have been some changes since then, such as the newest technique of rehydroxylation, but much in this volume is still viable.

Vermes, Geza. *The Complete Dead Sea Scrolls in English*. New York: Penguin, 1998. One of the definitive publications in English of all the Dead Sea Scrolls, including the multiple fragments from cave 4.

Vivian, R. Gwinn, and Bruce Hilpert. *Chaco Handbook: An Encyclopedia Guide* (Chaco Canyon). 2nd ed. Provo, UT: University of Utah Press, 2012. A definitive handbook written by two of the foremost experts on Chaco Canyon; well worth reading if you plan to visit the site.

Walsh, John E. *Unraveling Piltdown: The Science Fraud of the Century and Its Solution*. New York: Random House, 1996. One of the accounts of the Piltdown Man hoax, written in a readable and accessible manner.

Weisman, Alan. *The World without Us*. New York: St. Martin's Press, 2007. An intriguing thought experiment and investigation into what would happen if humans were to suddenly cease to exist; the book gave rise to a National Geographic Channel special and speculation by archaeologists about how our civilization might be interpreted—and misinterpreted—by future scientists.

White, Gregory G., and Thomas F. King. *The Archaeological Survey Manual*. Walnut Creek, CA: Left Coast Press, 2007. One of the newest manuals available regarding archaeological surveying procedures.

Wilkinson, Toby. *The Rise and Fall of Ancient Egypt*. New York: Random House, 2013. Universally hailed as one of the most interesting and readable accounts on the history and archaeology of ancient Egypt, this volume will be of interest to many who are fascinated by Egypt.

Williams, Gareth. *Treasures from Sutton Hoo*. London: British Museum Press, 2011. An excellent volume on the finds from Sutton Hoo, including many that are on display in the British Museum.

Wood, Michael. In *Search of the Trojan War*. 2nd ed. Berkeley, CA: University of California Press, 1996. One of the best books written by a nonarchaeologist on the archaeology and history of the Trojan War; accompanied the BCC series of the same name. Highly recommended for those interested in the topic.

Yadin, Yigael. *Masada: Herod's Fortress and the Zealots' Last Stand*. New York: Random House, 1966. Yadin's best-known book, this is his account of the excavations at Masada, written for the general public in an accessible and jargon-free style.

Image Credits

Page 7: © chameleonseye/iStock/Thinkstock.
Page 8: © ajlber/iStock/Thinkstock.
Page 24: © edella/iStock/Thinkstock.
Page 41: © Photos.com/Thinkstock.
Page 59: © Photos.com/Thinkstock.
Page 62: © TonyBaggett/iStock/Thinkstock.
Page 83: © marekuliasz/iStock/Thinkstock.
Page 99: © Michal Boubin/Hemera/Thinkstock.
Page 119: © FSYLN/iStock/Thinkstock.
Page 138: © Lindrik/iStock/Thinkstock.
Page 153: © swisshippoiStock/Thinkstock.
Page 156: © JoseIgnacioSoto/iStock/Thinkstock.
Page 170: © Westersoe/iStock/Thinkstock.
Page 189: © Lefteris_/iStock/Thinkstock.
Page 192: © Rostislav Ageev/iStock/Thinkstock.
Page 193: © Dorling Kindersley/Thinkstock.
Page 208: © NicoPelon/iStock/Thinkstock.
Page 209: © cmart7327/iStock/Thinkstock.
Page 228: © Martin Bahmann/Wikimedia Commons/CC BY-SA 3.0.
Page 246: © RobertHoetink/iStock/Thinkstock.
Page 248: © IMNATURE/iStock/Thinkstock.
Page 267: © amite/iStock/Thinkstock.
Page 283: © Steven Frame/Hemera/Thinkstock.
Page 318: © miquelpijoan/iStock/Thinkstock.
Page 321: © urf/iStock/Thinkstock.
Page 339: © arogant/iStock/Thinkstock.
Page 354: © crystaltmc/iStock/Thinkstock.
Page 356: © Photos.com/Thinkstock.
Page 375: © Simon Dannhauer/iStock/Thinkstock.
Page 378: © flowersandclassicalmusic/iStock/Thinkstock.
Page 394: © John Kershner/Shutterstock.
Page 397: © BerneyMax/iStock/Thinkstock.
Page 415: © snoofek/iStock/Thinkstock.

Page 417: © KenWiedemann/iStock/Thinkstock.
Page 433: © Dmitry Rukhlenko/Hemera/Thinkstock.